The Municipal Budget Crunch

The Municipal Budget Crunch

A Handbook for Professionals

Edited by ROGER L. KEMP

McFarland & Company, Inc., Publishers
Jefferson, North Carolina, and London

LIBRARY OF CONGRESS CATALOGUING-IN-PUBLICATION DATA

The municipal budget crunch : a handbook for professionals /
edited by Roger L. Kemp.
p.   cm.
Includes bibliographical references and index.

ISBN 978-0-7864-6374-9
softcover : acid free paper ∞

1. Municipal budgets — United States.
2. Municipal finance — United States.
3. Municipal budgets — United States — Case studies.
4. Municipal finance — United States — Case studies.
I. Kemp, Roger L.
HJ9147.M77   2012   352.4′82160973 — dc23   2012014085

BRITISH LIBRARY CATALOGUING DATA ARE AVAILABLE

Front cover image © 2012 Shutterstock

Manufactured in the United States of America

*McFarland & Company, Inc., Publishers
Box 611, Jefferson, North Carolina 28640
www.mcfarlandpub.com*

To Anika,
the best and the brightest

Acknowledgments

Grateful acknowledgment is made to the following organizations and publishers for granting permission to reprint the material in this volume.

City of Westminster, Colorado
Colorado Municipal League
Detroit Free Press
e.Republic Inc.
Government Finance Officers Association
International City/County Management Association
Iowa League of Cities
League of Minnesota Cities
Maine Municipal Association
Municipal World Inc.
National Civic League
National League of Cities
Penton Media, Inc.
Stanford University
World Future Society

Table of Contents

Part III. The Future

Appendices

Preface

Citizens in cities throughout the country routinely expect their elected and appointed public officials to balance the budgets for their respective organizations, with the goal of maintaining public services and keeping taxes at a minimum. It is also safe to say that, while everyone uses selected public services, no one knows all of the public service options available to them. Generally, when public officials reduce their operating budgets, citizens don't mind what they "cut," so long as it is not a service that they directly use.

In the past, fiscal problems (e.g., budget increases and revenue shortfalls) could be city or state specific, but during the past few years the fiscal problems being faced by all levels of government — local, regional, state, and national — are related to generally tough economic times. Local governments — counties and cities — generally cannot greatly influence their local economies, especially when the economic problems are statewide and national in nature. Also, when a higher level of government has fiscal problems, the government usually resolves them by giving fewer funds to lower levels of government. This is especially true for the national government as well as our 50 state governments.

The types of budget reduction and revenue enhancement practices evolving in America are being generated by public officials in individual local governments. Public officials at these levels of government are doing their best to be creative to maintain existing levels of public services, to keep their taxes to a minimum, and serve the public in the best possible manner. Public officials typically "do their own

thing" in their respective communities. This reference work assembles, for the first time, the best practices in budgeting processes, revenue generating options, and financial management services, based on a national literature search and makes this information available for the first time to citizens and public officials throughout the nation in a single volume.

The goal of *The Municipal Budget Crunch: A Handbook for Professionals* is to educate citizens and public officials on these evolving state-of-the art budgetary, revenue, and financial management practices. This volume is divided into three sections for ease of reference. The first section introduces the reader to relevant state-of-the-art topics related to public budgeting, revenues, and financial management practices. The second section, and by design the longest, includes numerous case studies, or best practices, on how local governments are initiating measures to balance their respective budgets while maintaining acceptable levels of public services and while keeping tax increases to a minimum. Such practices are critical to maintaining the quality of life in cities and towns throughout the country. The third section focuses on the future of city budgets, revenues, and the public services that they finance. In short, this section provides a summary of the evolving options and best practices available for charting the financial future of America's cities.

Several appendices have been assembled to promote a greater understanding of this new and evolving field, as well as provide resources for those citizens and public officials seeking additional information on the current local government fiscal movement. Valuable local, state, and national online resources are provided in this section.

Based on this general conceptual schema, the sections of this book are highlighted and briefly examined in greater detail below.

Cities and Taxes

The first section sets the stage for the fiscal crisis being faced by public officials and citizens in America's cities, ways cities are coping with these economic hard times, and legal and service implications of budget reduction decisions that include staff reductions. These chapters provide an overview to this subject and set the foundation for the various evolving best practices that are presented in the second section.

Briefly, these chapters focus on the various budgetary practices and fiscal management options that are generally available to local governments. These topics include an examination of the measures that should be taken to ensure a city's long-term fiscal well being. Lastly, this section sets forth and examines the financial measures that should be taken to restore the aging public infrastructure throughout the nation, much of which was built decades ago with the financial assistance of the federal and state governments.

These chapters provide the framework and background against which the best budget reduction and financial management practices that have emerged in cities across the United States in recent years are examined. The purpose of providing this information is so the reader can feel comfortable when reviewing the best practices examined in the second section.

Best Practices

The various cities, towns, and communities examined in this section, including the states in which they are located, as well as the highlights of the evolving best practices in the new discipline of maintaining the existing level of public services while making every effort to hold down taxes, are listed below in alphabetical order.

These case studies represent an important and significant research effort to obtain a body of knowledge on the best practices available in the dynamic and still evolving field on ways to hold down taxes while maintaining satisfactory levels of public services. The best practices section includes an examination of nearly 40 local governments, which are located in nearly one-half of the states.

CITIES

Ann Arbor	Peoria
Arlington	Philadelphia
Auburn	Portland
Boca Raton	Provo
Chandler	Redlands
Charlotte	Roanoke
Chicago	Rochester
Cincinnati	Rockland
Colorado Springs	St. Paul
Coral Springs	San Diego
Denver	San Jose
Des Moines	Sandy Springs
Elgin	Savannah
Eugene	Seattle
Gardena	Springfield
Hanover	Walnut Creek
Harrisburg	Waukesha
Las Vegas	West Palm Beach
Lewiston	Westminster
New York	Worcester

STATES

Arizona	Nevada
California	New York
Colorado	North Carolina
Florida	Ohio
Georgia	Oregon
Illinois	Pennsylvania
Iowa	Texas
Maine	Virginia
Massachusetts	Utah
Michigan	Washington
Minnesota	Wisconsin

BEST PRACTICES

Use of economic development practices to increase revenues.

Sharing public services to reduce costs.

Consolidation of municipal services.

Development of long-range financial plans.

Use of citizen volunteers to provide public services.

Implementation of employee wellness programs to reduce health benefit costs.

Using citizen input to make public budget decisions.

Improving the publics' trust in their municipal government.

Using citizens to evaluate their public services.

Public policies that focus on financial planning practices.

Use of service performance results to make future budgetary decisions.

Use of citizen input on the value of their public services.

Using trained public managers to address outstanding fiscal issues.

Using citizens to revise and improve a city's budgetary process.

Using professional public managers to improve city finances.

Implementation of generic public service and cost reductions.

Modifications and revisions to the existing property tax structure.

Reassessment of a city's basic public service levels.

Considering property tax relief options for senior citizens.

Providing special public services to low-income citizens.

Using performance measurements to improve the budgetary process.

Reconsideration of contracting public services to the private sector.

Use of new financial management assessment processes and practices.

Use of both employee and citizen input to balance public budgets.

Use of citizens to help provide selected public services.

Encouragement of citizens to provide selected tax relief options.

Seeking out possible additional funding sources.

Public services are directly impacted by senior citizens.

Use of flexible staff schedules to save budgetary funds.

Solicitation of feedback on public services from municipal employees.

Contracting public works services to the private sector.

Use of budgeting for results process as a new financial practice.

Implementation of joint purchasing programs.

Reduction of energy related budgetary expenses.

Implementation of new budget processes and practices.

Reduction of health care costs for aging municipal employees.

Provision of successful social service programs to citizens.

Use of performance results to improve public services.

Use of independent sources to measure public service performance levels.

The Future

The final section examines budget, revenue, and financial management trends and practices that are evolving in our nation's local governments. The topics examined include emerging financial constraints and new public service opportunities, and how public officials in cities throughout the country are redefining the quality of life in their respective communities. Other important topics concerning the future of public budgeting and financing include an examination of the condition of America's public infrastructure and how cities can use technologies to provide and enhance their public services. Lastly, a summary of cost-reduction and revenue-enhancement measures are examined to give citizens and public officials an overview of the various budgetary, financial, service level, and revenue options available to them as they cope with economic hard times in the future.

These readings reflect the various initiatives and best practices being taken by public officials, many times with the assistance of citizens and employees, to balance budgets with the goal of maintaining essential public service levels while not increasing taxes. These practices are still evolving, are dynamic in nature, and represent the new focus of public officials in cities throughout the nation when it comes to budgeting and financial planning and management practices. Modern budget and financial planning practices that achieve these goals are being developed and implemented with greater frequency by public officials during the pasts few years.

This volume represents an important codification of knowledge in this new field. Most citizens, including the public officials that represent them, are busy coping with the budgetary and financial problems in their respective communities. This research brings together evolving best practices in a new field brought about by recent economic hard times, which directly impacts the availability of revenues to finance public services in cities throughout America. It is important that public officials work with citizens as they cope with the financial constraints brought about by these negative economic conditions, and their resulting operational constraints.

Appendices

This is the first edited reference work on this topic that offers options for public officials and citizens in communities to consider and use in their budgeting and financial planning practices. To this end, several important reference resources have been assembled and are included as appendices. Brief descriptions of the seven appendices are highlighted below for reference purposes, and to facilitate future research and obtaining relevant information from these valuable resources.

Local Government Financial Terms. Because the new field of cities and their evolving budgeting and financial management practices relates to existing budget and financial practices, a list of commonly used public finance and budget terms is included for reference purposes. These terms are frequently used by municipal government financial professionals. These terms will make it easier for public officials and citizens to understand and monitor local public budgets and finances.

Regional Resource Directory. This ap-

pendix includes a listing of all of the community governments included in Part II, Best Practices. Readers wishing to follow up on any of the best practices contained in this volume are provided with immediate access to each government via its website. In those communities with the council-manager form of government, it is suggested that inquiries and questions be directed to the office of the city manager. In those cities with the strong-mayor form of government, it is recommended that all inquiries and questions be directed to the office of the mayor. Additional information, including possible personal contacts, may be obtained from these municipal websites.

National Resource Directory. This listing includes all major national professional associations, foundations, membership organizations, and research institutes serving public officials, professionals, and concerned citizens. Many of these organizations focus on various issues relating to community public budgeting and financial management concerns. The website is listed for each major organization and association. These groups frequently focus on current issues and problems relating to municipal budgetary and financial management.

City Management Officials State Chapter Directory. Many states have statewide chapters of the national professional association for local government management officials, the International City/County Management Association (ICMA). Those states with ICMA chapters, or closely related organizations, have their websites listed.

Finance Officials State Chapter Directory. Many states also have statewide chapters of the national professional association for finance managers, the Government Finance Officers Association (GFOA). Those states with GFOA chapters, or closely related organizations, have their respective websites listed.

State Municipal League Directory. Most states have a professional municipal association, which serves as a valuable source of information about their state's city governments. State leagues typically have copies of municipal laws, policies, and budgets available for public officials and citizens in their state to review. The website for each state's municipal league is listed.

State Library Directory. Each state has a central state library, and each one typically contains copies of state laws and policies concerning municipal budgeting and financial management practices for their state, as well as for cities within their state. These libraries serve as an excellent resource for both citizens and public officials. The website for each state library is listed.

The editor hopes that the information contained in this volume will assist citizens, local public officials, and leaders of community organizations as they attempt to make sense out of the many best practices emerging in the dynamic and evolving field of municipal budgeting and financial management practices. The future of America's municipalities depends upon the proper planning and management of their available financial resources through the best budgetary and financial management practices available. Citizens not only expect but demand that prudent measures be adopted and implemented in these areas to insure that their public services are provided at the lowest possible cost.

PART I.
INTRODUCTION

CHAPTER 1

The Fiscal Crisis and America's Cities
Derek Okubo

America's communities are facing the worst fiscal crisis since the Great Depression. Over the past few years, sales tax receipts, an important source of revenues, have plummeted. Developers went bankrupt, meaning fewer permit fees for commercial and residential buildings. Banks remain very cautious about lending money, adversely affecting development and business growth. A reduced number of shifts in local plants means lower revenues from utility fees. Even municipalities that have been fiscally prudent or conservative by not incurring large debt face potential threats that could plunge them deeper into crisis:

- Uncertainty with health insurance and pension costs for government staff
- Aging communities that could put pressure on health services
- Older infrastructure
- The possibility of a natural disaster or pandemic and its impact on already tight budgets
- Unfunded mandates from the feds and states that will trickle down to local governments, forcing them to make cuts that they have been able to avoid to this point

Unfortunately, the full measure of this fiscal crisis may not have been felt yet, thanks to the reliance of local governments on property tax collection and the fact that assessments don't immediately reflect fluctuations in the economy. Although recent economic reports show improvement in the economy, past experience suggests that for local government the worst effects won't occur until eighteen to twenty-four months after the low point of the recession.

The last time there was a national economic crisis, the federal government moved in to help struggling communities. With a huge budget deficit facing the federal government, however, such a rescue seems unlikely. Already, the amount of local revenues from federal sources has declined from about 17 percent in the 1970s to about 5 percent today.

To become more efficient and fiscally responsible, local governments and institutions must change how they do business, to:

- Move beyond the historical turf wars that have existed between government entities to develop new partnerships and joint services
- Find ways of linking budgets directly to performance assessments and outcomes that are visible to the public
- Engage the public in making informed de-

Originally published as "Fiscal Sustainability and Local Government," *National Civic Review*, Vol. 99, No. 4, Winter 2010, pp. 31–34, by the National Civic League, Denver, CO. Reprinted with permission of the publisher. www.wileyonlinelibrary.com/journal/ncr.

cisions about budgets in an efficient, responsible, and productive manner

Interviews with Public Managers

In November and December 2009, the National Civic League interviewed city and county managers from across the nation (both coasts, north and south, and in the heartland) regarding the financial crisis facing local municipalities. They made themselves fully available and were eager to share their frustrations, surprises, and hopes. In this summary, we have excluded names and communities for confidentiality reasons.

The first question we asked managers was very general: "How is the economic crisis manifesting itself in your community?"

The managers gave many examples that fell into a small number of categories.

Assessed property valuations have dropped, which has an impact on revenues for schools and local government. Sales tax revenues have remained flat or fallen (the range was 3–14 percent). Unemployment was rising in these communities, which created an increased need for human services, for as service-oriented non-profits and other organizations struggle, residents turn to local government for help. County managers have seen growth in requests for social services, mental health services, and food stamps (in one community requests have increased by as much as 25 percent).

Budget issues at the state level are having an impact on another county, where there has been an increase in county jail population as the state cuts back and places prisoners in county jails to finish their sentence — a case of the state pushing the costs down to local counties. Residential development has slowed considerably, in some communities nearly to a full stop. Commercial development in most cases is continuing. It hasn't stopped but has slowed or stayed the same.

Employee costs are going up in all jurisdictions, as much as 10 percent per year for employee costs for the next few years in California, said one respondent, and "that is a conservative estimate." Delinquency in payments to local

government is up. Code enforcement reports are up, as people's ability to fix problems is affected by the downturn.

Local government contributions to community amenities have been cut drastically or confined to:

- Museums
- Playhouses
- Economic development corporations
- Downtown partnerships
- Municipal bands
- Senior centers

City staff members are being forced to learn how to finance commercial developments to keep things going until the financial markets stabilize. Most communities are imposing hiring freezes and have experienced layoffs (mostly through attrition), but some have had to lay off staff in areas that were once considered untouchable. As one person put it, "When cities are laying off police and fire, that is a bad sign." Some managers expressed frustration about the seeming denial of elected officials and residents. In every case where the managers vented their frustration, they noted a higher degree of denial on the part of elected officials and residents, some of whom seemed to think that money was still available somewhere within their budgets. As a result, they were unwilling to make cuts or were asking for more money for their "pet" programs.

One city manager said he will know things are turning for the better in his community when he sees improvement in three key indicators: new housing starts, increased lending of money for local businesses and developers, and improvement in the municipal bond market. "Disaster may be too strong a word," another manager said, "but this is definitely the worst financial crisis that I have seen. I've seen three recessions, and we recovered within six to twelve months. People are now recognizing that we still haven't seen bottom. 2010 is going to be worse revenue-wise in California."

Some, however, have said that the economic crisis gave them an opportunity to make cuts that needed to be made years ago but were politically too difficult to make at the time. In California, "Local government types are taking on these issues and are dealing with them," said one manager. "Younger city managers are more open to public engagement, and we need that with this crisis. We need community engagement because there is no way local government can come up with the answers ourselves. We need the dialogues on the priorities. That is the silver lining — that partnering with the community is happening out of necessity. Communities have learned from Vallejo's experience and that concessions have to be made" by everyone. (Vallejo, California, was unable to balance its budget and avoid municipal bankruptcy.)

We asked those public managers whose communities seemed less severely affected by the downturn what has saved them from seeing a greater impact on their community. The most common answer was proactive thinking and being ahead of the curve. The downtown economic downturn following the attacks on September 11, 2001, had caused financial challenges for some communities. Those financial difficulties revealed that the local governments needed to diversify and understand their revenue streams. Putting these new systems and approaches in place has helped them cope with the 2009 economic crisis.

Some communities experienced fortuitous advantages. For instance, in one border community the population at a military base substantially increased, causing growth in revenue. In the meantime, violence in a neighboring community led to a number of more affluent residents moving to their community. Some California cities (perhaps about 5 percent) had lower budgets and wealthier but shrinking populations (therefore less service costs). They also never had big retirement packages for staff thanks to fewer workers.

One manager noted that residents in his community were still spending money, but they were spending it differently. Instead of frequenting high-end shops, they were shopping at the medium- to lower-range stores. This revealed that a diversity of retail options for residents was crucial to sustaining their tax base.

In almost every case, managers in communities less adversely affected than neighboring cities believed it was due to the practice of being smart with development and avoiding debt. For example, one community reported that after September 11 it suffered a significant decrease in sales tax, at one point dropping 13 percent in one quarter (and at that time it was 30 percent of their revenues). This fact revealed that the city government was highly susceptible to economic downturns by being so dependent on sales tax, so it adopted new approaches for diversifying revenue. As a result, this community was not affected as badly as others with this latest downturn. This manager reminded us that the NCL-led, community-based strategic planning process revealed the need for diversification, and the stakeholders drove a property tax increase to help. It passed and was one area that helped create significantly more balance.

Since 2001, this community has been building up its fund balance after making a policy that 20 percent of all revenues must be set aside in a rainy day account. In 2009, the fund helped cover the costs to repair or replace capital equipment without affecting other areas. The fund has continued and now makes up 20 percent of their fund balance. They have not had to lay off people, nor stop any projects, but they must be conscious of how they manage and schedule projects.

Many city managers mentioned that the economic crisis has given the "sustainability mind-set" new salience. Being smart with development and avoiding sprawl in previous years left with them lower infrastructure costs and service expenses than in other growing communities (focusing on urban boundary planning, and redevelopment). In addition, focusing on economic sustainability in years past has helped create a local mind-set (buy local, eat local, use local transit) that has helped keeps sales tax revenues fairly stable.

The willingness of elected officials and staff to face the realities and make hard decisions was absolutely essential. A strong relationship between council leadership and the city manager was always necessary with this issue. Communicating with residents on the crisis — sharing important information and being willing to meet face-to-face — was also crucial.

Will the New Year Be Worse?

The responses to this question varied from uncertain to worse, to about the same, to better.

- Almost all said their sales tax projections for 2010 were flat, which they took as a positive sign that things were not getting worse (as many feared). 2008 projections foresaw a decrease that indeed materialized in 2009.
- Those who said they were uncertain or things were going to be worse were those local governments that had higher dependence on development and growth.
- Those who said things were going to be better were those communities that had been fiscally conservative for a number of years. These practices allowed them to minimize the negative impact of 2009.
- All communities were exploring innovative ways to finance development.
- Some have seen a small increase in applications for development, which gives them hope that things might pick up in the third and fourth quarter of 2010.

However, some managers said that things could get worse, even for those minimally affected, with a local disaster or more cutbacks and mandates from the state as they push costs down to the local level.

Long-Range Impact

When asked if they thought the crisis would forever change the way local government conducts business, the managers gave a range of answers. Those who answered, "No, it will not forever change the way local government conducts business" were already implementing preemptive measures or had conservative fiscal practices in place. Among the comments:

I disagree with any "sky is falling" mentality. Speaking with other managers, this crisis has helped us make changes that were needed but were politically difficult to move on. This has helped us make better business decisions.

I don't agree at all. In talking with other (good) managers, I think we always realize that we can't do everything and hard decisions have to be made. We have to be up front and deal with them. We are a resilient bunch.

I don't agree that it will forever change — forever is a very strong word. I treat it like a regional disaster. For example, in 2002 we were hit by a devastating ice storm and the perception was that the landscape was forever changed. Today we look at where we are, and we went through this disaster and recovered very well. Communities and local governments are incredibly resilient, and we can and will heal ourselves. Some people to tend to think that this crisis we are currently going through is like that — I don't believe it is.

"This is a perfect time to change," said one manager. "There is some validity in the premise ... but change with local government is so incremental. We need these major incidents [to occur] in order for government to change. Technology, global economy, recession ... we are in the beginning of recognizing what drives the economy and revenues for local government. It is finally taking place. I just know that the status quo cannot work. Grudgingly, some movement will happen here and there around the country because we are forced to change. Some may be longer-term changes, and the changes might not be obvious. I feel the change will be slow enough that we'll look back in 2020 and wonder what was going on that caused us to change the way we do business."

"Yes and no," said one manager. "We have had to change over time due to being a growing community. We were growing so fast we had to change. Now the bottom has dropped out, so we have to change again, only under different conditions. We are adaptive by nature." Another manager did not agree that it would change how government worked overall but would "force government to look at where they are getting their revenue from. Right now we are property- and sales-tax-dependent."

There were some managers who thought the changes would be permanent. "I'm trying not to be pessimistic," said one manager, "but this devolution started back in the 1980s. The feds started cutting back and passing them down locally to the states. In our state, we have a structural problem that will not go away even with a better economy. A lot of cities are going to have less to provide services because the costs are going up and we have less revenue. I don't see that going away with an aging population, aging infrastructure — costs are going to continue to go up. Federal, state, and local governments need to change. Local governments are going to take the brunt."

"I believe we are going to be locked in for a long time," said another. "We don't have a lot of diversity revenue-wise and within our community retail-wise. There is a lot of leakage, where residents are going elsewhere to shop at the large national retailers." Another said yes, but only in specific areas: "For instance, I don't see any changes happening in the way police departments work, but I do with fire departments."

What Governments Are Doing Differently

Every manager I interviewed said the financial crunch had adversely affected the local government. The differences were a question of degree. Local governments have made changes in their approaches to several areas. An important one was innovative revenue generation. Communities were looking at things such as banking and development collaboration with local government, new developer fees, new impact fees, and new user fees. Innovations with health insurance costs for staff included partnering with health insurance providers and focusing on prevention by incorporating ambitious wellness programs to keep premiums down.

Communities are exploring new partnerships to offer services across jurisdictions, setting aside turf issues and collaborating on services. For example, some are combining police and fire dispatch services. Communities are revisiting their relations with employee unions and asking community users to pony up. Another example: it looked as if an ice rink that was maintained by the city would be closing because of costs. The users stepped up to pay for the costs through their team fees, therefore keeping the rink open.

Communities are thinking more about smart development, incorporating sustainability practices for the long run. Staff members are learning more about how to finance commercial development and how to diversify revenue sources by broadening sources beyond large box retailers to include high to low end. They are taking a hard look at sales and property taxes. They are exploring new technologies to assist with services.

Local governments are being forced to increase spending on social programs for the poor, including such things as assistance with utility fees, energy assistance, and water fees. Recognizing that people cannot afford house repairs, some cities are finding partners to help subsidize costs, or pull volunteers together to help. Some managers believe there is a need to explore different government structures among the state, counties, cities, and towns to find more effective and fair ways of addressing revenue issues.

There seems to be more of a mind-set of paying attention to results — actual impacts rather than outputs. "Government has been exceptional in measuring numbers or outputs — not outcomes," said one manager. They see the need to change the structural system of "how many" to "how effective are we?"

Local officials, both elected and appointed, are finding it necessary to spend more time educating themselves and others about the existing tough realities, including scheduling more face-to-face meetings with staff and constituents. They feel the need to design processes to tackle issues that put people in the mind-set of problem solving, not a "what am I going to lose" mode. They are encouraging staff members to search for solutions and assist in implementing the solutions. Referring to mayors and city councils, one manager said: "As leaders, they have to be willing to go out into the communities and meet with them. Now more than ever. We've been fortunate that our leadership has done so."

How Will the Crunches Affect Citizen Engagement?

Every manager said that the financial crunch has created more scrutiny of local government and how it is operating, but residents' expectations haven't changed toward basic services even though the money to cover them has dwindled. The managers reported that the scarcity has created a self-survival mentality among many, resulting in a lot of parochial attitudes and conflicting forces that need to be brought together to identify shared priorities and partnerships. Many reported that they feel incivility among residents has increased. A few managers felt that the health care public forums held in the fall of 2009 initiated a circus atmosphere for public meetings, where it "became OK" for people to abandon civility and they were applauded for behaving that way."

Every manager said that citizen engagement is more important than ever. Among those reasons mentioned:

- Local governments need to know citizen priorities for services.
- Resident engagement means sharing in the problem solving and helping with the implementation.
- Resident input on solutions helped initiate their genuine participation as partners on community programs that used to be the sole responsibility of local government and has saved them from being cut.
- Communication with residents on the rationale (the whys) behind the cuts is crucial to building understanding to move toward problem solving.

Resident understanding means that although they may not agree with the decision, they understand why the decision had to be made. As one manager put it, what is critical is "strategic planning processes that include residents — local government needs to be even more strategic than ever."

Conclusion

Today's environment has created a need for different tweaks to public engagement ap-

proaches to challenging issues. Public forums must move away from placing constituents in the role of mere problem identifier and instead place constituents in the role of problem solver. Public officials are more courageous about making tough choices if they know they have buy-in from the public. In addition, as services to neighborhoods and commercial districts are being cut, it is often the most organized, most affluent, and most vocal groups that have the closest links to local officials. For people from local governments whom I talked to, this is unacceptable during these tough times, and intentional and deliberate efforts must be made to hear from those who cannot or will not participate in public processes. The tough decisions, they feel, must be shared by all, rather than imposed on the overlooked and underheard.

The timing of this current economic crisis offers municipalities and the communities they serve motivation to create effective methods of addressing complex challenges because the urgency to create change is ever present. People across all sectors recognize that change must occur and that it will not happen on its own. Nor is it the responsibility of one sector to do it alone. People must come together to make it happen. The tools that will be applied to help build fiscal accountability can be easily applied successfully to other issues that emerge, and therefore they are sustainable.

The irony is that restrictive budgets make some local government officials leery about pending precious dollars on seemingly nonessential "process" efforts, which underscores the need to improve the cost effectiveness of citizen-based efforts to address this fiscal crisis. When it comes to civic engagement, government officials have to become "better consumers." Effective processes, procedures, and facilitative leadership skills to coordinate partnerships and funding strategies across interests are required.

CHAPTER 2

Balancing Budgets with Job and Service Reductions

Christopher W. Hoene *and* Jacqueline J. Byers

Unemployment in America is a national crisis. It is also a local crisis. As individuals and families struggle to find work, make ends meet, and keep their homes amid an anemic economic recovery, they increasingly turn to local services for support. Local governments provide job training and assistance, transportation, support services for individuals and families in need, health care and education and afterschool programs that support working families. In many communities, local governments are also one of the primary employers.

Unfortunately, just as families are increasingly turning to local governments for support, local governments are facing their own fiscal crisis. The effects of the Great Recession on local budgets will be felt most deeply from 2010 to 2012.[1] In response, local governments are cutting services and personnel. This report from the National League of Cities (NLC), National Association of Counties (NACo), and the U.S. Conference of Mayors (USCM) reveals that local government job losses in the current and next fiscal years will approach 500,000, with public safety, public works, public health, social services and parks and recreation hardest hit by the cutbacks. Local governments are being forced to make significant cuts that will eliminate jobs, curtail essential services, and increase the number of people in need.

This report presents the latest survey results from local officials on job losses and service cuts. The survey results point to the urgent need for federal action to minimize layoffs and service cuts in order to help families and stabilize local economies.

The Economic Role of Local Governments

Local governments — cities and counties — are important to the vitality of families and local economies. They provide goods and services that are important to the quality of life of families, such as public safety, parks, libraries, housing and health services, and are central to the performance of local economies.

Local budget crises lead to job losses in both the public and private sectors. The business of local governments is often conducted through the private sector — construction and maintenance, garbage collection and recycling and tree trimming are just a few examples. The Economic Policy Institute estimates that for every 100 public sector layoffs there are 30 private sector layoffs.[2] Local government investment in transportation, water, sewer and communications infrastructure also leverages significant private sector growth by reducing

Originally published as "Local Governments Cutting Jobs and Services," *Research Brief*, July 2010, by the National League of Cities, Washington, D.C. Reprinted with permission of the publisher.

private sector costs and creating opportunities for additional investment. Local governments are also significant sources of employment. Local and state governments comprise one of the nation's largest employment industries, larger than the manufacturing and construction industries combined. Local governments account for seven in every 10 of these employees.[3]

Local governments across the country are now facing the combined impact of decreased tax revenues, a falloff in state and federal aid and increased demand for social services. Over the next two years, local tax bases will likely suffer from depressed property values, hard-hit household incomes and declining consumer spending.[4] Further, reported state budget shortfalls for 2010 to 2012 exceeding $400 billion will pose a significant threat to funding for local government programs.[5] In this current climate of fiscal distress, local governments are forced to eliminate both jobs and services.

Cuts in Local Jobs

In May and June of 2010 NLC, NACo and USCM conducted a survey of cities and counties across the country for the purpose of gauging the extent of job losses. The survey was emailed and faxed to all cities over 25,000 in population and to all counties over 100,000 in population. The survey results presented below are based on 270 responses, 214 responses from cities and 56 responses from counties.

The surveyed local governments report cutting 8.6 percent of total full-time equivalent (FTE) positions over the previous fiscal year to the next fiscal year (roughly 2009–2011). If applied to total local government employment nationwide, an 8.6 percent cut in the workforce would mean that 481,000 local government workers were, or will be, laid off over the two-year period.[6] Projected cuts for the next fiscal year will likely increase as many of the nation's local governments draft new budgets, deliberate about how to balance shortfalls and adopt new budgets.[7]

Local job losses are most heavily felt in public safety, public works, public health, social services, and parks and recreation. Local governments typically seek to shield direct services to residents from cuts during economic downturns and the cuts occurring in these services are indicative of the depth of the recession's impact on cities and counties.

Cities and counties almost always seek to protect public safety services — police, fire, and emergency — from cuts in personnel and funding. The need for these basic, or "core," services in terms of protecting the public against crime, fire, and disaster often increase during periods of economic downturn. The depth of the current downturn, however, means that surprising numbers of cities (63 percent) and counties (39 percent) report cuts in public safety personnel. For some communities this means fire and police stations that are closed and the potential for reduced capacity to respond to emergencies.

A majority of the surveyed cities (60 percent) and counties (68 percent) report making personnel cuts in public works. Public works services are highly visible to local residents — such as highway and road construction and maintenance and solid waste (garbage and recycling) disposal. Cuts in public works are common responses to economic downturns, but the range of local governments making these cuts in response to the current downturn is considerably higher than previously. For instance, in response to the 2001 recession, a survey conducted by NACo revealed that 26 percent of counties were delaying highway and road construction and 23 percent reported delaying highway and road maintenance.[8] Cuts in public works go beyond public jobs, with many of these services provided via contracts with private sector businesses.

Approximately half of the surveyed counties report personnel cuts in social services (52 percent) and public health (48 percent), services that are critical to local residents in need. Counties, and some cities, deliver significant services in these arenas, in many cases as extensions of state government programs. For example, many counties are the primary delivery agents for child welfare services, cash assistance payments to individuals and families in need and public health and medical services. Confronted with their own significant budget shortfalls, many states are cutting these programs. Yet, demand for these services tends to increase during periods of economic downturn. Personnel and other budget cuts will increase the already expanding pressures on case loads and the remaining personnel.

Park maintenance and programs for youth, such as afterschool educational and recreational activities, and seniors, such as meal delivery services, are also highly visible local services that often serve as the primary point of interaction for many residents with local governments. Approximately half of cities (54 percent) and counties (45 percent) report personnel cuts in parks and recreation services.

Many local governments are also making personnel cuts in library services, resulting in closures, reduced hours and cuts in programs. Libraries often serve as centers for job searches for residents without access to computers and the Internet, or provide afterschool programs.

City- and county-run schools and school districts are also facing significant cutbacks. Economic conditions have eroded local revenue bases and, particularly in education, state budget shortfalls are resulting in significant cuts to funding for local schools. In response, teaching jobs and special programs are being eliminated, class sizes are increasing and caseloads for school aides and counselors are on the rise.

The Need for Federal Action

While the nation's economy is slowly emerging from the worst economic downturn since the Great Depression, the consequences of the recession will be playing out in America's local communities for years to come. Since the onset of the economic downturn, local leaders have been forced to make tough choices in an effort to provide desperately needed services and to bolster their local economies while responding to large and often persistent budget shortfalls. With the nation's unemployment rate hovering around 9.5 percent and more than 8 million jobs lost since the recession began in late 2007, families are being forced to do the same.

To secure economic recovery, Congress and the Administration must act now to create jobs quickly and help stabilize local government economies. An immediate opportunity exists in the Local Jobs for America Act (H.R. 4812/S. 3500), which would provide $75 billion in targeted and temporary fiscal assistance over two years to local governments and community based organizations to save and create local jobs. Other opportunities include investing in infrastructure through targeted spending to local governments and ensuring that small businesses and local governments can obtain access to credit. Federal investment that helps save local jobs and preserve local services will help stabilize communities across the country and ensure that all of America's families are able to participate in the economic recovery.

REFERENCES

1. Christopher W. Hoene, *City Budget Shortfalls and Responses: 2010–2012*, National League of Cities, December 2009, http://www.nlc.org/ASSETS/0149CE492F8C49D09 5160195306B6E08/BuddgetShortFalls_FINAL.pdf.

2. Ethan Pollock, *Local Government Job Losses Hurt Entire Economy*, Economic Policy Institute, May 2010, http://www.epi.org/page/-/pdf/issuebrief279.pdf.

3. U.S. Bureau of Labor Statistics, www.bls.gov.

4. Local fiscal conditions typically lag economic conditions, in much the same way that state fiscal conditions lag economic conditions and the unemployment rate lags overall economic recovery. For local budgets, this lag can be anywhere from one to three years, depending on the factors driving the changes in the economy and the depth of those changes. Current economic indicators suggest that the U.S. economy passed the low point of the current recession in late 2009, which means that the low point for fiscal conditions will likely be experienced sometime in 2011. To illustrate this lag, the U.S. Census of Governments reports that local property tax collections began to decline in the first quarter of 2010, two-and-a-half years after the housing market began to decline in the summer of 2007.

5. Elizabeth McNichol, Phil Oliff and Nicholas Johnson, *Recession Continues to Batter State Budgets; State Responses Could Slow Recovery*, Center on Budget and Policy Priorities, July 2010, http://www.cbpp.org/cms/index.cfm?fa=view&id=711.

6. Total city and county employment statistics are drawn from the U.S. Census of Governments.

7. Not all cities and counties utilize the same fiscal year timeframes. The most common local government fiscal year runs from July 1 to June 30, which is used by 46 percent of the surveyed cities and 56 percent of the surveyed counties. Some local governments utilize a January 1 to December 31 fiscal year (28 percent cities; 21 percent counties), some use an October 1 to September 30 fiscal year (22 percent cities; 18 percent counties) and others use some alternate timeframe (4 percent cities; 1 percent counties).

8. Harry Hayes and Richard Clark, Counties in Crisis, Carl Vinson Institute of Government, University of Georgia, July 2003.

Editor's note: Contributions to this research were also made by Christiana McFarland, Will McGahan and Caitlin Geary at the National League of Cities, and by Kathryn Murphy and Deseree Gardner at the National Association of Counties.

CHAPTER 3

Prudent Options for Balancing Public Budgets

Roger L. Kemp

Public officials in communities across the nation have to balance their respective budgets, keep tax increases to a minimum, and make every effort to maintain existing public services. Particular fiscal problems can be state specific, but at this difficult time in our nation's history, all local officials must cope with these difficult issues.

Local government officials can make good use of lessons learned from the past. There is no need to reinvent the wheel when it comes to balancing public budgets in hard times.

The national pressure for cutback management began in the state of California a generation ago. At the time, I was both working for the city of Oakland, California, and preparing my doctoral dissertation. For my dissertation I chose the subject of coping with Proposition 13 because I had been assisting in developing the city's budget in response to the revenue reduction imposed by this citizens' mandate. The practices I learned from this experience, plus my other budget reduction experience that has been gained from serving in communities on both coasts of the United States since then, are reflected in this article.

Over the years, numerous budget development processes have projected, enhanced, and protected revenues; guided department managers and elected officials; and worked to ensure that public services were reduced only marginally, with the goal of balancing the annual budget in the most positive way possible.

Strategies, measures, tactics, and programs useful for today's public officials — both elected and appointed — are noted below. The purpose of presenting these options is to ensure that budget reduction practices and adoption processes are prudent yet optimize the use of existing revenue sources and make every effort to minimize the reduction of public services to citizens being served.

No new public services. During difficult financial times, there must be a policy of no new public services. No additional services should be added to the budget unless they are cost covering from a revenue standpoint. This means that, if user fees and charges cover the cost of providing the service, then it can be approved. If not, consideration of the service must be postponed until subsequent fiscal years. This is a fact of life when revenues are limited.

Implement a hiring freeze. One of the most obvious ways to save money is to impose an organization-wide hiring freeze. During these difficult financial times, elected officials early in the budgetary process should officially approve a hiring freeze. This creates immediate savings in salaries, fringe benefits, and other budget line items used in the provision of public services. Everyone should know that the elected officials are taking such action to avoid or at least minimize layoffs of employees and reductions of services later in the budget development process.

Form a union-management cost-savings committee. To balance public budgets, it is a positive measure to involve major stakeholders such as public unions in the process. The local government manager should meet with union representatives as appropriate (usually one member from each union) and ask for their cooperation in reviewing expenses and operations and in jointly recommending ways to save funds and avoid employee layoffs if at all possible. Asking elected officials for approval to form such a committee should have a positive effect because a message is being sent to citizens that both management and unions are involved in reducing the budget.

Update user fees and charges. Reevaluating the user-fee structure seems self-evident, but few cities and counties routinely update their user fees and charges for public services. Although the private sector updates prices annually because of increased costs, governments seldom perform this task with any regularity. User fees and charges should be updated to reflect the actual cost of providing the services rendered to the public. It is also appropriate to provide discounts or free-use periods to selected citizens subject to the approval of their elected representatives.

Check existing enterprise funds. The national trend is to create enterprise funds in which the user fees and charges generated by the service make it cost covering. These funds are appropriate when only the users of a specific service benefit from its provision (sewer, water, arenas, stadiums, museums, golf courses, parking, and the list goes on). As budgets increase for such services, the user fees and charges should increase also, to ensure that the revenues cover the entire cost of providing the service. If discounts are approved for certain groups, user fees and charges must be increased for other citizens who use the service in order to offset this revenue loss.

Create other enterprise funds. After you check your existing enterprise funds, also review your government's public services to see whether other services should be set up in this manner. Sewer and water services have long been cost covering from a revenue standpoint, but other public services must be considered for enterprise fund status when they do not benefit the entire community. If a public service benefits only certain citizens, then those users should pay for the cost of the service. Funding for golf courses, arenas, stadiums, zoos, and museums is headed in this direction.

Use one-time revenues wisely. It is not usually fiscally prudent to use one-time revenues or budgetary savings to fund future operating expenses. The only sound financial practice is to use one-time revenues or budget savings to fund one-time expenses, both operating and capital, as appropriate and subject to the approval of elected officials. Using one-time revenues and budget savings to finance operating expenses merely exacerbates an organization's fiscal problems in the future.

Always seek available operational grants. Make sure that the staff is informed and knowledgeable about all existing grants from other levels and types of governments as well as appropriate nonprofit foundations. Every public agency should attempt to take advantage of all external funding sources for which it may qualify, including grants made available from nonprofit foundations. Most public libraries have reference books that list both regional and national nonprofit organizations and the programs for which they provide funding.

Optimize the use of available infrastructure grants. The federal government has made these grants available in the past under different administrations. When city and county managers know these funds are available, they should have their elected officials approve a projects list and start preparing plans and specifications to fast-track major projects that qualify for this funding. It is common for a local government to spend money up front to obtain engineering services in order to have important projects shovel ready when the grant funds become available. These project-related costs are often reimbursed subsequently by such grant programs.

Take measures to accommodate the truly needy. Elected officials and their staffs should not forget that, when public services are reduced and user fees and charges are increased, special consideration should be given to truly needy citizens. Special provisions, as defined and approved by elected officials, should be made for these residents. Modest user fees and charges, along with discounted charges that can include free use during low-utilization periods, are entirely appropriate during difficult financial times.

Consider employee work furloughs. The use of employee layoffs to balance a public budget should be a last resort. Efforts should be made to work with employee unions to avoid layoffs. One of the options available to save public funds and balance budgets is to have an employee work furlough. This requires selected employees to take time off for a number of days, up to a few weeks, typically staggered throughout the fiscal year, to reduce costs and minimize disruptions to public services. Elected officials usually favor this option because public services are not reduced substantially.

Avoid employee layoffs. Several options are available to save money, balance budgets, and avoid employee layoffs. Management and union representatives can agree to open labor negotiations to discuss various cost reduction and expense deferral options. Because governments basically deliver services, most of which are provided by people, public budgets are driven by salaries and fringe-benefit costs. All of these expenses can be reduced or deferred to avoid employee layoffs and severe service reductions. This is an appropriate option for major budget reductions.

Follow prudent bonding practices. The staff should recommend, and elected officials should approve, fiscally responsible bonding practices for all bond-funded public projects. Revenue bonds can be used to finance those projects with a solid revenue stream. General obligation bonds are typically used to finance public improvements and land acquisitions when no, or minimal, revenues are generated by these projects.

General obligation bonds are backed by the full faith and credit of the issuing government and have lower interest rates than revenue bonds. Public officials should also have established cost-limit policies for capital projects, land acquisitions, and major equipment pur-

chases to qualify for bond financing. Also, some states provide bonding services to their local governments, which serves to aggregate purchases and thus provide lower interest rates for a bond issue.

Provide timely budget information to everyone. When reducing a public budget, make it a point to pursue all financial options to reduce operating costs and generate additional revenues. This means that all available operational and fiscal options should be listed and presented to elected officials for their review and consideration. It is entirely appropriate to start such budget review practices early during the fiscal year. This means that city and county managers should have their staffs prepare revenue projections early to allow time to work with department managers and employee unions to explore all service reduction, revenue enhancement, cost reduction, and expense deferral options.

Direct department heads to look for accrued savings. Early in a difficult fiscal year, a directive should be sent to all department managers asking them to review their approved budgets with the goal of holding down expenses, including employee-related expenses such as overtime as well as those operating expenses that can be reduced immediately without negatively impacting public services. Everyone should be told that this effort is being made to increase budgetary savings to offset the projected deficit for the coming fiscal year and to minimize possible future service reductions and employee layoffs.

Consider early retirement programs. Everyone agrees that senior employees cost more than entry-level employees. To the extent that an early-retirement program, such as a small pension incentive, can be offered to encourage senior employees to retire, it will save any public agency considerable funds in the future. New employees for most jobs start at the entry level, saving salary and fringe-benefit expenses. The hiring of new employees can also be deferred, if necessary. Early-retirement programs are considered a favorable expense reduction option by public unions and their employees.

Implement prudent financial policies. More public agencies should be approving prudent financial and budgetary policies, especially during these difficult economic times. This is a public and official way to give direction to all employees. Many local governments wait until there is a budgetary or financial problem before adopting financial policies.

Because of this, such policies sometimes tend to be problem-specific. Now is the time to proactively adopt sound fiscal policies. By doing this, public officials will give permanent direction to their staffs and mitigate the impact of future financial difficulties during the coming years. When such policies are established by elected officials, and approved publicly, they stay in place until they are changed by majority vote at a future public meeting.

Review existing funds for appropriateness. Periodically, when the annual audit takes place, the auditor and top management and financial staff should be requested to review all of the organization's funds, and their balances, for appropriateness. Some funds may have been established for a purpose that has been changed by subsequent circumstances or legislation.

The size of all existing funds should also be reviewed to ensure that the funds do not exceed the level desired when they were established. Any changes to existing funds, or their levels of funding, should be reviewed with elected officials and must be changed at a public meeting as a part of the budgetary process. Any excess fund balances, or funds no longer needed, can be transferred to the general fund to offset a potential financial deficit.

Rank public service levels. One of the greatest problems in reducing any budget is the highly political question of the relative value of various public services. Public services may be categorized into four service levels:

Level 1 comprises essential public services, which should not be reduced under any circumstances. Basic minimal levels of police, fire, health, and public works services fall into this category.

Level 2 comprises those programs that are highly desirable, but not absolutely essential.

Level 3 comprises the nice-but-not-necessary services that have significant value but do not provide essential or necessary services to the public.

Level 4 services can be described as the first-to-go programs because they are not essential and serve only a small portion of the community.

The criteria used to rank public services should be determined by elected officials as they consider budget reduction options.

Evaluate the impact of service-level reductions. To properly assess proposed service reductions, their relative impact on prevailing services must be determined. Many program reductions, because of existing personnel vacancies, may have no substantial impact on services; however, other service reductions may have a measurable impact. Four stages of service reductions can be used for this purpose:

Stage 1 reductions would reduce a substantial portion of a program or eliminate the program entirely.

Stage 2 reductions would reduce a sizable portion of a program but would not affect basic services.

Stage 3 reductions would reduce only a small portion of a program and not affect essential public services.

Stage 4 reductions would have little or no impact on prevailing public services.

Management can recommend such criteria, but elected officials determine the final rankings.

Prepare public service impact statements. Last but not least, before final decisions are made on reducing a government's budget, citizens should be informed of the impact that a monetary decrease has on the services selected for possible reduction. Each budget reduction proposed should come with a public service impact statement. This information should be provided with the list of proposed budget reductions given to elected officials.

The statement should also be made available to citizens at the public hearings and meetings held on budget reductions. If time permits, signs should be prepared and placed at those public facilities where services might be reduced. Public officials have an ethical obligation to properly inform the public of the operational impact of their financial and budgetary decisions.

There is no doubt that these are difficult financial times for local public officials who represent the citizens and manage their organizations. All of these financial, budgetary, and operational choices are difficult to make, but they are a sign of the times. The sorting and prioritizing of public programs, and the rational reduction of government spending, form the most pressing challenge facing public officials today. Analyzing the political and administrative choices implemented by other local governments over the years will facilitate the use of orderly and sound options by today's public officials as they balance their communities' budgets.

These suggested guidelines are offered with the intention of providing insight and clarity to this arduous process. Budget reduction and revenue enhancement strategies that reflect responsibility, not only to the beneficiaries of public services but also to those who must foot the bill, must ultimately prevail.

Welcome to the difficult world of sorting out the relative value of public services and making sound financial and budgetary decisions so that public budgets are balanced to meet available revenues!

CHAPTER 4

Saving Money by Contracting for Public Services

Amanda M. Girth *and* Jocelyn M. Johnston

With increased fiscal challenges for many cities across America, more local leaders have recently begun investigating alternative means for delivering services, namely contracting or privatization. While contracting is not a new concept, it does alter the service delivery landscape for city officials. More specifically, contracting requires a new set of local management skills and raises issues about the quality of contracted services, new costs associated with contracting, managing vendor competition and ensuring optimal contract performance.

American University, with the support of the National League of Cities, launched the Survey on Local Government Contracting to better understand how public managers view contracting in the nation's cities and towns. Public managers across the country provided critical insights into the "real time" management challenges of local government contracting, helping to highlight the importance of effective governing.

The results of the survey indicate that while municipal officials generally favor government contracting, many face significant challenges in holding contractors accountable for their performance. This may be attributed to the competitiveness of the market for the contracted service, management capacity of both the government and contractor, and the effective (or ineffective) use of performance incentives.

Attitudes About Contracting

The survey asked managers questions about their general attitudes on municipal contracting. Results indicate that managers generally:

- Support government contracting (93 percent);
- Prefer to provide services in-house if given the option (69 percent); and
- Believe that most public agencies do a good job at contract management (63 percent).

About one in two managers (47 percent) report the greatest drawback of contracting is the difficulty of holding contractors accountable for their performance. The greatest benefits of contracting are distributed across a number of factors, ranging from cost savings (35 percent), greater flexibility in service delivery (32 percent), staffing (14 percent), and higher quality services (13 percent).

Overall, most respondents (69 percent) indicate that their contracts produce high-quality services to citizens. However, there is less consensus among managers about cost sav-

Originally published as "Local Governments Contracting," *Research Brief*, February 2011, by the National League of Cities, Washington, D.C. Reprinted with permission of the publisher.

ings, as just over half (55 percent) report saving money from contracting services.[1] The vast majority of public managers (69 percent) are generally confident in their level of expertise to manage contracts. However, less than half report having the adequate staff (48 percent) or enough time (40 percent) to effectively manage contracts.

Competition in City Contracts

Just over half of managers surveyed (55 percent) report being satisfied with the market for their contracts. Respondents reveal that they would prefer to work with multiple vendors for their contracts, and 87 percent say that four or more is optimal. Yet one-quarter of the managers surveyed report they often resign themselves to working with a small number of vendors because their efforts to find more have failed.

When asked about their ability to find other vendors, managers reported that:

- It is difficult to find high quality vendors (34 percent);
- The number of contract bidders tends to reduce over time (22 percent), often because contractors buy each other out (14 percent);
- They continue to seek additional vendors for current contracts with the next contract cycle in mind (53 percent); and
- Finding vendors takes away from oversight work (23 percent).

In order to manage vendor competition, managers report using a variety of strategies to increase the number of vendors for government contracts and otherwise strengthen competition for their contracts. Perhaps most interesting is that two in five managers routinely report using mixed delivery (i.e., some portion of the service is contracted out while some portion is produced in-house) all (7 percent) or most of the time (34 percent), and about one in three (34 percent) actively create new vendors (i.e., encouraging outside organizations to set up new subsidiaries for contract work) at least some of the time.

Contract Performance

Public mangers also report mentoring and helping contractors with performance. Twenty percent indicate that they spend *a significant amount of time* helping contractors improve contract performance. More than half of respondents (52 percent) report mentoring contractors to ensure they will continue to bid on their contracts in the future.

When it comes to using performance incentives in dealing with contractors, managers indicate they are more likely to use sanctions to penalize for performance problems (66 percent) than they are to use rewards for satisfactory performance (23 percent).

To gather additional information on the ways in which managers address performance issues, respondents were asked to think of one specific contract that best reflected their experience with unsatisfactory performance. When faced with poor performance, 64 percent of managers surveyed elected to take formal action against the contractor, with the most common responses being financial sanctions or contract termination.

Finally, the ways in which managers reported measuring contract performance varied significantly. Managers report that contractors tend to fall short in performance primarily in the areas of responsiveness, quality and service continuity.

It is clear that performance problems do not generally take long to emerge; 78 percent of managers agree that performance issues appear near the beginning or midway through the contract. Managers also indicate that in many cases, their organization was highly dependent on the contractor that was failing to meet performance thresholds. More than half (56 percent) state that their organization did not have the technical expertise to provide the service in-house and 79 percent did not have the resources to provide service in-house.

These survey results suggest that when municipal leaders are forced to privatize city services, most place a strong emphasis on developing, enhancing and ensuring contractor performance. Whether that's through developing strong relationships, creating vendor competition, or holding contractors account-able, city leaders are generally aware that merely shipping responsibility outside of government ultimately will not improve public service.

About the Survey

The survey was sent to 2,195 city officials across the U.S., including 487 randomly selected city managers and 1,708 functional specialists who were primarily department directors and their representatives from building inspection services, human services, information technology, parks and recreation and public works. The survey was conducted from July to November 2009. Results are drawn from 332 respondents for a response rate of 15 percent. With this response rate, it is expected with a 95 percent degree of confidence (i.e., in 95 out of 100 random sample surveys) that if another random sample of municipal officials completed the survey, response results would be within 4.96 percentage points (+/- 4.96 percent) of the results reported here. Survey response rates based on population and region of the country are provided on the website of the National League of Cities (http://www.nlc.org/).

NOTE

1. Unless otherwise indicated, this means the respondent reported agreement (agree or strongly agree) on a five-point scale ranging from strongly disagree to strongly agree.

Author's note: The Survey on Local Government Contracting was conducted by American University with the support of the National League of Cities.

The authors wish to thank Christopher Hoene, director, Center for Research and Innovation, Christiana McFarland, research manager and program director, Finance and Economic Development, and Caitlin Geary, fellow Finance and Economic Development, at the National League of Cities for their assistance and support of this survey effort. The authors also would like to thank the 332 public officials who shared their time and responded to this survey.

CHAPTER 5

Innovative Staffing Options Help Balance Budgets

Laura Kushner

If you have read any newspapers, turned on the television, or opened a web browser lately, you will definitely agree that the world is changing rapidly and there are many challenges ahead for all of us.

For one, we've got the recession, which we all hope will be a short-term challenge. Beyond that, rising energy costs, shrinking revenues, a desire to "go green," the impending retirement of baby boomers, the pressure to provide services at low costs but keep employees motivated and productive — all of these forces are causing cities to think through their staffing strategies. Some of the more innovative opportunities cities are examining include options like flexible scheduling, telecommuting, and phased retirement programs.

Flexible Scheduling

The concept of flexible scheduling has been around for many years, and some cities have offered a flexible work schedule to their employees for decades. Usually, this means that the employee continues to work five days per week, but he or she has some flexibility around the "core hours" of the city. Core hours are generally defined as the primary hours in which most employees will be at work (e.g., 9 A.M. to 4 P.M.).

An employee who chooses to "flex" his or her schedule might be able to choose to work from 7:30 A.M. to 4 P.M., for example, or from 9 A.M. to 5:30 P.M. Coming in later can help accommodate a single parent who wants to see his or her children off on the school bus or employees who simply are not "morning people." Coming in early and leaving early is a nice option for employees who are more productive in the morning or who want to be home when their children get out of school. This flexibility contributes to a happy employee, which is likely to result in a high rate of productivity and retention.

More recently, however, several cities have begun experimenting with four-day workweeks for other reasons. With gas and energy prices rising quickly in the past year, some cities are considering whether they can save on their own energy costs by closing city hall one day per week. Other cities are looking at this option to provide better services to their customers and a nice benefit to their employees.

In other words, if employees work a 10-hour, four-day workweek, then city hall services can be open earlier in the morning and later at night. Customers gain because they can pick up their dog licenses before heading off to work. Employees get the benefit of an extra day off and savings on gas by one less day of

Originally published as "Innovative Staffing Strategies," *Minnesota Cities*, Vol. 94, No. 3, March 2009, by the League of Minnesota Cities, St. Paul. Reprinted with permission of the publisher.

commuting. In some situations this can be a true "win-win" for everyone.

Telecommuting

Telecommuting is often seen as the ultimate flexibility in scheduling, but in reality it may require a city to be more structured with its employees. Good telecommuting policies and programs should be well-defined as to what days and hours employees are considered to be "at work" and, in the long run, may leave less flexibility for the employee than what is required when they come in to city hall every day. However, telecommuting can be a great way to save money for both the city and the employee and, in some cases, actually increases productivity.

Take, for example, a city that is quickly outgrowing its city hall. Instead of remodeling to accommodate more office space, the city could consider offering a telecommuting option. The employees who telecommute may also save money on gas, dress clothes, and lunches. In some situations, the employee may be able to save on daycare costs, but this depends greatly on the individual circumstances. It is generally not a good idea for employees to have childcare duties while they are telecommuting.

Cities and other employers sometimes reject telecommuting as an option without considering some of the facts. One fact to consider is that telecommuting can be anything from working from home one day a month to working from home full-time. It can be limited to only those staff whose job duties do not require much interaction with other staff or customers. It can be allowed only during certain seasons or in certain departments. A telecommuting program can be as limited or as all-encompassing as the city needs dictate.

Now think through a typical work day. How many minutes does an average employee take chatting with co-workers about their children, politics, and the weather? How many minutes does an average employee take commuting to work? How much time does it take to travel to and from meetings? How much

time is wasted at the beginning of each meeting with social chitchat? Many of these activities are eliminated with telecommuting. Sometimes employees can be more productive at home than at work.

There are, of course, downsides to having employees telecommute. Social interaction with co-workers is good for teamwork and morale. More than one person has tried telecommuting and found that it wasn't right for them because they missed being around people and feeling like part of a team. There is also a certain synergy that comes from co-workers interacting— new ideas are generated and exchanged. Sometimes these ideas result in better ways to deliver services to customers, save the city money, or generate new revenues.

In many ways, a limited telecommuting program— limited to certain employees with certain types of jobs on certain days of the week— can give the city the best of all worlds. Keep the social interaction, teamwork, and synergy but gain some benefits in productivity and cost savings.

Phased Retirement

On February 12, 2008, the Social Security Administration issues a press release about the first baby boomer to begin drawing her Social Security retirement benefit. While the recent economic downturn may slow down the rate of boomer retirements, it's safe to say that the retirements will happen eventually. What this means for cities is that a tremendous amount of skill, ability, and just plain know-how will be walking out the city hall doors over the next two decades.

One way to make sure that boomers pass on their knowledge, skills, and abilities to the next generation is to adopt a "phased retirement" program. Under current Public Employees Retirement Association (PERA) law, if an employee wants to retire but the city wishes to temporarily rehire the retiree to train in a replacement, there is a limit on the amount of earnings the retiree can earn before it affects his or her pension.

Retirees under the state of Minnesota retirement plan, however, are able to phase into retirement by cutting back their hours by as much as 50 percent, draw their full pension, and earn a half-time salary. This can be a strong tool to entice a retiree to continue to work for a period of time while training in a replacement or documenting some of his or her job knowledge.

The League of Minnesota Cities is working closely with PERA to determine whether a similar program might work well for city retirees. There are some specific criteria that have to be met to allow a phrased retirement approach to be added to the PERA plan, but we are exploring all possible options to come up with something that may fulfill the flexibility desired by both cities and their employees.

Some Issues to Consider

Some issues to consider include four-day workweeks, telecommuting, and a phased retirement program. These options are explained in greater detail below.

CONSIDERATIONS FOR FOUR-DAY WORKWEEKS

- What do union contract provisions say about scheduling, if anything? Will this be a benefit extended to union employees? If so, is the city willing to negotiate on any aspects?
- What does the city's personnel policy say about scheduling? Does it need to be updated?
- Will city offices be closed any days? If so, what is the impact on customer service?
- How much can the city expect to save by closing one day per week?
- Will new employees be offered the schedule right away?
- How will the schedule affect payment of overtime (e.g., will it result in the employee working more than 40 hours in one workweek and less than 40 in another)?
- How will meetings be scheduled? Will the city require employees to adjust their schedules to attend meetings on their "off" days?

CONSIDERATIONS FOR TELECOMMUTING

- Is the home work environment safe and ergonomically appropriate?
- Will non-exempt employees who are eligible for overtime pay be eligible to telecommute? How will the city ensure that overtime rules are followed?
- What safeguards will the city put in place to make sure that telecommuting employees are actually working while at home?
- Will telecommuting employees be required to attend meetings in person or will they be allowed to participate by conference call?
- What equipment will the city provide and will it be supported by the city's technology services staff? What will happen if the employee damages the city's equipment or causes a virus to enter the network? Will the city pay for Internet access?
- How will the city ensure that the employee takes reasonable precautions to protect private data that is worked on from home?

CONSIDERATIONS FOR PHASED RETIREMENT

- Current PERA law does not allow a city to rehire a retiree unless there is a 30-day break in service and there is no prior agreement between the retiree and the city with regard to the rehire.
- Current PERA law limits the dollar amount that a retiree can earn after retirement without the earnings impacting his or her retirement benefit.
- Will allowing a phrased retirement program discourage up and coming employees from staying with the city for fear that they will have to wait too long to obtain promotions?
- What limits will the city place on a phased retirement program? Will it be limited to one year? How will the city determine which job classes to approve and which to disapprove?

CHAPTER 6

Evaluating the Results of Staffing Decisions Beforehand

Lisa Rund *and* Laura Kushner

During these tough economic times, your city may be evaluating its staffing levels, especially given the fact that the majority of any city budget is staffing costs.

Unfortunately, staffing decisions can also be legally risky decisions if the city hasn't thoroughly evaluated all of the options and potential consequences beforehand. Even with the most common employee cost-saving measures, there are critical factors for cities to consider.

Layoffs or Reductions in Force

Layoffs or workforce reductions refer to terminating employees due to budget cuts or reorganization. Layoffs can be temporary or permanent; permanent layoffs are often referred to as reductions in force (RIF).

Sometimes managers see layoffs as a way to deal with performance problems or misconduct, but that is a viewpoint that can get the city into trouble. For example, employees who are veterans, union members, or in some other protected class will probably have legal protection if they can show that the layoff was a pretext for getting rid of the employee.

When the city is considering a layoff, there are some critical questions to consider, including:

- What do the union contracts and personnel policies require with regard to a layoff? How is "seniority" defined?
- Do the union contracts allow subcontracting? If not, the city may have trouble subcontracting during the term of the contract.
- Were the *positions* to eliminate or combine determined *before* choosing the *specific employees* to layoff? This will help show the city is acting in good faith and not discriminating on the basis of a protected status.
- What benefits will the city have to provide to affected employees (e.g., severance, insurance, unemployment costs)? Severance pay is limited by state law and both state and federal law requires continuation of certain group insurance benefits. In addition, unemployment costs will often limit the amount that a city can initially save in salary costs by doing a layoff.
- Will any veterans be affected, thus requiring a written notice? While veterans are not entitled to a termination hearing upon layoff, the city should be ready to show that the layoff was done in good faith and not as a pretext for getting rid of the veteran.
- Have the business reasons been carefully documented for the positions eliminated and

Originally published as "Tough Times, Tough HR Decisions," *Minnesota Cities*, Vol. 94, No. 3, March 2009, by the League of Minnesota Cities, St. Paul. Reprinted with permission of the publisher.

the specific employees terminated within each position?

Hiring Freezes

A hiring freeze refers to a city policy of refusing to fill any position that becomes vacant during a specific period of time. Generally, this means any and all positions, but sometimes cities need to make exceptions to the hiring freeze. Some questions to consider include:

- Does it make sense to exclude some positions based on:
  - Safety or liability issue?
  - Revenue brought in by the position?
  - Special expertise provided by the position?
- What approval and documentation process will be used for exceptions?

Early Retirement Incentives

Early retirement incentives can be offered to employees who are eligible to retire. Incentives typically include retiree health insurance for a period of time or a set dollar amount. Incentives must be carefully structured to comply with Equal Employment Opportunity Commission (EEOC) guidelines. Some questions to consider include:

- Will incentives be offered to eligible employees across the board or only certain job classes? The city should be prepared to justify why it is limiting the incentive to certain job classes.
- Will the city be able to obtain union agreement? In most cases, the city needs the union's agreement to offer the incentive.
- Does the plan meet EEOC guidelines? Generally, the incentive must be completely voluntary and meet certain timelines for consideration, especially if the employees are being asked to waive their rights under civil rights laws.
- Are there clear parameters for eligibility (e.g., employees with 10 or more years of service, and who have met age and service require-

ments for a public pension benefit)? While the city can reserve the right to limit the number of employees that take advantage of the incentive, it should always be prepared to explain why any employee or group of employees is not eligible.

- What are the tax consequences of any benefits being offered? This is particularly important when the city is offering to pay retiree health insurance or put money into a post-employment health savings account.
- Is there an established "window of opportunity" when the offer is available? Giving a window of opportunity increases the likelihood that employees will take advantage when the city most needs it.
- Has the potential impact of losing a significant number of employees been considered and prepared for?

Voluntary Termination

Unlike early retirement incentives, voluntary termination programs do not require that an employee be eligible to retire. In a voluntary termination program, a group of employees is offered some type of severance payment in return for voluntarily resigning and signing a waiver of rights to sue or request a veteran's preference hearing. The severance payment must be more than the employee would be eligible for under regular city policies or union contracts. Although voluntary termination programs differ from early retirement incentives on eligibility factors, many of the same questions to consider apply:

- Will incentives be offered to eligible employees across the board or only certain groups of employees (e.g., recreation programmers)?
- Will the city be able to obtain union agreement?
- Will the plan meet EEOC guidelines?
- Is there an established "window of opportunity" when the offer is available?
- Has the potential impact of losing a significant number of employees been considered and prepared for?

- Does the severance payment follow guidelines in state law (no more than 12 months wages, six months for highly compensated employees)?

Wage Freezes

A wage freeze typically refers to withholding cost-of-living increases or across-the-board range adjustments for non-union employees. It can also refer to withholding scheduled step increases, merit increases, performance pay, or any other type of increase. Wage freezes for union employees must be negotiated with union representatives. Some questions to consider include:

- What do the union contracts or employment contracts require?
- What is the potential impact of freezing only non-union wages (e.g., retention, morale, incentive to unionize)?
- What types of pay will be included in the freeze (e.g., cost of living, step increases, reclassifications)?
- Will there be an adverse effect on pay equity?

A wage freeze bill has been introduced in the House and Senate (HF 586/SF 372). The bill prohibits all wage increases (except promotional increases) through June 30, 2011. Many union contracts are already settled for this time period and would not be impacted by the bill.

Unpaid Leave

Unpaid leave refers to asking or requiring employees to either take a period of time off unpaid or to reduce their work schedule for a certain period of time. Some questions to consider include:

- Will the unpaid leave be voluntary or mandatory? Mandatory, across-the-board approaches are seen as more fair but may disproportionately affect employees with lower salaries.
- Will the unpaid leave be across the board or targeted to certain job classes? A reduction in word schedules may work best when tar-

geted at certain job classes that provide less essential services.
- How will the work and pay be handled for exempt employees to comply with the Fair Labor Standards Act (FLSA)? When reducing the work schedule for exempt employees, the best practice is to help them identify which duties will no longer be performed or performed only when time permits. If requiring exempt (or non-exempt) employees to take leave without pay, the city may want to offer them the option of spreading the leave without pay over a period of time instead of taking it all in one month. This can help employees with personal budget issues.
- Will the unpaid leave be considered a temporary "layoff" under union contracts? This will help the city make the case with union groups that it has the right to impose the layoff or reduction in hours without negotiating over it.

Probably the most critical thing for cities to remember is to seek legal advice and document the business reasons for any employment decisions.

Streamlining Ideas

The League of Minnesota Cities was asked by the governor and legislative leaders to provide a list of streamlining ideas that would help cities deal with the consequences of city aid cuts. In turn, the League asked cities for their help compiling this list. Many of the solutions that cities have sent to us are related to staffing and human resources issues, including:

- Eliminate pay equity and comparable worth requirements for cities.
- Provide a state-mandated health insurance program for public employees at all levels, and mandate contribution levels like the Public Employees Retirement Association (PERA) does.
- Create a new level of PERA benefits for new hires with lower contribution rates and lower benefits.

- Reduce the Rule of 90 to 84 for PERA benefits to tempt people to retire early.
- Freeze the contribution formula for fire relief pension funds to assist cities with possible growth in contribution levels.
- Significantly amend workers' compensation laws to lower costs for cities, both on the premium side and on payouts to employees.
- Remove the eligibility of seasonal employees to receive unemployment benefits.
- Amend the Public Employee Labor Relations Act to reduce costs and regulatory burdens on cities.
- Address the problem of following the pay equity rules if the state is seeking a wage freeze.
- Allow cities to give performance bonuses to employees; this will provide an incentive for efficient operation of the city.

Note: For more information on the implications of cost-cutting staffing measures, visit the League of Minnesota Cities website (http://www.lmc.org/).

CHAPTER 7

Options to Ensure Fiscal Health During Tough Times

Alan Kemp

The collapse of the national housing market, the credit crunch and the subsequent slowdown in the economy in recent months is having and will have an impact on state and local government budgets. The economic downturn recently caused the State of Iowa to cut spending across-the-board 1.5 percent for FY 2009 and early budget estimates for FY 2010 are not optimistic as anticipated expenses meet declining revenues.

The 1.5 percent across-the-board reduction at the state level for the current fiscal year is estimated to save the state $91.4 million. These cuts include about $1.2 million for programs of particular interest to local government including reductions to the Community Development Block Grant Program, Iowa Power Fund and the Property Tax Credit Fund. State cuts for the current fiscal year are largely manageable for local governments. The big unknown is the level of reductions that will be needed for the state to balance its budget for FY 2010.

The same national economic trends impacting state government revenues will also influence local government budgets over the course of the next several budget cycles. The extent of this influence will largely depend on the health of your local housing market and the supply (and diversification) of sales tax generating businesses in and around your community. Iowa by most indications is better off than national averages, but it is still an appropriate time to prepare for tough budget times. This article is intended to provide general suggestions and advice on issues related to coping with reduced resources both in the short term and the long term.

Take a Deep Breath

While we are entering a period of instability, it is still important not to panic. It is crucial that decision making be strategic, measured, consistent with citizen priorities and sensitive to the concern of employees. Cities should examine all options, work closely with employees and the public, and make the choices that are best for the community. There are certainly some principles that city officials will want to keep in mind. Most important is the need for a long term strategy. As a practical matter, this implies services may need to be reduced if permanent savings are going to be realized. Short term solutions may be more popular, and may be appropriate to help make ends meet until other solutions are found.

If service reductions involve reduced maintenance standards or response times, it is

Originally published as "Ensuring Fiscal Health," *Cityscape*, Vol. 64, No. 8, February 2009, by the Iowa League of Cities, Des Moines. Reprinted with permission of the publisher.

likely that this should be formalized in some fashion. Consultation with the city attorney is imperative to determine the form and the substance of a policy decision of this nature.

City officials need to monitor the results of decisions made and make modifications as necessary. No one can fully anticipate the potential impact of such decisions, and even if that were possible, circumstances change. The service that seems optional today may be indispensable tomorrow. Citizen attitudes might also change.

Expenditures

As revenues decline, cities typically examine where they can reduce costs or eliminate expenditures. Cities may consider across-the-board reductions or may choose to examine specific expenditures within the budget. While across-the-board cuts seem equitable, they may not appropriately consider long-term projects that can be negatively impacted. Not all city programs and spending enjoy the same level of use, need and support. It is hard to treat fireworks for a 4th of July celebration and the clean drinking water in the same manner. Prioritization of spending is a difficult but necessary step elected officials must take during tough budget times.

In the short term, the city may propose delaying or altering a major project. For instance, the city may consider a water park to replace an aging swimming pool. The city may defer the water park until alternate funding can be found or alter the project to something less costly. In the long term, cities may decide to re-evaluate their capital improvement plans to prioritize and fund these major improvements deemed most necessary.

Cities can delay purchasing items, such as office equipment or vehicles, and attempt to extend the life of equipment or supplies, or lengthen the replacement cycle for vehicles. Such an approach must be taken carefully to avoid increased maintenance costs offsetting any potential savings. For the long term, cities should consider group purchasing options to maximize cost savings. Group purchasing pro-

grams, such as U.S. Communities located at www.uscommunities.org, allow cities to take advantage of discounts given to large entities. Cities can take advantage of State of Iowa contracts equipment. For more information visit www.iowadot.gov/purchasing/ or http://das.gse.iowa.gov/procurement/. Cities can also join with other political subdivisions, such as counties and schools, to identify commodities that can be purchased as a group.

Working with Independent Boards

Certain city departments enjoy a greater degree of financial autonomy, either by virtue of state law or by the nature of their operations. For example, utility boards typically have oversight of their operations. Library boards and parks and recreation boards may enjoy a significant degree of oversight of their budget and revenues. The degree of independence a board enjoys may be outlined in the city's ordinance. In certain cases, the city council may need to make reductions in the budgets that are overseen by an autonomous board. Communications between the city council, the board and their staffs will be the key to successfully addressing the required spending reductions. Both need to remember that the budget is only an appropriation. It is not guarantee of income. Both the city and the boards will need to work together in amending priorities and determining adjusted spending levels.

Personnel Changes

For most cities, personnel costs represent a high percentage of their general fund expenditures, in both wages and benefits. It is only logical that cities may look to staff reductions in order to reduce costs. Layoffs, hiring freezes and organizational restructuring are all options. Each of these, however, has potential costs and long term impacts, both on the city's budget, the efficiency of the organization and staff morale. Reductions in staff can be fairly expensive as a city needs to consider unemployment costs, unused vacation payouts and compensatory time liabilities. For these reasons, cities need to clearly understand their objectives, carefully consider their options and act prudently. Cities can also evaluate their benefits to determine if health insurance deductibles, employee contributions and rates are in line with market averages. As with most personnel issues, cities must consult with their city attorney to ensure they are protecting the rights of their employees and mitigating any potential liability.

Revenues

Regardless of your revenue sources, it is important to review your assumptions for how your city estimates revenues. How will those sources be impacted by national economic trends? Will funding be impacted by further state budget cuts?

The most common form of revenue for the city is the property tax. It is a 2009 legislative priority of the Iowa League of Cities, as well as a recommendation of the Legislative Property Tax Study Committee, to diversify revenues sources in hopes of reducing the reliance on property tax. While we hope to report success in obtaining alternative revenues for cities during the legislative session, there are several other options to the property tax that city officials can consider right now.

Many city services are supported through fees. Fees can be collected on licenses for animals or businesses, permits for housing or contractors, and entrance to recreational facilities such as a swimming pool. Services currently supported by the general fund can sometimes be converted to enterprises, such as garbage collection. Several cities have also started a storm water sewer utility. Fees may be more acceptable to citizens because a direct connection is drawn from the fee paid to the service provided. The amount of the fee should be enough to cover all the expenses of the service provided. Revenue generated beyond this could be challenged as an illegal tax. Surcharges added to existing utilities should be avoided as these can also be challenged as an illegal tax.

Another opportunity for supplementing revenue is through fines. Fines are intended to not only dictate behavior, such as obeying traffic laws, but also provide revenues to cover enforcement. Enacting traffic laws as city ordinance ensures the majority of the fine is refunded to the city. This is not the case if the traffic infraction is written under state law. Cities should also review their municipal infraction ordinance, or consider adopting such an ordinance. Any changes to fines or enforcement methods should be reviewed with the city attorney.

Conclusion

Reducing services or increasing revenues are not popular choices, but they are solutions to keep the fiscal health of the community intact during tough budget times. City officials will want to maximize public participation to ensure service cuts or revenue increases are accepted by the community at large. Such participation can deepen public understanding and begin building better community support for city services. City officials did not ask for this challenge, but it is up to us to face it. It will require that we use all the skills and assets in our communities.

CHAPTER 8

Strategies to Ensure
Long-Term Fiscal Health

Jeff Schott

As cities cope with the challenges of our current tough economic conditions, considerable attention is focused on immediate, short-term budgetary issues. The article "Ensuring Fiscal Health" in the February issue of *Cityscape*, discussed several helpful short-term approaches in dealing with these issues. But it is equally important that cities maintain a long-term outlook on their financial situation. The purpose of this article is to suggest several strategies by which cities can promote their long-term fiscal health.

Strategic Budgeting

Especially in periods of limited financial resources, policy makers should adopt a strategic approach to budgeting. Establishing priorities and developing benchmarks can provide direction to policymakers and help local governments stay on course.

The National Advisory Council on State and Local Budgeting (NACSLB) recommends a goal-oriented approach to budgeting based on the following framework:

PRINCIPLE I — ESTABLISH BROAD GOALS TO GUIDE GOVERNMENT DECISION-MAKING

- Assess community needs, priorities, challenges and opportunities.
- Identify opportunities and challenges for government services, capital assets, and management.
- Develop and disseminate broad goals.

PRINCIPLE II — DEVELOP APPROACHES TO ACHIEVE GOALS

- Adopt financial policies.
- Develop programmatic, operating, and capital policies and plans.
- Develop programs and services that are consistent with policies and plans.
- Develop management strategies.

PRINCIPLE III — DEVELOP A BUDGET WITH APPROACHES TO ACHIEVE GOALS

- Develop a process for preparing and adopting a budget.
- Develop and evaluate financial options.
- Make choices necessary to adopt a budget.

Originally published as "Strategies for Fiscal Health," *Cityscape*, Vol. 64, No. 9, March 2009, by the Iowa League of Cities, Des Moines. Reprinted with permission of the publisher.

PRINCIPLE IV — EVALUATE PERFORMANCE AND MAKE ADJUSTMENTS

- Monitor, measure, and evaluate performance.
- Make adjustments as needed.

Reconciling Short- and Long-Range Planning

Recognize the longer-term financial impacts of short-term budget decisions. Capital projects, debt financing of such projects, and many annual budget decisions affect budgets far into the future. Identify the projected operating and/or personnel costs associated with providing current and anticipated services, projects, and programs (adjusted for inflation) before committing to the initial funding of that item.

Guard against making short-term budget decisions at the expense of longer-term needs. Examples of such situations are unfortunately quite commonplace: spending down fund balances accumulated over a period of time for designated purposes (such as specific capital projects or equipment/vehicle replacement), deferring maintenance projects, or transferring funds from the general fund to enterprise funds (or vice versa) solely to prop up the fund in question.

Financial Planning and Analysis

A variety of financial planning and analysis tools can provide counties — regardless of size — the necessary information base and guidelines for effective strategic budgeting and planning. They can help policymakers evaluate the short-and long-range impact of budget proposals. They can help elected officials see the big picture and prioritize proposals or projects at the same time, rather than on an individual or stand-alone basis.

Financial Trend Analysis — A city needs to know the state of its financial condition. Periodic monitoring and evaluation of financial data and trends, including multi-year forecasting of revenues and expenditures, can help elected officials think strategically about priorities and needs.

Financial Policies — Financial policies establish guidelines pertaining to key elements such as revenues, operating expenditures, capital expenditures, reserve funds, fund balances, investments, debt management, enterprise funds, accounting, auditing, and reporting. Carefully developing and monitoring meaningful financial policies, such as establishing and maintaining fund balances as a percentage of fund expenditures or per capita debt service expenditures as a percentage, can provide very useful guidelines to assist elected officials in making difficult budget decisions.

Capital Improvements Program (CIP) — The CIP is a multi-year (typically three to ten year) program for the planning, scheduling, and financing of large construction, infrastructure and improvement projects, and purchasing of major pieces of equipment. The CIP helps prioritize capital spending needs and provides useful information about upcoming major expenditures.

Equipment/Asset Replacement Plan — Similar to the CIP, this is typically a five to twenty-year plan identifying the scheduled replacement of equipment, vehicles, facilities and other physical assets. Like the CIP, it helps policy makers anticipate and plan for upcoming major expenditures beyond the standard one-year budget cycle.

Contingency Planning — During times of financial uncertainty, it can be quite helpful to develop budget contingency plans, especially for revenue shortfalls. Certain revenue sources, such as local option sales taxes, can be extremely volatile during these periods. Developing advance contingency plans allows for more deliberate and careful analysis of alternatives and options as opposed to crisis mode emergency response.

Stimulating Economic Growth

As discussed in the recent white paper, "Navigating the Fiscal Crisis: Tested Strategies for Local Leaders," prepared by the Alliance for

Innovation and ICMA, one of the best methods for cities to stimulate their local economies may be to maintain current expenditures and expand capital improvements, provided local revenues, reserves, interest rates and federal programs make it possible. Of course, these conditions rarely occur during economic downturns. It is more likely that city expenditures get reduced, which in turn may negatively impact economic development in the community.

The white paper suggests that periods of economic distress may offer the most opportune time to promote local economic development efforts. Private sector firms tend to be more sensitive to the impacts of economic development incentives, because their profit margins may be smaller and their cash flow more constrained.

Recognizing that direct cash outlay may be problematic for local governments during these downturns, the white paper identifies other opportunities to entice economic development, including infrastructure, skilled available workforce, job training, and educational institutions and streamlining project reviews. Finally, the white paper points out that a period of resource scarcity is an appropriate time for jurisdictions in a region to share economic development incentives and benefits.

Citizen Engagement

Effectively dealing with long-term financial issues is not easy. Difficult decisions have to be made. It is crucial to develop strategies and methods to inform, listen to, and involve a broad base of community members in this process. Such an approach benefits both citizens and elected officials.

FOR CITIZENS

- They learn more about the issues and decision-making processes.
- An effective citizen engagement process can lead to creating partnerships for solving problems.
- The process allows citizens to provide real input on policy decisions.
- The process can create a strong sense of buy-in and belonging.

FOR LOCAL OFFICIALS

- A citizen engagement process can demonstrate to citizens that certain public decisions are difficult and complex.
- The process helps citizens understand the financial pressures that affect services and programs.
- The process helps elected officials find out what citizens really think about important issues and policy decisions.
- The process can help defuse tensions between groups of people and between citizens and government.

Of course, the citizen engagement process is not absolute. Elected officials are still responsible for setting policies and making decisions for the community — and the local elected leadership team is still ultimately responsible for the overall success and vitality of the community — with citizen guidance, input and engagement.

CHAPTER 9

Financial Measures to Restore America's Infrastructure

Nancy Mann Jackson

When President-elect Obama promised to create millions of jobs "by making the single largest new investment in our national infrastructure since the creation of the federal highway system in the 1950s," a delegation of mayors had a few ideas about where to spend the money — more than 4,600 shovel-ready projects, to be more specific.

Bags of money do not arrive on local government doorsteps every day, but financing experts caution that, while federal funding may be welcome, it is not likely to arrive without strings attached. "What we've seen historically is that it's not a free checkbook," says Denise Beauchamp of Superior, Colo.–based Key Government Finance.

In most cases, local governments are required to match federal dollars, or use federal money only for very specific purposes. For instance, federal funds may not be eligible for equipment purchases, which may be needed to complete the infrastructure projects.

Meeting the Match

Even local projects that are largely federally funded likely will require local governments to come up with significant money for items or services that are not included in the federal grant or for required matching funds, according to Dennis Brown, vice president for State Government Relations at the Washington-based Equipment Leasing & Finance Association (ELFA). He notes that if federal monies do become available for local government projects, there is almost always not enough to complete the project or extraneous parts of the project that cannot be covered by the federal government.

Also, because loan money is scarce, city and county governments could face difficulties acquiring those matching dollars to make the federal program work. First, the lenders' traditional incentive for tax-exempt government loans has diminished in the current economy. Because lenders do not pay taxes on the income they earn by loaning to municipalities, they often can offer such customers highly competitive interest rates. "[However,] a tax benefit is only good if you have profits you want to shelter," Beauchamp says. "As profit margins decline among financial companies, their appetite for tax-exempt debt disappears."

As a result, the marketplace for government financing has shrunk significantly. Some players in the industry have withdrawn from the government finance space altogether, and some others are avoiding new deals with a "wait-and-see" attitude. "There are too few dollars

Originally published as "Capital Steps," *American City & County*, Vol. 124, No. 1, January 2009, by Penton Media, Inc., Overland Park, KS. Reprinted with permission of the publisher.

chasing too many deals," Beauchamp adds. And, if the current liquidity crisis continues well into 2009, more lenders are unlikely to flood the municipal financing space anytime soon.

When local governments find lenders that are still in the game, antiquated regulations keep them from borrowing large sums at highly competitive rates. Based on a 1986 regulation, when certain entities — such as city or county governments — borrow more than $10 million in a calendar year, their debt is considered non-bank-qualified. While banks have no legal restraints for the number of bank-qualified (BQ) loans they offer (provided to borrowers with less than $10 million in debt per year), lenders are limited in the amount of non-bank-qualified debt they can carry to 2 percent of their capital. Because the $10 million limit has never been adjusted for inflation, almost any infrastructure project makes it a non-bank-qualified borrower. And, because the limit is per-year rather than per-transaction, any debt a municipality issues, including municipal bonds, contributes toward the $10 million.

"If they build anything with bricks and mortar, it's over $10 million; any highway is over $10 million," Brown says. "Some finance sources are in a situation where they have a bucket for bank-qualified loans; the BQ bucket never fills up, and the non-BQ bucket stays full."

Expanding the Options

With fewer lenders available to municipal governments and outdated regulations limiting the number of loans active lenders can carry, cities and counties that need to match federal funds may be looking for new options this year. Municipal lease-purchase financing can be one method of stretching the federal dollars to move projects forward. "Under current laws, if [local governments] get all this money, it's still not going to cover the projects they need to complete," Brown says. "If [a city receives] an annual sum of $5 million and its infrastructure needs are $40 million, it can try to spread out that $5 million and leverage it into a $40 million lease for 10 years," he says.

Beauchamp says that government officials sometimes misunderstand the leasing option, especially if they confuse government leasing with commercial or consumer leasing. Unlike commercial leasing, municipal leasing always results in a purchase. "You make your final payment, and the asset is yours," Beauchamp says.

ELFA points out that there is not a lot of difference between straight lending and municipal lease-purchase. It amortizes just like a loan, but, because lease agreements are not restricted by the same limits as traditional loans, they offer a more readily available form of financing for government infrastructure projects and equipment.

Aside from considering lease-purchase agreements, municipal governments also should understand their bank-qualified status. ELFA suggests that if a small municipality that is a traditional BQ borrower is having trouble finding someone to buy their debt, they should be marketing themselves to a state-chartered bank, small bank or independent bank. That is because smaller banks, which do not have their own holding companies (or "non-banks") to handle non-BQ loans, can only carry BQ debt — and there is no limit to how much they can carry. Because lenders have more capacity to offer BQ financing, they can often offer better interest rates.

For those municipalities that borrow more than $10 million in a year, industry professionals recommend lobbying politicians to change the limit for BQ financing. The 1986 statute is "cutting out a lot of small banks [from providing financing] and small communities [from obtaining financing]," Brown says. "If it was changed to $10 million per transaction, it would open up the markets a whole lot."

Other proposals advocate tagging the limit to inflation. Regardless of how the change is determined, most in the industry agree that a change to the BQ limit would help both lenders and borrowers. "[If the limits remain consistent,] what ultimately happens is that banks have a continually shrinking market each year as prices for projects go up," Brown says. "Local government leaders who want to make a difference ought to be at Congress' doorstep saying, '$10 million doesn't go as far as it used to.'"

With a new president elected on a promise of change, now might be a good time for the request increasing the $10 million limit, Brown says. "That would be a lasting change and would make a difference," he says. "It would help small communities get access to funding from a lot more sources."

PART II. BEST PRACTICES

CHAPTER 10

Ann Arbor Uses Economic Development to Increase Its Revenues

Craig Chavez

Local governments of all sizes are coming up with creative solutions to their slumping economies. In this article about Ann Arbor, Michigan (population 114,000) two remedies that are working for Ann Arbor may help suggest similar solutions for circumstances in other communities.

Since there is a lag time of 18 to 24 months between changing economic conditions and their effect on revenue collections, many local governments are just now feeling the full impact of the economic downturn. Ann Arbor, Michigan, who has experienced a weak economy since 2001, can help other local government managers who are looking for solutions. This article shares Ann Arbor's story about its labor restructuring plan and its partnerships with surrounding local governments on collaborative economic development.

revenues will mean another 11 percent cut across the board, including the likely closure of some recreation facilities, and significant layoffs, beginning July 1, 2010.

The state of Michigan has further complicated Ann Arbor's financial scenario. Because the state's budget is in limbo, Michigan has reduced its revenue sharing between the state and its local governments. Roger Fraser, Ann Arbor's city administrator, said, "This is problematic because our budget was calculated with the state's contribution of revenue sharing. Its 10 percent reduction, announced in October, further compounded a bleak revenue outlook."

Although the current situation is bad, Ann Arbor's job restructuring and involvement in the creation of an economic development group called Ann Arbor SPARK have helped mitigate the negative effects of the current recession.

Introduction

In 2001, Ann Arbor had 1,000 employees. Today, it has fewer than 750 employees. Because of Michigan's statewide policies limiting property taxes, each fiscal year it became necessary to reduce expenditures to match limited increases in revenue. Now, after 11 percent expense reductions in the current year, slumping

Labor Restructuring

Several years ago, declining revenues, coupled with an influx of early retirements and a Byzantine organizational structure, created the perfect opportunity to reshape Ann Arbor's organization for the better. Following a major reorganization in 2002–2003, and with the help of a consultant, Ann Arbor's management and

Originally published as "Somber Spots and Bright Spots," *Public Management*, Vol. 92, No. 4, May 2010, by the International City/County Management Association, Washington, D.C. Reprinted with permission of the publisher.

human resources staffs involved line supervisors, employees, and their unions in the restructuring of various job functions.

Employees got together in facilitated work groups and used their hands-on knowledge to examine the work processes and make suggestions for process and staffing improvements. From these examinations, service area managers and human resources staff were able to work with the unions and create what they call "career progressions," which are new job classifications with clear, five-level pay and skill progressions. These job classifications and their required skills were formed with input provided by the employee work groups.

Before the restructuring, job descriptions and work structures were so separate and rigid that they hindered Ann Arbor's ability to function efficiently. Fraser said, "There were, for example, 32 different clerical job classifications, and, due to the work structure, any clerical job opening required a cumbersome posting process because the job classifications prevented people from being moved around as needed."

After the restructuring, all of the clerical positions were reformed into one job classification with a five-level skill and pay progression. Ann Arbor has seen similar benefits from restructuring other departments like field operations that include water, sewer, public works maintenance, and park services. With this added flexibility, Ann Arbor can now move employees around from an unneeded area, like parks maintenance, and have them work on snow removal during the winter.

Both the city and its employees benefited from the restructuring and the new career progressions. The employees received opportunities for increased pay and a new career path, and the city achieved needed flexibility. Richard Martonchik, Ann Arbor's human resources service partner and a member of the restructuring project, said of the labor flexibility: "It is useful during any economic downturn, especially during this recession. The restructuring allowed Ann Arbor to keep providing services even with the reductions in funding and staff.

SPARK

Created in 2005, Ann Arbor SPARK is a collaborative effort among the city of Ann Arbor, Washtenaw County, other local communities, Eastern Michigan University, the University of Michigan, Washtenaw Community College, and the private sector. The economic development group has three functions: traditional economic development, new business development and assisting start-ups, and managing employee talent.

Employee placement is done by partnering with local businesses that cannot find talented employees. SPARK also has ongoing programs of support for folks seeking jobs. With this effort, SPARK maintains direct contacts with thousands of talented job seekers. Through this and other imaginative tools, SPARK provides any given company the means to attract the best and brightest to that company. SPARK also holds more than 200 networking events a year, and these events assist small and start-up companies with every facet of business development.

SPARK puts a big focus on new business development. Through research, SPARK found that new businesses lacked the needed resources to thrive. The resource dearth included funding and business knowledge, so SPARK focused on increasing business education and funding. Entrepreneurs can attend SPARK networking events and learn from attorneys and other professionals about the basics of business.

The training includes such topics as business and patent law, information technology, developing business plans, and building and using professional networks. The training also includes how to get business funding.

Funding has been a crucial part of new business development. By working with local banks, the city of Ann Arbor, Washtenaw County, and the Michigan Economic Development Corporation (MEDC), SPARK has generated micro-loans from $5,000 to $50,000 that can be used for a variety of business needs. These loans are essential to start-ups who lack working capital in the best of times and especially during the down economy because the state of Michigan has seen a sharp increase in people trying to start their own businesses.

Although the demand for funding is high, start-ups were not able to borrow from banks. The SPARK microloans and training programs fill this gap and provide new and fledgling businesses with needed funding and knowledge. In addition to the microloan program, SPARK has committed nearly $9 million in venture capital funding to start-ups through the state-wide Michigan Pre-Seed Capital Fund. Michael Finney, SPARK's president and CEO, said, "We're successful because we're focusing on supporting businesses in every stage of development and growth and supplying them with the tools that they need to succeed."

SPARK, a private, not-for-profit company serves as the sole economic development agency for the region, consisting of 28 local governments and two major universities. This arrangement streamlines economic development, creates efficiencies, and eliminates economic turf wars between neighboring local governments. Instead of each local government funding its own economic development efforts, the governments now contribute to SPARK, and SPARK works to develop the economy in a broader and more efficient manner. This process pools resources and is especially useful in a tight funding environment.

During this fiscal year, Ann Arbor contributed $75,000 to SPARK, and Washtenaw County gave $250,000. Based on benchmarking, similar sized cities and counties typically spend $2 to $3 million to staff their own economic development organization.

By pooling resources, local governments in the county enjoy significant cost savings while benefiting from a $7 million economic development organization with 15 full-time employees. "By fostering a regional approach to economic development and working with partners in the Ann Arbor and the greater Detroit area, we've been able to achieve a high level of results in a collaborative environment," said Finney.

A Silver Lining

Ann Arbor's experience provides guidance to other local governments dealing with the recession. Although it was painful to reduce the number of city staff by 25 percent, and reduce recreation, police, fire and other services, Ann Arbor's labor restructuring softened the impact. In fact, Martonchik said, "The restructuring allowed us to maintain services even with reductions in staff, and up to this point the residents have hardly noticed changes in service levels."

SPARK also helped Ann Arbor navigate through the economic uncertainty. Pfizer was a major employer in the city, but when the company left, it took 5 percent of Ann Arbor's property tax revenues and 3,100 jobs with it. Yet, there was some relief, according to Fraser, because, "SPARK created 2,900 jobs after Pfizer left."

With the labor restructuring and involvement in SPARK, Ann Arbor used creativity and innovation to respond to budget shortfalls and a changing economy. This meant there was a silver lining to Ann Arbor's efforts. Despite various and increasing economic challenges, the city was able to develop better, more efficient ways of operating and minimize service impacts to its residents.

CHAPTER 11

Arlington and Other Cities
Share Services to Reduce Costs

Monte Mercer

Shared services, many of which are public-private partnerships (PPPs), refer to the operational philosophy that involves centralizing functions once performed by individual organizations. In day-to-day operations, problems and opportunities arise that are ideal for collaboration. This abundance of possible shared services and partnership opportunities can be overwhelming though, and it can lead to difficulty identifying which projects to try. The best determining factor for success is for the customer to be the driving force behind any collaborative effort.

The North Central Texas Council of Governments (NCTCOG) serves 240 member governments — or customers — of which 170 are cities. It has had the opportunity to spearhead a large number of shared services and PPP initiatives in recent years, and in this article I want to share what we've learned.

In fact, shared services fulfill NCTCOG's mission to strengthen the individual and collective power of local governments and to help them recognize regional opportunities, resolve regional problems, and make joint decisions. These initiatives are primarily designed to solve common needs of NCTCOG's member governments, but they often reach a statewide audience as well.

Steps for a Successful Collaboration

A common recipe for success can be applied to any collaboration effort. By nature, however, shared services are unique and have elements that will apply exclusively to each individual project. For projects to be successful, it is best to tailor an approach that takes individual differences into consideration for each shared services program.

After identifying a problem or opportunity that can be remedied through a shared services approach and also identifying the local government stakeholders, NCTCOG then takes the next step in the process and functions as the coordinating organization. This is followed by determining which entity or entities — also called organizations in this article — can serve as a project champion. Project champions need to be recognized leaders within the stakeholder community because they are crucial for the success of any shared services project, as they lend both credibility and energy to the project.

Create a Winning Approach

When deciding whether a proposed shared services project is feasible to pursue, NCTCOG

Originally published as "Shared Services and Cost-Saving Collaboration Deserve Respect," *Public Management*, Vol. 93, No. 4, May 2011, by the International City/County Management Association, Washington, D.C. Reprinted with permission of the publisher.

and the prospective participants use these criteria:

- Does it have the potential to save money?
- Does it have the potential to provide equal or better service levels?
- Can a governance structure or operational process be devised that assures that the participating local governments share in the control of the program?

If these questions can be answered in the affirmative, then we proceed to the next step.

Developing the Request for Proposals

The request for proposals (RFP) process begins with research by the planning organization, the project champions, and any other entity that desires to participate in identifying potential solutions to the chosen problem or opportunity. This leads to an understanding of the project dynamics and sets the stage for initial discussions with prospective private and public sector service providers. Conversations with service providers allow insight into opportunities for standardization and other cost-saving measures while validating the parameters necessary to create a credible RFP.

Identifying opportunities for standardization is one of the most important due-diligence steps, and it should be performed collectively. The 80–20 rule is a good guide for assessing opportunities for standardization. In other words, ferret out the things that each participant does in common 80 percent of the time so that they can be the focal point for maximizing efficiencies and economies of scale.

After this step is accomplished, it is essential to visit with the potential service providers and get their input and understanding of the program being suggested. Doing this allows potential failure points to be exposed.

It is recommended that a significant amount of time be spent with the subject matter experts (SMEs) and the technical experts from potential service providers during this step. Opportunities for cost savings using this approach will generally be significant.

Our experience has been that an element vital to crafting the RFP is understanding how the private or public sector provider will deliver the service. If the procurement is based solely on our understanding of the problem and the solution, we may inadvertently limit the opportunities to provide a more innovative and cost-effective approach to solving the problem.

When the due diligence has been performed, a nonbinding statement of interest is sent to potential users of the service. After these statements are returned, this information will be summarized for the RFP. One critical piece of information for the responders is an indication of the volume of activity or transactions that can be anticipated, as this will be important as pricing discounts are considered.

Participation usually far exceeds the initial statements of interest that are returned. As the RFP is developed, it may take several iterations to reach a version that satisfies all groups; therefore, maintaining some flexibility will allow for creative responses. The RFP should also be scalable to various group sizes. After the RFP draft is completed, it needs to be reviewed by the participants or a representative committee to create the official version.

It is helpful for the committee to be composed of SMEs. For best results, they should be from various-sized entities in order to gain varying perspectives concerning the shared services initiative.

After responses to the RFP have been received, a selection committee should meet to review the submittals. RFPs should be scored on the basis of predetermined selection criteria so scoring is unbiased.

Implementation

It is often a good idea to assemble a pilot group to participate in the initial implementation, again including entities of various sizes for this group. Pilot programs are an excellent way to discover unforeseen problems and remedy them before rolling out the program to a larger audience.

During this implementation phase, encourage communication among the stakeholders to get a reading of components working well and those in need of improvement. These are ready-made networks for exchanging ideas and information and are invaluable during the process. When the pilot has proved successful, a more robust rollout can be initiated.

Planning Organization and Facilitator

The streamlining of administrative activities is one of the biggest opportunities for shared services projects. Here are ways to streamline access to the project:

- The planning organization executes a master agreement with the selected service provider, and it is structured to allow the participating organizations to gain access through interlocal agreements.
- The participants execute an interlocal agreement with the planning organization.
- The participants can then engage the service provider through a service agreement to perform the required services.

The facilitator normally assumes responsibility for many of the administrative duties that would ordinarily be done by an individual organization or a service provider.

Participating Organizations

Participating entities can benefit significantly from shared services. Because individual purchasers are consolidated into an organized, volume-purchase arrangement, the participants are able to realize lower prices while still benefiting from a high-quality provider. This approach also eliminates the need for each entity to go through an individual selection process and to incur the costs involved in issuing and evaluating proposals. This is especially true for small to medium-size organizations.

NCTCOG has been able to leverage the collective bargaining power of several groups to negotiate a lower price for the contract. With the importance of cost reduction during these difficult economic times, it's notable that

NCTCOG's shared services programs have been able to generate savings of 25 to 50 percent for participants.

Service Provider

The service provider benefits by being able to reach many organizational clients with just one proposal, thus increasing its market penetration and enhancing its ability to sell other services in the future. The provider also benefits from the standardization of operations realized in the shared services arrangement, which reduces risk for the service provider and allows better pricing to be experienced by the participants.

The clients also can forgo the expense of conducting individual contract negotiations. All of these factors give a service provider ample motivation to reply to an RFP and to partner with the planning organization.

Examples of NCTCOG Shared Services

iCOMMUNITIES: A SUCCESS STORY

The iCommunities program created an extensive Internet mapping service that was combined with a set of powerful GIS, database, and Internet technologies. These tools allow local governments to distribute key information to their constituents and other communities within the region.

Residents are able to access specific neighborhood information such as zoning, building and activity statistics, and event notices. Information can be distributed to organizational staff on various program, asset, and work management activities. Traditionally, establishing a tool such as iCommunities would mean that each entity would incur hefty costs for hardware, personnel, and networking. Through this shared services program initiated by NCTCOG, cities can have ready access to this powerful tool for a low cost.

Participants pay a fee to support one network and a group of technicians who service the entire participant list. As individual participants request additional functionality from the iCommunities program, the enhancements become available to all participants. A base-level functionality is automatically applied to all participants.

Additional functionality is offered on a fee basis; specific features can be set up to accommodate unique needs of a specific organization and costs charged according to complexity and extra support needs. The sharing of knowledge and innovation is one of the most positive by-products of this collaboration.

The Small City Accounting Project: Lessons Learned

Even with the best of intentions, not all PPPs are successful. With each new collaborative effort, however, lessons are learned. NCTCOG's Small City Accounting Project is one such example. Riding on the success of a shared services initiative to acquire enterprise resource planning software to handle accounting, purchasing, and human resources functions for three large-member groups, participants decided that smaller entities could benefit from a similar project.

The project, unfortunately, never really progressed. The reason for this lack of advancement is that, although the larger entities were already interested in the concept and approached NCTCOG to facilitate the purchasing process, the smaller entities were contacted to determine their interest after all the parameters had been developed.

In this case, the project would have found more success had it been customer driven. The best shared services occur when the planning organization is either approached by the entity or seeks ideas from it directly.

Compensation Management Services: Looking to the Future

A current NCTCOG initiative is under way to assist with compensation analysis, design, and best practices implementation. Salary costs usually make up, on average, 70 percent of a local government's general fund budget. Yet tools that readily provide the ability to quickly and accurately analyze, monitor, and control these costs are lacking, as is the ability to assess the impact that changes to salary structures have on benefits and other components of compensation packages.

Various city managers in NCTCOG's 16-county region requested assistance in identifying potential solutions for evaluating these costs in real time. Through the procurement process, a vendor with a multifaceted web-based solution has been identified. The vendor's web tools have the capability to provide projections of personnel costs using scenario-based analytics, and they also contain current salary data so that any participating organization is able to determine the competitiveness of its compensation and benefit plan.

Other features make it easy to measure internal compensation equity. A major benefit of this program is that it increases the ability of an organization's human resources staff to carry out many functions that are currently done by consultants. This project was approved by the NCTCOG executive board in January 2011, and we are now in the implementation stage.

Strategy for Success

Consider this course of action for shared services success:

1. First and foremost, underpromise and overdeliver! It is important to establish achievable results. If you set unattainable milestones or goals, you can undermine your credibility.

2. Begin the procurement process with the end goal in mind. Look toward the future throughout the RFP research, development, and scoring process. With forethought, you can avoid many of the traps and delays that can evolve during the process. Look for opportunities to standardize because standardization is usually one of the largest contributors to reducing risk and achieving cost savings.

3. Use a grassroots approach based on a crawl-walk-run philosophy. It is best to start with a small pilot group and perfect the program before rolling out to a larger audience. Project champions are crucial in building a strong foundation for shared services projects as they have a real interest and commitment to performing the due diligence necessary to support the program and to assuring its success.

For more information on the NCTCOG shared services programs, visit the website at www.nctcog.org/sharedservices.asp. I think our recipe can be used successfully by other local governments that want to navigate the shared services options available today.

CHAPTER 12

Auburn and Adjoining City Consolidate Services

Liz Chapman Mockler

The twin cities of Lewiston and Auburn will embark late this month on a one-of-a-kind municipal collaboration effort when they essentially unite six planning and code enforcement offices into one operation.

Although the computer system necessary to bring the offices closer together is costly — at about $354,000 — that is far less than what the computer conversion would have cost if each city had approached it separately.

Also, officials from both cities expect to save a combined $36,000 annually, once the system by EnerGov Solutions of Duluth, Ga. becomes operational.

Aside from money, the benefits of the new system to both cities' staffs, contractors and developers, residents and, in later stages, neighboring communities, are both exciting and significant, said Laurie Smith, Auburn assistant city manager and chief project coordinator.

"It has been a great deal of work by staff, in part because we are developing something new," Smith said. "We're not just implementing an automated program. We're revamping everything we do."

Under the new system, Smith said, employees will be trained so they can work from one computer server from two locations. They also can work interchangeably in both cities, she said.

Gil Arsenault, Lewiston director of Planning and Code Enforcement, said the council and City Administrator Edward Barrett "showed tremendous confidence in the staff" and project by funding the conversion last fall, during one of the worst financial eras for local government in recent Maine history.

"It's been quite a collaborative effort," Arseneault said, noting that long-time Lewiston Deputy City Administrator Phil Nadeau also was an early booster of the project.

"Everyone is excited about the promise" the project represents for both commercial hubs, Arsenault said.

Tailor-Made

Garth Magness, director of Business Development for EnerGov, said the project underway in L/A is the first in Maine. The company has about 200 clients, he said, and about eight active projects around the country.

"The biggest challenge for the two cities was to identify those points of agreement regarding business processes," he said. "They found a lot of efficiencies they were not aware of prior to our analyses of their processes."

The new software "suite" includes six components tailored to the needs of the two cities.

Originally published as "L/A Unite Offices, Computer Systems," *Maine Townsman*, Vol. 72, No. 6, June 2010, by the Maine Municipal Association, Augusta. Reprinted with permission of the publisher.

Lewiston and Auburn rank second and fifth in population in Maine, at 35,756 and 21,151 residents respectively.

The goals of the collaborative effort are far-reaching, Smith said. The new EnerGov program is designed to:

- Enhance and streamline the planning, zoning, permitting and code enforcement operations of both cities, including equalizing building fees and allowing developers, builders and residents to do most of the required paperwork online on their own time.
- Align the two cities' planning and code processes for both commercial and residential development, including fees.
- Improve cost efficiency and operational effectiveness.
- Improve public access to planning, building and code enforcement reports and documents, including those dealing with inspections and violations.
- Reduce workloads for city staffs that already have been cut.
- Reduce errors.
- Reduce legal costs.
- Allow municipal officials to analyze data, evaluate the use of human and other resources and make adjustments where beneficial.
- Merge all functions of community, business and residential development permitting to allow the cities to continue working together, rather than competing, for new development.

"One of the most exciting parts of this project is that we (rarely) have an opportunity to review what we do and redevelop our business flow processes," Smith said. "This new program will allow us to redevelop the (land use) processes in both cities so that they are the same processes and the same timelines" to get things done.

Smith said overcoming the typical thinking that "this is the way we've always done it" was the first challenge L/A officials overcame in making such a change.

Ready, Set, Go

Auburn City Manager Glenn Aho arrived in the city from Lincoln in May 2008 and began looking for ways to run the city more efficiently while also improving customer service.

At first, he pitched the idea of a joint ordinance book for the two cities. The Citizens Commission on L/A Cooperation "liked the idea but were skeptical," Aho said. So the new manager decided to start by merging the Auburn code enforcement and assessing departments to reduce redundancy, including buying popular assessing software that allowed anyone to track code and assessing operations online.

That move alone improved service, cut costs and dramatically reduced foot traffic into city offices. After getting the "virtual assessing office" launched, Aho again approached the L/A commission about Lewiston and Auburn joining forces to expand the idea.

"We identified EnerGov as having exactly what we were looking for," including making the Land Use Department operations more user-friendly, efficient, accountable and transparent to the public.

Using GIS

A crucial element to making the new system work was finding a program that could be built upon the cities' Geographical Information System. EnerGov's software also allowed for that.

Magness, of EnerGov, agreed with Aho. "The cities had staff in place that understood the importance of geography and mapping in land-use planning," he said. "This project will expand and enhance the use of GIS."

Arsenault, closely involved in the project from day one, said he and other officials met in early June with L/A business leaders to brief them on the project and upcoming Web launch.

"I think the biggest value will be to small businesses that (operate) on both sides of the river," Arsenault said. "We met with a group of business leaders from both cities (on June 4) and they were very excited about what we've been doing and what we're going to do."

But the price was steep, Aho said, so he again returned to the L/A study committee to present the idea of essentially merging all planning and code operations using the EnerGov system — and splitting the costs and benefits.

"This is where Laurie (Smith) really got people involved" from both sides of the river and spearheaded getting the proposal approved by both city councils and then making the actual conversion, Aho said.

"EnerGov will do for L/A what technology has done for UPS," Aho predicted. "Instead of chasing paper, we'll be sending (computer) files around and getting people to electronically sign off. On the outside, our customer service will be far superior to anyone else's in the state, especially for the end-user, whether it's a developer or the guy who wants to build a deck."

Getting Close

The project's first phase is expected to launch on June 28. It is just the latest effort by Lewiston and Auburn to share and streamline services and save money.

Smith said the twin cities, separated by only the Androscoggin River, have explored for decades ways to join forces — especially in the demanding and expensive areas of economic development, code enforcement and permitting.

The cities' proximity and the development trends that have increasingly overlapped since the 1980s have given officials impetus to join forces wherever possible, Smith and others said.

In fact, official cooperation between the two municipal governments spans 133 years, according to L/A officials, beginning with the creation of the Lewiston and Auburn Horse Railroad in 1874.

"This project shows the (L/A) councils' commitment to being innovative," Lewiston's Arsenault said.

EnerGov Solutions markets itself as a global leader in developing land use and management software for government. The company works exclusively with municipal, county and state governments.

The company was selected from six firms after a Request for Proposals process that took nearly a year to complete.

The company was helping to get staffs from both cities trained in early and mid–June so the initial launch would go smoothly for both employees and contractors.

Public Benefit

By fall, the second phase of the project will give the public access to myriad information, including: who was issued permits for what; code violations against developers, builders, businesses and property owners; and, what is being planned for "mystery locations" where residents see a new project starting but little is known about what's going on — or up.

Contractors and property owners are expected to appreciate the new program once they are familiar with and confident in it, Smith said. For example, the computer suite will allow builders to request most of their permit documents online. It also will notify developers by email when there is a problem with a project. That should allow contractors to fix problems quickly and keep projects on time and within budget.

Applicants also will be notified by email if their work has failed to pass code or other legal requirements, again saving them time and money by being able to quickly address the issues.

Individual homeowners will be able to use the new program in the same way, also saving them time, money, frustration and travel to city hall.

After the new system has proven itself, other city departments, as well as those in the small towns that ring Greater L/A, will be able to link into the system, according to Smith, who was recently named the new Wiscasset town manager.

A regional system would bring even higher returns for both municipal government and the people it serves, she said.

"It is amazing software," Smith said, "that is revolutionizing how our cities do business."

Notes: Auburn has a population of 23,203, is 65.8 square miles, has 10,608 housing units, and a per capita annual income of $19,942. It was the first municipality in the state to adopt the council-manager form of government in 1917. It was the recipient of the All American City Award in 1967.

Lewiston has a population of 35,690, is 35.2 square miles, has 16,470 housing units, and a per-capital annual income of $17,905. It has four colleges within its boundaries, including Bates College. It was the recipient of the All American City Award in 2007.

(Source: 2000 Census Information)

CHAPTER 13

Boca Raton Develops Long-Range Financial Plans

Linda C. Davidson

Developing and adopting budgets that support strategic goals without exceeding available resources is a challenge at all times, but particularly when the economy is unstable. Elected officials are reluctant to raise taxes or adopt new fees, so government finance officers are faced with some tough choices. Jurisdictions can cut services, reduce costs, or explore and implement resilient alternatives — a combination of strategies to provide resources that will be sustainable in the future. Local governments need to react in the short term by providing current budget solutions, but also by developing the ability to plan effectively and efficiently, forecasting budgetary requirements based on current economic conditions. We need to use long-term financial planning to anticipate future needs and provide sustainability in our funding strategies.

Florida law dictates that local governments must adopt a balanced budget. Florida's ability to fund budgets on the state and local levels has been severely affected by the economic downturn. The state has also mandated significant property tax reform. Factoring in the foreclosure crisis, financial market conditions, reductions in sales tax and other state revenues, and declining property values, significant reductions in revenues and service delivery are expected at both the state and local levels. Ac-

cording to RealtyTrac, Florida had the second most foreclosure filings of any state in 2009, and high foreclosure rates continue to affect property values and tax collections.

Throughout Florida, local government finance officers have employed many strategies and approaches for dealing with the revenue shortfalls and reductions in services and personnel that have been required in the last several years. To diversify their financial position, many jurisdictions have adopted new revenue enhancements and fees, expanded their use of grants, prioritized services, and reduced operating costs (e.g., employee layoffs and furloughs, outsourcing of services, and regionalization and consolidation of services). They have also adopted budget policies that provide financial resiliency and direction that will be sustainable for the long term.

A recent survey prepared by the Florida Legislative Committee on Intergovernmental Relations (FLCIR) asked Florida cities and counties to detail the effects of tax policies and the economy. The majority of respondents indicated that their local governments will reduce their workforce, reduce services or the level of service, and contract out services or jointly fund services.

Originally published as "Budgeting for Sustainability: A Florida Perspective," *Government Finance Review*, Vol. 26, No. 2, April 2010, by the Government Finance Officers Association, Chicago, IL. Reprinted with permission of the publisher.

Revenue Enhancements

Fees provide a mechanism for collecting additional revenues while reducing the jurisdiction's reliance on property taxes. Local governments in Florida have adopted a wide range of fees, including program assessment fees (a common one is an annual fire assessment fee, based on property type and size, that recovers all or a portion of fire services), special assessments (to fund public improvements that benefit a property), and impact fees (to recover a portion of the public services a new development is likely to require). In addition, governments often receive fees from public/private partnerships.

Florida also has a large number of special districts that have been used to provide specific funding and services throughout the state. This method has been effective in funding the delivery of services for particular needs such as hospitals, airports, or downtown districts.

Additional property tax reform at the state level has been proposed, and there are other statewide initiatives that might limit the ability of local governments to enact or raise fees in the future. Such legislation will severely affect the ability of state and local governments to adopt resilient measures to provide the resources for future budgets.

Expanded Use of Grants

More and more local governments are using federal, state, and local grants to fund or supplement programs and to acquire or construct infrastructure. The Internet makes grant applications and reporting easily accessible. A local government should analyze the use of one-time grants for funding personnel or services very carefully, however, doing a cost-benefit analysis and looking at the long-term impact on operations. The amount of grant funding to be used for personnel might decline over extended grant periods, for instance, but the employees and associated operating and capital replacement costs will remain. Grants also require significant reporting and compliance efforts, so the economic benefit of each one should be evaluated, both short and long term.

The American Recovery and Reinvestment Act of 2009 (ARRA) provides a number of opportunities, but local governments should carefully evaluate the grant conditions and terms when determining their appropriateness. Funding through the ARRA is temporary and the grant requirements and commitments should be analyzed. For instance, if a local government chooses to apply for transit-related funding to operate a shuttle bus system, there are conditions as to how that shuttle system can be operated. One caveat is that the funds can only be used to pay union employees, which could negate the economic benefit of the transit grant if the cost of employing union workers had not been factored in.

The federal government has set up a one-stop shop for all federal grants. Information about ARRA-related and non-ARRA-related grants is available at www.grants.gov.

Service Prioritization

A local government needs to determine the cost of providing services to its residents, and then determine the priority of those services. Some are essential — police, fire, and solid waste collection — and some might be at the direction of local policy, such as beach renourishment. Other services are performed at the discretion of a local government, such as youth and recreation programs and beach maintenance. These services are not required, but local residents have come to expect them, and they have been strategic priorities for the local jurisdiction. There are also services that have historically been funded by the local government, including fireworks, holiday parades, or payments to non-profits for activities that benefit the local government and the community, and are frequently used to provide the local match for federal and state funds.

Each of these services needs to be evaluated and prioritized as part of the annual budget process. The budget should outline how these service priorities support the strategic plan and goals of the local government. The budget should detail the program costs and benefits, and the minimum amount of revenue required to fund the service. When service priorities are established, revenues can be estimated for the funding of these programs, and budgetary resource allocations can be made based on this prioritization of service delivery. (Florida requires notice to the public and several public hearings for the adoption of the annual budget.) Because of dwindling resources, many local governments in Florida have reduced or eliminated non-mandatory or non-core services, specifically cultural activities, non-profit funding, and other enhancement programming.

Reduction of Operating Costs

Many Florida municipalities have made significant efforts to review services and related operating costs during the annual budget process and to recommend reductions in operating costs when warranted. Over the years, local governments have expanded their services and personnel, and that expansion is not necessarily sustainable under current economic conditions. Due to the state-initiated property tax reform over the last several years, most local governments have recommended reductions in service, changes in employee benefits, and personnel cuts in an attempt to realign expenditure growth to anticipated revenue growth. Another option Florida governments have used is outsourcing functions such as building permit and plan review, engineering, and sanitation services, which can reduce ongoing operating costs significantly.

In Florida, some local governments have implemented a four-day work week and have closed their facilities one day a week to reduce costs. Others have permanently shut down libraries and park facilities, or have sold facilities. Some have increased the use of volunteers to provide services. Collective bargaining agreements in Florida cannot exceed three-year terms, and most local governments have negotiated or are in the process of renegotiating limits to salary growth and health insurance benefits, and have prospectively reduced pension benefits for union members to reduce long-term costs. There have been considerable scrutiny of personnel costs to reduce overtime and other benefits, delay salary increases, and use employee furloughs to achieve savings.

There are non-traditional approaches that can be used to stabilize costs. These include fuel hedging, using futures contracts and a fixed-price fuel supply, to help offset the volatility of fuel prices.

Regionalization or Consolidation of Services

Budgetary funding issues have caused more local governments to consider providing services with other governments in a collaborate effort to consolidate and reduce costs. The Government Finance Officers Association (GFOA) recommends that governments examine the benefits of alternative service delivery that involves shared service efforts in its best practice on *Alternative Service Delivery: Shared Services* (available at www.gfoa.org). The purchasing power of local governments can be improved by pooling purchases — the volume of transactions can help achieve better pricing and efficiency. There are 67 counties, 412 cities, and more than 1,600 special districts in the state of Florida, so there is ample opportunity to regionalize and consolidate service operations, and there has been an increased push in this direction, mostly for police and fire services.

In March 2009, Florida Legislative Committee on Intergovernmental Relations prepared an interim report, titled *Review and Consideration of Consolidation Models for Florida's Local Governments: Interim Project Update*, which was presented at the Florida GFOA Fiscal Survivor Series in August 2009. The presentation is available at http://www.floridalcir. gov/presentations.cfm.

Long-Range Financial Planning

In 2008, the GFOA's executive board approved a best practice on *Long-Term Financial Planning*. It says: "Long-term financial process is the process of aligning financial capacity with long-term service objectives. Financial planning uses forecasts to provide insight into future financial capacity so that strategies can be developed to achieve long-term sustainability in light of the government's service objectives and financial challenges."

For budget sustainability, local governments need to develop long-range financial plans to guide them in their future strategic and budgetary decisions. Long-range financial plans are financial forecasts that project revenues and expenditures over a period of time, typically 3 to 5 years, using past historical trends and future revenue and spending assumptions. They incorporate current economic conditions and the impacts of new or expanded facilities on operating costs. A long-range financial plan should provide an opportunity to evaluate current policies and practices before they create critical fiscal stress on the local government. The best-informed, most fiscally sensitive decisions will be those made with the longer-term implications in mind. A long-range financial plan should provide financial strategies and recommendations for sustainable budgetary actions.

Financial Condition Assessment

The Florida Auditor General's Office has developed financial condition assessment procedures that local governments can use to determine both their short-term and long-term

fiscal health. (The procedures are available at http://www.myflorida.com/audgen/pages/fca_procedures.htm.) These indicators, which were also presented at the Florida GFOA Fiscal Survivor Series August 2009, can be used to flag poor financial condition. The Web site contains an overview of the assessment tool, along with specific instructions for using it, as well as a comparison of various Florida cities, counties, and special districts. Using these assessment tools can assist in a local government in its long-range planning, but consideration should also be given to the condition of capital infrastructure.

Conclusions

Local governments must develop and employ strategies that will yield the anticipated results despite external conditions that provide swings in revenues and costs, over which we have little or no control. The strategies should include revenue enhancements, the expanded use of grants, service prioritization, reduction of operating costs, containment of long-term fixed costs, and the consolidation of services. Developing long-range financial plans that respond to an uncertain economy is a critical component to sustainability. Local governments need to adopt resilient actions to contain or control costs; otherwise, they will not have the ability to plan and react accordingly.

CHAPTER 14

Chandler and Other Cities Use Volunteers to Provide Services

David Bigos

Say that you're sitting there thinking, "I wonder what a typical day in the life of the Joe Chandler family is like." Well, it goes something like this.

It's 5:30 A.M., Joe — OK, OK, maybe closer to 6:00 — and you're awakened by the sound of your coffee maker perking up a nice Kona blend you recently purchased from the local farmer's market. You stroll to the kitchen to grab a cup, fix a little toast, go out and scoop the newspaper off the driveway, and head to the patio. Forecast says 77 and sunny ... again.

Your significant other joins you, and as you scan the paper you chat about last night's Art Walk — the monthly outdoor art and music collaboration among the city, the privately run Downtown Chandler Community Partnership, and local arts groups. And that is one attractive new ceramic cactus you folks picked up last night. Then there's this weekend's Multicultural Festival, one of several events that celebrate Chandler's rich diversity throughout the year.

You've read the paper, so fire up the home computer to check email. What's this? A-ha: the city has notified you about tomorrow's public meeting (one of several taking place throughout the community), seeking input on the budget via Twitter. Can't make it? That's OK, because the results will be tweeted as well. And there's more news on Chandler's Facebook page. You'll have to check that later, because it's time to get ready for work.

After a quick shower, it's off to work for you. Long commute? Naah. The job market here is holding its own despite a down economy. You're at your desk in fifteen minutes. But wait: Jill Chandler's got you beat — she telecommutes. There's a lot of that in this high-tech corner of the globe. Of course, on the way to your office you checked your messages from the cell phone; she checks hers in the den. You're busy people, Mr. and Mrs. Chandler! You've just arrived at work in Arizona's hottest business cluster, the Price Corridor. Decades of planning have made this area home to a diverse, sustainable workforce. It's just another day in techno-paradise.

Chandler is also a community of young, well educated people who enjoy a family-oriented lifestyle. Average age in the community is 32.9 years, and 69 percent of us have at least some college education.

With that said, it's Jill's turn to take the kids to school today. And the classrooms are wired too! Thanks to all those corporate partnerships in the classroom. In fact, they know more than the both of you when it comes to computers. What an asset. What a future! After

Originally published as "Chandler, Arizona: Telling Our Story," *National Civic Review*, Vol. 99, No. 4, Winter 2010, pp. 26–33, by the National Civic League, Denver, CO. Reprinted with permission of the publisher. www.wileyonlinelibrary.com/journal/ncr.

work, Joe, you pick up the kids from the Intel Computer Clubhouse at the new Boys and Girls Club. You remember the day not long ago when you both voted in a city bond election to build the $7 million facility, which is also one of the few clubs in the country constructed to LEED-certified environmental standards.

The kids are safe at home, and you stop for a bite to eat before heading to class at the University of Phoenix. Just a few months away from that master's degree, Joe Chandler! During dinner, you contemplate the truly global society we live in. You finally arrive home from your long day, play with the kids, and pet the dog.

Of course, the Chandler family understands the many challenges of the day as well. Located on the edge of the Phoenix Metropolitan area, Chandler, like its neighbors, has been hit hard by the recession. Revenue deficits in the tens of millions have been met with elimination of more than 130 city positions through freezes and retirement buyouts. Dozens of capital projects have been delayed or put on hold indefinitely, as have raises and cost-of-living increases for municipal employees.

For the past year, Chandler has also renewed emphasis on low-income areas of the city through volunteerism, with a mayor's initiative called For Our City that is bringing together service clubs, church groups, and other organizations to create a massive volunteer pool. Coordinated in part by the city's diversity office, it is also looking at the overlap of services to better serve those less fortunate in the community who may have been overshadowed in the past. The Chandler Human Relations Commission also reaches out to all segments of the community with an annual series of educational forums, festivals, and workshops to bring the community together and celebrate its diversity. The commission is just one of more than two dozen appointed citizen groups that offer direction and advice to the Chandler City Council on topics ranging from neighborhood issues to public housing concerns to domestic violence education. The mayor has also established commissions advocating for youth (daughter Jane's a member!), the elderly, and the disabled.

To date, few services have been affected by the recession, and layoffs have been avoided. Although the city's financial foundation is truly being tested, past fiscal policies (which include a deep pool of cash reserves and a low employee-to-resident ratio) have been applied, allowing the city to weather the storm better than most, at least to this point. The city has partnered with school districts to jointly fund facilities, among them a performing arts center, three pools, and two branch libraries. Chandler also collaborates with the state's universities to bring a research element to the city. And we partnered with the Town of Gilbert, a neighbor to the east, on a joint water treatment plant that saved the two municipalities $22 million in construction costs and $1 million annually in operations.

Chandler collaborated with several neighboring cities last year to form a Gang Fusion Center, which allows rapid sharing and dissemination of information as it relates to area gangs to combat a growing problem. The city also partnered with local nonprofits to battle such issues as the lack of proper health care for young children and underage drinking. Additionally, city officials initiated the Chandler Coalition for Youth, a group of area nonprofits, educators, businesses, and city staff members who developed an inventory of services to identify areas that were lacking, as well as areas of overlap.

These efforts have led to Chandler being named to the 100 Best Communities for Young People by America's Promise, a national partnership led in part by General Colin Powell. Chandler was one of just a few dozen cities to be a winner three years running. It was named a Most Playful City by Ka-BOOM! for three straight years. Ask residents what they enjoy about their community, and they're sure to include our award-winning parks system in their response. But we don't just build parks, we create them through creative community partnerships. Examples include a bike park and skate park, designed in part by a committee of local youths. The new Paseo Vista Recreation Area was built atop the city's old landfill. And with input from the city's Pakistani community, we built the region's first cricket field. It's all about the family in Chandler, friend.

As you turn out the lights, you look back on just how connected you've become in this multifaceted community. With a glow from the new moon peeking through the windows, you ponder how to make your chosen hometown an even better place for all, before nodding off.

And there you have it. A day brought to you by the City of Chandler, Arizona.

Challenges

Since the early to mid–1990s, Chandler has been one of the fastest-growing cities in the country, nearly tripling in just twenty years.

1990— 90,000 residents
2000—176,000 residents
2010— 253,000 residents

This type of growth places many strains on a municipality and its citizenry, including infrastructure expansion, provision of basic amenities, and fostering a sense of community among newcomers.

One other significant event occurred in the past decade that has also taken a toll on residents and their connection to the community. Construction of two freeways basically dissected this 72-square-mile city into thirds. Freeways create not only obvious physical barriers but also psychological barriers, blocking people from vital city services and social outlets.

Connecting with Newer Residents

Having a city with distinct geographical areas broken up by freeways and complicated by the presence of five distinct school boundaries has left many Chandler residents lacking any real sense of community. Consider southeast Chandler. As the latest growth area in the city, the vast majority of new residents located here in the past five years.

In that time, they have experienced constant road and utility construction, development of few public amenities, and little else. Chandler is faced with the challenge (read: opportunity!) to connect with residents, ask for patience as infrastructure growth catches up with the housing boom, and create a true sense

of "place" once the distractions of new development have gone away.

A second challenge is the need for renewed emphasis on older neighborhoods and low-income communities. A true test is to keep up with growth, but it is equally challenging to deliver the resources to areas in decline. Community sustainability, instilling pride in older neighborhoods, and refurbishing parks, streets, and other aging infrastructure could be a full-time task, were it not for the continued growth we face.

Like most communities, Chandler also has pockets where the socioeconomic conditions fall at or below the poverty level. Neighborhoods in decay, lower employment, low- and no-income families, aging populations, and lack of social services and other resources all leave some residents doing without even the most basic services such as medical care. Chandler is also seeing a growing problem with youth related crimes, with spiking arrests and liquor law violations.

Failure to address these two critical challenges would lead to long-lasting government distrust, resident apathy, crumbling neighborhoods, and other urban decay problems.

Chandler Heights Community Facilities

The Chandler Heights Community Facilities are aptly named; the multiple facilities placed on this 113-acre site serve the greater community good in a variety of ways. The entire lifecycle of this $27 million project is filled with examples of interdepartmental cooperation and innovation that enabled the City of Chandler to address several community needs, including water conservation, public safety, environmental education, and parks and recreation.

The project originated with one city department, municipal utilities, but eventually evolved to include police and community services. The original purpose was simple and clear: to create a surface and subsurface water recharge facility to place reclaimed water that had been piped to the site from the city's Airport Water Reclamation Facility, located several miles away.

Chandler, like most Arizona cities, requires reuse of all effluent produced by its wastewater treatment plants. Seasonal changes in supply necessitate that this reclaimed water be held someplace for storage and recovery as part of the city's comprehensive reclaimed water management plan. In 2001, the Municipal Utilities Department acquired 113 acres of undeveloped farmland in southeast Chandler to build the Chandler Heights Recharge Facility, for the purpose of effectively managing these seasonal demand variations in the reclaimed water supply.

When municipal utilities staff determined the recharge project would not require all 113 acres, they looked for other uses that could benefit the residents in this rapidly growing section of the community. At the same time, the Community Services Department was seeking land in the area for a new park and recreation amenity, and the Police Department was looking for space for a substation that would improve response time and add security for this part of the city. Despite the seemingly disparate objectives of the three departments, their common needs and the opportunity to share this land resource resulted in a partnership in the project that became collectively known as the Chandler Heights Community Facilities.

The project rapidly evolved and grew in complexity. A master plan was created in 2003 and unveiled to the public in October 2004 for input. The plan included four acres allocated for a 20,000-square-foot police substation that includes community meeting space, and a thirty-one-acre park, which would include a five-acre urban fishing lake and an 11,000-square-foot, multigenerational Environmental Education Center. The remaining seventy-eight acres would go to water recharge basins. After another public meeting and discussion in December 2005, designs were finalized. The project was completed in April 2008.

Nearly the entire project was funded through system development fees (SDF). The city began charging SDF in 1997 to help offset the cost of growth and subsequent expansion of resident services. In addition, these fees, charged for all new private development, allow the city to build projects like this to serve the community and environment. The remaining funding was obtained through a bond and a generous contribution from a private developer.

The police substation opened in January 2008, making a significant impact as response time to priority one calls have decreased from six minutes twenty-one seconds to five minutes thirty-four seconds in just two years. This statistic and an increased presence of officers have made for a safer, more welcoming area of the community.

The wetlands are a hit as well. Recharge basins have created a lush surface with streams and vegetation establishing an ecosystem that attracts many types of migratory birds and serves as a sanctuary for other wildlife. Each basin has an area that is constantly submerged, resulting in a wetland habitat. These submerged areas create a network of ponds connected by a system of small streams. The continuous flow of reclaimed water to the ponds helps to maintain a healthy wetlands ecosystem.

In addition, each basin has habitat islands that are not subject to flooding during recharge. The habitat islands maintain a level of isolation and encourage wildlife use when other areas that are more accessible to the public are occupied. Miles of walking trails surround the basins, and wildlife-viewing blinds have been strategically placed to accommodate bird watching, enhancing the educational opportunities of the habitat.

Adjacent to the wetlands is the more actively used part of the facility: Veterans Oasis Park, which includes a fishing lake that is stocked several times a year through the Urban Fishing Program of the Arizona Game and Fish Department.

The lake uses water that was recharged into the aquifer through the wetlands and then recovered by an onsite well. Filling the lake from the recovery well, circulating and oxygenating the water through an aeration system, and emptying the lake through evaporation and irrigation demand that all contribute to maintaining a healthy lake environment.

The unique combination of a recharge facility, wetlands, urban fishing lake, and park also serves as a fertile learning environment for educating the public and demonstrating the importance of water recycling and reuse, conservation, and respect for nature. The 4.5 miles of trails that wind throughout the area are equipped with interpretive signage to explain the ecosystem and water resource management behind the lake and the wetlands. There are also habitats for butterflies and hummingbirds, an outdoor amphitheatre, a learning-oriented playground for kids, and multiple picnic ramadas and shade structures.

The park was designed for passive recreation, which includes hiking, stargazing, bird watching, and other noncompetitive activities. The aim is to get people outside to enjoy nature and learn about their ecosystem.

That is what makes the Environmental Education Center (EEC) so critical to the project's success. The EEC serves as the gateway to the park and a welcome place for visitors. It offers year-round recreational and educational opportunities for residents of all ages. The center has an information desk, nature discovery room, exhibit areas, and classrooms with specialized glass doors that can be opened to allow instant access to the park's true classroom — nature.

Just as the wetlands attract wildlife to this spot, people are flocking as well and coming together to form new groups to interact with nature. About twelve thousand people use the EEC every year, and more than 430 volunteers donate about eighteen hundred hours annually to the center. They include Green Teens, Desert Rivers Audubon, Arizona Herpetological Association, Mother Nature's Storytime — all initiated and driven by residents like you, Mr. and Mrs. Chandler.

Chandler Care Center

The Chandler CARE Center (CCC) is a schoolbased, community-linked program of the Chandler Unified School District. Established sixteen years ago, the Chandler CARE Center opened a new, 8,800-sqaure-foot free-standing facility this March after outgrowing its three-classroom space in an elementary school. Through a true community alliance, dozens of local donors, including the City of Chandler, have allocated funds and services necessary for success.

Every year, the Children's Clinic delivers free acute-care medical treatment to more than thirteen hundred uninsured poverty-level babies and youths in Chandler, many of whom are treated repeatedly every year. With the new facility, administrators expect the number to at least double. In addition, twenty-six hundred immunizations are given annually. The new CCC facility has four dental operatories, with the capacity to treat an average of 150 patients weekly.

Annually, more than seven thousand needy Chandler residents receive food, clothing, or household items at the Chandler CARE Center. In the past fifteen years, the CCC has given medical assistance and immunizations to more than fifty-one thousand uninsured youths in need.

Many medical, dental, counseling, and service organizations donate their professional services at the Chandler CARE Center on a scheduled, rotating basis, so there is no charge to any child, family, or the school district for services.

The CCC promotes school readiness, attendance, and academic success by supplying medical treatment, dental treatment, immunizations, counseling, social services, parent education programs, and referrals for youths from birth to eighteen years old. The intended population of the CCC is uninsured children from families with little or no income living anywhere in the City of Chandler, regardless of the school district in which they reside. Historically, 88 percent of patients and clients are poverty level Hispanic families, with a majority residing in the city's redevelopment area.

The Chandler CARE Center is a program of the Chandler Unified School District (CUSD), supplying the fiscal infrastructure and administrative oversight needed to direct this comprehensive community based program. The CUSD also furnishes maintenance, insurance, and utilities for the Chandler CARE Center. The Chandler CARE Center incurs little actual operating expense because of its longstanding community partnerships with many local entities. In fact, out-of-pocket expenses for the

CCC are only 22 percent of its actual operating budget because virtually all the professional services are donated.

The goals of the Chandler CARE Center have varied little over time and include improved medical and dental health of uninsured youths from birth to eighteen, more children (from birth to eighteen) who are up-to-date on immunizations, access to free mental health services by licensed clinicians, improved school attendance, and an overall influence on the academic achievement of students from no-income, low-income and non-English-speaking families. It is a holistic family approach that also includes increasing the number of parents who communicate effectively in English as well as the number of parents who provide effective parenting skills.

Community collaboration has been the key to the success of the CCC, and the Children's Clinic is a keystone service to that end. It offers free acute-care medical treatment, well-child checkups, TB skin tests, and sports physicals for uninsured Chandler youths from families with little or no income. The medical staff of the Children's Clinic comprises volunteers who donate their professional services on a scheduled, rotating basis. Volunteer organizations include private practitioners as well as staff from larger entities such as CIGNA and Banner Health.

Children also receive free eye examinations and glasses from the Lions Club, Wal-Mart, and a local eye doctor. Additionally, free vouchers are available for needed medications, medical lab tests, and medical imaging. This funding is furnished in part by the City of Chandler Social Services Commission and donations from CUSD employees. To help the Children's Clinic leverage this funding, several local businesses offer services at 25–70 percent off their customary price.

The CCC also holds a weekly immunization clinic at no charge in partnership with Catholic Health-Care West and the Chandler Fire Department. The Chandler Public Library staff distributes free books in English or Spanish to children in the clinic, while taking the opportunity to register parents for library cards at the same time.

Dental services are yet another service component of the CCC. Catholic HealthCare West gives free fluoride varnish treatments, dental cleanings, and X-rays. Volunteer dentists offer restorative services.

A prime factor contributing to the success of the Chandler CARE Center is its historically stable source of income from the City of Chandler, including a $500,000 grant toward the new building. Other funding is directed toward CCC's operations and three employees from the city and private donors. The CCC also has a solid cadre of local, volunteer doctors who have been supplying free medical treatment for many years.

The Chandler CARE Center has been recognized numerous times for its unique ability to make medical services, educational opportunities, and social services available to no-income and low-income children and families in such a collaborative, cost effective manner. Those honors include the 2008 Making a Difference for Women Award from Soroptimists International, the 2007 AZ Leader Force Blue Ribbon Model Program for Healthcare from the Collaboration for a New Century, the 2002 Leadership for Learning Award from the American Association of School Administrators, and the 2001 MAGNA Award from the National School Boards Association.

The center's administrator, Susan Horan, could fill volumes with her stories of the help given to local families. Students diagnosed with life-threatening ailments who would have otherwise never visited a doctor for reasons of cost or for escaping the keen eye of a teacher have been healed, more often than not at no charge to the family. There are tales of kids showing no fear in sometimes dire or even bizarre circumstances because of the friendly surroundings of the center and its dedicated and caring staff. This community can embrace these stories because of the generous contributions of so many.

In summary, the Chandler CARE Center has a long history of successfully delivering the health care and social services that uninsured poverty-level children need if they are to enter and succeed in school. In the last five years, the CCC has come a long way. With its new center built firmly on a foundation of community support, the CCC will continue as a recognized model for improving the health, wellbeing, and educational achievement of needy youths and parents.

The Chandler Coalition on Youth Substance Abuse

In 2006, a group of young residents gathered to identify issues critical to Chandler's youth. These kids, peer leaders in an organization called ICAN (ICAN used to stand for "Improving Chandler Area Neighborhoods," but it now simply goes by its four-letter name), identified underage drinking as a critical issue among teens in the community. From that dialogue, the Chandler Coalition on Youth Substance Abuse (CCYSA) was formed.

ICAN is a nonprofit organization with a mission of offering free programs that empower youths to become productive, self-confident, and responsible citizens. For the past eighteen years, ICAN has joined with local community partners to initiate proactive prevention efforts to direct young people away from the streets and into more positive programs.

The organization conducts substance abuse and gang prevention programs for high-risk youths age five to eighteen in the Chandler Redevelopment Area (an area of approximately two square miles in the city's downtown core).

At the heart of the coalition are the ICAN Peer Leaders. This group is tasked with learning leadership skills at ICAN and applying those skills through at least one monthly community service project. These kids were the driving force in gathering a coalition of community stakeholders to serve as their advisors on addressing the issue of underage drinking. They included Mothers Against Drunk Driving, the Arizona State Liquor License and Control Board, the Mayor's Office, Chandler police and fire departments, Neighborhood Services, and the CUSD. Leading the process themselves and engaging ICAN staff, the teens developed and implemented a comprehensive community development strategy to address underage drinking, with three main goals:

1. Decreasing alcohol advertisements and signage visible from the street, erected by merchants in the Redevelopment Area
2. Decreasing the number of adults willing to buy alcohol for underage drinkers
3. Decreasing merchant sales to underage drinkers through increased carding

Through mobilization of coalition members, the teens organized and carried out several steps based on the three goals. They researched and gathered data to support their initiatives, while using the resources of the stakeholder group to achieve success.

Actions included identifying city ordinances on signage requirements, community education (including a thirty-minute show on the city's cable Channel 11), a survey of consumers, and many other strategies. Using these resources, the teens then collaborated with local merchants to remove alcohol signage, offered free training to merchants on ID'ing, and educated various sectors of the community on the risks of underage drinking.

The results: through the work of the coalition, the community benefits in many ways. By promoting laws and norms that establish healthy beliefs and clear standards on underage drinking, the overall health of the community is positively affected. Violence within the city is reduced, economic stability is promoted, and savings to the community are reaped from lessened demand for future health and social services related to alcohol abuse.

The measurable achievements of the group included:

- A 72.2 percent decrease in adults willing to purchase alcohol for a minor
- A 36 percent decrease in merchants willing to sell alcohol to a minor
- A 20.9 percent reduction in alcohol signage within the Chandler Redevelopment Area

Some of the key findings are noted by the teens:

> Underage drinking is a very real problem for youth, and our goal is to help educate others about the dangers associated with alcohol abuse. The CCYSA gives us an outlet to impact this problem and become leaders in our community [Jonathon, age eighteen].

Underage alcohol-related emergency room visits increase by 56 percent on Friday and Saturday nights as compared to weekdays for youth living in the Chandler Redevelopment Area. Drinking alcohol just isn't worth the risk of harming yourself or others. By being an active member of the CCYSA, I'm helping educate others about this community health issue [Victoria, age fourteen].

Selling alcohol to minors is unsafe, irresponsible, and illegal. The average age for a youth to first use alcohol in Chandler is 12.6 years old. I'm helping the CCYSA make a difference through education with merchants in our community, to keep youth in Chandler safe and alcohol-free [Isabel, age sixteen].

The Chandler Coalition on Youth Substance Abuse has also garnered regional and national attention. In 2008, the National Association of Social Workers named the coalition members State Citizens of the Year. In 2009, the MetLife Foundation honored the group as one of six programs recognized nationally for innovation in youth prevention programming.

Changing Lives

CCYSA is not only changing the norms existing in our community for the health and safety of our youths but is also profoundly influencing those involved in the program. Finally, consider Daniel. At seventeen, he first encountered ICAN's Peer Leadership program. Before getting involved, he wasn't proud of his choices; he was hanging out with gang members and drug users, and he started to get involved in both (introduced to him at alcohol and binge drinking parties). Here is what Daniel has to say:

At the time, I didn't think there were any other alternatives, and if there were I didn't see them clearly enough. I didn't think I had a real future back then. We just got through each day and went on to the next, not thinking about the consequences of our actions ... alcohol had a lot to do with that.

One day, it kind of hit me when I got in trouble at school. I was in trouble, and I wasn't doing much to stop it. Detective Kelley from Chandler Police Department, who was involved with CCYSA activities, asked me to make a choice to stay out of trouble. He said ICAN and CCYSA would help me do this.

After six months of being involved, I have done all of the outreach projects and I feel really good about it. We are doing something positive for our community and for the kids that live here. We are really making a difference.

ICAN and CCYSA accepted me when I came to them and helped me turn things around. I have met positive people who encourage me. I really feel lucky to be a part of ICAN and CCYSA. And it's nice to see so many people from our community who care enough to make a difference.

By accepting and mentoring young people like Daniel, so many more Chandler youths stand a chance for success and a life without the harmful effects of underage drinking. Through a no-nonsense plan, recruiting like-minded community individuals and organizations, the peer group was able to make significant strides in the community. Signage, education, a few taps on the shoulder to point out indiscretions in the law, and a whole lot of determination have led to a remarkable story with equally remarkable results.

CHAPTER 15

Charlotte and Other Cities Implement Employee Wellness Programs

Robert Barkin

Public employers who have become experts at trimming their communities' annual budgets now are working just as hard at trimming their employees' waistlines. With health care taking an increasing portion of their expenses, local governments are promoting wellness programs to improve employees' health and control costs.

Today, two-thirds of public employers offer wellness programs, with 40 percent providing stand-alone programs and 25 percent offering wellness initiatives as part of group health plans, according to the 2007 Public Employee Benefits survey from the Brookfield, Wis.–based International Foundation for Employee Benefit Plans (IFEBP). In fact, wellness education is the most popular public sector initiative, followed by health screenings, health risk assessments, health fairs and subsidized flu shots, according to the survey. "With health care costs still rising, it's one area where we can still have an impact," says Catherine Reese, senior benefit analyst for Charlotte, N.C.

Charlotte has developed a Wellness Works initiative that teaches the city's 6,000 employees how to prevent illness and helps them practice healthy lifestyles. "If we prevent illness, we save money," says Christina Fath, Charlotte wellness administrator. "And, there's the public health issue. Wellness is the first key piece. If we can get control of health issues, society will benefit, as well."

As other communities — like Sarasota County, Fla.; and Maricopa County, Ariz.— join Charlotte in trying to change employee behavior, they are experimenting with incentives and methods that will produce the most positive results. The return on investment still may be difficult to calculate, but the communities believe the efforts eventually will pay dividends.

The reason public employers are looking for ways to cut health costs is easy to understand. In 2004 (the most recent data available), national health care expenditures were nearly $1.9 trillion, more than double the $717 billion spent in 1990 and more than seven times the $255 billion spent in 1980, according to the U.S Department of Health and Human Services (HHS) The year-over-year increase in 2004 from 2003 was 6.8 percent — more than twice the inflation rate.

The 2004 figure represents 16 percent of the Gross Domestic Product (GDP), which is three times larger than the industry's share in 1960. Per capita health care expenses more than doubled from 1990 ($2,821) to 2004 ($6,280). U.S. health care spending is expected to increase at similar levels for the next decade, reaching $4 trillion in 2015, or 20 percent of GDP.

Originally published as "Scaling Back," *American City & County*, Vol. 122, No. 5, May 2007, by Penton Media, Inc, Overland Park, KS. Reprinted with permission of the publisher.

Healthy Bodies, Healthy Budgets

State and local governments have additional burdens because their employees are heavy users of the heath care system. For example, public employers pay almost double the cost for health insurance than do private sector employers, according to a 2005 study of employee benefit programs by the Washington-based Employee Benefit Research Institute. That is partly because teachers and professors, who are higher paid, have better benefits and are more heavily unionized, so employers pick up more of their health care costs. Even when teachers and professors are not included, though, the costs for other subgroups, such as service personnel, remain significantly higher because they include higher risk professions, such as police and fire.

In addition, mounting evidence suggests that the costs of health care are concentrated in a small segment of the community, and that by reducing that segment's use of the system, overall health care costs could fall significantly. For example, according to HHS, the top 1 percent of users of the health care system are responsible for almost 25 percent of the nation's total health care costs, while the bottom 50 percent of health care users, who have little or no health care costs, are responsible for less than 5 percent of total health care costs. By attacking the health issues afflicting the heaviest users of the system, health providers believe they can have the greatest effect on reducing health costs.

Charlotte used claims data from its health care providers to focus on the health issues that appear most predominant, says Anna Ellis, the city's benefits manager. Charlotte's Wellness Works initiative incorporates education with activities that encourage employees to know their health risks and take action to combat them. The city publishes articles in the employee newsletter about the benefits of exercise, and it stuffs paychecks, sends emails and mails postcards to workers' homes with messages about everything from exercise tips to suggestions for healthy breakfasts.

On-site screenings for blood pressure, cholesterol and weight management are scheduled at the locations where many public safety and public works employees work. "The key to success is making it easy for employees to take an interest in their own health and welfare," Fath says. "We go out to the locations at 5:30 or 6 in the morning to be there when employees concentrate."

In addition, the city has tried to inject a little fun into the wellness mix, by creating a walking competition. Groups of four employees from all ranks of the city's work force, including department heads and city managers, were challenged to compete with each other to walk the most miles. The group that walked the most after six weeks received a trophy. "We're hoping that people will continue to keep walking together," she says, "and we're seeing some evidence of that."

Investing and the Returns

If education and competition are not enough to inspire employees to take care of themselves, communities are using financial incentives to encourage them. About two-thirds of public employers offer one or more types of incentives for participation in wellness programs, according to the IFEBP study.

Maricopa County has invested in education and aggressive programs that require significant resources. For example, the county has opened a free gym that is open 24 hours every day, and if employees accept additional personal responsibility, their medical care costs will be reduced. In addition, this year the county is initiating a diabetic management program that would pay for a substantial part of their medical costs — if their doctors' regimens are met. "If they follow their doctor's instructions, they will receive free medicine and supplies," says Pat Vancil, the county's employee health initiatives manager.

The county currently spends $609,000 on diabetes medicine and supplies, and will add another $229,000 for the new program. The savings for the county, Vancil says, will come with the reduced long-term expenses from the various diabetes-related illnesses, which would only be exacerbated if sugar levels are not monitored and prescribed medications not taken. "We want people to take an active role in their health care," she says. "If people get involved, they take some control of their own well-being."

Public officials, while acknowledging the overall health benefits of wellness programs, also are looking for evidence that they are worth the implementation cost. A number of studies indicate that wellness programs can help save money.

Surveys cited by the University of Michigan Health Management Research Center found that wellness programs yielded net savings of $3.44 to $13 for every dollar spent on programming. The university also studied the combined effect of several health risks on health care costs. In the study, a no-risk group (those who never smoked, of moderate weight and walked for at least an hour each day) had average adjusted health care costs of $171, while costs for a group with all three risks were 42.6 percent higher.

By attacking some of the key factors in poor health — smoking, obesity and lack of exercise — wellness advocates argue they can improve the lives of their workers as well as reduce how they affect health care costs. The university study noted that wellness programs yielded the greatest benefits when they included health education, an employee assistance program that focuses on drug treatment and mental health care, early detection programs and a fitness program.

Sarasota County, Fla., is incorporating all of those tactics — including employee incentives for health risk assessments, preventive care and healthy living programs — into its wellness program. The county also has begun targeted intervention — including disease management, outreach and education — for high-risk employees. As a result, county health costs fell to 6.95 percent in plan year 2004–2005, versus 13.7 percent nationally, and they did not increase 2005–2006, versus 12.4 percent nationally.

Ultimately, Sarasota County officials want to educate employees on the relationship between their own health habits and the rising cost of health premiums for the entire work group, showing that healthy habits can go a long way to reducing the overall cost. "Making the connection between medical costs, health risks and personal financial security is the key," says Steve Marcinko, manager of employee benefits and wellness for the county.

But, while reducing the county's health care costs is one goal, that is not the primary message, Marcinko says. "First and foremost, wellness is about people and improving the quality of life."

CHAPTER 16

Chicago Uses Citizen Input to Make Budget Decisions

Josh Lerner

In Chicago's Rogers Park neighborhood, April 10, 2010, was a day of reckoning. Over the past year, dozens of community members had been organizing an experiment in democracy — ordinary residents were going to decide directly how to spend city budget dollars. Not just give their opinions, but actually make decisions. The organizers showed up early in the morning to the large school cafeteria that was hosting the final public vote. No one knew, though, if people would really turn out.

They did. In a few hours, over twelve hundred people flooded the school to learn about the thirty-six spending proposals and vote for their favorites. The Chicago experiment is one of over a thousand cases of participatory budgeting, a global best practice of local democracy, according to the United Nations. In 2009, Alderman Joe Moore invited my organization, The Participatory Budgeting Project, to help launch the first U.S. process in his city ward. As budget crises deepen and trust in government plummets, Moore is one of many voices calling for more democratic and accountable ways to manage public money. Could participatory budgeting be a solution?

Reinventing Democracy in Brazil

Citizen participation in budgeting is not a new idea. In small towns in New England and elsewhere, residents have long been able to decide spending through town hall meetings. Larger cities often hold budget consultations to collect input on spending priorities.

In 1989, the Brazilian city of Porto Alegre launched a new kind of democratic process, called Orçamento Participativo (participatory budgeting, or PB). It scaled up the grassroots participation of town meetings to the city level by combining direct and representative democracy. Through PB, citizens have decided how to spend part of the city budget through an annual series of neighborhood, district, and citywide assemblies. At these meetings, community members and elected budget delegates identify spending priorities, deliberate on these priorities, and vote on which projects to implement. Each year, tens of thousands of people participate, deciding up to a fifth of the city budget.

The results have been dramatic and well documented by researchers such as Boaventura de Sousa Santos and Gianpaolo Baiocchi. In 1989, only 49 percent of the population had basic sanitation service. After eight years of PB,

Originally published as "Participatory Budgeting: Building Community Agreement Around Tough Budget Decisions," *National Civic Review*, Vol. 100, No. 2, Summer 2011, pp. 30–35, by the National Civic League, Denver, CO. Reprinted with permission of the publisher.

98 percent of households had water and 85 percent were served by the sewage system. In the same time span, half of the city's unpaved streets were paved, and the number of students in elementary and secondary schools doubled. New public housing was built at increasing rates, and bus companies expanded service to previously neglected neighborhoods. Even the number of neighborhood associations increased. These changes have benefited slums and low-income communities in particular. Although a 2004 change in government weakened PB, the process has persisted for two decades.

From Porto Alegre to the World

After emerging in Porto Alegre, PB was soon adopted throughout Brazil, then elsewhere in Latin America. In the past decade, it has become popular in Europe, Africa, and Asia. By 2007, over twelve hundred cities were practicing it. Countries such as the United Kingdom and Dominican Republic have passed laws requiring that all local governments implement PB, and the United Nations and World Bank have named it a best practice of democratic governance. States, counties, schools, housing authorities, and community associations have also used PB for their budgets.

The first North American experiments occurred in Canada, and outside of city hall. In 2001, Toronto Community Housing, the second-largest public housing authority in North America, launched PB for its capital budget. Each year since then, up to six thousand tenants have decided how to spend $9 million for building and grounds improvements. An hour away, in the city of Guelph (population 115,000), PB grew in a coalition of grassroots neighborhood groups. Starting in 2001, the Neighbourhood Support Coalition began using a deliberative process to allocate roughly $250,000 annually from various government and foundation sources. Most recently, the Montreal borough Plateau Mont-Royal implemented PB in 2006, 2007, and 2008 for up to $1.5 million of its capital budget.

The hundreds of examples around the world are not cookie-cutter copies, but they are based on a common approach: needs assessment, deliberation, decision making, and implementation. First, community members identify spending priorities and select budget delegates to represent their neighborhoods. With help from public employees, the delegates transform the community priorities into concrete project proposals. Community members then vote on which projects to fund, and the city or institution implements the top projects.

Elected officials still retain plenty of power, but they share some of that power with constituents. Typically, less than 20 percent of the total budget is put on the PB table. This is both a little and a lot. It is a small portion of the budget but a large chunk of the discretionary funds — the money that is actually in play each year, not set aside for fixed costs such as wages and infrastructure maintenance. The funds may be for capital or operating projects, depending on the city.

Why has PB been so popular? Most people seem to be motivated by six main benefits:

1. *Democracy.* Ordinary people have a real say — and they get to make real political decisions. Politicians build closer relationships with their constituents, and community members develop greater trust in government.

2. *Transparency.* Budgets are policy without the rhetoric — what a government actually does. When community members decide spending through a public vote, there are fewer opportunities for corruption, waste, or costly backlash.

3. *Education.* Participants become more active and informed citizens. Community members, staff, and officials learn democracy by doing it. They gain a deeper understanding of complex political issues and community needs.

4. *Efficiency.* Budget decisions are better when they draw on citizens' local knowledge and oversight. As John Dewey said, "The man who wears the shoe knows best where it pinches." Once they are invested in the process, people make sure that dollars are spent wisely.

5. *Social justice.* Every citizen gets equal access to decision making, which levels the playing field. Traditionally underrepresented

groups tend to participate more than usual in PB, which helps direct resources to communities with the greatest needs.

6. *Community.* Through regular meetings and assemblies, people get to know their neighbors and feel more connected to their city. Local organizations spend less time lobbying and more time deciding policies. Budget assemblies connect community groups and help them recruit members.

Perhaps because of such broad support, there have also been some problems, mainly with translation, co-optation, and tokenism. Advocates in some countries, such as Germany, have translated "participatory budgeting" to mean any kind of public involvement in budgeting. Public consultations, dialogues, and hearings that have taken place for decades suddenly become "participatory budgeting," even though these processes have little in common with the Porto Alegre model. In many cases, this practice has helped governments legitimize old (or new) consultation practices that give citizens no power to decide spending.

Meanwhile, the World Bank has aggressively promoted a trimmed-down version of PB in Africa and elsewhere, under the banner of transparency and good government. Coincidentally (or perhaps not), this has helped deflect blame for economic problems away from international institutions and toward local governments. As in Germany, notions of social justice have been mostly set aside. In the United Kingdom, advocates have launched over two hundred PBs, but most involve less than $100,000, sparking concerns about tokenism.

In the past twenty years, PB has captured the imagination of people around the world thanks to its core concept: citizens deciding public spending. This idea has inspired excitement because of its potential to reinvent democracy by empowering ordinary people to become policy makers. As PB appears on the radar in the United States, will it give citizens real decision-making power? Or will it just become a new name for budget consultations or token participation?

Putting Democracy on the Menu in Chicago

Surprisingly, Chicago was the first testing ground for participatory budgeting in the United States. The city is notorious for its patronage system and lack of transparency, but this same system also created space for experimentation. To compensate for the mayor's near omnipotence over citywide issues, city council members have each received about $1.3 million in annual discretionary "menu money" since 1994. The aldermen, as they are known locally, are free to spend this money at their will in their wards. Usually they fund items such as street repairs and lights, from a set menu. Some fail to spend the funds, and others have been criticized for doling them out as patronage.

In 2007, Alderman Joe Moore learned about PB at a session we organized at the U.S. Social Forum, a national gathering of progressive activists. Since 1991, he had represented Chicago's 49th Ward, which includes the Rogers Park neighborhood and over sixty thousand residents. Moore had already been outspoken on hot-button issues in the city council. *The Nation* magazine named him the "Most Valuable Local Official" in the country, in recognition of his successful sponsorship of a resolution against the Iraq war, measures requiring living wages for employees of big-box retail stores, and environmental restrictions on Chicago's coal power plants. But in 2007, he barely won reelection amid criticism that he had neglected local ward issues.

When Moore first heard about PB, he was inspired, but not to action. As he later reflected, "I thought: Great idea — too bad I'm not mayor!" Only in 2009 did Moore fully grasp that he could use PB for his menu money, as a way to better address local issues. That February, he proposed that we work together to launch a pilot initiative. Together with my colleague Gianpaolo Baiocchi, I spent the next year helping Moore and his office plan and carry out the PB process.

Despite full support from Moore, we faced some challenges. For one thing, the 49th Ward is extremely diverse. Over eighty languages are spoken within its less than two square miles. The ward is roughly 30 percent Latino, 30 percent African American, 30 percent White, and 10 percent Asian. Retail strips are surrounded by apartment towers and single-family homes. Also, ward politics are feisty. The locals repeatedly warned us about virulent bloggers and combative organizations. How does one of the nation's most diverse neighborhoods bring opinionated residents together to make difficult budget decisions?

As Megan Wade Antieau and I explained in *YES!* magazine, we started in April by inviting leaders of all the ward's community organizations and institutions to an introductory workshop. To build community buy-in, we then invited them to join a Steering Committee. Over thirty groups signed up, including nonprofits, community-based organizations, block clubs, schools, churches, and even the Hare Krishna temple. Through several workshops and meetings, we worked with the Steering Committee to map the PB timeline, structure, and rules.

The public process kicked off with nine neighborhood assemblies starting in November. After presentations explaining the menu money and the budgeting process, residents divided into groups of five to ten. Guided by volunteer facilitators, they brainstormed spending ideas on flipchart, identified their top priorities, and picked community representatives who would transform those priorities into concrete proposals. After the assemblies, these representatives, along with Steering Committee mentors, split into six thematic committees: Streets, Traffic Safety, Parks and Environment, Transportation, Public Safety, and Art and Other Projects.

The committees met regularly over the next four months to review the initial ideas, develop proposals, and consult with experts. Members also went out into the field to do their own research. The Public Safety Committee, for instance, visited the 911 center and met with the police. As community representative Marilou Kessler explained, "Everyone [on the committee] came — about fifteen to sixteen people on a workday. It was astonishing cooperation." The trip shifted the committee's priorities. They learned that security cameras are used only occasionally and are not continuously

monitored. After police explained that lighting is more effective at deterring crime, the committee prioritized streetlight proposals over camera proposals.

Since the initial neighborhood assemblies attracted less than three hundred people, the alderman and the Steering Committee offered other ways for residents to contribute ideas and feedback. First, the alderman's office posted the ideas from the initial assemblies online and distributed them via e-mail. To complement the face-to-face discussions, the Steering Committee set up a PB blog and individual blogs for each committee. Community representatives posted photos and surveys about their project ideas and collected suggestions from the stream of blog comments. In early March 2010, the community representatives held three more neighborhood assemblies (including one in Spanish) to present their spending proposals and get final feedback.

After a last round of revisions, the community representatives presented a ballot of thirty-six specific budget proposals and then helped organize a publicity campaign. The Art and Other Projects Committee put together a poster exhibition of proposals at Mess Hall, a local cultural center. Andy De La Rosa, an artist on the committee, found himself swayed by the proposals from other committees. "This is all extra," he said of his committee's proposals for murals, artistic bike racks, and historical markers. "I hope people vote for the streets."

On April 10, all ward residents age sixteen and over were invited to vote on the proposals at a local high school. Voters did not have to be registered or even citizens — they just had to demonstrate that they lived in the ward. The week before, 428 residents had already voted early at the alderman's office — more early voters per day than during the 2008 presidential election.

On the final voting day, a stream of people filled the school cafeteria. They read over posters explaining the proposals, consulted with community representatives from each committee, and then voted for up to eight projects on paper ballots. In the end, 1,652 residents voted. This number vastly exceeded expectations, considering that it was a brand-new process with little media coverage and no other elections or ballot measures to inspire turnout.

The $1.3 million was enough to fund the fourteen most popular projects. The proposal to fix sidewalks received the most votes, and other funded projects included bike lanes, community gardens, murals, traffic signals, and street lighting. Every committee had at least one proposal funded. Most of the projects are currently being implemented or have already been completed.

Moore quickly pledged to make PB an annual process, and the second year began with a new round of neighborhood assemblies in September 2010. As in other cities, the process evolved slightly, based on lessons learned. The Steering Committee was replaced by a new Leadership Committee, which included not only organization representatives but also community representatives from the first year. After seeing that street repairs received little funding the first year, the new leaders proposed adding an additional question to the final ballot, asking what percentage of the budget pot should be set aside for streets.

Building a More Participatory Democracy

The experience in Chicago highlights some challenges and opportunities for participatory budgeting in the United States. The biggest challenge is a familiar one: How do you attract diverse participants, beyond the usual suspects? In Latin America, poor people turn out in droves for PB, partly to fix urgent problems, such as unpaved streets and open sewers. In the United States, these basic needs are already met, and infrastructure repairs, such as street resurfacing, are more often priorities for wealthy homeowners.

In the 49th Ward, turnout was no more diverse than in other local community meetings. While every community was represented, on average participants were older, whiter, and more likely to be homeowners than in the ward as a whole. Latino turnout was especially low, probably because of distrust of government and worries about immigration status. Had turnout been more diverse, would funding have been allocated differently?

More important, what can be done to include underrepresented groups? In the 49th Ward, we invited organizations working with these groups to lead the process, provided Spanish-language assemblies and materials, did targeted outreach to key community groups, and scheduled meetings at convenient locations and times for working people. Other approaches were not adopted due to limited funding or interest, such as using experienced facilitators, including fun activities and entertainment at assemblies, and providing child care, food, and interpreters. Low-income residents might have been more interested had funds for programs been on the table. More use of Facebook and other social media might have attracted more youth participation.

PB also requires that politicians, public employees, and citizens adapt to new roles. Politicians need to give up control over some decisions in order to gain community support. Their staff members need to spend more time facilitating discussions and providing technical assistance. Citizens need to move beyond complaints and become comfortable deliberating and making decisions.

In Chicago, people generally rose to these challenges, but the adjustments were not easy. Some community leaders were reluctant to take ownership, deferring to the alderman's office. Staff members were already overwhelmed with work, and at first they struggled to keep up with the new responsibilities. Facilitating democratic participation involves a lot of face-to-face conversations, phone calls, and e-mails. In most citywide PBs, a whole office manages the process. In small jurisdictions such as the 49th Ward, there is much less staff capacity. Only when Moore hired a designated PB coordinator, Nicole Summers, did the process take off.

Despite these challenges, the Chicago experiment illustrated ways to bring people together to make tough decisions. Sure, residents had conflicting ideas about how the money should be spent. But now they had space to negotiate these differences and focus on the common good. Community representatives showed an impressive ability to move beyond their initial assumptions and priorities. At first, "Everyone was complaining about their block," said Laurent Pernot of the Transportation Committee. "But now every single committee has taken stewardship of the whole ward as their mission."

In a time of downsizing, PB showed how government can harness citizen energy to get things done. Staff members had little time to research spending ideas, but enthusiastic residents came to the rescue, once they had the power to make a difference. For example, to identify sidewalks most in need of repair, Transportation Committee members walked almost every block of the ward, in the middle of the Chicago winter. "I will never look at sidewalks the same way again!" reflected Dena Al-Khatib, one of the sidewalk inspectors.

Perhaps most important, PB can help establish government as a valuable public good — an idea that is very much under attack. Once people see that public dollars are being spent for useful projects, government seems more worthwhile. As Moore wrote in a letter to constituents, PB "exceeded even my wildest dreams. It was more than an election. It was a community celebration and an affirmation that people will participate in the civic affairs of their community if given real power to make real decisions."

If citizens have enough time, information, and support, they will make good budget decisions. And if elected officials agree to carry out these decisions, people will turn out and come together. By giving up some power, Alderman Moore gained more public support, recently winning reelection with 72 percent of the vote. Several other Chicago aldermen have also pledged to implement PB, and politicians from New York to California are considering launching their own initiatives. With enough political will, a new kind of grassroots democracy may be sprouting up.

REFERENCES

Baiocchi, G. "The Citizens of Porto Alegre." *Boston Review*, March/April 2006. Retrieved March 23, 2011, from http://bostonreview.net/BR31.2/baiocchi.php.

_____. *Militants and Citizens: The Politics of Participatory Democracy in Porto Alegre*. Stanford, CA: Stanford University Press, 2005.

Lerner, J., and M. Wade Antieau. "Chicago's $1.3 Million Experiment in Democracy." *YES!*, April 20, 2010. Retrieved March 23, 2011, from http://www.yesmagazine.org/people-power/chicagos-1.3-million-experiment-in-democracy.

Santos, B. "Participatory Budgeting in Porto Alegre: Toward a Redistributive Democracy." *Politics and Society*, 1998, *26*(4), 461–510.

CHAPTER 17

Cincinnati and Other Cities Improve Public Trust in Government

Sheryl Sculley

The state of our economy has organizations looking for ways to reduce waste and increase the public trust. The city of San Antonio, Texas, has been aggressively working on this issue for nearly 25 years. By creating the office of municipal integrity (OMI), we established a team to investigate and prevent fraud, waste, and abuse.

OMI Then and Now

In 1985, city leaders became concerned about contracts that possibly were fraudulent and personnel issues that required internal investigating. In response to these concerns, they created OMI that year and modeled it after similar programs in Cincinnati, Ohio, and Phoenix, Arizona. By creating OMI, the city took a proactive approach to prevention of fraud, waste, and abuse, and, in the process, inspired renewed confidence in local government.

On August 1, 2006, we strengthened OMI by creating Administrative Directive 1.75, which clearly delineated roles and responsibilities across the city for combating fraud, waste, and abuse. Since a later adaptation of Directive 1.75, OMI now reports directly to an executive committee known as the OMI Committee. It comprises representatives from the city manager's office, the human resources office, the police department, and the city attorney's office.

The OMI Committee meets monthly and carefully reviews each investigation for thoroughness and completeness. Executive review at that level enables management to make real-time assessments of fraud, waste, and abuse; to track trends; and to craft appropriate interventions.

Currently, OMI consists of two investigators and a third senior investigator who supervises all investigations and acts as liaison to city executive leadership. Although all OMI investigators are civilian, two of them have extensive law enforcement backgrounds and the third has a professional background in federal substance abuse programs.

The most crucial responsibilities of the OMI staff are interviewing witnesses and determining the subjects of the investigations. Daily tasks for OMI investigators include data collection, analysis, and surveillance.

Ethics and Fraud

Research shows that high ethical standards play an important role in how employees con-

Originally published as "Reducing Fraud, Waste, and Abuse in Local Government," *Public Management*, Vol. 93, No. 1, January/February 2011, by the International City/County Management Association, Washington, D.C. Reprinted with permission of the publisher.

duct themselves at work. With this in mind, in March 2006 we implemented mandatory ethics training for approximately 10,000 city employees. Employees received written material as well as a specially produced video that was designed to illustrate real-world scenarios where employees made decisions concerning common ethical situations.

There is evidence that fraud appears to be growing nationwide.[1] It's difficult to determine whether this is a result of recent economic downturns or the fact that in recent years more focus has been placed on fraud. In response to this trend, the San Antonio directed increased fraud prevention training for city departments that OMI identified as being at risk.

At-risk departments were identified as those with extensive cash handling, contract procurement, and regulatory functions. By the end of fiscal year 2008, OMI provided tailored fraud training to more than 1,000 employees citywide. This training continues today as investigators are commonly asked by department heads to provide fraud prevention and fraud awareness training to their personnel.

Curbing Fraud, Waste, and Abuse

OMI investigates employee misconduct ranging from misuse of position and misuse of city resources, to more serious cases of theft and fraud. In 2009, OMI saw a 40 percent increase in cases investigated and resolved. The conclusion rate of these investigations ranged from a one-day turnaround to several months of intensive data tracking as well as surveillance within the community.

In a recent investigation, OMI investigators identified a fraudulent billing scheme being carried out by two employees. The scheme involved the receipt of payments being made by citizens toward brush collection fees. After the investigation was closed successfully, not only did the two employees resign but deficiencies in the on-site payment register, weight scale system, and security video were identified and corrected.

Moving Forward

The need for internal investigations within the public sector is an issue that should be taken seriously as the budgets that organizations use to fund daily operations. San Antonio was at the forefront of fraud prevention and investigation decades ago.

Today, OMI investigators continue their mission of curtailing fraud, providing awareness, and increasing public trust and transparency within our local government. With new ideas and insight, OMI is the gold standard that other organizations can follow as all of us continue to uphold the public trust.

NOTE

1. "Occupational Fraud: A Study of the Impact of an Economic Recession" (Austin, Texas: Association of Certified Fraud Examiners, 2010), www.acfe.com/occupational-fraud/occupational-fraud.asp.

CHAPTER 18

Colorado Springs Uses Citizens to Evaluate Public Services

Zach Patton

On a hot afternoon in late summer, the city pool at Monument Valley Park in Colorado Springs, Colo., usually would be teeming with children and families — the kids splashing, swimming and soaking up the August sun. But this year, the pool stayed quiet. Budget cuts forced the city to close all its swimming facilities. A few of them were taken over by a private swim club, but the ones that couldn't find a backer, like Monument Valley, remained shuttered.

"This place ought to be packed," says Kim King, administration manager of the Parks, Recreation and Cultural Services Department, as she stands outside the fenced-off pool in Monument Valley Park. "This should be crawling with kids. But there's nobody here."

Nearby, King points to a set of public restrooms housed in a small Spanish-style building clad in yellow stucco. Those are closed too, with signs on the door: "NOTICE: Due to budget reductions, this facility is closed indefinitely." Opposite that building is a moderate-sized pond with a small island in the middle. Today, the pond stands empty. The city can't afford to maintain it, and the water's been reduced to a stagnant, scummy puddle.

Times are tough in the Springs, as veteran residents call it. Like cities throughout the country, this town has been hit hard by the re-

cession. But its fiscal problems are especially severe. The city is famously right-wing, and property taxes here are some of the lowest in the nation — in 2008, the per capita property tax was about $55. City revenue instead comes mostly from local sales taxes. As a consequence, Colorado Springs is feeling the downturn's effects faster and more sharply than other cities. At the close of 2009, the city found itself facing a nearly $40 million revenue gap for this year.

So to save money, the Springs slashed its budget and enacted a series of severe service cuts to save money. One-third of the city's streetlights were turned off to reduce electricity costs. The city stopped mowing the medians in the streets. (At one point earlier this summer, the medians were so overgrown with weeds that the city was in violation of its own code for property maintenance.)

The parks department was hit especially hard — its budget was gutted from $17 million in 2009 to just $3 million this year. In addition to closing the pools and restroom facilities, the city pulled out all the trash cans from its parks, since it could no longer afford to collect the garbage. Four community centers and three museums were put on the chopping block, although private donations and some emergency public funds are keeping them open for the rest of the year. With maintenance money wiped

Originally published as "Doing Less with Less," *Governing*, Vol. 23, No. 12, September 2010, by e.Republic Inc., Washington, D.C. Reprinted with permission of the publisher.

out, the vast majority of the city's parks were left to wither and brown in the summer heat. Former flower beds downtown are now just messy tangles of weeds.

And it's not just aesthetics. As money has gotten tighter over the past two years, the city has cut some 550 employees from its work force by eliminating positions or through outright layoffs. Of the 1,600 municipal employees left, 1,200 are police officers or firefighters. Municipal bus service has been reduced by 100,000 hours, meaning buses no longer run in the evenings or on weekends — a problem in a place where the vast majority of transit riders have no alternative way to get to work. The police department auctioned its three helicopters on the Internet. Spending on infrastructure projects has essentially ceased, and the city faces a $700 million backlog in capital needs.

It's a crisis, to be sure. But in this politically conservative, tax-averse town, it's also something of an experiment. After the impending cuts were announced in fall 2009, the city put a property tax increase on the November ballot. The measure was soundly defeated. Thanks to Colorado Springs' Taxpayer Bill of Rights (TABOR), which actually predates the state of Colorado's TABOR by a year, any proposed tax increase must be voted on by the citizens. With their vote, residents made it clear they'd rather suffer service cuts than see their taxes raised.

As a result, other cities are watching, waiting to see if this exercise in stripped-down government might actually serve as a model during tough economic times. City Councilmember Sean Paige is one person who thinks scaling back government's role in the Springs is a good thing. "People in this city want government sticking to the fundamentals," he says. "There's a crybaby contention in town that says, 'We need to raise taxes and we need to get rid of TABOR.' But I think the citizens have made it clear that this is the government people are willing to pay for right now. So let's make it work."

Colorado Springs' service cuts made national headlines when they were rolled out this past spring and summer. After reading the media stories, one half-expects the city to look like some urban dystopia: fallen trees in the

streets, boarded-up buildings, roads left dark by switched-off streetlights, drivers swerving around giant, unfilled potholes.

But when actually walking around Colorado Springs, things don't look that bad. The city is hemmed in to the west by Pikes Peak and other spires of the Front Range (the original "purple mountain majesties" in *America the Beautiful*, which was written here in 1893). Take away the mountains, though, and Colorado Springs could be any mid-sized American city. Downtown consists of a clutch of dun- and clay-colored mid-rises along broad, flat avenues. There's a small, walkable strip of bars and outdoor cafes.

This city of about 420,000 residents also has something of an earthy, hippie side: Acacia Park, a leafy square at the north end of downtown, is ringed by art galleries, an indie music store, a Tibetan imports place, a hookah bar and an Afghan kabob joint. There's even a feeling of progressive urban planning that belies the town's Libertarian reputation. More than 70 miles of on-street bicycle lanes thread their way across the city, and the city manages another 100 miles of urban trails for jogging and hiking. Green spaces downtown are filled with eclectic sculptures by local artists.

In fact, it's easy to walk around the place and wonder what all the fuss is about. So what if there are a few weeds in the medians? Or if some of the streetlights have been turned off? Is that such a price to pay for low taxes and limited government?

Colorado Springs may have gained a reputation as a bastion of right-wing values and small-government ideals, but the city hasn't always been quite so conservative. Thanks to several military bases nearby, as well as the United States Air Force Academy, there's long been a Republican bent to the area. But it wasn't until about 20 years ago that the Springs began to shift to the Christian right. In the 1980s, in a bid to diversify the area's economy, the city began actively courting non-profit organizations to relocate to Colorado Springs. Dozens of groups moved in, especially religious ones.

At one point, Colorado Springs was home to the national headquarters of more than 80 religious organizations, including, most famously, the socially conservative Focus on the Family, which relocated there in 1991. By 1993, Focus on the Family ran a 45-acre campus on the north side of town, with 1,200 employees. Other, similar groups followed, earning Colorado Springs the nickname of "the Evangelical Vatican."

As local politics have swung to the right, Colorado Springs has become more virulently opposed to taxes: Since 1990, the local property tax rate has plunged 41 percent. The local TABOR law, implemented in 1991, imposes an inflation-based cap on the amount of revenue the city can collect. Any revenue over that limit must be returned to taxpayers. That's kept the city government lean and small, even before the recent round of cuts.

The proliferation of non-profit groups has had another effect — a strong current of can-do volunteerism in the community. As the government has scaled back its services, private organizations have, in many cases, stepped in. In addition to the citizen groups that have taken over some of the pools and one of the city's community centers, companies and non-profit foundations have helped raise funds for visitors' centers and other facilities. At the Phantom Canyon Brewing Company in the center of town, the front of the menu implores diners to "Save the Fountain!" by purchasing a new signature ale — some of the proceeds go to keeping the water turned on at the Julie Penrose Fountain, a giant metal loop that rains water down on kids in America the Beautiful Park. The city cut funding for the fountain a couple years ago.

As the cuts worsened this year, the city has increasingly relied on these volunteers' efforts. By lining up residents to "adopt a trash can," the city's been able to return about one-third of the rubbish bins that were removed from municipal parks. Citizens can "adopt a street light" on their block and have it turned it back on by paying a donation — between $100 to $240, depending on the type of light. The city has even discussed an "adopt a median" program, recruiting residents to trim the medians with their own lawnmowers.

"This city has really stepped up, and I'm proud of it," Paige says. "It's almost like we're moving to a do-it-yourself model."

But that's a concern for some, including Paige's fellow City Councilmember Jan Martin, who authored last fall's proposed tax increase that would have covered this year's shortfall and prevented the service cuts. "Right now, in this crisis, we've sort of lost the sense of the common good," she says. "There's a real sense of, 'I'll take care of mine. You take care of yours.'"

Look a few years down the road, she says, and the city's rich areas will prosper while the poorer sections of town will suffer. "The parts of the community that can't afford services will continue to deteriorate," Martin says. "And the neighborhoods that can afford to pay for street lights, parks, trash removal and medians will continue to prosper and be beautiful. I worry we're creating a city of haves and have-nots."

For now, the outpouring of volunteer support has mitigated some of the most visible impacts of Colorado Springs' budget cuts. But there are bigger, longer-term issues, says Interim City Manager Steve Cox. "We get a lot of attention for the trash cans and the street lights, but that's just scratching the surface. There are deeper problems than that."

One of those problems is public safety. Everyone agrees that the police and fire departments should be last on the list of cuts. Still, those departments have had to reduce services as well. In addition to selling off helicopters, the police department has slashed its ranks, says Chief Richard Myers. Property detectives have been cut by one-third, and the department has completely wiped out some units, including its fugitive-investigation group. "We've eliminated entire street teams out of our regional drug unit. In 2011, we're significantly shrinking the number of school resource officers. Our specialty units are just imploding."

In all, the department is down about 80 officers, from a high of 689 a few years ago. That's a significant cut, but what's worse is that the force already was stretched thin. "Most police departments in comparable cities would have 750, 800, maybe 900 police officers," Myers says. "Now we're down in the low 600s, and the city isn't shrinking." Even more challenging, Myers says, is that Colorado Springs covers such a large area of land. Geographically, the city is huge: Boston, Miami, Minneapolis and San Francisco could all fit within its borders.

With a dwindling number of cops serving a growing population across a vast tract of land, residents are feeling the cuts. Officers no longer can respond to as many incidents in person — if someone breaks into a car or steals a kid's bike, the police just take the crime report over the phone. And it's unlikely they'll have the resources to follow up on it, Myers says. "We're struggling with the fact that so many people can be victimized by property crimes and have it treated more as an insurance report and a cursory tick mark on the tote board, rather than us helping them try to solve their crime."

Technology is a problem, too. The police department already was lagging in technology before the latest cuts. Investing in them now would be impossible. For example, Myers points to in-car video cameras, a tech upgrade he implemented at his previous two posts as police chief in other cities. "That's standard in police departments; it's a routine tool in law enforcement," he says. "We don't have a single one in a squad car here."

Despite all the reductions, Myers says he can't point to an uptick in crime. But he worries about the longer-term implications of a bare-bones force. Myers says he firmly believes that a proactive, decentralized style of policing, as it was proven in the 1990s, reduces crime, increases the public's confidence in the police and increases the collaborative kind of policing where citizens and police work together for long-term solutions. "And to now see us moving more and more and more to almost a completely reactive style of policing is just difficult for me to tolerate."

Still, he says he recognizes that tough times call for tough measures, and if this is the police department Colorado Springs is willing to pay for, so be it. "My mourning period is over, and the focus now is on redefining the new norm. We're past doing more with less," he says. "We're doing less with less."

Colorado Springs' fiscal day of reckoning has arrived. But the reason other cities are watching the Springs is because what happens here isn't necessarily just an extreme experiment in do-it-yourself government — it could be the future.

Thanks to the city's heavy reliance on sales taxes, the revenue crisis was brought to bear last year. In other municipalities, where revenues rely more on property taxes, the problems may only be beginning. "Cities are really going to be hard hit at least through 2011," says Christiana McFarland, director of finance and economic development programming for the National League of Cities (NLC). Because property taxes are based on periodic assessments, there's an 18- to 24-month lag before the city feels the full effect of the downturn. "We're anticipating property tax revenues will take a huge hit this coming year."

And cities already have been making cuts, according to NLC surveys. More than two-thirds have delayed investments in infrastructure or capital improvements. Another 22 percent have made cuts in public safety; 27 percent have reduced their spending in human services; and a full 71 percent have already been forced to make cuts in personnel. "With the budgets already cut down to the bone," McFarland says, "they're going to start digging into the marrow."

The big question is whether the cuts are part of a crunch-time crisis, or whether they represent a new era in smaller government. For her part, McFarland says she doesn't think the Colorado Springs model can be a long-term solution. "Cities need to get back to a basic level of delivering services, particularly in public safety."

Meanwhile in Colorado Springs, the crisis is spawning broader conversations about what citizens expect government to be. "It really brings you to some fundamental questions that elected representatives should be asking themselves," Martin says. "It forces you to prioritize and decide, what is the role of government? And what services should the city be providing?"

One thing seems certain in the Springs: The service cuts are here to stay. Thanks to TABOR, it could be years before the city is even able to return to 2009 spending levels. The pools may reopen and the medians may get mowed, but those services will likely be performed by the private sector. As public funds start to trickle back in — and local sales tax revenues have been on the uptick so far this year — they'll go toward rebuilding the police department and adding back some of the bus routes. And for many, that's just the way things should be. "I think we're plowing fertile new ground here," Paige says. "And I think we can make it work."

CHAPTER 19

Coral Springs and Other Cities Focus on Financial Planning

Shayne Kavanagh

The concept of sustainability has captured the attention of local government leaders across the United States and Canada over the past few years. This includes finance officers, as the term "financial sustainability" has come to signify practices such as directing one-time revenues away from recurring expenses and taking into account long-term maintenance and operating costs when planning and evaluating capital projects.

However, the current recession has taught us that sustainability is a necessary but insufficient condition to ensure the ongoing financial health of local government. A sustainable system is balanced, but an external shock (such as a severe economic downturn) can unbalance the system and perhaps even cause its collapse. Local governments will continue to be faced with serious challenges from the outside, including but not limited to economic adjustments, natural disasters, and important policy changes by other levels of government. As such, finance officers must strive to help their organizations go beyond sustainability to a system that is adaptable and regenerative — in a word, resilient.

A sustainable system is balanced but potentially brittle. A resilient system not only survives shocks, it thrives.

Jamais Cascio, a fellow at the Institute for Ethics and Emerging Technologies, identifies eight essential characteristics of a resilient system[1]:

- **Diversity**: Avoid a single point of failure or reliance on a single solution.
- **Redundancy**: Have more than one path of escape.
- **Decentralization**: Centralized systems look strong, but when they fail, the failure is catastrophic.
- **Transparency**: Do not hide your systems. Transparency makes it easier to figure out where a problem may lie. Share your plans and preparations, and listen when people point out flaws.
- **Collaboration**: Work together to become stronger.
- **Fail gracefully**: Failure happens. Make sure a failure state will not make things worse.
- **Flexibility**: Be ready to change when plans are not working. Do not count on stability.
- **Foresight**: You cannot predict the future, but you can hear its footsteps approaching. Think and prepare.

This article explores these characteristics as they relate to creating a financially resilient

Originally published as "Building a Financially Resilient Government through Long-Term Financial Planning," *Government Finance Review*, Vol. 25, No. 6, December 2009, by the Government Finance Officers Association, Chicago, IL. Reprinted with permission of the publisher.

government and the central role that long-term financial planning plays in financial resiliency. The Government Finance Officers Association (GFOA) interviewed officials at several local governments that have been practicing long-term financial planning for a number of years (some as long as 15 or 20) and have, as a consequence, achieved financial resiliency.

The rest of this article will describe how long-term financial planning supports three of the most important characteristics of resiliency: diversity, decentralization, and collaboration. To read about how long-term financial planning can support all the characteristics of a resilient system, please see the GFOA's full-length report on financial resiliency at www.gfoa.org/ltfp.

Diversity

Avoiding a single point of failure or reliance on a single solution:

- Keep a multifaceted perspective on financial health.
- Maintain a diversity of funds to reduce reliance on the general fund.
- Enlarge the base of supporting constituents.

The most fundamental aspect of "diversity" in financial planning is a multifaceted perspective on financial health. The viewpoint should not be limited to revenues and expenditures: land-use patterns, demographic trends, and long-term liabilities (such as pensions) must all be carefully monitored. For example, long-term financial planning has highlighted the connection between land-use policy and financial condition for many of our research subjects, thereby directly influencing land-use policies. In Florida, sales taxes are distributed by the state on a per-capita basis, rather than the point-of-sale method used in many other states. As a result, cities in Florida lack the powerful incentive for commercial development that many other cities have. The City of Coral Springs, Florida, however, has recognized that commercial properties are not subject to the

same property tax restrictions as residential properties, and commercial properties therefore remain important net contributors to financial health.[2] This nuance has led Coral Springs to emphasize diversity in local land use, while many other cities in the area are primarily residential. In another example, the City of Sunnyvale, California, like many cities in the state, is part of the California Public Employees' Retirement System (CalPERS). Warned by CalPERS about potential rate increases, the city performed an independent analysis and discovered that it might experience a 35–45 percent increase in required pension contributions in the future. This has allowed the city to begin planning now to mitigate and absorb this risk.

Another common theme among our research subjects is diversity in the funds maintained. Different funds can be used to account for non-current liabilities such as OPEB, workers' compensation, depreciation, and replacement of assets. Self-supporting internal service funds contribute to efficient overhead services. These practices reduce the burden on the general fund and keep it from becoming a single point of failure.

Finally, Mentor Public Schools in Ohio has consciously cultivated constituent diversity. In any school district, parents in the district are going to be the most engaged constituents. Taxpayers who do not have children, however, are an indispensable source of funding. Therefore, Mentor Schools takes special care to demonstrate its financial responsibility to parents and non-parents alike, and to find out what non-parents think of the school district's performance. For example, Mentor Schools has an important pay-to-play component to its extracurricular activities (it is not 100 percent tax supported) and has been mindful of keeping its asset portfolio consistent with future service demands — for example, two properties were recently sold, thereby eliminating maintenance costs, generating a one-time revenue, and placing the property back on the tax rolls. Enhancing financial management credibility by taking highly visible actions like these enlarges Mentor Schools' base of supporters.

Decentralization

Centralized systems look strong, but failure is catastrophic:

- Make managers manage their cost and revenue structures.
- Engage departments in identifying issues, analyzing them, and developing strategies.
- Engage departments in financial modeling and forecasting.
- Develop an organization-wide strategic framework that departments can innovate within.

Decentralization is about engaging operating departments in financial planning so all departments think more strategically about finance. Long-term financial health does not rely solely on the efforts of central administration.

The bedrock of decentralization is for all departments to be responsible for their own budgets. For instance, a large county in the western United States made departments more responsible for program revenues by directly linking their program revenue income to budget allocations. A Midwestern city was having trouble controlling overtime, so it moved all funding for overtime into a central budget. Departments then had to manage their overtime requests more carefully because all overtime was drawn from a single, more transparent funding source.

Sunnyvale goes beyond these fundamental steps by making departments fully responsible for their long-term cost and revenue structure, including the operating impact of proposed capital projects. In fact, there was recently a high level of interest in a new park in the community, and the recreation director was one of the most vocal advocates of putting a long-term maintenance funding strategy in place before committing to building the park.

With this basic ethos of making managers manage their budget in place, it becomes possible to take a decentralized approach to financial plan development. Through its financial planning process, the finance and operating staff at the City of San Clemente, California, identifies a number of "critical issues" that could af-

fect the future financial health of the city. A number of cross-functional "issue teams" are then formed to analyze each issue and suggest strategies. San Clemente has found that staff members are eager to participate on the teams (some even requesting a spot a year in advance) because they know the decisions made during the planning process are important and positive involvement is a key to advancement at the city. The consistent and meaningful involvement of departments in identifying issues, analyzing them, and developing strategies is a recurring theme in financially resilient governments.

Engaging departments in financial forecasting and modeling is an underappreciated practice — it hones their understanding of financial condition, and, hence, their perception of the need for a solid, long-term financial strategy. It also improves the quality of the forecast. Hanover County, Virginia, realized that the new economic reality made historical data less useful than it had been in making projections. Qualitative judgment was more important than ever. The county formed cross-departmental teams to examine major revenue sources and develop key forecast assumptions. For example, community development, economic development, and assessor personnel were all involved in analyzing the property tax.

Finally, and perhaps most importantly, long-term planning fosters a strategic framework for creating value for the public through government programs. The long-term plan articulates the service objectives the government is striving for and defines the parameters within which the government will pursue these objectives. Departments can then develop their own plans and budgets, yet remain aligned with the big picture. A plan drives action and prevents paralysis by analysis or inertia. The plan grants permission to try new things to further the plan's objectives.

All these characteristics promote the innovation needed to adapt to changing financial conditions. When it is accepted that everyone is working toward the same objective, innovation is more likely because commonality of purpose makes "failure" permissible — if the innovation was intended to achieve a high-priority strategic goal, then the effort is respected.

As an illustration of how planning can create shared goals, Hanover County has found that its planning process has been very important in creating value for teamwork across departmental lines. In Hanover, objectives are established through the planning process, and reliable information about the objectives and financial conditions is then disseminated. The county then works on creating communication channels across departmental lines where information sharing is important. For example, training and professional development is often one of the first expenditures to come under pressure during a revenue downturn, yet training is a primary source of the innovations needed to improve cost-effectiveness. Hanover has used its planning process to establish and support an objective for high-quality professional development across the organization, including encouraging joint training opportunities across departments.

Collaboration

Working together to become stronger:

- Build the service priorities of elected officials into the plan.
- Give elected officials a role in the planning process that they can thrive in.
- Orient elected officials to the planning process.
- Use key indicators to help elected officials stay abreast of financial condition.

Elected officials have an incalculable impact on financial health because they have the final say over tax policies and budgets. Therefore, resilient governments have close collaboration between elected officials and staff. It helps both groups become more savvy financial decision makers, to better recognize problems, and to enact appropriate solutions.

The first step is to engage elected officials by building their service priorities into the financial plan. In addition to demonstrating that the plan is relevant to their service goals, this step provides a common basis for participation in the planning process. Although not every official will be comfortable discussing financial issues, all can discuss and appreciate service issues.

The next step is to give elected officials a role in the actual strategic planning process. As part of this process, they help identify and confirm critical issues, such as setting service goals, they also help identify issues that affect the financial health of the city, and ultimately they review and approve the critical assumptions behind the staff's suggested financial strategies — assumptions that will shape how the annual budget is developed.

When new officials are elected, they must be introduced and acclimated to the planning process. Resilient governments have a formal orientation program and provide periodic refreshers. San Clemente, for example, has an annual compliance self-review of its financial planning portfolio. The city has found that this is a good way to keep elected officials engaged with these fundamental precepts of good financial stewardship. In addition to these formal mechanisms, regular one-on-one meetings on financial issues give officials a chance to ask questions that they might not be comfortable asking in a public meeting. The impact of all of these efforts is to create a culture on the governing board in favor of financially resilient decisions. Once in place, the culture can become self-sustaining as new officials are subject to peer pressure and existing officials take their own actions to promote resiliency (such as Sunnyvale's aforementioned charter amendment, which was driven by public rather than staff action).

Finally, key indicators of financial condition should be established and communicated to help elected officials remain confident that they have a handle on financial condition. Mentor Public Schools, for example, keeps its board up-to-date on three key indicators:

- Percentage of budget spent on personnel (with 85 percent as an upper threshold).
- Recurring revenue versus expenditures (including biannual forecast updates).
- Enrollment trends versus staffing (keeping student to staff ratios consistent).

Conclusion

Financial resiliency is essential to continuing a consistent program of public services despite the current volatile economic environment. A number of local governments from across the country have achieved financial resiliency and realized benefits such as top bond ratings and a soft landing in the current recession. Most importantly, though, these governments have been able to maintain the trust and confidence of their constituents and continue to create value for the public through government action.

NOTES

1. Jamais Cascio, "The Next Big Thing: Resilience," *Foreign Policy* (May/June 2009).
2. "Net contributor" means that a constituent contributes more in tax revenues than he or she uses in services.

CHAPTER 20

Denver and Other Cities Use Performance Results to Make Budget Decisions

Melanie McKinney-Gonzales

Do more with less. It is a common refrain these days. Government entities always try to do more for less, particularly when budgets are tight.

Performance management, benchmarking, pay-for-performance, and best practices are popular techniques many have experimented with to improve productivity and efficiency. Several larger Colorado cities — including Denver, Colorado Springs, Loveland, Fort Collins, Greeley, Thornton, Longmont and Westminster — have successfully implemented such programs.

The success and improvements touted by governmental entities and the private sector have many municipal managers wondering: Could this work in my municipality? If you are a manager or mayor in one of the 165 Colorado communities with a population under 2,000, you may have considered some of these programs but decided they demand too much time or finances for your small staff and budget to meet.

When asked by the author what projects would be useful from an intern, Bayfield Manager Brett Boyer said he, "had wanted to do performance measurement but was skeptical if it would work in a small town. We went forward anyway."

A six-month study performed in south-western Colorado offers some insight about how smaller communities might implement and use a performance management system. The study suggests that smaller municipalities can make good use of performance measures.

Benchmarking, or performance management, as it will be referred to here, is the practice of using performance measures to make management decisions, such as staffing, resource allocation, program prioritization and improvement, and budgeting.

Performance measures are the quantifiable data that can be collected that show the workload, efficiency and the effectiveness of services.[1]

Performance standards can be measured internally over time or externally by comparing with other jurisdictions or companies.

Internal comparison involves collecting the same information over several months or years and looking for trends or changes in the measure. For example, comparing the average length of time to process a building permit in 2002 to the average length of time to process a building permit in 2001 within the same jurisdiction would be an internal comparison. Internal comparisons help managers identify whether service delivery is improving over time or whether a department is facing changing demands.

External comparison involves collecting

Originally published as "Can Performance Measures Add Up for Small Cities, Towns?," *Colorado Municipalities*, Vol. 80, No. 5, October 2004, by the Colorado Municipal League, Denver. Reprinted with permission of the publisher.

similar measures from multiple municipalities or jurisdictions and exchanging the data. Comparisons between organizations can help identify excellence as well as where improvements might be possible.

Three major obstacles are repeatedly cited by small communities for not initiating or participating in a performance-measurement project: lack of time and resources, cost of participation in existing programs, and lack of other, similar-sized communities with which to compare information.

"The biggest challenge for us," Boyer said, "has been the time it takes to maintain the data and having a central person to put it together. We are a small staff in a growing town and everyone is very busy."

Despite the obstacles, the recent study shows that performance measurement in small communities can be done successfully and provide the same type of valuable information that leads to innovative changes as larger communities. To make this type of management tool feasible for these smaller jurisdictions, the measurements must be structured to eliminate or minimize the obstacles.

For six months in 2003, three Colorado towns participated in a performance measurement project to determine its effectiveness and feasibility in jurisdictions with limited staff, budget and other resources. The communities that participated were Bayfield, Mancos, and Olathe in La Plata, Montezuma, and Montrose counties respectively. The towns have similar populations (between 1,100 and 1,700) staff sizes (between 9 and 17), and departments (administrative, public safety, public works, and parks and recreation).

Olathe Director of Operations Bill Sale said, "I think the project was most helpful in pointing out what performance aspects of our jobs are measurable and how those can be measured."

The most significant hurdle for any small community is the time and staff size available to complete any project. Performance measures are no different.

Reviewing the extensive lists of measurements many large cities or counties use is daunting for any small-town manager. Many of these measurements also may seem superfluous in a small-town environment. The most crucial aspect of creating a performance measurement system for small towns is to refine and limit the overall number of measures required to be collected by staff.

Bayfield, Mancos and Olathe did just that.

Staff from the Town of Bayfield developed the original list of measurements that were thought to be important or useful. These lists were refined by the Bayfield manager and then by the managers and staff in Mancos and Olathe. Additional changes, additions and deletions were made to the list of measures throughout the course of the six-month project. No changes were made that rendered the measures incomparable with previously collected data as that would prevent longevity and consistency of information.

According to Boyer, "The measurements are being used in the front office for administration, billing and accounts payable, Public Safety, Public Works and Parks and Recreation. We have not developed any more to use. With time perhaps we will. Again the key was to keep it simple, useful and relevant."

This study developed for the communities of Bayfield, Mancos and Olathe did not require any participation fees. Without the pressure of participation costs, the managers and staff were able to concentrate solely on developing appropriate measures that fit their organizations. The resulting lists of measures at the end of the six-month project period are by no means a finished product. A crucial aspect of any well-developed performance measurement system is the constant reevaluation and refinement of measures, though care should be taken not to compare data that was measured or collected differently.

Nevertheless, the lists of measures produced in the course of this study are an invaluable starting point for any small jurisdiction to adopt and adapt to their individual needs or for a small group of towns who wish to compare their data.

At the end of the project, managers and staff in Bayfield, Mancos and Olathe had a better understanding of what performance measures were and how they could be used to improve services.

Olathe's Sale said, "We continue to improve our service based on conclusions drawn from the performance data gathered. However, we no longer formally collect data as we did for the project. Each department head and I have established methods of measuring certain aspects for our performance based on the model we used."

In Bayfield, data was going to be used to determine if a second court session should be added each month. The Olathe manager learned that Mancos and Bayfield do not read water meters during the winter months and was interested in learning if this change could be implemented in Olathe also.

Boyer reported, "For the most part each department is still tracking and using the measurements that were established. It has been difficult to follow up on data collection and use."[2]

Conclusion

With a minimal amount of measures, performance analysis and management is a realistic option for small municipalities. All three managers who participated were satisfied with the results and found it a useful management method for monitoring and improving services. They indicated that it is a feasible and effective tool for small municipalities and stated that they would encourage other small municipalities to at least become familiar with this management tool if not implement it.

"The most significant benefit," Boyer said, "is knowing where each department is with certain key indicators and then using those as benchmarks for monitoring and improving performance. As managers, my department directors and I could be better at utilizing the data. Time will tell if we are successful. The biggest challenge for us has been the time it takes to maintain the data and having a central person to put it together."

No municipality should exclude it as a possibility because of their size. Small municipalities are able to implement this type of system if it is done properly and with their unique needs in mind. The analytical data may not always be used in a small government environment where personal connections and informal relationships are highly valued as well, but decision makers should ideally try to have analytical data available to them even if it is not used to make a final decision. The "art" of public management is knowing when and how to implement the "science" of any given method.

"Overall, it has been a good step for us," Boyer said. "It is not without gaps, failings and grumblings ... but it is a management tool that even for small towns is beneficial."

Notes

1. There are primarily three types of performance measures. They include output-workload, efficiency, and effectiveness. Output/workload deals with the number of services performed or jobs/projects completed. Efficiency includes the amount or number of jobs or services that can be performed for a measured unit of time or cost. Effectiveness includes the number of services performed or jobs/projects completed that did not require follow up maintenance, repair, or additional services within a reasonable period of time.

2. Examples of these performance measures are explained below. For output/workload the number of meters replaced, the total miles of roads plowed, maintained, etc., and the gallons of water treated. For efficiency the number of labor-hours required to replace a water meter, the dollar cost per lane-mile of roads maintained, plowed, etc., and the dollar cost per gallon of water treated. For effectiveness the number of wataer meters fixed or replaced that did not need additional services for 6–12 months, road maintenance jobs that do not need additional maintenance for 12 months, the number of days that treated water did not meet state standards and the number of customer complaints about water quality.

CHAPTER 21

Des Moines and Other Cities Seek Citizen Input on Public Services

Barbara J. Cohn Berman

Local governments supply basic services to the public that enable us to plan and conduct our daily lives. Although responsibilities vary from place to place, these services usually include police and fire protection, roadway and other infrastructure maintenance, traffic control, management of parks, water supply, emergency services, public education, public libraries, code enforcement, recreation, services for children and for people with special needs, and more. We depend on these services being delivered predictably and well; we pay local taxes to ensure this outcome. Yet information to the public about how our local governments are doing is made available inconsistently, if at all.

Regular reporting to the public about the range of government performance has not been commonplace, but involving the public in selecting information to be measured and reported is even more infrequent. Constructive conversations between the public and government on the subject of performance measures and reports are rarer still. Yet our research at the Fund for the City of New York's Center on Government Performance revealed that the public assesses government by using indicators that differ from some of government's standard measures. Hence, engaging the public is criti-

cally important if we are to have government actions aligned with the public's needs.

The idea that local governments should produce measures of their performance is not new, and the practice of doing so has expanded in recent years. Governments keep tabs on and produce reports that are used for accounting, auditing, budgeting, and management purposes as well as to comply with legislative mandates. They compile data about revenues and expenditures. They count work that comes in (such as the number of applications and complaints) and work produced (such as applications processed, tons of refuse collected, lane miles paved). These are data usually described as operating statistics — inputs and outputs. They are often used for internal management and budget purposes only. The data are significant and necessary for any well-run government.

However, the measurement and reporting of the results of governmental efforts — the "outcomes" — are still uncommon in government reports. Yet we learned that it is the results of governmental efforts that the public sees and wants. In this context, the public is variously described as the ultimate stakeholder and consumer of government services, not to mention the electors of its government leaders and the taxpayer supporting governmental efforts.

Originally published as "Involving the Public in Measuring and Reporting Local Government Performance," *National Civic Review*, Vol. 97, No. 1, Spring 2008, pp. 3–10, by the National Civic League, Denver, CO. Reprinted with permission of the publisher. www.wileyonlinelibrary.com/journal/ncr.

Private sector organizations measure and produce reports about their performance to investors and shareholders. For them, success is measured ultimately by profitability and the various elements that influence profit. Government performance has no single criterion of success. While private sector organizations must find out if they are meeting their customers' needs and expectations in order to survive, grow, maintain, or increase their market share, there is no comparable, compelling survival requirement for local governments to consult with their constituents.

Public hearings, when required to be held or customary in a jurisdiction, are one way for some members of the public to express their views regarding programs or legislation. Typically, the only people attending the events are those who are directly affected by the issues getting a "hearing." What often transpires is a series of prepared statements met with respectful silence or defensive answers instead of dialogue. At worst, these are confrontational exchanges with little learned or changed on the part of government or the public.

One could argue that people make their decisions at election time, exerting the ultimate influence on their local government leadership and direction, and therefore additional public input is not needed. Yet the process and results of local elections do not include members of the public weighing in on their satisfaction with how specific services are delivered or how responsive government officials are to their needs. Nor does the election process give the public an opportunity to learn about the scope of its government's activities and reasons why their government is doing what it is doing.

The gap in information flow and communication between the public and local government probably accounts for the feeling expressed frequently in our focus groups that people think they are powerless to affect changes in city services. "You can't change the system" or "You can't fight city hall" are typical comments.

To be sure, local government's work is not easy. It must reckon with a plethora of local, state, and federal laws, regulations, and codes, sometimes inconsistent with one another. Intractable problems need to be addressed even if local government policies and practices are not responsible for them. Local media cast bright lights, crises occur, and gearing up for the next election is omnipresent. Some local government functions require special technical, technological, engineering, legal, medical, or other expertise that is difficult to explain to the general public or too technical for most people to want to know or to have an opinion about.

It is easy to understand, then, why governments proceed to manage, make decisions, and set priorities that are not informed by the public's will or needs and for the public to be out of the loop in learning about why, when, and how their local governments are taking actions that affect their lives, in big and in small but important ways.

A major push by the Alfred P. Sloan Foundation started in the mid–1990s to narrow this gap, beginning with our work at the Fund for the City of New York's Center on Government Performance and continuing into what has become a national and even international initiative. Over the past thirteen years, much has been learned, tried, and set into motion. Although not yet the norm, a movement and increased willingness on the part of governments to consider new ways to listen to and communicate with the public seems to be afoot, along with new interest from nonprofit organizations to engage in performance measurement and reporting about local government activities.

Of course, local government is not required to accept the public's recommendations that emerge from any of these initiatives, but when citizen surveys, focus groups, and other types of carefully planned, inclusive feedback sessions are designed and conducted with outside nonpartisan, professional assistance they offer opportunities for government to hear from the public in new, nonconfrontational, constructive ways. When done with sincerity and demonstrated respect for the public, people can feel a new level of confidence that their government cares about them.

Beginning in 2003, forty-seven governments have been participating as Trailblazers, initiating citizen informed performance measurement and reporting, as grantees in programs run by our Center on Government Performance at the National Center for Civic Innovation, the national sister organization of the Fund for the City of New York. The Sloan Foundation also supports these programs. The grantees experiment with various ways to disseminate their performance reports to the public for the first time and to obtain the public's reaction to the content and style of the reports.

Public Versus Government Perceptions on Performance

Reports from Trailblazer grantee governments and focus groups conducted by the Center on Government Performance, Fund for the City of New York, reveal a number of differences in how the public judges local government performance and how local governments tend to measure and report about their performance:

- The public is interested in outcomes and the quality of work performed. Governments report about workloads, costs, and number of full-time employees.
- People do not care about which agency or level of government is responsible for what. Governments report performance by agency and level of government — local, county, state, federal.
- People expect services to be coordinated even if they are delivered by different agencies, governmental bodies, and contractors hired by government. Typically, governments report performance by agency.
- People rate government performance by their first impressions, including how they are treated, how accessible an office and information are, and how clean a facility is kept. Few governments gather data about these matters or report about them.
- People understand that government work is complex and often difficult. They do not expect perfection and instant responses, but they do expect to be treated with courtesy, respect, and compassion. They think that government employees must exhibit knowledge in their area of work, be helpful

and responsive, take initiative to solve problems, and give timely responses. They also think that government should deliver evenhanded treatment to all people, in all neighborhoods. Typically, data about the interactions the public experiences with government are not acquired, analyzed, or reported.

Here are examples of specific services local governments supply and the indicators that some governments report about them, as contrasted with the cues and results the public looks for:

A. Public Libraries
- Government measure: number of reference queries; number of feet of shelf space
- Public measure: staff helpfulness; availability of materials needed; accessible hours

B. Emergency Medical Services
- Government measure: response time
- Public measure: response time plus knowledge and responsiveness to the problem at hand

C. Health Code Enforcement
- Government measure: number of restaurants and food stores inspected
- Public measure: cleanliness and food safety ratings for each restaurant and food store

D. Roadway Maintenance
- Government measure: number of work requests; roadway lane miles resurfaced
- Public measure: smoothness score; number of major jolts encountered per mile; quality of roadway repair and smoothness after repair; need to repair again after a short time

E. Street Cleanliness
- Government measure: tons of refuse collected
- Public measure: absence of litter; reliable schedule for refuse collection

When some local governments asked members of their public for feedback about traditional performance reports, people said the reports were hard to understand, ponderous, and otherwise unappealing. They said that many of the measures were irrelevant and inconsequential to them.

Nonetheless, people in their focus groups and ours said they wanted and needed information from government. When asked to describe the types of reports they would like, they said they wanted:

- Reports and information presented clearly and simply
- Honest reports about how government programs are working
- All the news, not just good news
- To understand the challenges that their government and their community are facing
- To know how and where they can obtain additional information about services and key issues
- To be able to evaluate information for themselves, without spin
- To know what other jurisdictions are doing and how they are doing in comparison

In many jurisdictions, new findings and lessons are emerging that are consistent with our first research efforts in 1995: people do care about their local government's work, they want and need information about what their government is doing, and they understand that much of what local government must do is difficult and complex. They do not expect perfection, but they want to be treated with respect and courtesy, expect responsive and reasonably timely reactions to their questions and requests, and want to know how they can obtain information about government's programs and activities. Conversely, they consider it intolerable if their government agencies and employees are inaccessible, disrespectful, nonresponsive, or goofing off.

New Measures and Data Developed After Listening to the Public

Developing these new measures of government performance is not always easy and may require discovering new ways to collect and analyze data. In the process of doing so,

however, we are finding that governments are realizing that some of the data they have been collecting are rarely used and are not particularly useful. On the other hand, the public's response to the new measures is positive and also relevant to government's benchmarking, strategic planning, and management improvement work. Three examples describe initiatives undertaken by our Center on Government Performance to apply the public's perspectives to some government services and obtain data that both government and the public can trust.

First, we learned from focus group participants that people judge government performance by a range of conditions they see on city streets. Knowing that there are no measures or reports that synthesize them since many governmental agencies, units within agencies, public utilities, private organizations, and individuals have responsibilities for these conditions, the Fund for the City of New York's Center on Government Performance created ComNET (Computerized Neighborhood Environment Tracking).

ComNET is now a major national citizen engagement initiative and has inspired related programs throughout the United States and abroad. With its use of handheld computers, ComNET enables community groups to gather information about all the problems on city streets (fire hydrants impaired, litter, abandoned vehicles, graffiti, and so forth) in an accurate and verifiable manner. Our software requires precise information about the problem and its location and associates conditions found with agencies responsible for repairing them. Via a Web-enabled database, clear reports and charts are produced containing unemotional, verifiable information that enable communities and government to have constructive conversations about mutual concerns. As of this writing, ComNET has been implemented with local community groups in eighty-three neighborhoods in New York City, Seattle, Des Moines, Durham, Yonkers (N.Y.), Irving (Texas), Worcester, and elsewhere.

Second, after learning that people rate government agencies by how they are treated, we introduced the Citizen Gauge concept. An impartial Website (http://www.fcny.org) that can be hosted to collect people's reported experiences and ratings of their encounters with government, it encourages reports about positive experiences as well as information about where improvements are needed.

Third, every focus group we conducted wanted to talk about the condition and maintenance of city roadways. People said that bumpy roads and potholes were unacceptable, a safety hazard, and a reflection of poor workmanship and lack of government pride. As a result, we created Smoothness and Jolt Scores for city roadways, using profilometry equipment that generated verifiable, reliable measures of roadway surfaces. Focus group participants defined the ratings to be used ("good, fair, poor, or terrible") after riding on sample roadway segments. They also told us when a bump in the road should be counted as a "jolt." There was a high correlation between the focus group's judgments and the profilometer readings. We conducted two surveys of almost seven hundred miles of city streets each, using these measures and producing reports at the community level.

The Elements and Language of This New Movement

As with many things that are new, terminology is created. During the past thirteen years of this Sloan Foundation initiative, several descriptors have been used, are sometimes used interchangeably, and are still being honed. For now, the following distinctions are useful.

Performance measurements and reports that are referred to as "citizen-based," "citizen-driven," or "citizen-initiated" literally emanate from outside government — either directly from existing citizen groups or from nonprofit good government organizations, advocacy groups, and universities that work directly with the public. They often conduct research, collect data, produce reports, confer with government about their findings, and make recommendations. They can focus on particular government services such as the condition of public parks, the reliability and rideability of public transportation, or the adequacy of public schools.

Or they may cover a broader range of governmental services.

The term "citizen-informed performance measurement and reporting" is used when local governments take the initiative. In the best examples, they reach out to a broad, representative swath of their public and invite them, in nonconfrontational settings, to comment on existing governmental performance measures and reports. These local governments often ask professional market or other researchers to design the manner in which members of the public will be selected, help create the survey or other research instruments to be used, have professional moderators conduct the sessions with the public, and help interpret the results.

As people look at performance measures and reports now, it can be useful to consider two sets of questions.

First, *who is doing the measuring?* government itself? an advocacy group? an objective outside organization? Who decides what is being measured? How are the data derived? Does the public have the means to be informed about what is involved in the measures? Are the methods used credible to the public? Is there a process in place so that the public can identify measures that are meaningful from their perspective?

Second, *who is doing the reporting?* government itself? an advocacy group? an objective outside organization? Who has access to the reports? Does the public have a way to influence the content or style of the report? Do the reports cover all major local government functions?

It is fitting now to view various aspects and implications of this maturing initiative, which, if sustained, can invigorate public participation and influence in their local governments. One can think of no better place than the *National Civic Review* to present the first single publication devoted to this subject.

This issue is devoted to presenting perspectives and examples from government, communities, nonprofit organizations, researchers, and the academy about this body of work that started thirteen years ago. This knowledge and information involves new ways for government employees to think about their work and new ways for the public to understand, sometimes influence, and appreciate government. Though still developing, these efforts are moving us along a path of establishing government practices that are more open to the public, enabling opportunities for the public and government to communicate with one another more productively, using data they both understand and can trust, and helping to bring government employees back to the reason many entered public service in the first place: to serve the public and make their part of the world better.

There are many telling examples of what has been tried and learned over the past thirteen years. Many professionals are contributing, from think tanks, nonprofit good government groups, professional associations, universities, community organizations, youth-serving institutions, consulting firms, and government itself. It has been daunting to select among them for this issue, but space and time limits what we can include here. The compelling judgment was to include various perspectives and results with the hope that more will be added to the literature and the practice in the near future.

The opening article by Ted Greenwood, program director of the Alfred P. Sloan Foundation, describes its approach in developing their wide-ranging program starting in 1995. The underpinning of their concern is to ensure that the public receives accurate and full information about its government's performance.

The next article in this issue describes the eleven year journey that the city of Des Moines, Iowa, embarked on to achieve what is now a multiple award-winning citizen-informed performance measurement and reporting practice. The trip was fraught with obstacles and detours, many of which spurred unusual, creative solutions. With a new understanding of the public's concerns, they responded to what they learned and have evidence that the citizenry recognizes the changes. Des Moines assistant city manager Michael Matthes tells their story in such an engaging way that his next award may be one for being able to add humor and clarity to a complex and serious subject. The City of Des Moines is a Trailblazer grant recipient of the National Center for Civic Innovation.

If governments are going to be the ones to spearhead development of citizen-informed performance measures and reports, there must be a sea change in how public servants are trained, how their jobs are described, and how their own performance is evaluated. Typically, learning how to be responsive to the public is not part of formal university curricula or in-service training. There are few courses and little practice in designing and understanding citizen opinion and satisfaction research. Job descriptions and individual performance ratings rarely include standards for being respectful and responsive to the public.

Two articles address these matters. First, Marc Holzer, dean of the School of Public Affairs and Administration and Board of Governors Professor of Public Administration at Rutgers University-Newark; and Younhee Kim, assistant professor there, discuss their experiences at Rutgers in crafting degree and responsive nondegree offerings about citizen influenced performance measurement for students and practitioners of public administration, candidly pointing out some of the challenges for universities and making some recommendations.

Second, Brooke A. Myhre uses the City of San Jose's experience to highlight how government employees can and need to be a critical part of the effort to work effectively with performance measurement and public involvement. During a twenty-eight-year career in local government linking performance monitoring and improvements, budgeting, management practices, and workforce development, he was involved in the award-winning Investing in Results program to transform the government of San Jose into a customer-focused and results-driven organization. San Jose received a Certificate of Distinction from the International City/County Management Association for its performance measurement work.

We have much to learn from how the private sector conducts market research and trend analyses. Madelyn Hochstein, president of DYG, the world renowned social research firm, has years of experience crafting original research used by industry leaders, federal agencies, and major nonprofit organizations. She helped our

Center on Government Performance at the Fund for the City of New York design its extensive and comprehensive focus group research, which revealed many important findings, including the fact that the public often assesses local government performance differently from government's typical measures. That finding is now being confirmed in many other cities in this country. She has advised grantees in the National Center for Civic Innovation's Trailblazer Government Performance Reporting program and government finance officers on how to conduct credible research to learn about the viewpoint of the public. We asked her to identify some tips for those who are thinking of starting a "listening to the public" initiative and to comment about whether an increase in the public's interest in local government performance is part of any of the trends that her organization tracks.

Roberta R. Schaefer is the founding executive director of the Worcester Regional Research Bureau (WRRB) in Worcester, Massachusetts. Worcester civic leaders formed the WRRB twenty-two years ago because they felt the need for an organization to conduct independent, nonpartisan research on public policy. Schaefer describes the evolution of her research bureau since 2000, when it sought hard data to assess an element of Worcester's strategic plan: "improve municipal and neighborhood services."

She amassed data using one of the best known and widely used examples of citizen-driven performance measurement, ComNET, developed by the Fund for the City of New York in response to our findings that people judge cities on the basis of a whole array of things they see on the streets. Anne Spray Kinney was budget director for Milwaukee, Wisconsin, and executive director of the Milwaukee Metropolitan Sewerage District. After leaving government service and becoming a senior partner in the Public Strategies Group, she helped local and state governments reinvent themselves by becoming more efficient and responsive. Today, she is director of research and consulting for the Government Finance Officers Association (GFOA), the 101-year-old organization that serves more than seventeen thousand finance officers in the United States and Canada by identifying and developing financial policies and practices and promoting them through education, training, and leadership. In her article, Kinney reminds us that measurements and reports alone are not sufficient and performance improvement should be the goal. She also presents research findings and raises questions to consider, including if and when, perhaps, citizen involvement can overreach into government's realm.

In another article, Ted Greenwood argues that the government performance measurement and reporting initiatives the Sloan Foundation is helping to support should combine forces with the long-standing Community Indicators movement. If governments do citizen-informed performance measurement and reporting and community indicators include government performance measures, then detailed government performance measures will be linked with high level community indicators, making performance measures more relevant to citizens and community indicators more able to influence government actions.

CHAPTER 22

Elgin and Other Cities Use Public Managers to Address Fiscal Issues

Elizabeth Kellar

What are some of the driving forces that are shaping local governments in the years ahead? Five mega issues emerge from conversations with national and local leaders:

- Long-term economic outlook.
- Strained relationships with state governments.
- Demographic changes.
- Resource challenges.
- New media and technology.

One might expect local government managers to be daunted by these issues. Instead managers interviewed for this chapter conveyed resolve and a sense of mission about what they can do to help their organizations and their communities adapt to these challenging times.

Economic Realities Squeeze Employees and Benefits

The economic recovery has been slow, and unemployment remains high. In 2009, most local governments adjusted to the downturn in revenues by imposing hiring freezes and holding the line on employee pay and benefit costs. During 2010, however, more local governments have had to lay off employees and make changes in benefit packages.

According to September 2010 data from the Bureau of Labor Statistics, local government employment, excluding jobs in education, is down 167,000 jobs, or 2.6 percent, compared with November 2008. Analysts do not expect state and local revenues to return to 2008 levels until 2013.

In writing about the National League of Cities (NLC) annual survey, "City Fiscal Conditions in 2010," in October 2010, authors Christopher W. Hoene and Michael A. Pagano found that "the declines in 2010 represent the largest downturn in revenues and cutbacks in spending in the history of NLC's survey, with revenues declining for the fourth year in a row."

Local governments also face serious challenges because of funding losses in pension plan assets. The downturn in the stock market in 2008 dramatically reduced the value of equities in public and private retirement plans alike. Aggregate funding of state and local pension funding levels has declined from a respectable level of 84 percent in 2008 to 78 percent in 2009.

Because public pensions typically "smooth" upturns and downturns over a period of three to five years, the full impact of the 2008 equity losses will not be evident until 2013. A recent

Originally published as "Mega Issues Drive Local Changes: Managers Tackle Future Challenges With Resolve," *Public Management*, Vol. 93, No. 1, January/February 2011, by the International City/County Management Association, Washington, D.C. Reprinted with permission of the publisher.

study published by the Center for State and Local Government Excellence found that in the United States the ratio of pension assets will decline, on average, to between 66 and 76 percent of liabilities by 2013, depending on stock prices.[1]

There is, of course, considerable variation in funding levels. Some plans have no financial issues at all while others have a major unfunded liability. In 2009, for example, 11 percent of the 126 pension plans studied were funded at the 40–59 percent level, and 10 percent of plans were 100 percent funded.

Future funding levels will depend on many factors, including increases in contributions and how well the stock market performs. The authors at the Center for Retirement Research at Boston College examined three scenarios for stock market returns to see what pension funding levels would be if stock prices are flat, grow modestly, or grow robustly. No one can predict future stock returns, but most analysts urge governments to be conservative in their estimates.

Because of the funding issues and an intense media focus on employee benefits, many local and state plans are undergoing changes. Typically, there are reduced benefits for new employees and higher contributions from both employers and employees.

Michigan and Utah have replaced their defined-benefit plans with a hybrid plan for all public employees. The National Conference of State Legislatures (NCSL) reports that more states have enacted significant retirement legislation in 2010 than in any other year in memory.

As Ronald K. Snell, director, State Services Division, National Conference of State Legislatures (NCSL), explains, "The economic recovery alone won't solve the funding issue. There are structural issues that have to be addressed that were adopted during more optimistic times." California's decision in 1999 to reduce the retirement age from age 60 to age 55 for general government employees and from age 55 to age 50 for public safety employees is often cited as a key factor for that state's large unfunded pension liability.

Strains with State Governments

Because of the loss of revenues, some state governments have looked to local governments as a place to shift responsibilities they struggle to pay for. But perhaps no state has as difficult a relationship with local governments these days as California.

Chris McKenzie, executive director, League of California Cities, wrote in *Western City*, September 2010, "How a state government can say on the one hand it is serious about job creation (and the attendant revenue benefits it brings to the state) and on the other hand kill jobs in the private and public sectors by raiding and borrowing local government funds is beyond local officials' comprehension." The voters in California agreed. They passed Proposition 22 in November 2010, which prevents state lawmakers from tapping local fund to plug state budget holes.

Scott Hancock, executive director, Maryland Municipal League, said at the 2010 ICMA Annual Conference in San Jose that local governments "cannot count on states to be a benevolent parent anymore."

Leon Churchill, city manager, Tracy, California, noted that, although state government has lost considerable credibility, residents in Tracy recently approved a local sales tax increase as a vote of confidence in what the city is trying to do. Tracy's experience is not unique. From California to Oregon to Michigan, substantial majorities are voting to support local ballot measures.

Daniel Gilmartin, executive director, Michigan Municipal League, sees an opportunity for local governments to reinvent the way they do business. "There's sustainability about what local governments do," he said. "Those cities and regions that focus on quality-of-life issues and have a strong education system and workforce will have the greatest opportunities."

Churchill and Gerald Newfarmer, president and CEO, Management Partners, Cincinnati, Ohio, have spearheaded a discussion of state-local relationships within ICMA's Government Affairs and Policy Committee.

They would like to see the state-local partnership restored with some core principles in mind, including a respect for local government autonomy. They also see opportunities for local governments to help shape the future by promoting shared services and more regional strategies.

Older, More Diverse Demographics

Our communities and our workforces are aging. The millennial generation, including those age 14 to 32, is larger and more diverse than the aging baby boomer population that is starting to retire. These realities are prompting many organizations to look at planning for succession, training to help retirees update their skills so they can return to work, and using technology more creatively to improve productivity and increase flexibility.

James Ley, county manager, Sarasota County, Florida, says he has brought in retired managers as "roving resources" to tackle issues that need attention throughout the organization. Sarasota County has increased flexibility by creating a separate system for hiring employees for particular needs.

Kim Walesh, chief strategist, San Jose, says it is important to engage residents in their 20s and 30s as they often feel left out. Social media and wiki planning are good tools to reach them. She notes that younger residents are often more diverse than others and that this cohort includes entrepreneurs and immigrants, the "secret sauce to Silicon Valley's success." At the same time, she observes that immigration into the United States is expected to plateau.

An increasing number of local government employees are eligible to retire in the next five years — about 30 percent nationwide. What are managers doing to ensure that employees are ready and able to meet the needs of our communities in the future? Here is the landscape in three different communities, some of which are undergoing major change.

Elgin, Illinois, Faces the Future with a Plan

"One of the best things for Elgin may have been the rising cost of energy," muses Sean Ste-gall, city manager, Elgin, Illinois. "During the housing boom years, the city acted more like a suburb and created developments with cul-de-sacs. The pain of the Great Recession changes behavior. In the past year, we've reached a consensus that we should act like who we are."

Elgin is a city of 106,000 where many residents commute to jobs in Chicago. Its website boasts that it embraces newcomers and long-term residents alike. Among Elgin's assets are three train stations, a bus station, a rural sector, and a historic downtown.

The city recently adopted a comprehensive plan that takes advantage of those assets and outlines a way forward. The plan seeks to connect all of the cul-de-sacs that sprang up with the housing boom with the city's traditional urban street grid. To capture the city's new direction, there's even a slogan: "We are the city in the suburbs."

Elgin strives for a balance of housing options and prices to meet the needs of residents at all stages of their lives. Recreational facilities, commercial structure, and higher-density housing are planned around transportation corridors and located near employment centers. The downtown is viewed as the "heart of the community," with plazas and parks and improved access to the riverfront.

The Congress of the New Urbanism (CNU), an organization that promotes walkable, mixed-use neighborhood development, sustainable communities, and healthier living conditions, has seized on Elgin's initiative to make it a pilot for the nation.[2] Working with city leaders, CNU identified barriers to the city's goal of strengthening a sense of place in neighborhoods.

The priorities of the Illinois Department of Transportation, for example, have been to improve vehicle flow and to build highways. The interests of local businesses and pedestrians have not been as important to the department. As a result, highway development blocked many residents from walking to parkland or other amenities that were just blocks away.

Even when Stegall contemplates the serious challenges ahead, he maintains a positive attitude. "It's our job as managers to keep cities moving as our county goes through this transition." Like most cities, Elgin has been hard hit by the economic downturn.

The city had to lay off 80 employees and cut $15 million from its general fund budget of $70 million in the first year after the recession. Unions also have agreed to make concessions in their compensation and benefits.

Despite the cutbacks, Elgin has doubled its budget for employee education and training. With fewer employees, Stegall says it is essential that they are well educated, well compensated, and well prepared. They also need good technology tools. Elgin has an in-house technology group that is supplemented by consultants. The group is using technology to help departments work together more seamlessly in the field. Instead of tweaking private sector software for their needs, they are examining work flow processes and writing their own code. The goal is to make it easy for an employee to use the software for required reports.

The aging of the community has not gone unnoticed, either. Stegall says that many retirees want to return to work to replenish their savings. Others want to do something meaningful in retirement. Elgin is creating an office of volunteer services to leverage this untapped resource.

Elgin recognizes that competition for water will be a major issue in the decades ahead, not only for Elgin but also for surrounding communities. It draws water from the Fox River, a tributary of the Illinois River, a source that is reliable and less costly than either Lake Michigan or aquifers, the primary source of water for most other Chicago area cities.

Hennepin County, Minnesota, Provides Flexibility to Employees

Like the community it serves, the Hennepin County, Minnesota, workforce is aging. Some 30 percent of its employees are eligible to retire in the next five years. County Administrator Richard Johnson says that the pace of retirements has slowed since the economic downturn. This gives the county some breathing room to focus on succession planning and to prepare the workforce that will be needed in the future.

One initiative that has worked well for Hennepin County's human services employees is the results-only work environment. Employees have laptops, control their own schedules, and come and go as they please, using a hoteling office space as they need it. Because social workers and others need to be out in the community to do their jobs, it makes sense to provide this flexibility, Johnson says. The program may be expanded to other employees selectively.

While technology has driven some changes, Hennepin County anticipates that the state's continuing economic difficulties will be the dominant factor. As a new governor and several new state legislators take office, they face a state budget deficit of $5–$7 billion. Johnson says that a deficit of that size is unlikely to be closed without both tax increases and spending cuts.

Johnson reflected on the growing tensions between local and state governments over the past 10 years. While there once was a partnership and a distinction of roles, it is now common for the state government to shift responsibility to local governments without providing a source of revenue to pay for the service. Local governments have been forced to squeeze operations and raise property taxes. Cutbacks have reached the point where residents will experience such service reductions as longer wait times and delays in processing applications.

Hennepin County continues to enjoy a relatively good relationship with its 1.2 million residents. Unlike some states, there has been little backlash against public employees in Minnesota. That may be because Minnesota has managed its pension funding issues in an assertive way, raising contributions for both employers and employees and reducing the cost-of-living adjustment for current retirees.

Water management is a significant issue for the county because there is fragmentation caused by many different water and soil conservation districts. Some of these entities can raise revenues while others cannot, so one part of the county will have costs and service levels different from another part. Hennepin County is large enough to bring the groups together to clarify who is in charge and to address issues of equity, stream management, and lake management.

New Media Tools Fuel False Information in Cape Elizabeth, Maine

Michael McGovern, town manager of Cape Elizabeth, Maine, notes that community engagement has been affected by technology. Certain community groups use a software program that makes it easy to collect e-mail addresses. A taxpayer group made up of mostly wealthy individuals was established two years ago and more than once has spread false information.

Group members often apologize privately for spreading the false information, but then they put out the same false information again. Some individuals have, for example, criticized Cape Elizabeth for having a generous pension plan when, in fact, 15 years ago it switched to a defined-contribution plan for all employees except police.

Four weekly newspapers and one daily cover the community, which has fewer than 9,000 residents. One of the weeklies signed on a blogger who writes negatively about the town. Most town staff members have stopped reading the blog as it was demoralizing to them.

Fortunately, Cape Elizabeth has an excellent town council that sorts through the issues thoughtfully. In one case, some residents have called for a regional or consolidated fire service even though the change would actually increase costs in Cape Elizabeth as the neighboring community has higher costs for its fire service. Cape Elizabeth's current fire service consists of a call company with one full-time employee, the fire chief, and a total budget of $150,000.

State and local relationships are always challenging, particularly during times of economic constraints. The amount received through revenue sharing from the state of Maine is exactly what it was 10 years ago because there is less money in the pool and the state has changed the formula. What this means is that revenue from property taxes increased 70 percent during the 10-year period, yet Cape Elizabeth's total revenues have remained flat for three straight years.

The revenue squeeze last year required the city to lay off employees for the first time. The only upside to the recession is that the bidding environment has been competitive so the city has benefited from lower prices, particularly in the construction area.

McGovern says, "Water has never been an issue in Maine, but energy is. When we look at the need to replace the boilers in the high schools, for example, we consider the possibility of a boiler that can use either oil or wood chips. We also consider options for solar panels to heat water in the summer months.

"The U.S. Department of Energy gave the state of Maine a grant for energy efficiency improvements that required some of the dollars be shared with local governments. Cape Elizabeth received an $85,000 grant to make lighting upgrades that improve energy efficiency. The project is already finished, and we expect the investment will pay for itself in two years."

Aging Workforce and Talent Challenges

Cape Elizabeth has 50 employees, and 20 percent of them have 25 years or more of service. Because of the recession and investment declines, no full-time employees have left the town voluntarily in the past three years.

Cape Elizabeth's workforce demographics may be younger than many others. Typically, state and local government employees are five to seven years older than their private sector counterparts. They also are more highly educated. The recession has prompted most local government employers who are eligible to retire to work longer, but in California, retirement-eligible employees have been retiring in greater numbers.

Most Americans are not thinking about future workforce gaps when unemployment is running close to 10 percent. But managers are increasingly looking at succession planning issues, knowing they soon will have critical vacancies that must be filled. Finding, developing, and retaining talent is one of the most important legacies that a local government manager can leave behind.

As ICMA Executive Director Bob O'Neill recently wrote in a "Management Insights" column for *Governing* magazine, "The future is coming fast, start preparing now." For a profession that likes to fix problems, the opportunities have never been greater.

NOTES

1. "The Great Recession and the State and Local Government Workforce," Center for State and Local Government Excellence, 2010, http://tinyurl.com/yejvvtc.

2. Christopher W. Hoene and Michael A. Pagano, "City Fiscal Conditions in 2010," National League of Cities, October 2010.

3. Alicia H. Munnell, Jean-Pierre Aubrey, and Laura Quinby, "The Funding of State and Local Pensions: 2009–2013," *State and Local Pension Plans* 10 (April 2010): pp. 5–6.

4. "Renewing Elgin" (Chicago: Congress for the New Urbanism, n.d.), www.cnu.org/sites/www.cnu.org/files/Elgin_final.pdf.

CHAPTER 23

Eugene Uses Citizens to Improve Its Budget Process

Donald J. Borut, Melissa Germanese *and* William Barnes

Changes in economies at the local, national, and global levels are creating enormous new challenges for America's citizens, communities, and their leaders — and enormous opportunities as well. The current crisis dramatically highlights and drastically alters our situation and prospects. It also further illuminates underlying patterns.

How and where Americans work, what they need to know, what skills they need to have, whom they compete with for jobs and business, what rules govern behavior — all of these are changing. It is way past time for the nation's people and their elected officials to think and act differently in response to these changes. Our conclusion is that *to do better economics, we must do better politics.*

The U.S. and global economies are characterized by their dynamism, by what Joseph Schumpeter called the "creative destruction" that fuels innovation, opportunity, and growth. However, that same dynamism, as it plays out in communities across the nation, is an ongoing source of insecurity and turmoil for many Americans (during times of trouble and even during times of growth). The members of the National League of Cities — mayors and city council members across the nation — hear their constituents' concerns *every day* in town hall forums, community meetings, and coffee shops.

Although we must work to address the continuing fallout from the current economic and financial crisis, we also need to get a better handle on the underlying, structural changes buffeting local, regional, and national economies, and on how to respond to those changes in effective ways.

The nation's citizens, communities, and leaders must create:

- *A new social contract* among the American people that encourages and enables individual responsibility and constructive civic engagement, and that brings a "common good" framework to public and policy discussions of the economy and other issues.
- *Shared understandings* of the fundamental economic issues confronting America today, understandings that are not clouded by partisan considerations and that recognize the importance of strong local and regional economies to U.S. economic success.
- *A well-functioning intergovernmental system* that enables and demands that all levels of government — federal, state, and local —

Originally published as "Governing Economies in the Twenty-First Century," *National Civic Review*, Vol. 98, No. 2, Summer 2009, pp. 31–36, by the National Civic League, Denver, CO. Reprinted with permission of the publisher. www.wileyonlinelibrary.com/journal/ncr.

work together effectively to strengthen the economy and address other priorities.

- Now is not the time to wax nostalgic for the "old" economic system or "old" forms of leadership. Rather, it is a time to follow the words of President Abraham Lincoln's second annual message to Congress in 1862: "As our case is new, so we must think anew and act anew."

The Common Good and an Engaged Citizenry

Too many of America's leaders have largely abandoned the common good as a framework when discussing the economy and other key issues. As a society, we have lost a shared sense of why government exists, and in what instances it can be a force for good.

In a 1996 report, "Connecting Citizens and Their Governments," the NLC Advisory Council contrasted two models of democratic governance. The first model is the vending machine: people put in their taxes and fees and expect that much back in services. In the second model, which we referred to as "barn raising," people focus instead on what they can achieve collectively, both through government and by working together in their communities.

Delivering basic services efficiently is critical to good government, but the vending machine model can contribute to a sense among citizens that they are merely customers of government. The needs of the community as a whole become secondary to people's interest in knowing they are getting at least their fair share of services and attention.

As a result, people can lose sight of government's role in protecting and advancing the common good and of their own role as citizens in influencing government actions and decisions. In fact, many public officials — the leaders of our local, state, and national governments — have often fallen into the trap of *demeaning* government as a force for collective problem solving.

"People no longer understand what taxes have to do with their lives. There is a lack of understanding that only government can solve certain problems," said Stuart Comstock-Gay, director of the Democracy Program at Demos, in a 2008 presentation to the NLC Advisory Council.

Bringing back the common good as a focus of public discussion and government policy, whether on the economy or other issues, requires elected officials at all levels to embrace a fundamental shift in how citizens and governments work together.

Local, state, and national leaders must embrace new strategies for involving citizens in the work of identifying key challenges and opportunities facing cities and the nation, and how the government and other sectors should respond. The result of this work: solutions that can credibly and realistically promise to reap rewards not for a limited few but for entire communities and regions and the nation as a whole.

How to engage citizens in the work of public problem solving is the focus of the work of NLC's City Futures Panel on Democratic Governance. The panel defines "democratic governance" as "the art of governing a community in participatory, deliberative, and collaborative ways."

In the course of its deliberations and research, the National League of Cities identified a number of successful principles that can guide leaders at all levels as they set out to restore a common-good framework to the crafting of public policies. These principles are the following:

- Reaching out through an array of groups and organizations is critical for mobilizing large numbers of citizens, and many kinds of people.
- Most public problems cannot be solved without the effort, energy, and ideas of citizens and their organizations (churches, associations, businesses, and nonprofit groups).
- Large-scale, open-minded deliberation, where citizens consider a range of policy options, results in public decisions that are fairer, more informed, and more broadly supported.
- Giving people a sense of "political legitimacy" — a sense of status and membership

in their community — promotes individual responsibility and leadership.

As local fiscal conditions continue to spiral downward, for example, many cities are combing their budgets, trying to find the "right" balance among service cuts, fee increases, hiring freezes, and delaying capital projects. The right balance, however, is not easy to pinpoint and requires placing values and making judgments about particular services, activities, and amenities. Many communities are using the opportunity to approach tough, complex, and controversial budget decisions by seeking input from the community about their wants and needs, their evaluation of services, and their priorities.

Engaging the community in the budgeting process is one way to help make more informed decisions, strengthen trust with constituents, and ease some of the political risks that come with budget cuts.

Although a process to solicit and incorporate the visions and expectations of the community-at-large is more time-intensive and costly and requires greater demands on city staff, the process has longer-term positive consequences, such as a greater sense of community and shared responsibility. The process requires that residents not only offer input but also help implement and support changes, creating a situation where residents engage with local government to protect and advance the needs of the community as a whole, instead of a vending machine model of government.

Local governments should be prepared to demonstrate how community input was used and continue the engagement process. Communities can incorporate initial input into a budget and then conduct ongoing engagement to measure citizens' support for the plan and continue community engagement.

For example, the City of Eugene, Oregon, actively engages with the community on an ongoing basis in a number of ways, including citywide surveys, targeted questionnaires, community forums, and project workshops. The city has several standing citizen commissions, including a citizen budget committee, and a network of additional advisory panels of community members.

This ongoing, multifaceted dialogue with the public furnishes the city with an understanding of community needs and priorities that the staff and city council rely on to help in the budgeting process. Last year, the council adopted a budget that maintained a stable level of services by finding savings and efficiencies to cover a few carefully considered changes to address the community's priorities.

Even with a larger challenge this year due to the current economic environment, the city expects to be able to move closer to a long-term sustainable budget by implementing a combination of efficiency measures, user-fee increases, and service adjustments based on staff and community input.

"We benefit from actively engaging many residents in our budget process and service delivery," said Eugene City Manager Jon Ruiz. "Because of the involvement of the public and the good decision-making of our city council and Citizen Budget Committee members, we know our budget reflects the community's current priorities and we are in a better position now to handle the current economic crisis."

Understanding Economic Change

American workers and their families and employers are operating on a different economic playing field from what they knew in much of the twentieth century, with different rules and requirements, players, and expectations.

Making matters still more challenging, America has been adrift amid these changes. The nation lacks a fresh, constructive, and actionable *shared* understanding of the fundamental economic issues confronting America today. Working with residents, political leaders at all levels need to create a new narrative about what is happening in the economy — and what it takes to produce better outcomes for people, not just for financial mechanisms and institutions.

It is not enough to rely on national statistics to show what's changing in the economy — because national averages do not reflect the wide variety of day-to-day reality where people live in America's cities, towns, and regions.

Prior to and beneath the current crisis, fundamental shifts are occurring. Here is how we see what's changing, on the basis of what we see and hear in the communities we serve.

The Geography of the Economy Is Changing

The globalization of the economy and the advance of technology have made national and state boundaries less important. But contrary to conventional wisdom, the world is *not* flat. Place still matters. In many ways, place matters now more than ever before. The real contest today is among communities, not nations.

Over the years, research by NLC and others has affirmed the existence of local economic regions that encompass center cities, surrounding suburbs, and contiguous towns and rural communities. The "national economy," NLC has asserted, is not one gargantuan, homogeneous entity but rather a "common market" of these local regions. What happens in these regions to strengthen *their* local economies, in turn, is what drives the overall economic success of the United States.

All politics is local, the saying goes. Well, it's time for America's leaders to remember that economics is not solely a national or international phenomenon; it's local, too. It is time to ground both political and economic conversations in a real sense of what is happening to people in America's cities and towns.

The Nature of Economic Activity Is Changing

What matters to local and regional economies is not what national statistics say about the status of manufacturing versus services as a focus of economic activity. Rather, local, state, and national leaders should be focused on bigger questions such as:

• *How can we support high-growth, high-wage jobs?* Jobs themselves are changing in both the manufacturing and service sectors, and they will continue to change. In today's knowledge economy, the education, skills, and capacities of workers, entrepreneurs, and managers are crucial to success for businesses, communities, and nations alike.

• *How can we develop the infrastructure that will ensure the economic prosperity and vitality of America's cities and towns?* We can no longer ignore the role of infrastructure — our nation's roads and railways, air and sea ports, transit and water treatment systems, even broadband access — in enabling us to compete economically as cities, regions, and a nation.

• *How can we support innovation and home-grown, entrepreneurial businesses and help them grow?* According to the U.S. Small Business Administration, small businesses in the United States employ half of all private-sector employees and generate 60 to 80 percent of net new jobs. Even though economic development at all levels traditionally has focused on the "great buffalo hunt" of attracting and retaining large employers, today it is equally if not more important to support home-grown, entrepreneurial businesses.

Raising these questions, and seeking answers, will help elected leaders and their constituents go beyond the headlines to develop a better sense of how the nature of economic activity is changing in America today, and how government and others can best respond.

Insecurity and Inequality Are on the Rise

Economic change always produces winners and losers. But the changes we've seen in recent years are different. The pace and the nature of these changes have contributed to growing inequality as an increasing number of Americans face diminished opportunities to achieve the American dream.

Wages have stagnated for thirty years. As a result of these and other facts, the American dream of a level playing field where everyone has a chance to succeed remains unfulfilled. In 2006, the top 20 percent of households took home more than half (50.5 percent) of the nation's total household income, and their share continues to grow. Meanwhile, the share of income earned by those at all other income levels has been in steady decline over the last two decades.

The growing disparities in our society hurt the performance of local, regional, and national economies by lowering efficiency and productivity, sapping demand for goods and services, and consuming resources — for public safety, social services, and other needs — that could be used more productively in other ways.

America Is Living Beyond Its Means

Public and private debt in America is at a record level. America is starved of the public resources it needs to invest in infrastructure, skills training for workers, and other priorities that are sure-fire ways to strengthen local and regional economies.

Of course, it is not only government that is living beyond its means. A financial system boom based on high leverage has collapsed, causing widespread pain. Americans themselves have been saving less and taking on increasing debt.

Everybody doesn't have to agree on everything that's happening; it would be foolish to expect they would. People are going to have differing perspectives on the economic challenges facing their communities and the nation. The goal should be to find common ground and common interests. What changes in the economy can everyone acknowledge and understand? On what issues can people see opportunities to work together? What are the outlines of a widely shared vision of success?

During the NLC Forum on Economic Vitality in Denver in 2005, Susan E. Clarke, a professor at the University of Colorado at Boulder and author with Gary L. Gaile of *Local Politics in a Global Era: Thinking Locally, Acting Globally,* pointed out the importance of "telling stories" to make sense of globalization and other economic trends. We all need narratives that help put events and trends into a local context, that are a foundation for hope, and that create a basis for policies responding to the real eco-

nomic challenges facing American communities today.

Elected leaders make a difference, Clarke added, by engaging stakeholder groups and citizens in a process of developing an overarching economic strategy. The strategy must make sense in terms of the community's history, its assets, and its goals — its "story." Articulating this story publicly and persuasively is a key role for leaders.

With public understanding and agreement, America's communities can begin the hard work of crafting proper responses to today's economic challenges and opportunities. Making the needed adjustments in economic policy and our approaches to economic development is not just technical or programmatic work. Mainly, it's about leadership and citizenship, beginning with a commitment to fixing America's broken intergovernmental systems and to resurrecting the common good as a framework for action on the economy and other issues.

The Intergovernmental System

The U.S. intergovernmental system is broken. As NLC concluded in its report "Taxing Problems": "A decline in a sense of shared responsibilities among federal, state, and local governments for funding and delivering public services is resulting in unproductive, combative, and often-conflicting policymaking" (2006, p. 10). Getting government right and getting the relations among governments right is a key challenge, not only for public officials but also for all citizens. So the urgent need of fixing the intergovernmental system is part of the "shared understandings" that are important for democracy to work the way it should.

If leaders at all levels can come together to address the systemic problems that stand in the way of economic solutions, they also will strengthen their collective capacity to address other complex policy challenges facing America today. This shifts the discussion of how to strengthen intergovernmental relations from a largely academic argument to an urgent priority for all levels of government. It also makes the work of strengthening economies a platform for achieving broader changes in governance.

Limitations in the U.S. intergovernmental system thwart leadership at all levels in strengthening local and regional economies. The unraveling of the intergovernmental system over time is rooted in a number of factors:

- *"Pass-the-buck" federalism.* The federal and state governments have scaled back their responsibilities in critical areas such as affordable housing, infrastructure, and community development. As a result, local governments are left with the responsibility for activities and investments that are crucial to strengthening local and regional economies — and cities and towns lack the resources needed to nurture economic success.
- *Hyperpartisanship.* All too often in today's politics, policy debates that could yield true collaboration and action to address problems and opportunities facing our communities and the nation degenerate into electioneering, name calling, and political posturing. National interests are pitted against local interests and party interests are elevated above the common interest.
- *Divided governance.* There has been a misguided focus in recent years on trying to totally separate functions among local, state, and federal governments rather than finding ways for them to work together. In this environment, examples of intergovernmental collaboration, vertical and horizontal, are viewed as anomalies or as negligible because they are not perfect.

- *Outmoded revenue systems and inadequate public resources.* There is a mismatch between twenty-first-century economic activity (the growing service and knowledge sectors) and a revenue system based on nineteenth- and twentieth-century assumptions of the production of goods. This mismatch has created long-term structural imbalances at all levels of government, while growing antitax fervor among citizens and their elected leaders has constrained the search for new solutions.

Even amidst the current crisis and confusion, with a new administration and Congress in Washington, and with Americans eager for a sense that government can respond effectively to the real needs people see in their communities and their lives, we believe that America has a unique opportunity, right now, to build a better future. It will be a future built on a shared vision for our common well-being, with all levels of government working together, with citizens engaged as active partners in leading our communities and our nation, with local and regional economies driving national economic success.

REFERENCES

Clarke, S. E., and G. L. Gaile. "Local Politics in a Global Era: Thinking Locally, Acting Globally." *Annals American Academy of Political and Social Science* 551 (1997): 28–43.

"Connecting Citizens and Their Governments." Washington, D.C.: National Civic League, 1996.

"Taxing Problems: Municipalities and America's Flawed System of Public Finance." Washington, D.C.: National Civic League, 2006. Retrieved April 10, 2009, from http://www.nlc.org/topics/index.aspx?SectionID=public_finance.

CHAPTER 24

Gardena's Public Manager Improves City Finances

Lynn Peisner

Gardena, Calif., residents have been stopping police officers to gush over the city's bright new red curbs, which, for years, were weathered to a barely traceable pink. Freshly painted tow-away zones may not raise eyebrows in most communities, but in Gardena, they symbolize a new day. With two infamously cursed business schemes that left the city on the hook for more than $26 million and an ousted city manager who served jail time on several charges, including embezzlement, city employees say the 1990s were like a black cloud. Today, they say life here, like the new curbs, is vibrant.

But more than the curbs, Gardena residents are grateful police officers are even around to hear their comments at all. Public safety was just one of many city services that were scaled down in the decade it has taken Gardena to rebuild its finances and finally commence work on the economic development that could take it from being a Freeway City to the kind of place people want to settle down. It has been a long road to renewal, but the journey would not have had a chance of ending successfully without the dedication of Gardena's City Manager Mitchell Lansdell. For his savvy, patience and determination in pulling his city out of the red and saving it from ruin, American City & County has chosen Lansdell as the 2007 Municipal Leader of the Year.

A City's Fall

In the South Bay area of Los Angeles County, Gardena may be more notorious for its local government's blunders than for its showy card clubs, such as Larry Flynt's Hustler Casino. But, it was not always that way. In the 1980s, Gardena was thriving. By 1985, the city's general fund had a $12 million reserve, community programs were healthy and one-third of the city's police-vehicle fleet was replaced every year.

But as the 1990s approached, the city — with a tax base comprised of property tax, sales tax, card club revenue, utility user fees and a percentage of motor vehicle license fees — continued to spend money at the same rate even though revenues were decreasing. Eventually, the city dipped into its surplus until it was gone.

To generate additional revenue, a few council members devised two business projects local media would later describe as "colossally miscalculated." The first program made Gardena, in 1993, the first city in the United States to sell liability insurance to other cities. The city formed Municipal Mutual Insurance Co. (MMIC) and borrowed $10 million from Gardena's general fund, with the idea of regaining its initial investment plus profits in a market

Originally published as "Saving Grace," *American City & County*, Vol. 122, No. 12, November 2007, by Penton Media, Inc., Overland Park, KS. Reprinted with permission of the publisher.

where municipal insurance rates were soaring. In some cases, insurance carriers would not cover cities at all.

But, in the years it took for the state to approve MMIC's permit, the insurance market changed, and local governments began finding cheaper liability insurance. In the first couple years of the program, MMIC sold one policy — to the city of Gardena. With seven total policies sold by the mid–'90s, MMIC was unable to pay back the $10 million and had picked up additional debt.

By 1995, instead of disbanding and cutting its losses, MMIC abandoned the municipal insurance business to focus on the workers compensation insurance market. But, the company again foundered. When all was said and done, MMIC put Gardena in the hole for $20.6 million.

In 1991, the city launched its second business venture, the First-time Homebuyers Program, which loaned money to first-time homebuyers for their down payments. After five years of enjoying interest-only loans, program participants were expected to refinance their mortgages to pay off the city.

That program, too, was jinxed. The real estate market crashed, and 33 of the 73 loans the program issued went to foreclosure. The city stopped issuing loans in 1997, but by then, the general fund had accrued an additional $6.2 million debt.

The total debt of $26.8 million from the two failed programs consumed most of the $40 million general fund. "Basically, both programs were well-thought-out and served a good public purpose," Lansdell says. "Unfortunately, we just did not implement them in a way that allowed them to be successful."

Two Japanese banks held the notes for Gardena's debts and aggressively began seeking repayment. In 1997, facing an unbalanced budget, the city council was projecting to spend a considerable amount of money more than was available.

While Gardena was hemorrhaging dollars in its insurance and real estate businesses, its former city manager was discovered using precious city funds for personal vacations that included high-priced hotel rooms, first-class plane tickets and other unmentionable expenses. Following a grand jury investigation, the city manager was charged with several counts, including embezzlement, falsification of public records and misappropriation of city funds. He was fired and ultimately convicted on several of the charges.

Lansdell, who as assistant city manager had been watching his city plummet, was appointed acting city manager in 1997. He may not have had big shoes to fill, but when Lansdell took charge, the challenge before him was larger than life.

The Matter of Running a City

Working on the sidelines since 1985, Lansdell hit the ground running. According to his colleagues, he assessed the damage and set in motion the steps toward a long-term solution to his city's fiscal crisis. However, first he had to stave off the city's creditors long enough to get organized. By 1999, both banks allowed the city to pay interest only on their loans for five years.

Next, he had to secure the trust and confidence of city employees for his plan. He held several meetings to explain to everyone the challenges that lay before them. The city would have to operate on a shoestring until the debt could be repaid. "For years, the problems weren't really talked about," says Gardena Chief of Police Ed Medrano. "I think whatever they could keep close to the cuff they did, so when Mitch took over, he had to expose everything that was going on — all of the problems that people were not paying attention to. But we were always informed, and he didn't pull any punches. He didn't say, 'Things are going to be great, just hang tight.' He told us it was going to be difficult. But we have a plan."

At Lansdell's first city council meeting as the acting city manager in November 1997, his plan to trim $2.8 million out of the adopted budget was approved. The city cut staff levels 14 percent across the board by instituting a hiring freeze to avoid layoffs, drastically reduced capital projects (including sidewalk, street and tree maintenance) and cut operational expenses to keep the general fund deficit to $5.2 million, as opposed to the projected $7 million to $10 million in 1998.

When the five-year, interest-only period on the loans ended, Lansdell presented the banks with a revitalization plan that included revisiting fee increases, the potential of tax increases, and the sale of city assets. Discussions and proposals continued between the city and the banks until January 2006, and while Lansdell was keeping the city running and providing only the most necessary services, Gardena was still far from being able to pay off the $26 million principal.

Talk of bankruptcy plagued city hall, and when news that Gardena had contracted a law firm that specializes in municipal bankruptcy became public, the town panicked. "Eliminating the debt by any means possible was the only thing that was going to save the city," says D. Christine Hach, assistant city manager.

The Turning Point

By January 2006, Sumitomo and Union banks were fed up with negotiating with Lansdell and asked for a meeting with Mayor Paul Tanaka. "They weren't getting an agreement [from me]," Lansdell says. "They wanted to be fully paid, and I still wanted to pay them what I thought I could afford to pay."

Bank officials hoped that talking to someone else would yield different results. "In Japan, much like other parts of the world and even in a couple of major cities in the United States, they recognize one person and one person only as being the true 'boss' of the city," Tanaka says. "I told Mitch, 'I'm the elected official, but you're the expert, you've been handling this thing for years.' He said, 'They're done talking to me.' So I had to do an exhaustive study on this entire debacle."

Lansdell briefed the mayor on what he thought the deal points would be. After listening to the bankers' positions, the mayor, in a decisive gesture, told the representatives that they would either work out a repayment deal with Lansdell by the end of the day, or the city would file for bankruptcy. "It did take all day,

but at the end of that day we came up with the memoranda of understanding that was approved by city council in March of 2006," Lansdell says.

The agreement required Tanaka and Lansdell to convince Moody's and Standard and Poor's to re-establish the city's rating and apply for new bonds that would pay back Sumitomo and Union banks the full principal at 85 cents on the dollar. Lansdell decided to seek a repayment plan comparable to a home loan by turning its existing adjustable-rate, interest-only, five-year balloon payment into a 30-year, fixed-rate mortgage. The payments would be more affordable, interest would not fluctuate, and there would be no more fees of several hundred thousand dollars every time the loan needed to be refinanced, which was happening almost every six months.

"We then had to go out and meet with the financial institutions Moody's and Standard and Poor's because we were basically junk," Tanaka says. "Nobody would invest in us. After I told them my own personal story, my commitment to the city and the fact that I believed we had the best leader a city could have in Mitch Lansdell, they gave us an investment-grade rating, and within four hours, 21 or 22 million dollars worth of bonds were sold at 85 cents on the dollar that the banks had agreed to, and the entire cloud of bankruptcy was lifted. It was an amazing day."

The Future, Finally

Since the city's debt restructuring was completed and Gardena has been financially solvent for the past two years, Lansdell has begun rebuilding city staff and green-lighting previously stalled capital projects. The first priority was to re-staff the police department, which should employ 100 officers, according to Medrano, but in 1999, had declined to 65. "We're up to 92 officers already, and I'm well on my way to getting 100," he says.

In the past two years, the city council has approved Lansdell's recommendations to purchase five new patrol cars as well as an asphalt roller and a trailer for the public works department — the first new equipment purchased with general fund money in a decade. Gardena's general plan also was updated in 2006 for the first time in 30 years, and Lansdell is setting his sights on economic development for mixed use in several neglected areas of the city, although voters have defeated the formation of a redevelopment agency three times. Lansdell is pursuing designation of certain areas as enterprise zones for state tax credits.

Lansdell also has launched the Artesia Specific Plan to develop 23 acres off one of the many freeways surrounding the city. Last year, Artesia Square, a 7-acre development approximately in the middle of the 23 vacant acres, was approved. The grading permit has just been issued, and the development includes 13,380 square feet of commercial-retail space, 4,764 square feet of restaurants, 63 residential units and 35 live-work units. Mixing uses on one property is a popular concept in neighboring communities, but Artesia Square will be the first for Gardena. A $52 million dollar transit facility also is under construction and will figure significantly in revitalizing the north end of town.

It is hard to imagine that one person could have single-handedly reversed the tides leading Gardena to blight and bankruptcy, but those who work with Lansdell insist that is the case. "There is no one person who is more responsible for turning the city around," Tanaka says. "He's smart. He's politically astute. He has an incredible work ethic. And, I think most importantly, he's just a good person. That makes a big difference. He's got a good heart, and when you combine all those attributes, you get a great leader."

CHAPTER 25

Hanover and Other Cities Implement Generic Service Reductions

Joe Casey *and* Shayne Kavanagh

During the early stages of a financial recovery, jurisdictions need to take action right away to begin to stabilize the situation — before the leaders of the recovery process will be able to conduct a detailed diagnosis of the causes of distress and develop a response tailored to the situation. At this point, the organization can turn to generic retrenchment techniques — techniques that are safe to apply with little or no foregoing diagnosis of the situation, which are especially useful at the start of the recovery process. Generic techniques have the following essential characteristics:

- **Short time-to-benefit ratio**. A yield occurs in a very short period of time.
- **Not complex**. It is easy to understand the short-term benefits and long-term ramifications. It is also easy to explain to others.
- **Reversible**. It can be undone with reasonable effort. Since generic treatments aren't applied with much diagnosis, it is better if they can be reversed if needed. For example, a hiring freeze can be fitted, or a new fee can be repealed or reduced.

This chapter presents a number of generic retrench techniques, divided into categories such as personnel, revenues, supplies and materials, and more. The experiences of Hanover County, Virginia, are presented as an example.

Examine each technique to see if you can benefit from it.

Personnel

Stretch professional development funds. Training is usually one of the first things cut during a retrenchment, but training sessions are often where employees get new ideas on how to be more efficient. Rather than cutting training completely, consider a cost-sharing arrangement with employees. This reduces the budget for training without eliminating it and may lead employees to be more selective about which training sessions they attend. Memberships in professional associations are another form of development. Rationalize spending on membership in these groups by verifying that memberships are directly relevant to the duties of the employees involved and that the memberships are being actively used. You may also find that multiple employees have individual members for the same association when a collective membership is available.

Use unpaid or lower-cost labor. Hanover County found $30,000 in potential savings by using prison work release labor to clean kennels and perform other duties for its animal control program. Interns or community volun-

Originally published as "Generic Retrenchment Techniques: Any-Time Responses to Financial Distress," *White Paper*, 2010, by the Government Finance Officers Association, Chicago, IL. Reprinted with permission of the publisher.

teers can also provide low-cost labor to perform public services. When using this technique generically, it is probably best to limit it to lower-risk services. For example, while use of citizen volunteers in public safety roles has potential, it probably needs more study and forethought than can be brought to bear in the earliest stages of the recovery process.

Share personnel. There may be opportunities to share personnel across departments. Sharing personnel helps prevent layoffs by better distributing human resources to where they are most needed. There is often potential for sharing administrative assistants, for example. You might also look to see where the organization is hiring contracted labor and see if in-house resources could be used instead (which might help prevent a layoff).

Hanover found opportunities to share personnel with its county attorney, public works, community development, and public safety functions. To illustrate, a number of county employees (who were not employed in public safety) were working in volunteer fire fighting and emergency medical service (EMS) capacities for the county on their off-time. The county found a way to temporarily re-assign these employees to public safety to cover vacancies in fire and EMS. This allowed the county to retain necessary coverage levels for public safety services while avoiding layoffs in other departments.

Reassess personnel equipment needs. During times of higher revenues, personnel may have been assigned equipment that isn't completely essential to the job, and the government may now be willing to live with the lower level of service associated with eliminating that equipment. Hanover County reassessed the need for individual cell phones, personal digital assistants, uniforms, individual desktop printers, and take-home vehicles, saving almost $100,000 annually.

Allow voluntary part-time status. Letting employees volunteer to move to part-time status is a relatively non-controversial way to save money on salary costs (and fringe benefits that are based on salary). In fact, some employees might welcome the opportunity to move to part-time status. However, managers should think about repercussions such as the newly part-time workers' continued eligibility for fringe benefits and effects on scheduling. Despite the risks, this can be considered a safe generic technique because it can be easily reversed. In fact, managers might want to make it clear that part-time status is provisional, with a defined sunset date for the initiative. This will allow managers to assess the effects and rescind the decision, if necessary, without adversely affecting morale.

Short-term hiring freeze. A short-term hiring freeze that lasts a few months or simply extends the time a position is vacant might provide some immediate financial relief. This kind of hiring freeze would not usually require formal proceedings such as governing board approval. A longer hiring freeze would require more careful analysis, including deciding what departments and functions are affected (e.g., will public safety positions be exempted?), calculating how overtime costs will be affected, and identifying potential risks to critical services.

Rethink staffing ratios. Fixed staffing ratios can potentially transform personnel from a variable to a fixed cost. See if staffing ratios can be reconsidered to provide more flexibility in how staff resources are used. For example, Hanover County identified more than $1.5 million in potential savings from changing ratios for sheriff personnel per capita, teachers to students, and fire fighters per truck. While this technique may not lead to immediate savings by itself, it does form the basis for important discussions about staffing levels that could lead to significant savings later.

Revenues

Raise fees where appropriate. A review of fees may show that certain fees have not been raised in some time, in which case an increase might be appropriate. Public managers will have to use their judgment to determine where it is feasible to raise fees immediately and where further study will be required. Fees with the following qualities are candidates for an immediate increase:

- there has been no increase in a number of years,
- there is reasonable basis to assume that the cost of service has increased,
- the governing board and management expect high levels of cost recovery,
- those paying the fee are clear beneficiaries of the service, and
- there is existing statutory authority for raising fees.

Implement new fees where appropriate. Over time, the government might have come to provide a number of services that, while small and seemingly innocuous on their own, add up to real money. It may be appropriate to start charging a fee for these services, especially if the beneficiary of the service is a distinguishable constituent. For instance, Hanover County identified the potential for $50,000 in new revenue for its animal control service by starting a licensing tag program for cats. Hanover found that it was spending just as much, if not more, on animal control for cats, thereby justifying the fee. Again, public managers will need to use discretion to determine where a fee can be implemented right away and where more study will be required. To illustrate, a number of communities have implemented EMS fees, where accident victims are charged a fee for EMS response to the scene. While the accident victims are clearly the beneficiary of the service, such fees can be controversial and may require more deliberation.

Reexamine inter-fund charges. Just like user fees, inter-fund charges can sometimes become outdated. There may be obvious and widely agreed upon opportunities to update these charges to help the funds that are experiencing distress. This is another technique where the public manager must exercise discretion. A clear and compelling case for updating or adding a charge exists in some cases, but in others, the matter may require further study and discussion lest the charge degenerate into cross-fund subsidization.

Think more entrepreneurially. Government may have valuable assets that can be transformed into ongoing revenue streams. For example, Hanover County made more space

available for cellular service antennae leases and began selling methane from its landfill for a total of more than $100,000 in new annual revenues.

Supplies and Materials

Reduce paper costs. Using electronic documents can reduce printing and material costs in a number of ways. For example, the City of Redwood, California, purchased about $7,000 worth of iPads for its City Council, and it expects to save more than $30,000 a year in printing costs as a result.[1] Simply posting reports on the Web instead of printing them out could also save money — Hanover County plans to save 10 percent on its printing costs this way. You can also stop buying paper products such as calendars and day planners that are replicated in office productivity software such as Microsoft Outlook. Finally, modern office productivity software packages have graphic capabilities that reduce or eliminate the need for preprinted stationary and letterhead.

Save energy. Energy efficiencies are a great way to save money while fulfilling the green goals that many governing boards have adopted. This could include improving turn-off habits, initiating tighter temperature controls, keeping fleet tires properly inflated, and better managing routes and fuel.

Re-examine maintenance and replacement standards. The organization's maintenance standards might have been established years ago, when products were not as durable as they are today. For example, Hanover County identified the potential to save $200,000 per year by changing the standard for servicing buses from 30 to 45 days, a change that is acceptable because engines and buses are built much better than they were 20 years ago, when the standards were originally developed. In other cases, the organization might simply be willing to live with a lower standard of maintenance. Hanover County plans to save more than $100,000 a year by reducing standards for internal mail delivery, grounds maintenance, painting, and custodial services. The county also identified $350,000 in one-time savings that could be achieved by accepting higher mileage and years of service on ambulances and fire trucks before they have to be replaced.

Rethink lease agreements. Governments may rent properties that they could own for a lower net cost. Check to see if depreciating property values and the strength of the government's borrowing capacity might allow it to make financially savvy purchases of property that it currently rents. Hanover County projected $30,000 in annual savings from eliminating more than 30,000 square feet in rented space in favor of county-owned space.

Process Redesign

Share cashiering resources. More than one department probably has cash receipt functions, and sharing these services could help reduce personnel costs. Hanover County saved $40,000 a year by using the treasurer's office's cash receipt capabilities to cover the needs of the utility billing department.

Share constituent contact intake. It is not uncommon for multiple departments to have personnel who are responsible for taking calls directly from the public and greeting walkins. There is a significant amount of waste inherent in this arrangement because these individual constituent service agents often have a fair amount of downtime, and due to the nature of the work (i.e., constant interruptions), they are not usually very productive in using that downtime to accomplish other tasks. Consolidating constituent contact intake into one shared unit reduces downtime and allows the constituent service agents to specialize their skills. While some governments have gone so far as to implement a fully realized call center and 311 number, Hanover County found the potential to save $50,000 a year by directing the county's existing main number to a designated call-taker in the county administrator's office; improving signage to better direct visitors to the contact intake agents for the departments they want, rather than relying on dedicated receptionists to direct visitors; and making more effective use of the county Web site to provide services, thereby eliminating the need for some constituents to visit county offices.

Eliminate low or no-value tasks. Quality guru W. Edward Deming taught that most business processes contain up to 95 percent waste. A financial challenge may provide impetus to eliminate tasks that provide little or no value to the customer, but have remained in place regardless. Give managers permission to identify and eliminate this kind of work. Hanover County identified a number of such tasks, and eliminating some of them generated substantial savings. For example, the county found that it was placing notices of public hearings, job openings, and other advertisements in multiple area newspapers. This was an expensive and unnecessary approach (state law requires advertising in only one paper). Consolidating ads resulted in project savings of $20,000 a year. In the assessor's office, tax assessors would traditionally visit properties to reassess them, a time-consuming task. The assessor's office identified the potential for $150,000 in annual savings by eliminating the visit and instead using satellite photos to conduct routine reassessments. The assessor uses the photos to verify that nothing has changed from what was expected at the property.

Scope of Services Provided

Cut the most discretionary of spending. The organization may have certain programs that are widely recognized as "nice to have," but not essential to the mission. It may be possible to cut these programs, at least to some extent, in the early phases of the recovery process, if there is a shared understanding of the depth of the financial challenge and the logic of cutting this type of spending. Hanover County, for example, had traditionally operated a cannery for the benefit of local food growers (growers could take their produce to the cannery to be canned). A cannery is not essential to the county's core functions, so might be a place where spending could be reduced.

Reduce the scope of capital asset investments. A common response to fiscal distress is to defer or eliminate capital project spending, but jurisdictions need to make sure they aren't hurting themselves in the long term. For instance, a jurisdiction might have to rely on obsolete and potentially unsafe assets if it fails to invest in new ones, or new assets might be needed to preserve the economic vitality of the community. However, it might be possible to make a quick and low-risk decision to simply scale back on the asset purchase by reducing the amount purchased or by foregoing premium features. Hanover County found that it could save $100,000 by reducing the scope of a project to upgrade its communication system. The county reduced the number of ratio channels the system accommodated and the total number of radio towers by three (thereby accepting a lower level of coverage). The new communication system was still an improvement over the old one, but the county avoided the cost associated with premium features. Retaining the three radio towers would have improved radio coverage to 97 percent from 95 percent, but county officials decided it wasn't worth the added cost.

Make minor reductions in service levels. You might be able to make minor reductions in service levels at the earliest stages of the recovery process. If decision makers understand the depth of the financial challenge, they are more likely to accept some immediate reductions in services. Examples might include reducing library hours, reducing the number of issues of a community newsletter, or closing a community center for holidays.

Rethink subsidies. Your jurisdiction might have given subsidies — to internal programs, outside agencies, or constituencies — which could be reviewed for continued relevance and affordability. For example, tax exemptions may reduce revenue yields while only benefiting a narrow segment of the community. Local government may also have institutionalized financial support for good ideas that came from advocacy groups or elected officials who are no longer in office, but these programs may, in fact, be ancillary to providing essential core services. While reducing these subsides right away might be politically challenging, you can begin by cataloguing subsidies as a starting point for the discussion of their continued feasibility.

Fund Balances

If the government has built up fund balances in good times and has an explicit policy about how this money may be used to mitigate budgetary distress, then fund balances could be a useful generic retrenchment technique. The fund balance policy needs to describe:

- who can authorize use of reserves;
- the target level of reserves the government seeks to maintain (so the jurisdiction can assess the impact of the proposed use on actual reserve levels);
- how much of that target is authorized for budgetary stabilization specifically (versus responding to extreme events, for example); and
- the permissible uses of the reserve (can reserves be used only for non-recurring expenditures, or can they be used for recurring expenditures, in the context of a long-term plan to reach structural balance?).

If a government does not have a strong fund balance policy, then using reserves might not be a good generic technique because many of the decisions that would otherwise be framed by a policy will have to be thought through.

NOTE

1. Katharine Lackey, "iPads Saving Cities Paper Costs," *USA Today*, August 10, 2010.

Editor's Note: Hanover County, which is located in central Virginia, has a population of more than 100,000 people. Hanover has a total budget of $400 million and a general fund budget of $200 million. It is one of the smallest counties in the United States with a triple-A bond rating. In addition, the county recently received a Senate and Productivity and Quality Award and was chosen as one of the America's Promise Alliance's "100 Best Communities for Young People."

CHAPTER 26

Harrisburg and Other Cities Revise Their Property Tax Structure

Walter Rybeck

How did some local governments generate adequate revenue during a failing economy, reduce property taxes for most homeowners, entice new private development without subsides, retard sprawl, and keep housing affordable? Certainly a timely question. During this prolonged recession, shrinking funds are forcing localities to cut back on services when they are most needed by people suffering from loss of homes and jobs.

Several dozen cities dug themselves out of a hole by reengineering their property tax. They reduced taxes on homes and other buildings and raised taxes on land. Pennsylvania's capital city demonstrates the potency of this medicine.

In 1980, Harrisburg, Pennsylvania, was cited by HUD as one of the nation's most distressed cities. It had lost 800 businesses and a third of its population in 20 years. Mayor Stephen Reed initiated the two-rate tax in that era, reducing the tax rate on buildings to one-half the rate on land.

Reed, who continued as mayor until January 2010, credits the reform with playing a major part in reversing the city's downward slide. Most of the 5,200 stores and housing units that were boarded up when he took office are replaced or back in use. Since then, new construction and rehabilitation of existing structures increased the city's taxable real estate

from $212 million to over $1.6 billion. Businesses on the tax rolls rose from 1,908 to more than 9,100 by the start of 2009. Seeing these positive effects, Harrisburg reduced its tax rate on improvements to one-sixth the rate on land.

Tax hikes on idle sites induced owners to put them to use, discouraging sprawl. Reed said, "Unused urban land is what pushes development into open spaces. Many states try to save farmland by buying development rights. That's expensive. Without spending a dime, we achieved the same goal with our two-tier tax."

Upside-down property tax. The conventional property tax combines two distinct taxes, one on land and one on improvements. Taxpayers dislike the tax on buildings — for good reason. The more they invest, the higher their tax. In contrast, owners who let structures deteriorate are rewarded with lower taxes. Taxing good buildings heavily and poor buildings lightly is like giving blight and slums an engraved invitation to invade a city.

That's only the half of it. The good part of the tax, on land values, generally is too low, especially on vacant sites. Assessors look at the non-existent income streams of bare lots and mistakenly assign low values to them, ignoring their potential. This promotes land speculation, a prime cause of runaway housing prices, sprawl, and recessions.

Originally published as "Retooling Property Taxes," *Public Management*, Vol. 92, No. 2, March 2010, by the International City/County Management Association, Washington, D.C. Reprinted with permission of the publisher.

How so? Speculators hold prime sites vacant, waiting for population growth and local government services to make these sites more valuable. Plots kept in cold storage create an artificial shortage of developable sites. This drives urban land prices up, drives growth to the outskirts, and fuels more speculation until a boom, based largely on thin air, goes bust.

Virtues of taxing land. Taxing land more and buildings less takes the profit out of speculation, putting land users rather than land holders in the driver's seat. Unlike taxes on most anything else, taxes on site values reduce land prices. Good things flow from this remarkable fact, as these examples show.

Aliquippa, Pennsylvania, not only lost jobs when LTV's steel mill closed 20 years ago, a court order reduced LTV's property tax from $1 million to $200,000. The city reduced tax rates on buildings, making the tax rate on land 16 times higher than on improvements. This enabled Aliquippa to collect $450,000 from LTV's valuable site, and it nudged LTV to promptly find new occupants for its plant. Within a few years, the city treasury had a surplus. City Administrator Thomas Stoner says the two-rate tax "favors residences and puts more weight on industrial properties." This Rust Belt city still struggles economically but its housing costs remain affordable.

Peoria, Illinois, adopted tax reform under an enterprise zone law to revive a seven-mile strip of obsolete factories and blighted warehouses. This area along the Illinois River employed 2,000 people in 1980, down from 50,000 in its heyday. Taxes on new or renovated buildings were reduced 75 percent for five years, 50 percent for the next five. Reductions did not apply to land values. The city offered no subsidies to entice new firms. Building activity mushroomed, land values rose, and so did tax revenues. The dollar value of industrial and commercial building permits quickly rose from 8 percent to 29 percent of the citywide total. Tax incentives favoring instead of discouraging growth worked their magic.

Southfield, Michigan, attracted impressive growth after Mayor James Clarkson and assessor Ted Gwartney in the 1960s corrected the city's under-assessment of land. Land was assessed too low at 10 percent of value and buildings too high at more than 70 percent of value. Assessing both at market value touched off dramatic expansion. Average homeowners won a 22 percent tax reduction. Detroit, literally across the street, failed to follow Southfield's lead and was in decline long before the fall of its auto industry. Note that Southfield did not adopt a land tax. Its turnaround came from simply obeying the law of the conventional property tax and assessing both land and improvements at current value.

Getting Started

Local governments can replicate these successes by taking these steps:

1. Get state legislators to permit taxing land and buildings at different rates, if not already allowed.

2. Keep land assessments at current market value to get maximum mileage from the tax. (Inequitable land assessments in 2000 scuttled the two-rate tax in Pittsburgh, which had been a shining example of urban revitalization via tax reform.)

3. Run a computer simulation of a two-rate tax — lower rates on improvements, higher rates on land — to identify who pays more or less, to determine the optimum shift, and to avoid surprises. Organizations like the Center for the Study of Economics in Philadelphia, which designed many of the Pennsylvania reforms, can provide guidance on this phase.

4. Start with a revenue-neutral reform. If the community generates the same tax receipts citywide as under the traditional system, opponents cannot mischaracterize the tax shift as a tax increase.

5. Set land values rates as high as politically feasible. Everybody loves lower taxes on homes. The initial rate on land, however, should not be set so high that owners of vacant sites, whose taxes will rise, might defeat the measure. Once in operation, rate differentials can gradually be widened. In 2009, for example, Altoona, Pennsylvania, expanded its land tax rate to 27 times higher than its tax on buildings;

and DuBois, Pennsylvania, last year reduced its building tax rate to only 0.2 percent, so its land tax rate is 44 times higher, or 8.8 percent.

Incentives vs. police powers. New London, Connecticut, became notorious when the Supreme Court affirmed its right to condemn and replace good homes with commercial development. Widespread outcries arose against such aggressive use of condemnation powers. In July 2009, Governor Jodi Rell signed an act permitting New London to launch a land value tax pilot project that is now being designed. This use of tax reform to stimulate a local economy, as an alternative to manipulation of property rights, will be important to track.

Missing tool. Harrisburg and the other cities cited used many measures in addition to tax reform to spur renewal, fiscal stability, and economic growth. This land tax attacked the land speculation that often undermines the effectiveness of those other measures. Shifting taxes off buildings onto land is a vital but missing item in the tool kit of most local governments.

The reform changes urban dynamics.

Lower taxes on improvements promote development instead of penalizing it. Higher land taxes return to the local government the site values that result directly from improved public services and facilities. Land taxes also spur in-city growth, opening the way to new enterprises and jobs. They keep housing prices from soaring into the stratosphere — and then tumbling. To save localities and prevent the next crash, the land tax has the earmarks of a reform whose time has come.

Landowners with little or no improvements on prime sites pay relatively minimal taxes under the conventional property tax. Shifting taxes off improvements and on to land values means their taxes go up. In Allentown, Pennsylvania, for example, the publisher of the local newspaper held acres of central city sites used for surface parking lots, and he managed for years to get the mayor to veto the two-rate tax approved by a majority of council persons, until council eventually won the day. In West Virginia, powerful coal interests, who pay low taxes on their assets, have consistently blocked the legislature's efforts to give cities and counties the option of using a two-rate tax in that state.

CHAPTER 27

Las Vegas and Other Cities Reassess
Their Basic Services

Karen Thoreson *and* James H. Svara

The impacts of the fiscal crisis that is engulfing local governments in the United States have the potential to fundamentally reshape local governance. For a growing number of cities and counties, the shortfalls are substantially diminishing their resources and their capacity to deliver the range of services they provided previously. In a fiscal crisis, an immediate reaction is often to stop spending wherever possible and impose cross-the-board budget cuts. However, research on previous cutback periods indicates that reactive approaches are often counterproductive.[1] Uniform cuts applied across an organization do not distinguish essential from less important activities or productive from unproductive operations.

In a period of retrenchment, change is unavoidable because the decline in resources means that the government cannot maintain the status quo. Many officials have asserted that "a crisis is a terrible thing to waste," and it is common to hear brave calls to take advantage of trying times to make constructive changes. Pressing need can unleash the creativity of participants in the local government to come up with innovative possibilities. And, in fact, analysis of the conditions that engender award-winning innovation stresses the importance of crisis or challenge as a stimulus to change. In this sense, the experience of innovative local governments supports the aphorism that "necessity is the mother of invention." Unfortunately, given what we have learned from previous cutback periods, necessity can simply be the mother of reaction. Often, those governments that handle cutbacks well are those that have made preparations in advance of the crisis or have strong organizational capacity for leadership, analysis, and decision making. Recognizing the value of these factors is important for understanding why some organizations succeed and other decline.

Local Governments in
Fiscal Crisis

In the middle of 2009, ICMA conducted a survey of 2,214 city and county administrators for local governments exceeding 2,500 in population. One question asked respondents about the effects of the fiscal crisis on their communities, and their answers ranged across the spectrum as follows (n = 2,116)[2]:

- No impact: 0.5 percent (10)
- Minimal impact: 17.5 percent (370)
- Moderate impact: 44.5 percent (941)
- Significant impact: 30.8 percent (651)
- Severe impact: 6.8 percent (144)

Originally published as "How Local Governments are Navigating the Fiscal Crisis: Taking Stock and Looking Forward," *The Municipal Yearbook 2011*, by the International City/County Management Association, Washington, D.C. Reprinted with permission of the publisher.

Despite some positive signs in the economy, hardly any local governments are escaping any negative consequences, and nearly half are experiencing serious effects. According to the ICMA survey, the degree of impact increases with larger population size, especially in cities. For cities over 100,000 in population, more than three in five are grappling with major budget problems. In counties, the problems are somewhat greater as county size increases; however, the relationship is not as strong. According to the National League of Cities' *City Fiscal Conditions in 2010* report, nearly nine out of ten cities were less able to meet financial needs in both 2009 and 2010 than they were in the past.[3] Because of lags in property tax assessments and collections, declining property values continued to push down property tax receipts in 2010 and are expected to remain flat or decline further in 2011. Sales taxes did not decline as much in 2010 as they did the previous year, but they were still down 5 percent from 2009.

As a consequence of these conditions, local governments have been challenged to make immediate responses to the crisis; however, the fiscal strain continues, underscoring the need to develop new approaches for the future. As stated in a 2009 article in the *Harvard Business Review*, "It would be profoundly reassuring to view the current economic crisis as simply another rough spell that we need to get through. Unfortunately, though, today's mix of urgency, high stakes and uncertainty will continue as the norm even after the recession ends."[4] When the Alliance for Innovation issued *Navigating the Fiscal Crisis: Tested Strategies for Local Leaders*, a white paper prepared for ICMA in 2009, it was not yet clear that the navigation challenge was not a quick plunge down icy rapids but rather a protracted effort to stay afloat and maintain a positive course through seas that will continue to be turbulent.[5]

Since the early months of 2009, the Alliance for Innovation has been monitoring how the budget crisis was affecting 11 local governments across the United States and what approaches were being taken to handle budget retrenchment. These governments (shown with their estimated 2009 populations)—Hickory, North Carolina (40,469); Jefferson County, Colorado (536,922); Las Vegas, Nevada (567,641); Overland Park, Kansas (174,907); Phoenix, Arizona (1,601,587); Polk County, Florida (583,403); Prince William County, Virginia (379,166); Rancho Cordova, California (62,939); Rockville, Maryland (62,105); San Antonio, Texas (1,373,668); and Washtenaw County, Michigan (347,563)—all have been members of the Alliance.

The governments vary in the severity of the financial difficulties they face—from Las Vegas and Phoenix, which are experiencing dramatic declines in sales taxes and development-related revenues, to San Antonio and Rockville, which have had only a modest loss of revenue at this point. Some governments have experienced protracted fiscal strain because of the shrinking traditional industrial base in Michigan and North Carolina and the state-imposed cuts in local taxes that preceded the fiscal crisis in Florida. What these governments have in common, however, appears to be a general and long-term commitment to change.

Management Capacity at the Start of the Crisis

Research on previous cutback periods shows that governments with strong management capacity are more likely to respond quickly and adopt proactive rather than reactive approaches.[6] All the local governments being monitored had generally established the policy and management preconditions that would enable them to anticipate a change in economic conditions and make adjustments based on strategic choices. Almost all of them had in place a set of strategies, goals, and priorities before the downturn began. When choices were made about what programs and services to continue or cut, these governments could be guided by goals that were already established rather than set in response to crisis conditions. They were also able to identify changes in financial conditions before those changes were generally obvious.

Hickory and Washtenaw County, for example, had experienced severe declines in 2002–2003 and took advantage of that experience to respond to the current crisis. Jefferson County had developed a five-year forecast in early 2006 that focused on ongoing and one-time revenues and historical costs and recognized a structural deficit that needed to be corrected. Phoenix had detected early signs of revenue decline in late 2006; Las Vegas and Polk County recognized the downturn in 2007, and Las Vegas has been able to track the severity of the crisis. Prince William County, through its five-year budgeting process, noted the steep increases in foreclosures and made adjustments quickly. These governments generally measure performance and can assess relative levels of effectiveness and efficiency. San Antonio has been working for the past three years to evaluate and in some cases eliminate lesser priority or inefficient programs. Many of the governments had taken functions related to development and new construction and had organized them into an enterprise fund that links the number of staff members with the level of activity, and permits "automatic" expansion and contraction of service levels and staffing. Phoenix had accumulated substantial reserves in its property tax collections for repayment of bonds.

From conversations with individual managers and small focus groups, we were able to form some impressions about the contribution of managers. There is an almost paradoxical contrast between the depressing conditions that local governments face and the enthusiasm expressed by city and county managers regarding the challenge before them. "Getting us through this crisis," one manager said, "is why I am a city manager." There is the widely shared view that the most serious fiscal crisis in 80 years gives them the opportunity to demonstrate extraordinary leadership that draws on all their knowledge, values, and skills. Indeed, many managers seem to shine in situations requiring fundamental adjustments. The anecdote presented above exemplifies their interest in reshaping the local government to meet their demanding professional standards.

The jurisdictions that have goals and priorities in place are using them as criteria for making cuts. In 2009 Las Vegas reassigned a department director to head a fundamental service review team (with assistance from an outside consultant). The team identified $150 million in needed cuts over four months, and nonessential services are being modified, consolidated, or in some cases eliminated. Jefferson County plans to be looking at lower-priority programs and determining their ongoing relevance to its mission.[7] Although few cuts have been made so far, the county anticipates that programs with less priority will be downsized or eliminated in 2011. San Antonio has been working for the past three years to evaluate and, where warranted, eliminate lower-priority or inefficient programs; through that work, the city has eliminated $12.6 million in budget expenditures to date. In contrast, Phoenix has used its "Renewing Phoenix" project undertaken in 2008 to improve performance measurement as guide to its budget response, which resulted in budget cuts of $291 million and the elimination of over 1,500 positions in programs that were judged to be less important and underperforming.

Specific Actions by Monitored Cities and Counties

Beyond these budget-balancing efforts, the communities we monitored have undertaken a range of actions to change the scope of their services and the way they provide them. Their actions have been divided into three broad categories: innovations and improvements in current practices, organizational redesign, and new partnerships. Many of the actions span the categories. For example, Prince William County developed a new priority-based budgeting system that incorporates organizational redesign and ensures that the five-year budget is balanced every year. The county executive says that looking long term creates discipline in the staff and elected officials to look at how to pay for services and infrastructure in good times and bad. Partnering is enhanced by holding a "Budget Congress" where representatives of all key sectors of the county listen to all new budget requests and make recommendations to the county board on what to fund. This allows each sector to understand how cuts or additions may affect how they offer services.

It is worth noting the lessons that have been learned from communities that have long been engaged in budget balancing. Both Washtenaw County and Hickory mentioned a sort of "budget-cutting fatigue." Having been at the reduction game for nearly a decade, they both noted that employees, elected officials, and the community are tired of the relentless budget tightening. Hickory said that as they looked to create more shared services, some community members were asserting that they didn't want to do with less anymore! A different view was provided by Rockville, which experienced perhaps the least impact of the financial crisis of any community monitored. Although the city was never in desperate straits, its elected officials and leadership nevertheless perceived that the crisis provided them with an opportunity to correct past actions and put the community on an even stronger financial foothold.

Some examples of new approaches from the monitored cities and counties as well as from other governments are highlighted in the sections that follow.

Innovation and Improvement

Innovation can be defined as the creation of a new process, approach, or program that achieves better results than what had been in place previously.

Innovation had been taking place in local governments prior to the current budget crisis; however, the depth of the new fiscal realities has allowed local governments to redefine policies and standard operating procedures in ways that might not have been politically possible before. Furthermore, despite budget limitations, local governments continue to innovate in other areas, as evidenced by case studies submitted to the Alliance for Innovation in 2009 and 2010. Some examples of these innovations are as follows.

- Jefferson County, Polk County, and Prince William County, as well as Downers Grove, Illinois, have developed new budgeting systems that place greater focus on prioritization, outcome measurement, and long-term perspective.

- Las Vegas, suffering from some of the highest foreclosure rates in the country, has created "Stop NV Foreclosures," a new program that focuses effort on preventing foreclosures rather than dealing solely with the aftermath of residents losing their homes.

- Phoenix has included $10 million worth of savings in its fiscal year (FY) 2011 operating budget that would come from innovations and efficiencies identified during the course of the year. By December 2010, a team consisting of city staff and citizens came up with more than $10 million in general fund savings and more than $25 million in savings to all funds by eliminating positions, consolidating departments and functions, revising some transit services, rebidding some contracts, and realizing nearly $800,000 in "givebacks" from 100 private sector business partners who agreed to reduce contract fees.

- Johnson City, Tennessee, has revamped its economic development approach in a program called "Will This Float?" Focusing inward on the talent of local entrepreneurs, it has paired those emerging businesses with venture capital investment firms looking for new ideas.

- Novi, Michigan, has established a joint Public Safety Administration Team that unifies the police and fire service under one administrator while allowing each department to still retain its mission independence. This change has allowed for cost savings, significantly greater collaboration and improved databases, and systems more focused on results in this Detroit suburb.

Organizational Design and Process

Many communities have responded to the crisis by rethinking their general or strategic plan. Others have looked internally to how they could redesign fundamental processes to improve performance. An important feature in these efforts has been the involvement of a diverse set of actors.

- Polk County uses a "managing for results" approach that focuses on the delivery of seven classifications of services, from the basic needs of recreation and cultural arts.[8] The county establishes what citizens' expectations for service delivery are and then measures on a quarterly basis how it is doing in meeting those expectations.
- Speak UP Winnipeg, Manitoba, has designed and implemented its first community planning process. To develop a collaborative vision, the city has connected directly with over 42,000 Winnipeggers: its website has had over 8.5 million hits, over 26,000 visitors, and over 1,650 posted blog comments. At a cost of $3.2 million, the 25-year development plan is uniquely suited this large Canadian city. As this *Year Book* goes to press, the plan is still awaiting provincial approval.
- "Durham First" in Durham, North Carolina, has brought a new focus to its staff through an emphasis on a "culture of service." The program highlights the benefits of being a public servant and the rewards of providing service to the community and to the organization.
- Philadelphia, Pennsylvania, has established public service areas in its most vulnerable neighborhoods. Working with local residents who set the agenda for change and have a say in service delivery, the city is changing the way it interacts with its neighborhoods and citizens.
- Downers Grove has developed a system for "budget prioritization" that helps staff, elected officials, and citizens identify and select the community's core services. That process has guided a challenging budget process and helped set a tone for service delivery in future years.
- Wellington, Florida, has established a safe neighborhood initiative along with the Palm Beach County Sheriff's Office, which provides police service under contract. The initiative has mobilized the entire city organization to refocus city resources on reaching citizens and children in vulnerable neighborhoods. Police services are provided through a contract with the Palm Beach County Sheriff's Office. Through this focus the city has achieved measured results, such as a 25 percent drop in serious crime, including drug cases and burglaries, over the previous year. There has also been an increased number of reports from residents to code compliance officers where vandalism or code violations have taken place. Before the Safe Neighborhood program was implemented, 90 percent of the calls were reactive responses to trouble. By the end of 2009, that volume was down to 25 percent, meaning that three-quarters of the deputies' calls were proactive stops to check on residents or area businesses.

Partnerships

Developing new partnerships includes engaging diverse stakeholders to join in efforts that create synergy, cost savings, and a new approach to providing local services.

- Phoenix and Polk County both have embraced the opportunity to work with citizens through robust volunteer programs.
- San Antonio has developed a partnership with Goodwill, a nonprofit organization, to provide preventive health education at existing Goodwill facilities and job training to the unemployed and underemployed.[9]
- Vista Grande Joint Use Library in Casa Grande, Arizona, has developed an improved, high-tech, and cost-saving facility that both the city and the school district use to the benefit of all local citizens.
- Alachua County, Florida, has converted its conservationist principles into a dozen partnerships that leverage financial and human resources for comprehensive open space and land stewardship.

Looking to the Future

The fiscal crisis is producing change and rethinking, but substantial innovation is only beginning. There are impediments to mixing creativity and crisis, particularly in the initial period of downturn. Resources are limited for investing in innovation, and a lot of time and attention is being given to making reductions rather than improvements. At the same time, however, the sustained crisis is forcing local governments to go beyond immediate actions that produce savings in one budget year but cannot be repeated or sustained. We do not yet know what the full extent of change in practices will be. This is the point at which innovation may be more evident as the rebuilding process begins. During final interviews with our 11 communities, officials were asked to look to the future and describe what they expect the "new normal" will look like. Here are insights from their comments.

There will be much greater focus on and discipline related to core priorities.

Each local government spoke to this in its own way. Most plan to continue a focus on core services — those that reflect the revised priorities of citizens and officials. They are also looking to build capacity through reserves and financial modeling systems to ensure that they are better able to weather any future crisis without having to cut into core services or the resources needed to provide them. Rancho Cordova, California, quickly responded to the downturn by eliminating nonessential services and reducing contract staff in areas where requests for services had dropped. Las Vegas established an essential service review that identified core services and corresponding cuts in programs that did not address those needs. Communities that were not monitored through the two-year-long project are also stepping up.

Growth for our community or region will probably not be same again — maybe ever.

A number of local managers noted that as the community grew in good times, their organizations grew dramatically as well and were able to add increments to program funding with little annual review. These governments also expanded their infrastructure to attract new growth. But changing economic conditions and demographics are expected to mean a decline in growth, and any new growth is more likely to be accommodated through in-fill development. New investments are not expected soon, but the most frequently mentioned areas for new investments are sustainability, economic development, and technology.

Community expectations will need to shift.

Many managers said that "we can't be or have everything" anymore. For decades local governments have been using tax revenues to subsidize services that might not be considered public goods. Now, however, citizens should expect to pay closer to the full cost for specialized services that benefit an individual (e.g., recreation classes, fairground use, some library services, parking meters) rather than the whole community (e.g., streets, public safety, elections). Moreover, citizens can no longer look to government to solve their problems, nor should government view citizens as passive consumers to services. Increasingly, service needs and community problems must be addressed through a partnership between government, community organizations, and citizens. This new approach is a major theme in the white paper on citizen engagement recently released by the Alliance.[10]

Service production and delivery will need to change.

As a consequence of these changed expectation, service delivery will continue to change. Some governments are stressing a "rightsourcing" approach, critically reexamining the mix of services delivered internally and through outsourcing. Many local governments are exploring how to better involve citizens in the delivery of public services. A shift from a government-centered modeled to coproduction with citizens is anticipated. Neighborhoods will shift from a dependent to an interdependent state. The approaches include increasing opportunities for volunteerism; encouraging neighborhoods to raise funds to support nearby parks and other amenities; and generally including residents in decision-making roles in areas that affect their quality of life. In general, this trend could greatly affect how local governments operate in the future.

Conclusion

It appears that the overall response to the current fiscal crisis has been more proactive and strategic than it was in earlier retrenchment periods. In the past, most governments simply hunkered down and made across-the-board cuts without making distinctions between programs. Today, local governments are making both general cuts and targeted reductions. Guided by existing priorities, over three in five local governments throughout the country with significant or severe budget reductions have made targeted cuts, and about half have made cuts to all departments.[11] In many of the monitored communities that made budget adjustments guided by existing priorities, the next step is to reexamine the priorities themselves and fundamentally rethink how the local government functions.

The crisis has prompted deep reflection on what the role of local government will be in the future. It has not been a temporary downturn followed by a return to previous conditions. The duration and severity of the crisis have raised questions about how government is financed, what services it provides, and how it interacts with citizens and other organizations in addressing community needs. The new reality has set the stage for true discourse among officials and citizens on the future of communities and the local governments that serve them.

Notes

1. Charles H. Levine, "More on Cut-Back Management: Hard Questions for Hard Times," *Public Administration Review* 39, no. 2 (1979): 179–183.

2. Gerald J. Miller, "Weathering the Local Government Fiscal Crisis: Short-Term Measures or Permanent Change?" *The Municipal Year Book 2010* (Washington, D.C.: ICMA, 2010), 34.

3. Christopher W. Hoene and Michael A. Pagano, *City Fiscal Conditions in 2010* (Washington, D.C.: National League of Cities, October 2010), nlc.org/ASSETS/AE26793 318A645C795C9CD11DAB3B39B/RB_CityFiscalConditions2010.pdf (accessed December 2, 2010).

4. Ronald Heifetz, Alexander Grashow, and Marty Linsky, "Leadership in a (Permanent) Crisis," *Harvard Business Review* (July/August 2009), coffou.com/bm-doc/leadership-in-a-permanent-crisis.pdf (accessed December 2, 2010).

5. Gerald J. Miller and James H. Svara, eds., *Navigating the Fiscal Crisis: Tested Strategies for Local Leaders* (white paper prepared for ICMA, Arizona State University, January 2009), icma.org/en/icma/priorities/public_policy/policy_papers (accessed December 2, 2010).

6. Robert J. O'Neill, Jr., "Excelling in Times of Fiscal Distress," *Governing* (October 1, 2008), governing.com/columns/mgmt-insights/Excelling-in-Times-of.html (accessed December 2, 2010); James H. Svara, "Innovation and Constructive Change in Cutback Management: A Compendium of Research and Commentary by Local Government Leaders" (background paper for *Navigating the Fiscal Crisis*; see note 5).

7. Jefferson County has determined that a low-priority activity such as the fairground can continue as it is entirely self-supporting; see Scott Collins, Brandon Hanlon, and Ed Scholz, "Faltering Economy: Time to Thoughtfully Challenge the Status Quo," *PM Magazine* 91 (June 2009): 6–9.

8. For more information on this program, see Karen Thoreson and James H. Svara, "Award-Winning Local Government Innovations, 2009," in *The Municipal Year Book 2010* (Washington, D.C.: ICMA, 2010), 43.

9. For more information on this program, see Thoreson and Svara, "Award-Winning Local Government Innovations, 2009," 39.

10. James H. Svara and Janet Denhart, eds., *Connected Communities: Local Governments as a Partner in Citizen Engagement and Community Building* (white paper prepared for the Alliance for Innovation, Arizona State University, October 15, 2010), transformgov.org/Documents/Document/Document/301763 (accessed December 2, 2010).

11. Miller, "Weathering the Local Government Fiscal Crisis," 36; James H. Svara, "Local Government Leadership in the Fiscal Crisis in the United States of America," *International Journal of Policy Studies* 1 (July 2010): 18.

CHAPTER 28

Lewiston and Other Cities Consider Property Tax Relief for Senior Citizens

Douglas Rooks

Kathleen Chase served for 16 years as the assessor for Wells. Back in the 1980s, when property values along the Route 1 commercial zone began skyrocketing, she came across an elderly woman who was trying to hold onto her home and large plot of land, but couldn't afford to pay the escalating property taxes.

"In the course of a few years, the value of her property went from $160,000 to $800,000," Chase said. "She was trying to pay a $7,500 tax bill with an income of less than $25,000. She was legally blind and she had no family to help."

This was back when the state's circuit breaker tax relief program had started, and for a few years "that worked just fine," Chase said. But when state revenues began declining, the Legislature capped reimbursements and the woman ultimately sold her property and moved away.

Chase decided that, if she ever had a chance to do something for people like that elderly woman, she would. This year, she did.

In her second term as state representative for Wells, she became ranking minority member on the joint Taxation Committee. From that post, she convinced her committee colleagues, and then the full Legislature, to unanimously adopt her bill, LD 1121, which authorizes municipalities to adopt tax-deferral programs

for seniors. Wells is now one of the towns considering such an ordinance.

But the prospect of a new locally administered property tax relief program concerns some municipal officials — and the debate over whether, and how, to design such programs has just gotten started.

In general, tax assessors like Chase have the most sympathy for elderly residents who feel they are being taxed beyond their ability to pay. She notes that the criteria to qualify for tax deferrals is fairly stringent — seniors must be 70 or over, have lived in their homestead for at least 10 years, and have incomes less than 300 percent of federal poverty guidelines.

Property taxes are deferred, not forgiven, and the heirs or property buyer must pay the full amount, plus interest, when the resident dies or the property is sold.

Questions from Tax Collectors

Tax collectors, however, have many questions about the program. Vera Parent, Tax Collector for Peru and president of the Maine Municipal Tax Collectors and Treasurers Association, wonders whether the existing system couldn't serve elderly taxpayers in this situation.

Originally published as "Debate Over Senior Property Tax Deferrals," *Maine Townsman*, Vol. 72, No. 9, October 2010, by the Maine Municipal Association, Augusta. Reprinted with permission of the publisher.

"There are no limits on the town's ability to abate taxes," she said. "There are other ways to handle the situation some taxpayers find themselves in."

Others wonder whether, if the Legislature considers this such a high priority, it couldn't create a state program to accomplish the same end, without asking towns and cities to take it on.

As it happens, the state did authorize such a program not long after the circuit breaker was enacted, but only a handful of taxpayers are still enrolled. When Chase first proposed her bill, it took the form of reopening applications to this nearly forgotten state program, enacted in 1989, that helps pay the property tax bills for seniors in exactly this situation.

David Ledew, director of Maine Revenue Services' property tax division, said 175 taxpayers signed up for the program before the Legislature, amid falling revenues, suspended enrollment.

"They reopened applications briefly twice, but then closed them for good," Ledew said.

In its peak year, fiscal 1992, the state was reimbursing municipalities $132,000 for 158 taxpayers who had taxes deferred. As residents died or sold their properties, enrollment dwindled to just 14 taxpayers by fiscal 2005. Only seven remain today, and their cases need to be administered each year.

In the meantime, concern about excessive property taxes rises each time there's a real estate boom — including the latest that ended with the 2008–09 recession — and various solutions are offered.

Chase and Ledew both said that by January of this year, when the Taxation Committee was again discussing the held-over bill, there was no possibility of a state appropriation.

The state also enacted significant reductions in the circuit breaker tax relief program for individuals, reducing the maximum reimbursement from $2,000 to $1,600. The Legislature cut the Homestead Exemption from $13,000 to $10,000, only half of which is reimbursed by the state.

By that time, Chase had decided a local program might work better anyway.

"There's a reluctance among some people, particularly elderly people, to get involved in a state program. They're more comfortable with something closer to home," she said.

Ledew essentially said there are some reasons why a state program might work better, at least under the original design.

"In theory, this could be administered more efficiently at the state level. The state has expertise and knowledge, and can do things that municipalities are not as familiar with," he said.

Before the Legislature cut back, MRS planned to add staff to handle applications and write rules — hiring that was never carried out.

Ledew said a lack of reliable funding has been a problem for senior deferrals and other state tax relief programs, including municipal revenue sharing.

He noted that in the mid–1990s, tax-deferral reimbursements were briefly cut to 90 percent, which prompted a number of taxpayers to leave the program.

Municipal and state budgets are fundamentally different in the way they are constructed, Ledew said.

"When the state faces a revenue shortfall, it starts looking for somewhere to cut, and that usually means everything," he said.

Municipalities, by contrast, "start with a budget plan, and then assess the taxes to pay for it," he said. Towns may cut back programs, but look at funding them first before making that decision. Under these circumstances, it seems a better bet that a municipal tax deferral program will continue as envisioned than one administered and funded by the state.

Towns Have a Choice

The new law permits, but does not require, municipalities to run their own property tax deferral programs. It became effective in July and towns are now discussing whether they want to participate. Among municipal officials, opinions differ about the need for and practicality of the program.

Assessors like Chase tend to be the most supportive. They often work with annual or periodic revaluations of property and see the effects of dramatic rises in the assessed value of commercial property or shoreline lots on the coast and interior lakes.

Tax collectors, who would administer the program, have more reservations. Paul Labrecque, Lewiston's tax collector, said situations where elderly taxpayers face unaffordable tax bills are rare. Over two decades, he can think of only a half dozen cases where substantial abatements were requested. Applications for poverty exemptions are even rarer.

Labrecque is concerned about the ability of municipalities to administer such programs. "The way I read this, the municipality has to file a lien on the property every year," he said. "Otherwise, the claim isn't legal."

Ledew confirms that this is the case — each year, the state files a list with the county registries. That recurring work is something for municipalities that don't have managers or that elect their tax collectors and treasurers to consider, before enacting local ordinances.

"If you have new people on the job, without the institutional memory, it could be an issue," Ledew said.

Labrecque said that Lewiston does set up payment plans and finds other ways to help people pay taxes. "We'll work with them to the umpteenth degree if they ask."

Whether many elderly taxpayers are "taxed out of their homes" can be seen in different lights. Some observers, such as Rep. Chase, say that most people would rather sell and move than ask for what they see as a form of charity. It is this group, supporters say, who would be most likely to use the deferral program.

Interest in Belgrade

Dennis Keschl, town manager of Belgrade, says there is considerable interest among the board of selectmen in offering a deferral program. Last year, Belgrade was one of a number of towns setting up a program, authorized by the state the previous year, that allows seniors to volunteer to work for the town and be forgiven up to $750 of their tax bills.

"We have a lot of lakefront and typically those lots have greatly increased in value," he said.

"We don't expect to have dozens of applicants — maybe there would just be two or three — but it may really help certain individuals."

Keschl has seen how some elderly residents struggle on fixed incomes. He recalled one case when a couple whose home had been in the family for seven generations had to come up with $11,000 for a drilled well.

"I don't know how they did it, and now the well is contaminated, too," he said. "We're trying to help them raise enough money so they can afford to buy a filter."

A committee will begin meeting shortly with the goal of writing an ordinance that can be considered at the 2011 Town Meeting. Figuring out how budget for the program, and whether there need to be any additional eligibility requirements, will be part of the discussion, Keschl said.

Another municipality actively considering a program is Wells. Selectmen Chairman Bob Foley said it was clear after an initial meeting in July that, "We like the concept of the program and see the need."

There are a number of issues that need to be addressed, however. One is that Wells has a number of homesteads where ownership has been transferred to a family trust or other legal entity, but whose residents — with lifetime tenancy — might be eligible.

"I don't see that the state law addresses that situation, so we might have to," he said.

There are also instances where mobile homes are located on leased lands, or where the owners have an agreement to convey the property to a land trust. "We don't want to discourage people from applying but we have to make sure we're covered legally," he said.

Local Budget Impact?

Perhaps the biggest municipal concern is how deferred taxes will be reflected in the annual budget.

"At some point, the program should pay for itself," said David Ledew at MRS. "There will be enough properties exiting the program and producing revenue for the town to balance the ones being enrolled."

Ledew acknowledged that the break-even point "is somewhat hypothetical." In some towns, it might take four years to reach, in others 10 or more.

In Lewiston, Labrecque wonders whether smaller towns might have more difficulties finding the right balance.

"We have a revenue stream of $45 million so it's hard to see much of an impact there," he said. "But what about a town with a much smaller budget?"

Ledew thinks one advantage of a local program is that it's easier to keep tabs on the properties enrolled. In one case, a taxpayer involved in the state program moved to a nursing home but the property remained unsold and deteriorated for years before the taxpayer died.

"We were concerned about whether we'd even get our money back. We did, barely, but that's the kind of situation you need to watch," he said.

CHAPTER 29

New York Provides Special Services to Low-Income Citizens

Gordon Berlin *and* James Riccio

It is hard to design public policies that are durable in good times and in bad. Since the social safety net was first conceived in the United States as a response to the Great Depression, policymakers have attempted to balance two competing goals: reducing poverty while limiting dependence on public handouts. Just as it would have been difficult to foresee the booming 1960s from the depths of the 1930s, few predicted today's severe downturn during the roaring 1990s. Then, with economic cycles seemingly in check and unemployment at historic lows, the nation moved to tie the social safety net more closely to work — by greatly expanding the Earned Income Tax Credit and placing time limits and strict work requirements on the cash welfare system, Temporary Assistance for Needy Families (TANF). In the grip of the Great Recession's aftermath, the wisdom of building a safety net around work alone is in question.

But what might work better? Can we strike a better balance between protecting vulnerable families in the short run without exacerbating the intergenerational transfer of poverty? Can we maintain a focus on work without impoverishing families in periods when work is scarce?

In March, MDRC released early evaluation results from Opportunity NYC–Family Rewards, New York City's bold (and controversial) demonstration and evaluation of a conditional cash transfer (CCT) program to help families break the cycle of poverty. Family Rewards offers cash payments to poor families to reduce immediate hardship and poverty but conditions this assistance on families' efforts to improve children's school performance, family preventive health care, and parents' work and training — in the hope of reducing poverty over the longer term. Thus, the evaluation seeks to answer two basic questions: (a) does the program quickly increase families' resources and improve the conditions in which children are raised, without causing any substantial reduction in parents' work efforts — an unintended consequence that income transfer programs risk — and (b) does it support families as they invest in education, preventive health care, and work, which can help them exit poverty sooner and reduce the chances of their children being poor as adults? Although it is much too soon for a final judgment (the study will continue through 2014), the MDRC report assesses early progress against these twin goals.

The initial findings show that Family Rewards substantially reduced current poverty and material hardship and had a range of modest

Originally published as "Paying for Good Behavior: Does New York City's Experiment with Conditional Cash Transfers Offer Lessons for the Safety Net in the United States?," *Pathways*, Summer 2010, by the Center for the Study of Poverty and Inequality, Stanford University, Stanford, CA. Reprinted with permission of the publisher.

positive results in improving some education, health-related, and work-related outcomes. Yet, the press coverage was largely and perhaps not surprisingly negative, given that the initiative has provoked criticism from both the left and the right. At the risk of oversimplifying, the right argues that "it's wrong to pay people for what they should already be doing" and the left says "it's demeaning to assume that poor people aren't doing the right thing and wrong to make them jump through hoops for money."

What both sides seem to ignore is that the United States (with the support of both Democrats and Republicans) has already made the majority of its safety net conditioned on the work effort of beneficiaries. Are there lessons from New York City's CCT experiment that might speak to the inadequacies of a predominantly work-based safety net? Before addressing this question, let us outline what Opportunity NYC–Family Rewards is — and what MDRC's evaluation has found so far.

Opportunity NYC–Family Rewards

Opportunity NYC–Family Rewards was launched by Mayor Michael Bloomberg and New York City's Center for Economic Opportunity in 2007 as an experimental, privately funded[1] program to help families in six of the city's highest poverty communities break the cycle of intergenerational poverty. Inspired by Mexico's pioneering Oportunidades program, CCT programs have grown rapidly across lower- and middle-income countries, and evaluations have found some important successes. Family Rewards is the first comprehensive CCT program in a developed country and, as such, has been the focus of much attention domestically and internationally.

An incentives-only program (with no social services or case management component), Family Rewards is coordinated by a private, nonprofit intermediary organization, Seedco, in partnership with six community-based organizations. It is being evaluated by MDRC, which helped design the initiative, through a randomized control trial.

The program includes an extensive set of rewards, most of which are available for three years, with the following conditions:

Education-focused conditions, which include meeting goals for children's attendance in school, achievement levels on standardized tests, and other school progress markers, as well as parents' engagement with their children's education.

Health-focused conditions, which include maintaining health insurance coverage for parents and their children, as well as obtaining age-appropriate preventive medical and dental checkups for each family member.

Workforce-focused conditions, aimed at parents, which include sustaining full-time work and completing approved education or job training activities.

Overall, the program offered 22 different incentives during its first two years, ranging in value from $20 to $600. Recognizing that poverty's causes would differ between developing and developed countries, the program designers purposely chose to test a wide variety of rewards, including academic achievement and parent's work, education, and training, activities that were not rewarded in Mexico or most other developing countries. The objective was to see where incentives would — and would not — work. By rewarding a wide range of activities, the program also gave families many different ways in which to earn money, and it was able to avoid attaching overly large amounts of money to any one activity or outcome. Based on assessments of the program's early operational experiences, including the complexity of administering so many different rewards, along with preliminary impact evidence, a number of rewards were discontinued for the third year. This was done to simplify the program, lower its costs, better align it with need, and make it easier to replicate should it prove to be successful.

Program Implementation

Overall, the rapidly launched program was successfully implemented after a first year in which operational kinks were being worked out. Families were substantially engaged with the program, earning reward payments of more than $3,000 per year, on average, during each of the first two years. Nearly all families (98 percent) earned at least some rewards in both program years (mostly in the education and health domains), and 65 percent earned payments in every period in which rewards were available.

The Evaluation

The evaluation uses a randomized control trial involving approximately 4,800 families and 11,000 children, half of whom can receive the cash incentives if they meet the required conditions, and half who have been assigned to a control group that cannot receive the incentives. The period covered in the report, beginning in September 2007 and ending in August 2009, encompasses a start-up phase as well as a stage when the program was beginning to mature. The report presents early findings on the program's effects on a wide range of outcome measures. For some measures, the results cover only the first program year, while for others they also cover part or all of the second year. No data are available yet on the third year. The evaluation findings are based on analyses of a wide variety of administrative records data, responses to a survey of parents that was administered about eighteen months after random assignment, and qualitative in-depth interviews with program staff and families.

Early Effects on Reducing Material Hardship and Poverty

The effects on reducing poverty and material hardships and on other economic outcomes were substantial. Family Rewards:

Reduced the share of families living in poverty by 11 percentage points and cut "severe poverty" (defined as having income less than 50 percent of the federal poverty level) by nearly half, reducing it from 30 percent of the control group to 17 percent among the program group.

Reduced measures of material hardship, including difficulty providing enough food for one's family (by 7 percentage points) and not being able to "make ends meet" (8 percentage points).

Increased the likelihood that parents had bank accounts by 22 percentage points, increased their

savings, and reduced their use of alternative banking institutions, such as check cashers, by 7 percentage points.

Increased the percent of parents who paid their children an allowance, the amount they paid, and share who required children to earn the allowance by completing an activity.

Effects on Children's Education

Overall, Family Rewards has had no effect so far on elementary and middle school students' attendance or achievement. (The absence of effects on attendance was not surprising given the high rates of school attendance, averaging about 90 percent, among younger students.) However, a survey of parents indicates that Family Rewards increased the likelihood that middle school students became involved in school-related activities, such as programs to help with schoolwork or homework, school clubs, school musical programs, and dance or art lessons. In addition, parents of elementary school students were somewhat more likely to help their children with homework and to enroll them in an afterschool program that helps with homework.

Among high school students overall, Family Rewards increased the proportion of high school students with a 95 percent attendance rate by 5 percentage points — but has had no overall effect on student achievement. However, among the subgroup of incoming ninth-graders who scored "proficient" in eighth grade — that is, the students who met minimum academic standards necessary to perform high school level work and thus could take advantage of the performance incentives (although many still struggle in high school) — there were positive impacts:

Reduced the proportion of students who repeated the ninth grade by 6 percentage points.

Increased the likelihood of having a 95 percent or better attendance rate (in year 2) by 15 percentage points.

Increased the likelihood of earning at least 22 credits (11 credits per year are needed to remain on track for on-time graduation) by 8 percentage points.

Increase the likelihood of passing at least two Regents exams (New York's statewide achievement exams)[2] by 6 percentage points.

Effects on Family Preventive Health Care

The health-related incentives of the Family Rewards program were designed to encourage low-income families to maintain insurance coverage and to adopt better preventive health care practices. It turned out that a higher proportion of families than the program's designers had expected were already receiving health insurance coverage and practicing preventive health care. This finding may reflect the success of efforts by New York State and New York City to expand access to health coverage in recent years. Although the high rates of insurance coverage left little room for improvement on this outcome, the analysis found that Family Rewards still had small, positive impacts on a variety of health-related indicators (which are often difficult to move):

> Increased families' consistency of health insurance coverage (by 2–3 percentage points).
>
> Reduced reliance on hospital emergency rooms for routine care (by 2 percentage points) and increased receipt of preventive medical care.
>
> Increased receipt of at least two preventive dental care visits by 10 percentage points.

Effects on Parents' Work and Training

Family Rewards' early impacts on employment outcomes are mixed. The findings point to gains in the likelihood of full-time employment and average earnings but not in jobs covered by the unemployment insurance (UI) system. According to an 18-month survey of parents, the program increased the likelihood of working at the time of the interview by 6 percentage points, driven by an increase in full-time work. At the same time, the program also led to a small *reduction* in average quarterly employment rates (by 1.4 percentage points) in *UI-covered* jobs over a 12-month follow-up period, according to administrative records data. However, the effect on average annual earnings from such jobs (a decline of $286) was not statistically significant.

Some jobs are not covered by the state's UI system, such as self-employment, federal government employment, and out-of state work. The UI system also misses informal (casual or irregular) jobs that are never reported to state agencies. It is not clear why the effects of the program would vary across types of employment. Perhaps for some parents, non–UI jobs were easier to get in a period when the economic downturn was accelerating, particularly those that offered the full-time hours necessary to qualify for the program's work rewards. Such jobs may also have been more attractive options if they were more conveniently located, easier to obtain, or offered more flexible schedules than UI-covered jobs.

With regard to incentives for training, Family Rewards had a small but statistically significant impact (of 2 to 3 percentage points) on increasing the likelihood of receiving a training certificate or associate's degree.

Longer-term follow-up will be important for assessing how the program's marketing of the workforce rewards, which was intensified in years two and three, coupled with the trough of the labor market at that time, affect these results. Still, it is noteworthy that, despite transferring substantial amounts of cash to families, the program has not led to any appreciable reduction in work effort.[3]

Implications of the Early Results

Evaluations in other nations have convincingly shown that CCT programs can reduce poverty and improve the consumption of goods and services (for example, food consumption) among very poor families — but these results were seen in countries with undeveloped or nonexistent safety net systems. These CCT programs have also had some positive effects on human capital development outcomes, including school attendance, nutrition, and infant growth. In school attendance, the magnitude of Family Rewards' effects is roughly comparable to what has been found in evaluations of CCTs in other countries. In other areas, for example, school achievement (as measured by standardized tests) and parents' work, education, and training, Family Rewards is among the first to have found any effects.

The initial results from the New York City project show that CCTs can make an immediate difference in the lives of poor families in a developed country by increasing family income by 23 percent on average. Nearly all families were able to qualify for at least some rewards, mostly in the education and health domains — meaning that, even in a depressed labor market, poor families could make non-work efforts that would bring needed income. This income reduced measures of economic hardship as well, which are notoriously hard to move. It is important to emphasize that these effects on poverty did *not* lead to major unintended consequences, such as substantial reductions in work effort.

While many families were rewarded for efforts they would likely have undertaken without the program, Family Rewards did have modest effects on behavioral outcomes in each domain, suggesting that an income-transfer program with achievable conditions attached can provide a modest boost in positive behaviors. It's too early to say whether these effects will be sustained or grow or whether they are worth the cost — questions that will be answered as MDRC follows these families for another year in this three-year program and then two more years after it ends this summer.

In the meantime, the nation is looking for ways to strike a better balance between fighting dependence and fighting poverty in its safety net programs, to meet short-term needs while investing in better long-term outcomes, and to do so in a way that is more responsive to economic downturns and poor labor markets. Early lessons from Opportunity NYC–Family Rewards suggest that cash transfers with reasonable conditions attached can be a feasible and effective way to boost the income of poor families, raising some out of poverty, while maintaining the ethos of reciprocity and responsibility that is valued by American society (and certainly its elected representatives). But if policymakers are interested solely in CCTs as an inducement to change behaviors thought to be at the heart of long-term and intergenerational poverty, the early effects in this area will have to grow over time to be truly cost-effective. Longer-term results at the three- and five-year points due in 2011 and 2013 will provide those answers.

NOTES

1. These funders include Bloomberg Philanthropies, The Rockefeller Foundation, The Starr Foundation, the Open Society Institute, the Robin Hood Foundation, the Tiger Foundation, The Annie E. Casey Foundation, American International Group, the John D. and Catherine T. MacArthur Foundation, and New York Community Trust.

2. Regents exams are administered to all public high school students in New York State. Students must pass at least five tests in specified subject areas in order to graduate with a diploma recognized by the New York State Board of Regents, which sets standards and regulations for all public schools.

3. The impact evaluation tests the program's effects on a large number of outcome variables, raising the risk that, with so many estimates produced, some will appear statistically significant simply by chance. However, positive effects take on more credibility when there are many of them, and when they are part of broader pattern of results, as is the case in the findings that are emphasized here. For example, the positive effects on more-proficient high school students held across a range of outcome measures. Equally important, the lack of education effects for elementary and middle school students and for less-proficient high school students held across most of the outcomes examined for those groups. Furthermore, in each of the behavioral domains examined, many of the positive effects were on activities or accomplishments for which incentives were offered, such as insurance coverage and dental visits in the health domain, high attendance and passing Regents tests in the educational domain, and full-time employment in the work domain. In other words, the effects highlighted by the study were not simply a random assortment of positive impacts.

CHAPTER 30

Peoria Uses Performance Measures to Improve Its Budget Process

Peter Christensen *and* Katie Gregory

The City of Peoria, Arizona, is no stranger to performance management. For years, the city has worked to refine a system that has become a useful tool for making budgetary decisions and promoting accountability throughout the organization. The city has received recognition for its efforts from the Government Finance Officers Association's Distinguished Budget Presentation Award Program and from International City/ County Management Association (ICMA) Center for Performance Measurement. Still, Peoria has a long way to go to connect all the dots of its strategic planning and performance measurement systems and become a truly data-driven organization.

Peoria's New Reality

Stretching across 176 square miles in the northwest corner of the Phoenix metropolitan area, Peoria is a full-service municipality with a population of a little more than 150,000 and a general fund budget of more than $150 million. Peoria operates under the council-manager form of government, with a mayor elected at large and six council members elected from geographic districts. The city manager oversees more than 1,100 employees in 14 departments.

Peoria is known for quality schools and well-planned residential neighborhoods. The community also offers outstanding recreational amenities, including Lake Pleasant (Arizona's second largest lake), the Peoria Sports Complex (the spring training home of the San Diego Padres and Seattle Mariners), and the award-winning Rio Vista Community Park. The hotels, restaurants, and automobile dealerships surrounding the sports complex form an entertainment district that is a major source of revenue.

During the first decade of the new millennium, Peoria was one of the fastest-growing cities in Arizona and the United States. The city's growth spurt came to a screeching halt in 2008, however, with the onset of the housing crisis and recession, and growth-related revenues have all but dried up. Like other Arizona cities, Peoria is highly dependent on sales and income taxes (the state shares sales and income taxes with cities and counties), which have also fallen off dramatically over the last two years. Almost overnight, the growth focus that had dominated Peoria and its neighboring communities for so many years gave way to an entirely new reality that would require creative thinking and innovative management tools.

Originally published as "Becoming a Data-Driven Organization," *Government Finance Review*, Vol. 26, No. 2, April 2010, by the Government Finance Officers Association, Chicago, IL. Reprinted with permission of the publisher.

Performance Management

Early on, Peoria's leadership embraced performance management as an important tool for managing programs and services and for allocating city resources. The city has incorporated the recommendations of the GFOA, ICMA, and other leading organizations into its performance management program. For example, performance measures are organized by program areas, are based on service goals and objectives, measure outcomes as well as efficiency and outputs, and are reported over a three-year timeframe.

Some departments and programs lend themselves more easily to performance measurement than others. The most effective programs use performance measures and the associated program descriptions, goals, and objectives to tell a story. For these programs, an outsider would be able to pick up a performance report and quickly understand their purpose and key functions, and form opinions about whether they are achieving desired outcomes in an efficient manner. Many of the organization's successful programs have incorporated satisfaction surveys to measure the extent to which outcomes are being met in the eyes of their customers.

The city has taken an active role in comparative performance measurement, or benchmarking. Since 2005, Peoria has participated in ICMA's Comparative Performance Measurement Program with some 150 other cities across the country. Recognizing the difficulties inherent in benchmarking, namely the need to normalize data in order to facilitate meaningful assessments, the city nonetheless believes there is value in comparing performance across jurisdictions. This is particularly true when comparing cities in the same state or region. As such, Peoria is one of 11 cities that participate in the Arizona Consortium. The consortium focuses on sharing core service data and provides an opportunity to follow up on service delivery techniques that have proven to be effective, efficient, and successful.

The collection and reporting of good performance data is the foundation of a useful performance management program, but not the end thereof. Unless this information is used to make decisions about resource allocation and service delivery, it is really little more than window dressing. Although Peoria still has a long way to go, the city strives to integrate performance data into its decision making. To date, Peoria has been most effective at incorporating performance data into the annual budget process. Executive leadership and city council members are given performance information during their budget sessions, and they often use this information in their review of funding recommendations.

Faced with a substantial budget deficit and the need to adapt to a new revenue base in a slow-growth environment, Peoria's leadership has emphasized a new way of doing business that relies heavily on performance management concepts. The focus of this effort has been to deliver core city services as efficiently and effectively as possible by aligning resources with strategic goals and using performance data to measure the results. To this end, Peoria has completed a citywide organizational restructuring and developed a new organizational strategic plan based on city council goals and citizen survey feedback.

As part of the ongoing fiscal 2011 budget process, each department was charged with developing a department operating plan. The purpose of these plans is to encourage departments to think strategically and align their service activities and resources to achieve program and organizational goals. Each operating plan is supposed to include a department mission and vision, discuss council and organizational priorities that influence their operations, describe the key functions of the department, identify the desired outcomes of each key function, and estimate the resources needed to achieve those outcomes. Peoria's management team is using these plans to balance the 2011 budget and make the difficult decisions required to do so.

Lessons Learned

Through years of trial and error, Peoria has learned several important lessons in implementing performance measurement in a local government organization.

An incremental process. Effective performance management systems do not happen overnight, nor is there a mile marker to indicate that your organization's system has "arrived." An effective performance management system incorporates the basic elements identified by the GFOA and other leaders in the field, and is constantly evolving and adapting to the changing needs of your organization.

Flexibility is key. Not all performance measures are created equally, nor should they be. Flexibility from department to department and program to program is both necessary and desirable. Don't fall into the trap of forcing your entire organization into the same mold. Whatever technology you use to collect and report on performance measures should be sufficiently flexible to accommodate different approaches.

Rightsize your system. When it comes to performance measurement, less is often more. Don't measure or report on things that are neither meaningful nor useful, particularly if you're doing so just for the sake of impressing people with the sheer volume of information you can collect. This approach often backfires, overwhelming stakeholders to the point of undermining the entire effort. Know your audience and tailor your reports to the different needs of different stakeholders.

Don't punish honest reporting. It should come as no surprise that some departments attempt to manipulate their performance measures to make themselves look good. Obviously, such behavior undermines the integrity of the entire system. Auditing is one way to keep data manipulation in check, but it is costly and time consuming. Leaders can often remove the motivation to skew performance measures by creating an environment that emphasizes continuous learning and improvement, and does not punish those who fall short of their targets.

Wanted: organizational champions. It sounds clichéd, but it's difficult to imagine a successful performance management system that does not have the full support of the city manager or administrator. Lacking this imperative, few departments will invest the energy and effort needed to do performance measurement justice. Finding individuals within the departments who believe in performance measurement and will champion the cause among their co-workers can be the difference between a satisfactory system and a truly effective one.

Coming Soon: PeoriaStat

Even though Peoria has been successful in using performance measures in the budget process, it has struggled to keep performance measurement relevant once the budget process has concluded. A number of departments do a good job of using their performance measures to manage programs and services, but there is little emphasis on performance measurement on a citywide level outside of the budget process. To remedy this and to incorporate performance measurement into the city's larger strategic planning and decision-making processes, the city is preparing to begin a new performance initiative known as PeoriaStat.

As it is currently envisioned, PeoriaStat will involve monthly performance reporting by departments and regular review sessions. These review sessions will occur monthly, with each department participating at least quarterly. The department head will meet with the city manager, the two deputy city managers, and the performance measurement coordinator to go over the department's key outcomes. The intent is not to belabor the minutiae of performance measurement, but rather to act as a catalyst to continuous improvement through regular evaluation of programs and services important to city stakeholders.

CHAPTER 31

Philadelphia and Other Cities Reconsider Their Contract Services

Russell Nichols

Last summer, residents of Maywood, Calif., woke up one morning to find the government as they knew it gone. After years of corruption and mismanagement, the small, blue-collar city south of Los Angeles fired almost all of its employees, dismantled its police department and contracted with a neighboring city to take over most municipal tasks. On July 1, local officials announced that Maywood had become the country's first city to be fully outsourced.

It was an unprecedented move spurred by a loss of commercial liability insurance and Workers' Compensation. As the city drowned in deficits and faced multiple lawsuits, city leaders saw outsourcing as a light at the end of a collapsing tunnel.

But it was only a mirage.

Bell, Calif., the city that Maywood officials had tapped to run its services, erupted with a pay and pension scandal, forcing several top Bell officials to resign. By September, Bell had scrapped its contract with Maywood, leaving the city to fend for itself and find new contractors for its outsourcing hopes.

The search for financial salvation is sweeping the country as local governments grapple with waning sales and property tax revenues. The economic recession has strangled budgets, forcing layoffs and the disbanding of departments. Feeling pushed to the brink of bankruptcy, cities are trying to find effective ways to make do with less. Maywood, in its outsourcing attempt, may be the most extreme example, but in California and other states in the past decade, more public officials have turned to outside sources for help in providing services at a lower cost to the state.

In theory, the idea of contracting public services to private companies to cut costs makes sense. If someone is willing to fix streets or put out fires for less money, that should be a plus for a government's bottom line. Many state and local governments have identified hundreds of millions of dollars in savings by hiring outside contractors — or a neighboring city's services — to handle tasks like trash collection, pothole repair, and water and wastewater treatment.

But according to analysts, outsourcing is by no means a perfect solution. Some agencies don't have the metrics in place to prove in advance that outsourcing a service will save money. Problems from poorly conceived contracts can create cost increases that surpass the costs of in-house services, and if there's shoddy contract oversight, a government is vulnerable to corruption and profiteering. The privatization of public services can erode accountability and transparency, and drive governments deeper into debt. "Governments at all levels are just desperate to balance their budgets, and they're

Originally published as "Selling Out," *Governing*, Vol. 24, No. 3, December 2010, by e.Republic Inc., Washington, D.C. Reprinted with permission of the publisher.

grasping at privatization as a panacea," says Susan Duerksen, director of communications for In the Public Interest, a project that examines privatization and contracting. "But there's evidence that it often is a very bad deal with hidden costs and consequences when you turn over public service to a for-profit company."

Various governments — from small towns all the way up to federal agencies — have been sending public services to the private sector since the 1980s. The trend stems from the common belief that private companies can help governments save or make money by doing jobs faster and cheaper, or managing a public asset more efficiently.

This past March, for example, New Jersey Gov. Chris Christie created the state Privatization Task Force to review privatization opportunities within state government and identify barriers. In its research, the task force not only identified estimated annual savings from privatization totaling more than $210 million, but also found several examples of successful efforts in other states. As former mayor of Philadelphia, Pennsylvania Gov. Ed Rendell saved $275 million by privatizing 49 city services. Chicago has privatized more than 40 city services. Since 2005, it has generated more than $3 billion in upfront payments from private-sector leases of city assets. In 2005, West Virginia Gov. Joe Manchin worked to transform the state's Workers' Compensation Commission into a private insurance carrier, BrickStreet Insurance. That has led Workers' Compensation rates to decline about 30 percent statewide, translating to more than $150 million in annual employer savings.

"Sterile philosophical debates about 'public versus private' are often detached from the day-to-day world of public management," the New Jersey Privatization Task Force reported. "Over the last several decades, in governments at all levels throughout the world, the public sector's role has increasingly evolved from direct service provider to that of an indirect provider or broker of services; governments are relying far more on networks of public, private and nonprofit organizations to deliver services."

The report took careful note of another key factor: The states most successful in privatization created a permanent, centralized entity to manage and oversee the operation, from project analysis and vendor selection to contracting and procurement. For governments that forgo due diligence, choose ill-equipped contractors and fail to monitor progress, however, outsourcing deals can turn into costly disasters.

No industry has gone through greater outsourcing catastrophes in the past year than government IT. Last fall, Texas cut short its seven-year contract with IBM, an $863 million deal that called for IBM to provide data center and disaster recovery services for 27 state agencies. When an audit criticized the state's Department of Information Resources for lax oversight, inadequate staffing and sloppy service, the partnership fell apart. In Virginia, the state's 10-year, $2.3 billion IT contract with Northrop Grumman to run the state's computers, servers, e-mail systems and help desk services also has been plagued by inadequate planning, cost overruns and poor service.

Technology plays such a critical role in the storage and delivery of vital data that even minor delays and deficiencies can disrupt business operations, such as car registration renewals, and unemployment and medical care services. In August, a storage area network failure in Virginia knocked two dozen state agencies' computer systems offline in another devastating blow to the state's IT outsourcing contract. A week later, the state Department of Motor Vehicles still couldn't process drivers' licenses at customer service centers because databases were down.

"The problem is that outsourcing deals are really about risk," says Adam Strichman, co-founder of Sanda Partners, an outsourcing consultancy. "You're taking the risk of the unknown and dumping that on your supplier," he says. "You're outsourcing a problem to a company that has limited control over the root cause of the problem." The only way for a public-private partnership to work, he suggests, is to drive transformation from within the agency. And that's the hard part. Red tape usually prevents governments from making significant modifications, and private companies lack the authority to enforce real changes. When such a public-private stalemate stunts a project, it helps to have an exit strategy.

Those risks extend beyond the technology world. In 2009, in the wake of an audit of economic development agreements between Niagara Falls and two developers, New York state Comptroller Thomas P. DiNapoli discovered that the projects faltered because the city failed to monitor development contracts. One of the projects, a downtown retail mall, has been vacant since 2000; the second project, which began in 1997, yielded nothing more than a rudimentary building foundation.

"Before governments hire outside contractors, it's important to examine the cost-effectiveness," says Nicole Hanks, deputy press secretary of the state comptroller's office. "More times than not, it's less expensive to use state workers instead of outside contractors."

A good outsourcing deal starts with a thorough cost-benefit analysis to see if a third party can effectively deliver services better and more cheaply than public employees. Strichman says governments should hire an outsourcing consultant who can provide an independent assessment. But even with a consultant, conflicts of interest can tarnish a golden opportunity. After all, private companies may want to provide a service efficiently and well — and often do — but governments must ride herd on implementation of the contract. As Duerksen points out, a company's motivation "is not the common good; it's profit. If they can cut corners in any way, they often do."

In that regard, the provider that offers the lowest bid might not be the best option. But with his experience in several large-scale government outsourcing deals, Strichman has seen first-hand that in a bidding war, the company that has "a liberal interpretation for the lowest price wins," which inevitably leads to strife when high expectations meet underachievement. "Anyone can bid any outsourcing deal 5 percent cheaper, but the problem is you don't know what they cut out," he says. "When price reductions appear unrealistic, there's no magic. They are unrealistic."

Even with the proper oversight channels, policies won't work if departments don't participate. In 2005, the Wisconsin Legislature passed a law that required a cost-benefit analysis be completed for any purchase of service more than $25,000. The law outlines analysis procedures and reporting requirements. Soon after, the Contract Sunshine Act was enacted, requiring all Wisconsin agencies to provide online information about state contracts in excess of $10,000.

The laws were created to promote transparency and to ensure that agencies complete an effective cost-benefit analysis prior to procurements. But compliance has been low, says Janice Mueller, state auditor for the Wisconsin Legislative Audit Bureau. "We were asked to look and see why state agencies are not consistently reporting," she says. "It's really difficult to compel compliance."

In other cases, outsourcing efforts may be stifled by union contracts or a lack of available services. Mayor Sharon McShurley in Muncie, Ind., wanted to outsource the city's fire protection services to save money. But the city ceased its cost analysis after realizing that no such private services existed in the area. "It does tie our hands as administrators trying to figure out how to balance the budget and provide services with a reduction in revenue," she says. "I like the idea of outsourcing. Competition drives prices down. We don't have the revenue that we used to have."

CHAPTER 32

Portland Uses a New Financial Management Assessment Process

Michael Bailey, Karen Feher *and* Shayne Kavanagh

Every jurisdiction strives to achieve excellence in financial management. But knowing how effective you are means looking at each component of financial management to learn what is working well and what might benefit from improvement. The more thorough the assessment, the more the organization can do to ensure optimal performance.

In the United Kingdom, the CIPFA FM Model has been helping to define good financial management practices for local governments for decades. A large number of U.K. local jurisdictions use this self-evaluation tool to develop financial management approaches that fit their business goals and service aspirations. To help U.S. and Canadian governments build on this success, the Government Finance Officers Association has adapted the Chartered Institute of Public Finance and Accountancy (CIPFA) model for use in North America. The new version, called the CIPFA-GFOA FM Model, invites users to test their own financial management practices against professional best practices.

Financial Leadership

In addition to the immediately understandable benefit of pursuing world-class performance in financial management — that is, achieving fiscal efficiency and effectiveness throughout the organization — there are also other, perhaps less obvious, advantages. In this era of very tight budgets, combined with increasing scrutiny of how public funds are spent, it is useful to have a tool that reviews the jurisdiction's adherence to best practices. Good financial management is how managers meet their obligation to spend taxpayer money carefully, using it to improve services that affect the lives of citizens. An organization that handles its finances well has a solid foundation for providing services the public wants and needs, which is the business of every government manager.

The role of the finance officer requires leadership as well as stewardship. Finance officers are helping transform their organizations — a process that has taken on a new urgency as a result of the Great Recession. The FM Model is useful in helping leaders focus on and track improvement efforts. The model can help an organization ratchet performance up through an initial round of assessment and improvements, and then be used to revisit each area at a later time, so the organization can build on its successes, continually improving.

One aspect of good leadership is engaging

Originally published as "Improve Performance Using the GFOA's New Financial Management Assessment Tool," *Government Finance Review*, Vol. 27, No. 4, August 2011, by the Government Finance Officers Association, Chicago, IL. Reprinted with permission of the publisher.

others in the jurisdiction's improvement efforts. You achieve more buy in when you explain what you're doing and why, and the best practice target you're working toward. At the same time, feedback from disparate sources can point out problems you hadn't noticed, and point to solutions you hadn't considered. Engaging the following constituencies can be useful:

- *Customers.* The FM Model can help you analyze how easily other units within the government can access financial management services and how well their needs are addressed.
- *Stakeholders.* Demonstrating your efforts toward improvement can enhance your credibility with interested citizens, board members, and other managers, and further enhance your role as a trusted advisor.
- *The Community.* Community volunteers can participate or help with the evaluation and inform the local media of the project. While it might not be realistic to have citizens participate in a review of financial management practices, you might want to consider a public forum for the project itself. You could find that the community appreciates the efforts you're making; on the other hand, public scrutiny of internal financial processes could make the organization vulnerable, so it is important to weigh the pros and cons beforehand.

Using the FM Model

The GFOA-CIPFA FM Model is built around a number of "good practice statements"—fundamental statements of how a government organization should manage its finances. A series of detailed evaluation questions is associated with each of these statements, and answering these questions allows users to assess their jurisdiction's practices in light of each fundamental statement. The good practice statements cover each of the traditional subdivisions of financial management (e.g., budgeting, accounting, debt), and then they are divided into three styles of financial management and four dimensions.

Three styles. Governments can use the FM Model to chart a path of growth through the three styles:

- *Securing Stewardship.* The baseline style, the bedrock of financial management, emphasizes control, probity, meeting regulatory requirements, and accountability.
- *Supporting Performance.* A step beyond securing stewardship, the "supporting performance" step emphasizes responsiveness to the public; efficiency and effectiveness, and commitment to improving performance.
- *Enabling Transformation.* The highest level allows organizations to transform themselves into jurisdictions that are strategic and citizen-centered, oriented toward the future, proactive in managing change and risk, focused on outcomes, and receptive to new ideas.

Four dimensions. The four dimensions cover a blend of "hard" attributes — things that can be measured — and other features that are necessary for financial management to be effective. The four dimensions are:

- *Leadership.* Leadership focuses on strategic direction, business management, and how the vision and involvement of the organization's board members and senior managers affect its financial management. The tone set from the top is critical.
- *People.* The competencies and the engagement of staff is a crucial element.
- *Processes.* The organization's ability to design, manage, control, and improve its financial processes to support its policy and strategy also need to be examined.
- *Stakeholders.* Another key consideration is the relationships between the jurisdiction and any person or group with an interest in its financial health (e.g., governments, auditors, taxpayers, suppliers, citizens, partners). This dimension also deals with customer relationships inside the organization, between financial services and the operating departments they support.

Together, the styles and dimensions provide a nuanced perspective on financial management. The good practice statements and their associated evaluation questions explore each point of intersection between the styles and dimensions, and the results are tallied into a profile. The process allows finance offices to determine the extent to which their organizations embody any or all of these attributes, and to chart a path of improvement based on what the organization expects and needs from the finance function.

The FM Model is intended to be a collaborative tool. Members of the financial management team work together with internal (and sometimes external) stakeholders to conduct the evaluation. This approach provides a more accurate picture of financial management than one person's perceptions would, and it helps engage stakeholders in understanding how financial management works today and how it might change in the future.

Metro's Experience

Metro is the regional government for the Portland, Oregon, metropolitan area. The 28 jurisdictions it represents include three counties and 25 cities with a total population of approximately 1.5 million. Metro is a relatively young agency, with responsibilities that have grown steadily over the years. Founded in 1970 as a planning agency, it first expanded to do regional solid waste and transportation planning and to manage the Oregon Zoo and an urban growth boundary intended to reduce urban sprawl. In the 1980s, Metro acquired responsibility for wholesale regional solid waste operations, including managing a landfill and transfer station. When the Oregon Convention Center opened in 1990, Metro took on management responsibility for it and several performing arts venues as well. In the 1990s, the agency built a solid waste transfer station and assumed responsibility for an exposition center and the Multnomah County parks system. Metro voters also approved two substantial bond measures to purchase open spaces for future generations and several new regional parks.

Because Metro had no central policies or operating procedures, each new function imposed its own set of policies and procedures,

creating silos of financial operations and leading to duplication and inconsistent policies. Over the last several years, the organization has been working on breaking down these silos. It began by developing broad policies to guide operations in the areas of credit, investment, and capital asset management. Next, Metro merged the separate accounting funds each function had come with (except for those that had legal restrictions) into a consolidated general fund and changed its management structure to combine like functions into centers. It still lacked documented, consistent, agency-wide operational policies, however, as well as a central record of what already existed.

Metro was helping the GFOA adapt CIPFA's FM Model for North American use at the time (see the "Filling a Need" sidebar), and it became readily apparent that this tool could be quite useful in documenting processes and identifying areas that might need improvement. It is also a tool for documenting policies and consolidating existing procedures into one agency-wide procedure, when appropriate. Metro's finance team, comprising department finance managers and central budget managers and staff, realized that the model's dimensional nature melds the financial processes with the goals of the agency and the needs of stakeholders, pulling together all the important aspects of financial management. The model emphasizes stewardship and performance while providing opportunities for transformation to a higher level: from good financial management to great financial management.

The FM Model identifies all significant financial functions and requires documentation of how each function is fulfilled. This process helps the agency focus on needed improvements and provides peace of mind about the areas that are already operating well. Importantly, the FM Model's detailed list of questions for each good practice statement makes very clear what it means to meet that standard.

Metro took a team approach to evaluating its performance under the FM Model; all departments were represented. The organization also involved staff members who have technical knowledge about the process being evaluated or who perform the function. A broad view of the agency's existing processes and procedures began to take shape, and the organization started garnering agreement on what common policies could be developed.

Realizing that the first assessment would be the most time consuming, Metro decided to approach it on a two-year schedule. During the first year, team members reviewed the statements and graded the organization, providing documentation for their answers. In the second year, Metro reviewed the grading and finished the documentation. The agency is already using the process to identify areas of success and areas that would benefit from focused improvement. The FM Model has helped Metro achieve the following:

- A comprehensive review of financial management.
- An understanding of existing competencies in those functions.
- A method for verifying performance.
- A way to discover duplications of effort.
- A means for focusing on areas needing improvement.
- An opportunity to compare the agency's practices to industry best practices.

Conclusions

No matter how good an organization's business plan, comprehensive plan, or strategic plan, solid financial management is needed to support its goals and aspirations. The CIPFA-GFOA FM Model provides a way to create a healthy and engaging dialog within your jurisdiction about how the finance function is positioned to help accomplish the organization's goals. The FM Model will become an essential tool for those who are responsible for the finance function, helping them assess their performance and create a high performing unit that is able to secure stewardship, support organizational performance, and effect organizational transformation.

Filling a Need

The GFOA identified a need for jurisdictions to evaluate their financial management practices in the context of a national standard. After considering approaches such as an accreditation program, GFOA officials and board members concluded that the best approach would be to develop a self-evaluation tool based on the association's strong legacy of best practices, research, and consulting work.

The GFOA first checked to see if this approach was in place elsewhere. This search led to the Chartered Institute of Public Finance and Accountancy (CIPFA), a United Kingdom-based organization that is similar to the GFOA. CIPFA developed the CIPFA FM Model, which has been in use for a number of years as a self-assessment tool for public-sector finance departments. The two organizations formed an agreement to bring the FM Model to North America.

To adapt the CIPFA model for use by jurisdictions in the United States and Canada, GFOA staff reviewed the model against the association's publications and integrated it with GFOA best practices. The revised model was then examined by a task force of GFOA members, comprising practitioners who have served on GFOA standing committees or as instructors in GFOA training sessions, or have written for GFOA publications. After their own review, task force members field tested the model in their own organizations.

The resulting CIPFA-GFOA FM Model is a resource for the entire organization. Together, finance professionals, business managers, and boards can use the new FM Model to develop the approach that best fits their jurisdiction. The model can help create a profile of the organization's strengths and weaknesses, the organization's predominant style of financial management, and the degree to which that style supports the organization's strategic goals. It can also help assure board members about the organization's financial management practices. The model allows staff to test existing arrangements against the best practices it describes and to identify improvements, encouraging change. It also can be used as the basis for broader engagement with the customers and stakeholders of the financial management function, as well as bolstering the profile of the finance officer as a leader in the organization.

CHAPTER 33

Provo Uses Employees and Citizens to Balance Its Budget

John Borget

The City of Provo, Utah, has taken a unique approach to its budget process this year — a team approach that uses partnerships between employees and residents. Given the fiscal challenges the city was facing when its new mayor was elected in November 2009, he wanted to get a head start on the budgeting process for the coming fiscal year. The mayor was a newcomer to the public sector, coming from a private business and entrepreneurial background. He gathered together some of the brightest financial minds in Provo to serve as another set of eyes and ears and to provide input on how to prepare a budget in these difficult economic times.

Provo, a city of 120,000 residents in the heart of the Intermountain West, has a young, dynamic population. It is home to Brigham Young University, which has 35,000 students, and to many of the students at nearby Utah Valley University, with 23,000 students. Provo also has a strong and vibrant business community, and has been recognized as one of the most business-friendly cities in the United States.

But even with a robust local economy and a rapidly growing metropolitan area, Provo has been subject to the challenges of the current global recession. Like most cities in Utah, the city government's general fund revenue is largely dependent on sales tax and other revenues that are similarly reactive to the economy. During the boom years of the first decade of the 21st century, Provo's governmental services expanded, and the city funded a number of improvements in the quality of life of its citizens, including a new performing arts center, improvements to the city's aquatic center, new parks, and expanded police protection. So the city found itself in mid to late 2009 with increased demand for resources in an era of dramatically declining revenues.

Developing a Recommendation

Before taking office, the mayor-elect decided to form a Citizens Advisory Committee that would include bankers, budget officers, chief financial officers, a former council member, and certified public accountants, all of whom brought important and needed skill sets to the table. During the transition period between the election and the inauguration, members of this committee met weekly in the early morning hours, along with the city's finance team, to educate committee members about the city's financial status. This included updates on revenues, expenditures, employee compensation

Originally published as "Provo Brings Employees and Citizens Together to Identify Budget Cuts," *Government Finance Review*, Vol. 26, No. 4, August 2010, by the Government Finance Officers Association, Chicago, IL. Reprinted with permission of the publisher.

and benefits, budgeted expenditures, previous city budget philosophy, and budget cuts already in place. Key staff members including the assistant director of human resources, the public works director, and the energy department director were asked to present critical budget information to the committee. The education process took approximately two months.

Then, the mayor asked the committee to develop a recommendation to balance the general fund budget for fiscal 2011, which had an expected $3 million deficit. The city's largest revenue source is sales tax, which had declined more than 20 percent since the start of the recession. When faced with a budget deficit in the past, the previous administration had espoused a philosophy of reducing all department budgets by the same percentage across the board. The incoming administration, however, was facing budget cuts greater than 7 percent of operating expenses and took the position early in the process that it did not make sense to do an across-the-board cut. Such cuts would likely have a serious impact on vital services provided to residents. The new administration decided to take a "surgical approach" by evaluating the need for the city to continue providing all current services, along with its ability to do so, and scrutinizing all levels and functions of government. These kinds of budget reductions would be ongoing and should put the city in a better position for future years if the economy was slow to improve.

Seeking Employee Input

The Citizens Advisory Committee and the administration believed that employee input into the budget-cutting process would be valuable. They felt that a cross-section of employees would provide perspective and assist in analyzing the most effective ways of cutting the budget and minimizing the impact on services. Department directors were asked to recommend approximately five employees, who were selected to include front-line workers, supervisors, and mid-level management. These employees were respected by their peers and had a good understanding of the functions and services provided by the city and by their departments.

A meeting was scheduled with the mayor and the newly formed employee budget teams to provide direction. The mayor asked the budget teams to prioritize services and duties performed by their respective departments anal to give the Citizens Advisory Committee budget-cutting options to consider. The options were for cutting the operating budget by 5 percent, 10 percent, or 15 percent, and the recommended cuts were to be focused on those services that provide the least value or have the smallest impact to the citizens of Provo. While the administration believed going into the process that some departments might need to be cut by 15 percent, and others by only 1 or 2 percent, the budget teams were asked to consider options adding up to a 15 percent reduction so the committee would have a complete understanding of the options available for balancing the budget.

The budget teams were asked to closely scrutinize and question all services provided by the department. They were also asked to seek input from other employees in their departments, and to use any outside resources available. Each budget team was given approximately four weeks to do their analysis before meeting with the Citizens Advisory Committee to explain their recommended budget reduction options at the three different levels, and to answer any questions regarding their recommendations.

The presentations were comprehensive and provided a number of viable options for the Citizens Advisory Committee to consider. Many of the ideas presented had not been previously considered. The budget team reports provided detailed explanations regarding the recommended reductions, including the related service or function that would be eliminated and the consequence of eliminating the function or service.

In addition, the mayor provided a method for employees to contact him anonymously and provide any recommended ways to provide budget savings to the city.

Analyzing the Options

The Citizens Advisory Committee and the mayor also established a Budget Focus Committee, which consisted of the assistant director of finance anal three other respected and innovative employees from various city departments. The Budget Focus Committee functioned on a parallel track to that of the budget teams; it was asked to do an in-depth analysis of the budget saving ideas presented by the Citizens Advisory Committee, the administration, the budget office, and the employees. The Budget Focus Committee then presented its proposals to the Citizens Advisory Committee. Ideas that were considered included closing a fire station, outsourcing fleet and parks maintenance, reducing the use of city vehicles for commuting, consolidating customer service functions across city departments, and employee furloughs.

After hearing all of the recommendations from the budget teams and the Budget Focus Committee, the Citizens Advisory Committee gave the mayor a formal recommendation as to what ideas should be used to provide approximately $3 million in budget cuts in the general fund and another $2.4 million in other city funds. The general fund reductions consisted of approximately $1.7 million in personnel expenses, with the remainder coming from operational cuts or revenue strategies. Other funds identified $1.8 million in personnel expenses, and the remainder was derived from operational cuts and, in some cases, revenue strategies. As a result, 65 positions were eliminated — 31 through attrition, 34 through voluntary and involuntary reductions.

Conclusions

One of the lessons learned through this process is the need for government to be dynamic. As the economy changes, government needs to be responsive. If the economy is improving, government must be in a position to add resources, but if the economy is slowing, government must be in a position to cut resources. Jurisdictions need to be nimble in times of economic change, not only to be more responsive to economic changes, but in some cases to do a better job of anticipating the impact of such changes.

The recommendations that came from the Citizens Advisory Committee, employee budget teams and the Budget Focus Committee were impressive, and they were instrumental in helping the administration balance the budget during these difficult economic times. The decisions that were made as a result of the in-depth approach to the budget deficit were difficult and will affect the lives of a number of the city's employees. However, by making these difficult decisions today, Provo is positioned to effectively respond to the financial challenges it faces in the future. The city was successful in identifying cuts that will have a minimal impact on citizens because of the valuable input from employees and citizens. A majority of the cuts will be recurring or ongoing, thereby reducing the size of the government and better enabling the city to balance the budget in subsequent years.

Provo is truly a better community and a better governmental entity as the result of this process. By learning to be more nimble in responding to changing economic conditions, by bringing some of the best and brightest minds among its employees, citizens. and business leaders to bear on these challenges, and by being willing to make hard decisions to reduce ongoing costs and strengthen revenues, the city has not only balanced its budgets for the current and next fiscal years, but it is poised to come out of the current recession stronger than before and ready to maximize its opportunities in the years to come.

CHAPTER 34

Redlands Uses Citizens to Provide Public Services

John Buntin

"Stop! Taser, Taser, Taser!"

Triggers pull, nitrogen canisters pop and barbed darts clatter against body silhouettes taped to a wall. If the silhouettes had been people, five-second pulses of electrical current would have flowed into their bodies, toppling most of them to the ground.

"Don't aim too close to the heart," says Sgt. Jeremy Floyd. If someone's coming at you, he says, shoot for the lower abdomen.

Floyd, the training instructor at a Wednesday evening Taser recertification class in Redlands, Calif., is sharing the fine points of stun gun use with a small group of men and women, all of them outfitted in blue trousers and white shirts with police badges. The badges identify them as members of the Redlands Police Department, but things are not what they seem. For starters, Taser target practice isn't taking place at a police firing range. It's happening on the porch of the Joslyn Senior Center. And in a state where many sworn law enforcement officers retire in their 50s, most of these officers look, well, older. White hair is the norm here rather than the exception. There are other oddities, too. Police department physical fitness requirements often exclude individuals with disabilities, yet one of the men is firing from a motorized wheelchair.

That said, the men and women gathered on the porch are members of the Redlands Police Department, as their badges denote. But they are not sworn or paid officers. They're volunteers, part of the city's Citizen Volunteer Patrol (CVP) unit. And they're at the forefront of the one of the country's more ambitious efforts to integrate volunteers into the workings of local government.

At a time when most city and local governments are preparing to do less with less, officials in Redlands are taking a different approach: They're attempting to maintain current levels of service through other means. Ramping up the use of volunteers is one of them.

It's easy to see why. Three years ago, the police department in Redlands, a city of 71,000 people east of Los Angeles, had 98 sworn officers, 208 civilians and about two dozen volunteers. The police budget was $23.8 million, nearly half of the city's operating budget. Today, the department employs 75 sworn officers and 138 civilians and relies on 291 active volunteers, who last year contributed more than 31,000 hours of their time to the city.

The volunteers are not just answering the phones at police headquarters. They cordon off crime scenes, direct traffic, patrol the city's 14 parks, write parking tickets, assist with animal control and provide crowd control at special events. They are also trained to check in

Originally published as "Does Government Work Require Government Employees?," *Governing*, Vol. 24, No. 7, April 2011, by e.Republic Inc., Washington, D.C. Reprinted with permission of the publisher.

parolees, assist with records processing, help staff DUI checkpoints, take reports on routine property crimes, serve as the liaison with the local San Bernardino County district attorney's office, provide counseling to crime victims and monitor sex offenders remotely. In addition, they serve more traditional functions as volunteer reserve officers. Two volunteer reserve officers even conduct investigations alongside the city's detectives. One has his own caseload. Some of the volunteers — those who go through the special training session — are allowed to carry Taser guns for their own protection.

It isn't just the police department that's assigned volunteers to important duties. Eighteen months ago, when Les Jolly took over the city's Quality of Life Department, he started to develop a program that will soon field volunteer code inspectors. "Our staff was cut by over 10 percent this fiscal year," Jolly says. "If you don't think of creative ways to supplement what you do, then you are going to fail." Redlands also employs a part-time volunteer coordinator, Tabetha Johnson, who routinely works with local civic clubs to mobilize hundreds of volunteers for events such as Redlands' annual professional bicycle race.

"We have fewer resources," says City Manager N. Enrique Martinez. "We had to cut staff. My challenge is to maintain the same service level if not better. The public is not interested in whether you have 15 fewer people than before or not."

Nor should they be. At least that's the argument Police Chief Jim Bueermann makes. "The fallback position for most local government bureaucrats like me," he says, "is that it's so much easier to say, 'We have $3 million less so you are going to get fewer services.' But there are multiple ways to get to the outcomes that taxpayers expect their police department is going to deliver." Prominent among them are a greater reliance on technology and a greater use of volunteers. Call it do-it-yourself government. But can volunteers really put in the hours and perform sensitive, highly skilled jobs that take more than a friendly smile? Can they enable a government to do more with less? A close look at Redlands' experience suggests that under some circumstances, the answer just might be yes — although that might not translate into taxpayer support.

Jim Bueermann took command of the Redlands Police Department in 1998. A lifelong resident of the city and a 20-year veteran of the force, he knew his community well — the rough neighborhoods as well as the affluent enclaves where, starting in 1870, wealthy visitors from the Midwest and the East found an ideal retreat in Redlands' fragrant orange groves and snow-capped San Bernardino Mountains. Over the years, the visitors endowed their new community with such gifts as a symphony, a magnificent Moorish-style library, and perhaps most importantly, the University of Redlands. The city soon became known as "The Jewel of the Inland Empire."

That phrase is not heard much anymore. Today, the Inland Empire is defined more by foreclosures than orange groves. The problems of neighboring communities, such as gang-plagued San Bernardino, with which Redlands shares a border, have crept in. And, despite its relative affluence, Redlands has suffered through three years of declining revenues, which have resulted in budget cuts to city departments, including the police.

When the police department's workforce fell by a third, Bueermann turned to a city tradition: volunteerism. He accelerated volunteer-recruitment efforts and hired a volunteer coordinator to oversee his department's initiatives. In the process, Bueermann discovered something surprising. Volunteers are not deterred by requirements that are demanding and responsibilities that are real. They are attracted to them.

Veteran police officers discovered something too. When the volunteer program was starting out, says Lt. Chris Catren, "we were filling the gaps with volunteers." But as police came to realize that volunteers could do many of the routine tasks that had once constituted a significant part of their workdays — directing traffic, taking reports, delivering evidence to the district attorney's office, providing crime-scene control — they came to depend on them. "They are," Catren says, "as much a part of our service delivery model as the person in a black-and-white uniform with a badge and a gun."

The department has used volunteer officers to take on specific, new tasks, such as patrolling parks, municipal orange groves and desert areas that stretch across the 40-square-mile city. One such area is the Santa Ana river basin, known locally as "the wash."

The Santa Ana River, Southern California's largest, begins in the San Bernardino Mountains and ends in the Pacific Ocean at Huntington Beach. Once upon a time, mountain storms would send deluges of water coursing through the river's channel and into the sea. Today, subdivisions in Orange County occupy many of those floodplains, and the Seven Oaks Dam holds back the waters that would otherwise sweep those subdivisions away. But dams silt up. To maintain them, authorities must occasionally release water into the wash. That poses a problem because the wash also serves as home for the homeless.

In the past, police officers alerted encampments of the homeless to the coming water release so they could move to safer grounds. Now, the city relies on a group of volunteers known as the Citizen Volunteer Park Rangers to make sure the homeless are out of harm's way.

On a recent Friday afternoon, two uniformed rangers, Lee Haag, a retired Air Force officer, and Sherli Leonard, the executive director of the Redlands Conservancy, descend on their horses into the wash. A few weeks earlier, they had distributed fliers warning of the water release at two recently spotted encampments — one north of the Redlands Municipal Airport, the other in the lee of the Orange Street Bridge. Now they're checking the encampment near the bridge. As they approach, it is deserted except for a stray dog. As the horses climb out of the wash, the rangers encounter a woman out for a walk. She stops to pat the horses. Knowing that rangers are out patrolling the wash, she says, has made her day.

The creation of the Volunteer Park Rangers says a lot about how the city interacts with its volunteers. The ranger program started almost accidentally. Three years ago, retired audiologist Brad Billings read an interview in the local paper in which Police Chief Bueermann expressed a desire to organize a volunteer patrol to tackle problems of graffiti and disorder in the city's parks. Billings e-mailed the chief and two hours later got an e-mail back inviting him to a meeting. Their discussion was brief.

"Brad, it's yours," Bueermann told him. "Go for it." Bueermann appointed a sergeant to supervise the program but left it to Billings to organize, raise funds and run the initiative, which now numbers more than two dozen volunteers. Like the Citizen Volunteer Patrol, rangers received training, uniforms, iPhones (to mark the location of graffiti and other problems) and access to city equipment. Sending volunteer rangers into the wash is something many cities wouldn't do — even if the volunteers were trained and well equipped. Bueermann says such risk-taking is essential. "Too often we accept a lack of money as a reason not to do things," he says. "There are so many ways to get around that if we just accept a level of ambiguity, develop a tolerance for risk-taking and realize that sometimes failure is about learning."

As for Haag and Leonard, they say they have never felt unsafe.

Redlands is unusual for the depth and breadth of its volunteer activities, but it isn't alone. Confronted with the challenges of the Great Recession, cities across the country have begun to reconsider what can be done with volunteers. In December 2009, New York City Mayor Michael Bloomberg assembled 15 mayors to announce the launch of a new initiative, Cities of Service. Underwritten by both Bloomberg Philanthropies and the Rockefeller Foundation, the initiative provides cities with $200,000 grants to hire "chief service officers" to identify local priorities and develop plans to address them, using volunteers.

One of the mayors who appeared with Bloomberg was Nashville's Karl Dean. In January 2010, Nashville received one of the first $200,000 Cities of Service grants. Dean tapped Laurel Creech to run the program. Her first day of work last May coincided with the 100-year flood that submerged parts of downtown Nashville as well as several residential neighborhoods. From the city emergency command center, Creech worked with a local volunteer group, Hands On Nashville, to text thousands of volunteers with a request for help sandbagging downtown against the rising Cumberland River. Within three hours, more than a thousand volunteers were on hand.

Since then, Creech has developed a service plan that focuses on two issues — education and the environment. According to Creech, working with the heads of city agencies has been challenging. Although quite a few departments utilize volunteers in many ways, a lot of them don't use volunteers as effectively as they could or, she says, they "don't really know what suitable volunteer programs are and what volunteers can do and can't do. The challenge is getting them to recognize that there are opportunities for improvement."

Still, Nashville's chief service officer believes that volunteers will take on more and more tasks once performed by government employees.

In Redlands, that moment has already arrived. When budget cuts nixed the Redlands Police Department's plans to lease a helicopter from the county (at a cost of $500,000 a month plus operating costs) to provide air support, the department used drug forfeiture funds to purchase a 1967 Cessna 172, which it then kitted out with a $30,000 video camera that could be operated by a laptop in the back of the plane. To operate the plane, the department turned to volunteer pilots like Bill Cheeseman, age 70.

Cheeseman is a retired engineer who describes himself as "a gentleman acrobatic flier." On a recent sunny afternoon, he takes the plane up for a patrol shift. A police officer, Sgt. Shawn Ryan, sits in the back, along with his electronic equipment: image-stabilized binoculars, a laptop to monitor the police dispatcher and operate the video camera, as well as a LoJack system for detecting stolen cars. As the plane lifts off the runway of the Redlands Municipal Airport, a police dispatcher reports a recurring alarm in a neighborhood of mansions between Caroline Park and the Redlands Country Club. Two patrol cars arrive at the scene just minutes before the Cessna, which circles overhead.

Two officers from the patrol car have entered the house. They have silenced their radio. If there's a burglar inside, they don't want its squawk to announce their presence. Two thousand feet overhead, Ryan focuses on the house. "If someone runs out," he says, "we'll see them."

No one makes a run for it. The officers on the ground report that the wind was opening and closing an unlocked door. But even when the plane responds to a false alarm, it serves a useful purpose. One of Bueermann's first and most controversial actions as chief was to disband a "beat" system that assigned police officers to various sectors of the city, with little regard for actual crime rates. Needless to say, affluent low-crime neighborhoods were unhappy with the change. By putting a plane in the air — and highly visible police vehicles on the ground (albeit ones often driven by volunteers) — he's been able to assuage their concerns and free up his officers for the proactive police work of targeting gangs, guns and violence in the most dangerous parts of town.

It's the kind of creative problem-solving that has allowed the city to cut personnel by 16 percent without damaging city services, says Redlands City Manager Martinez. Last spring, San Bernardino County and the city of Redlands commissioned a polling firm to gauge public satisfaction with city services. Even though citywide staffing and funding have been cut and cut again since 2007, 81 percent of respondents said services were at least satisfactory — and 30 percent of that 81 percent actually rated services as better than satisfactory.

To Martinez, it was a testament to the creativity of city staff and the partnerships they have been able to build. "Less is not less," he says. "The way services have been delivered for the past 20 years is very labor intensive."

But the city's approach may also have lulled the citizens of Redlands into thinking that city leaders have solved the problem of doing more with less and that the city doesn't need more money to keep providing a top-notch level of service. Last November, when a measure to impose a half-cent sales tax surcharge to shore up city services went before the voters, it failed. In Redlands, the voters have spoken. Do-it-yourself government is here for good.

CHAPTER 35

Roanoke Encourages Citizens
to Provide Tax Relief
Ann H. Shawver

In March 2010, the Roanoke City Council took a bold step to support K–12 education, unanimously voting to increase the local meals tax by 40 percent at a time when anti-tax fervor was sweeping the Commonwealth of Virginia. Then the city worked with community and private organizations, using the tax increase to rally the public, encouraging them to eat at local restaurants in support of K–12 education. The program succeeded, in large part because of the clear and timely financial information provided to local media and the community.

Deciding to Focus on Schools

About a year before the recession struck, the city, the city council, and the school board started down a path to improve the performance of the city's public schools. The school board increased its level of commitment to improving school performance. New school administration was hired, and the city council increased its support.

The performance of Roanoke city schools was poor. The graduation rate was less than 50 percent, and almost 70 percent of students received free and reduced-rate lunches. Numerous schools were unaccredited, and some failed to achieve federal Adequate Yearly Progress standards. People who lived and worked in the Roanoke Valley often hesitated to send their children to Roanoke's public schools because of these performance issues, as well as social and behavioral woes within the schools.

Faced with deep cuts in funding from the commonwealth, coupled with a reduction in funding from the City of Roanoke under a local tax-sharing formula, Roanoke City Public Schools was expecting budget reductions of up to 10 percent from fiscal 2010 to 2011— in the range of $10 million to $14 million. Though the city council had provided funding above and beyond the tax-sharing ratio the year before, in an effort to maintain school funding, the cuts expected for fiscal 2011 appeared to be damaging to recent efforts to resurrect the schools.

Roanoke City Council members knew that for Roanoke's success in the arenas of economic development and quality of life, school performance had to improve. City council members feared that such progress would be impossible without adequate funding and that if funding to the schools was reduced, it could have permanent devastating effects.

Originally published as "Eat for Education: Roanoke, Virginia, Provides Fiscal First Aid for K–12 Education," *Government Finance Review*, Vol. 26, No. 4, December 2010, by the Government Finance Officers Association, Chicago, IL. Reprinted with permission of the publisher.

Two Cents for Two Years

During the early part of the fiscal 2011 budget cycle, one of the city council members came up with an idea to address the problem: a meals tax increase that would be dedicated to the city's public schools. After looking at the revenue that would be generated and the tax rates of surrounding jurisdictions and other Virginia localities, he made his case. He proposed increasing the existing meals tax by two percentage points, to 7 percent from 5 percent, effective from July 1, 2010, until June 30, 2012, at which time the rate would revert to 5 percent.

This idea immediately won praise from K–12 supporters, and it drew little criticism. Other alternatives were examined, but none provided as sizeable an impact on revenue — approximately $2.2 million per percentage point of tax increase. Other attractive features were that this plan taxed those who had the ability to pay for restaurant meals, and the tax was funded in part by non-resident visitors to Roanoke. As a city, Roanoke had the authority to increase its local tax without approval by the commonwealth and without holding a voter referendum. Roanoke leaders did not believe that this revenue initiative would have a major affect on people's dining habits, but some parties were concerned that this could be a risky move at a time of economic challenges because it would make Roanoke's meals tax rate the highest of any city in Virginia.

Alternatives

During Roanoke's budget season, city officials considered a number of alternatives to provide additional funding to the schools. One of these was an increase in the real estate tax, which would generate approximately $750,000 for each penny of increase. This option was not popular among elected officials, however, for several reasons. First, assessment increases throughout the past decade had left citizens skeptical about the fairness of how their homes were taxed. Roanoke's tax of $1.19 per $100 assessed value was already one of the highest rates in the immediate area, comparable with many urban communities in the commonwealth. In-creasing the real estate tax was also unpopular as a source of school funding because it would place an additional burden on elderly and others on fixed incomes.

Some elected officials and citizens inquired about the possibility of raising the local sales tax. While this was a logical suggestion, the city lacked local authority to increase this tax rate without approval by the general assembly — and language introduced in the 2010 session to give local governments such authority was soundly defeated.

As discussions progressed, some officials suggested considering the lodging tax for an increase, along with the prepared food tax. There were drawbacks to this idea, though, that led some Roanoke officials and community leaders to decide this tax would be a poor fit for support of the school division. First, increasing that tax by one percentage point would provide only $360,000 in revenue. Also, that revenue had historically gone to the local convention and visitors bureau.

Another idea was increasing the prepared food and beverage tax by two percentage points for two years or so, and then permanently increasing the tax by a lesser amount such as 1.5 percent. While the latter might have been a more sound solution from a budgetary standpoint, the "two percent for two year" proposal had already caught on by that point, and supporters of the concept were quick to condition their support on the requirement that it sunset in two years.

As required for all tax rate increases, a public hearing was held to allow citizen input. At the public hearing, numerous educators and school supporters voiced support for the increased tax, and the general citizenry voiced no opposition. The restaurant community, however, felt it had been singled out as an industry, and numerous restaurant owners took to the podium to object, although many felt that this tax increase was probably a done deal.

Forecasting the Impact

The city council unanimously approved the "two percent for two year" plan. The city had to consider any potential negative impact on the performance of the meal tax, given that it would be considerably higher than other communities in the valley — in fact, 7 percent would be the highest in the state. In preparing the fiscal 2011 forecast, the finance office determined an appropriate revenue estimate at the 5 percent level. Next, it determined the revenue equivalent of each percentage point of increase. In computing the expected revenue at an increased 7 percent tax rate, the incremental revenue for a two-percentage point increase was discounted by five percent. Thus far in fiscal 2011, this appears to have been a relatively conservative forecasting method, given the dynamics in place.

The Roanoke School Board was to receive nearly $4.4 million in funding from the tax rate increase. The money was dedicated to:

- Restoring K-8 staffing above the standards of quality minimums
- Restoring key high school positions
- Funding the Drug Abuse Resistance Education program
- Funding school resource officers
- Teaching elementary Spanish in grades 4–6
- Providing key central office staff
- Restoring athletics, chess club, and maintenance spending

In the end, the additional revenue meant restoring a majority of the positions that were to be cut when the fiscal year 2010–2011 budget was adopted, many of them teaching positions.

The Eat for Education Campaign

In the truest spirit of seeking ways for the community to work together in support of common goals, Roanoke's city manager quickly realized that an increased tax in the middle of an economic recession could only be viewed as a win-win situation if the city found a way to work with the restaurant community and generate support for dining in public restaurants as a means of supporting public education. Thus, the Eat for Education campaign was born. Fittingly, the city enlisted assistance from the same public relations firm that represented the restaurant industry when it resisted the rate increase.

There are five partners in the Eat for Education Campaign: the City of Roanoke, the Roanoke Valley Convention and Visitors Bureau, the Roanoke Regional Chamber of Commerce, the Roanoke Valley Hospitality Association, and Downtown Roanoke, Inc. (a not-for-profit downtown development organization). The campaign is also supported by the student chapter of the Public Relations Society of America at Radford University. This group is working with the public relations firm and the City of Roanoke's office of communications to promote the campaign and assist with details such as restaurant contacts, community outreach, and coordination with local organizations that can help promote the program.

The Eat for Education campaign was launched with a press conference on June 30, 2010. A Web site was created to promote the program (www.eatforeducationroanoke.com), and a letter campaign invited 130 locally owned restaurants — those with patrons most likely to be attracted by the project — to participate. The city's partners in the campaign also reached out to local restaurants. The Convention and Visitors Bureau provided free membership to all restaurants, along with dining out promotions on its Web site. The Chamber of Commerce tailored its Small Business Assistance Program specifically to address the special needs of restaurants. In addition, a video segment explaining the Eat for Education Campaign was aired on the local government access channel's "Inside Roanoke" program, explaining to citizens how the increase in the meals tax was entirely dedicated to public schools.

The city's Web site page contains a link to campaign information: the video segment, a link to the Eat for Education Web site, and graphic presentation explaining the allocation of the tax. The existing meals tax was already subject to a funding formula, so the graphic presentation was developed to show how the revised tax would be allocated. This was done to maintain full disclosure and to help the public understand how the full tax would be distributed.

Development of the Eat for Education campaign was timed so that the campaign would be in place by the start of the school year. Letters explaining the campaign and encouraging families to participate were distributed throughout the schools to take home to parents.

Ongoing Reporting

An important element of the Eat for Education program is transparency about the performance of the tax and how revenue compares to both the budget and the prior year. Roanoke's finance department has developed a tracking tool that models the typical ebb and flow of the meals tax throughout the course of the fiscal year, and this tool is applied to the fiscal 2011 revenue estimate to gauge the amount of revenue anticipated each month. At the end of each month, city accounting staff can review results and share the information with others. The local media have shown significant interest in the Eat for Education program and revenue results. Finance staff work to help media personnel understand how the growth or decline in the tax is measured, as adjusted for the change in tax rate to measure true economic performance.

As of September 2010, three months into fiscal 2011, meals tax results were relatively stable at a 0.5 percent increase from the previous year, when adjusted to eliminate the impact of the tax rate change. Actual meals tax results for the same period exceed budget by 3.3 percent.

In a further effort to keep citizens, business owners, educators, and the broader community informed, a Facebook page was also created for the program: Eat for Education Roanoke. This page shares public relations initiatives and is a good way to announce winners of the monthly drawings for restaurant gift certificates.

The tax has also been helpful in making city and school leaders and staff more aware of the value of dinning at restaurants within city limits. People keep this in mind when entertaining guests or planning events for groups, and they think about supporting Roanoke venues and the Eat for Education campaign. This awareness also helps support other retail in Roanoke.

The Questions

When the tax increase was put into place, citizens and the media immediately began asking questions about how it worked. There was a misconception that it was a state tax.

An interesting point to study will be whether the Eat for Education program helps Roanoke reduce its delinquency rate on prepared food and beverage tax. It is too soon to tell whether there will be an impact to this rate, which averages approximately 4 percent.

Another interesting element of the tax increase is the potential for debate about whether the tax increase is helping or hurting the restaurant business. Finance professionals must be careful not to get overly caught up in this debate, but they must be responsible for publishing information that is accurate, up to date, and easy to understand. Ironically, there are questions and debate about the stagnant or slightly declining performance of the tax, but naysayers seem to be forgetting that the reason a tax increase was needed was because the stagnant (and declining) economy had led to severe revenue reductions to the schools.

Elements of the Eat for Education Campaign

Restaurant enrollment. Restaurants that enroll in the Eat for Education campaign benefit from its marketing. Letters were sent to restaurants during the summer to invite them, and enrollment is optional and free of charge. The Eat for Education Web site publishes the list of member restaurants, including links to their Web sites. Restaurants that enroll receive a window cling they can display to announce their involvement.

Monthly drawing. When patrons of participating restaurants declare they are "eating for education," they are invited to complete an entry form (supplied to participating restaurants) for a drawing held each month. Participating restaurants each draw one form and send that name to Eat for Education headquarters. All names are placed in a hat and Downtown Roanoke draws names for $50 gift certificates that can be used at any of the participating restaurants.

School lunch day. Weekly, on a day to be selected, professionals will be invited to join the Eat for Education program by leaving their brown bags at home and dining out in support of education. Restaurants are encouraged to offer school-themed specials on this day.

Educator's day. One day a month will be Educator's Day, and showing their city school employee IDs allows Roanoke City School employees to take advantage of specials for breakfast, lunch, or dinner.

Family night out. This promotion, which will be rolled out soon, will encourage restaurants to offer family specials each Tuesday for a family night out.

Conclusions

The two-cent meals tax increase is an example of fiscal first aid. It also provides an interesting story about how government and private sector can work together, in this case through a public outreach program that supports the restaurant industry while publicizing the Eat for Education effort to raise funds for Roanoke Public Schools. Fiscal resiliency will mean finding ways to permanently reduce school system expenditures so the reduction in revenue can be absorbed when the tax increase sunsets in June 2012.

The city does not yet have enough data to assess whether the campaign is accomplishing its objectives. The only measure Roanoke officials have currently is the revenue collected for the meals tax, and so far that is exceeding expectations. However, city leaders believe the true success of the campaign will be measured not so much by how much revenue is collected or how many restaurants participate, but by the campaign's ability to affect public perception of the city as wanting to help the community. The hope is that, in addition to providing financial support to schools and helping to promote city restaurants in general, the campaign will create an atmosphere of good will toward Roanoke City Public Schools and our community for turning a negative (the meals tax increase) into a positive (supporting the school system) during difficult economic times.

CHAPTER 36

Rochester and Other Cities Seek Additional Funding Sources

Kathleen Gray

Communities are scouring state, federal and corporate bulletins for opportunities to fill holes in their shrinking budgets to pay for everything from fruits and vegetables for kids, to cops and firefighters on the street.

State and federal grants, along with gifts from corporations and foundations, are helping many cities pay for everything from essentials, like municipal services and capital building projects, to frills like recycling bins and public art that often are the first things to go in tough budget times.

"As elected officials have been given budget tasks" to cut a certain amount from their annual budget, "they're finding other sources of funding," said Oakland County Budget and Management Director Laurie VanPelt.

So in Oakland County, the district courts formed a nonprofit agency to help fund its drug court. Children's Village found more than $7,500 in state grants to pay for fruits and vegetables, salad bar equipment and nutritional education for juveniles being held in the facility, and the Oakland International Airport went after $2 million in grants to build an energy-efficient terminal in Waterford that is to be finished in August.

But grants often come with strings attached, meaning communities sometimes have to get creative.

Many people in Clinton Township wanted to jump at the chance earlier this year to submit an application for a $3.4-million Department of Homeland Security grant to rehire seven laid-off firefighters.

But township Supervisor Robert Cannon had grave misgivings: The grant required the township to promise not to lay off any firefighters for two years, or risk being forced to pay back the grant.

"Eight years ago, I would have grabbed the money, but it's a different time and a different economy," Cannon said.

The township is struggling with a 32 percent drop in property tax revenues and has 100 fewer employees than it did five years ago.

So the township came up with another plan: it voted last week to take pre-emptive action by laying off 12 firefighters and applying for the grant. That way, the township will be able to hire back many of the laid-off firefighters and maintain the size of the department.

But it's a risk, Cannon admitted, especially if the township doesn't get the grant.

"I hate to turn down what looks like free money, but it's never free," he said.

However, that hasn't stopped communities across metro Detroit from looking for ways to supplement their shrinking budgets:

Originally published as "Cities Use Gifts, Grants as Sources of Funding," *Detroit Free Press*, March 31, 2011, by the Gannett Company, Detroit, MI. Reprinted with permission of the publisher.

- Grosse Pointe, in partnership with Grosse Pointe Farms, got a Homeland Security grant last year for an emergency generator for their public safety departments. The request came in response to the widespread blackouts in 2003, when the departments had to operate off portable generators from the backs of pickups, said City Management Pete Dame — who was hired five years ago, in part, to help the city go after grants.
- In Rochester, as part of a $1-million grant from the Michigan Department of Transportation to rebuild Main Street through downtown, the city will redo its streetscapes by replacing lights, installing benches and improving crosswalks this summer. The city also got a $40,000 grant from DTE Energy last year to install a solar roof on the city's Fire Department headquarters.
- Clinton Township got $100,000 earlier this year from the local Mt. Elliott Cemetery Association to install a 3-mile walking/biking path to an arboretum in the township. They supplemented that project with a $200 grant for trees from the state Department of Natural Resources.

- Since 1995, the Community Oriented Policing Services Grants program has pumped $141.5 million into Wayne, Oakland and Macomb county communities to keep an additional 1,803 police officers on the street.

Some locals, though, don't want to depend on grants, especially for personnel costs.

Oakland County adopted a policy in the mid–1980s that mandates that when a grant that funds employees or programs ends, the job or program ends, too.

"The grants we go after aren't used to much to plug holes, but to enhance services. And when the funding goes away, the program goes away," VanPelt said. "We're just not going to accept funds with strings attached."

And that's a prudent course of action, said Arnold Weinfeld, director of strategic initiatives and federal affairs for the Michigan Municipal League.

"Communities really went after grants in the last few years, but given state and federal budgets, that's becoming more and more competitive, and more and more difficult," he said.

CHAPTER 37

Rockland and Other Cities
Are Impacted by Senior Citizens

Jeff Clark

If there is a color in Maine's future, it is gray — gray hair, that is. From summer residents returning to stay in retirement to resident Mainers choosing not to move to the Sunbelt after getting the gold watch, the state's population of older people has risen steadily in the past two decades.

And the impact older residents are having, and will have, on Maine's municipalities can only grow.

Since 2004, Maine has been the oldest state in the nation, and by 2009 the state had a median age of 42, compared to 36.8 nationally, according to the U.S. Census Bureau.

Research by well-known Maine economist Charles Colgan predicts that the over–65 age group will comprise almost 20 percent of Maine's population by 2020, climbing from about 16 percent today.

That likelihood is due both to the aging of the baby boom generation and Maine's attractiveness as a retirement home. By 2030, the state's over-65 population number is projected at 397,000 residents, or 22 percent of the state's total population.

Counterintuitive Trend?

Maine as a retirement Mecca may seem counterintuitive, but observers as far back as 1988 noted out-of-state retirees choosing the state over more traditional retirement magnets such as Arizona and Florida. Seasonal summer residents and regular visitors were making their homes here after decades of vacation stays, while others were drawn by the state's four-season lifestyle or the desire to be closer to children and grandchildren.

John Wasileski developed one of the first purpose-built modern retirement communities, the Highlands, in Topsham in the early 1990s. He later expanded the concept with an over-55 condominium housing development, Highland Green.

Depending on how the term is defined, Maine now has at least 45 retirement communities, almost all of them in small towns on the coast between Kittery and Bar Harbor. Not coincidentally, the coastal counties from York to Knox are predicted to have Maine's fastest growing elderly population in the coming decade, with strong centers of growth in the Ellsworth, Blue Hill and Bar Harbor areas.

Emergency Calls

"Our older population does require more services," acknowledged Belfast Mayor Walter Ashe, Jr., who has been active in city and state

Originally published as "The Graying of Maine: Its Municipal Impact," *Maine Townsman*, Vol. 73, No. 1, January 2011, by the Maine Municipal Association, Augusta. Reprinted with permission of the publisher.

politics for decades. "Years ago, our fire and po-lice departments weren't a quarter the size they are now. We get more emergency services calls, for example. The police force does a lot more home checks, that sort of thing."

"I think public safety is a good example of where towns will see an increased need for services," says Colgan, who now teaches at the Muskie School at the University of Southern Maine in Portland. "There will continue to be a strong demand for other amenities, such as walking trails and public libraries."

Belfast and communities like it can expect to see more of the same in the future, said Colgan.

"Small cities like Belfast and Rockland are drawing retirees because they offer access to local hospitals and other amenities," he said. "Falmouth, for another example, is attractive because it's next door to Portland. In those kinds of service-center communities, you will see the development of denser communities of older people."

"Definitely, yes, the retiree population is a factor looking forward in our planning," said Nathan Poore, Falmouth's town manager. "You have to plan appropriately to meet the varying needs of your residents."

The Oceanview at Falmouth retirement community has been part of the town for more than a decade. Its 255 residents, along with the many other retirees who call Falmouth home, are a reliable source of volunteers for everything from election workers to library board members. They also have been key supporters for the local mass transit bus system, which links Falmouth and Portland.

The flip side of the need for services is the willingness of seniors to get involved in their communities. Today's elderly are generally healthier, more affluent and better educated than at any time in the past. They also vote more regularly than any other age group.

They Vote, Seek Office

Senior centers and retirement communi-ties have become regular stops for candidates for elected office, said First Selectman Dick McLean, of Damariscotta, himself a retiree "from away" who has served on the board for 13 years.

Since many of the candidates themselves are retirees, "they're not going to the old folks' home to make sure they fill out the absentee ballots the right way," he quipped. "They're sit-ting at the tables with the old folks because they're older, too."

"They pay attention," said Ashe, the mayor in Belfast. "They vote. Plus, we have a lot of retired people involved in local politics and city boards and such. A majority of the city council is retired people. It's been a good thing. They bring a lot of experience."

McLean noted that three of the five Damariscotta selectmen are retirees. Retirees are also active on various town boards, councils, and committees, as well as local social organi-zations.

"We like to say we're retired, not tired," he joked.

McLean described a community where re-tirees group together and become active in many ways, from organizing book and garden clubs to opposing unwanted development, such as a proposal to build a Wal-Mart in the town in 2006.

"There's a real sense of involvement, I think," he said. "People want to be involved in their community."

Positives in Blue Hill

"These people have enriched our commu-nity," said Jim Shaw, a selectman in Blue Hill, home to the Parker Ridge retirement commu-nity as well as a significant number of other re-tirees. Shaw does not see a "disproportionate" drain on resources due to the older population.

"We're a pretty healthy lifestyle commu-nity," he said. "I don't think our emergency services have seen much strain. If anything, they've benefited. A lot of our volunteer fire-fighters are older people."

Shaw acknowledged that retirees have had an effect on town budget debates, although not in the way many might expect.

"The newer retirees from away are more

willing to support spending," he said, while long-time residents and natives "tend to be a lot more conservative on things like property taxes and spending. There may be a little debate from both groups about things like the school budget, but it's nothing like it was when I first moved here 30 years ago."

Colgan, the economist, predicted that, as seniors make up a larger portion of a community's population, "there will be real battles over schools. Schools are the biggest cost in a municipal budget, and I think we'll see real fights over education because older people don't have children in school."

If true, it has not happened yet. Ashe, McLean, Shaw, and others all described the elderly in their towns as sources of support for local education efforts.

"It makes sense that there should be some conflict," said Falmouth's Poore, "but I'm not seeing it."

Building Schools

Topsham town manager Jim Ashe (no relation to Walter) said the town has built a new elementary school and a middle school in recent years, both without opposition from the town's significant — and often vocal — retiree population.

"They do have an effect on local politics," he said. "We've seen groups of retirees turn out on some zoning and tax increment financing issues. With our town meeting form of government, you don't need a lot of people to make an impact if you organize. But they've always supported the schools."

"They're concerned about education like everyone else," Ashe added. "They've become citizens of the community, and they want to see the community thrive and become a place that can keep their grandkids around and give them good jobs."

The conflict, when there is any, seems to come more between retirees from away and locals.

"There are two distinct attitudes about the world here," Damariscotta's McLean said. "One is generally by those who have never been away and the other is by those who are from away."

He said it was characteristic of locals who had been born and raised in the area to resist change and perceived government interference.

"Those of us from elsewhere know that change happens, and you need to prepare for it," he said. "Things like design standards for buildings, for example. The natives will say we have never had any and don't need any, versus folks from New Jersey who have seen what happens (without standards) and warn that you won't like what you'll get without them."

McLean said there is a misconception about retirees who move to Maine later in life.

"Everyone has heard the old story about people from away who want to make Maine just like it was back home," he said. "Our retirees have seen the someplace else and they've come to Maine to get away from it. If anything, our attitude is just the opposite. We don't want to make this place like the one we left. We want to keep it the way it is."

CHAPTER 38

St. Paul and Other Cities Consider
Flexible Spending to Save Money

Claudia Hoffacker

As cities look for ways to provide better customer service, save money, and recruit and retain top-notch employees, they are trying some innovative staffing techniques. One of these strategies is staffing city hall 10 hours per day, four days per week (referred to as "4/10s"), and closing each Friday. Another strategy some cities are considering is telecommuting.

Four-Day Workweek

The City of St. Francis (population 7,201) moved to 4/10s last September as a year-long pilot program. "I'm excited that the Council will assess how things are going and decide whether to make the change permanent.

"It's a policy decision that doesn't have any cost. Hopefully, over time, it will have a positive financial effect," Hylen adds. "But it's a low-risk chance to change things up, and I'm glad that the Council is willing to try something new. And if it doesn't work, then we'll just go back to the way it was before. That's a really nice thing about this."

The main reason for moving to a four-day workweek was customer service, Hylen says. Since most residents commute out of the city to work, the longer hours give them a chance to do their business at city hall on their way to

work in the morning or on their way home in the afternoon. City Hall hours are now 7 A.M. to 5:30 P.M. Monday through Thursday, which is a typical schedule for cities trying this option.

Customer service was also the main driving force behind Albertville's decision to try a four-day workweek. "Overall, I think it's provided good customer service and that was the goal," say Larry Kruse, city administrator for Albertville (population 5,856).

Win-Win-Win

In Bayport (population 3,245), the city instituted a shorter workweek during the summer with four nine-hour days, and four hours on Friday. Last fall, the city began a four-day workweek. They say it's a win-win situation for resident, employees, and the city.

"The employees win," Bayport Administrator Mike McGuire explains, "because they get a three-day weekend every week and they save money on gas. The city wins because employees are happier, which will improve retention, because of a benefit that doesn't cost the city any money. The city will also save money. And the citizens win because city hall is open longer hours Monday through Thursday, and

Originally published as "Creative Staffing on a Budget: Flexible Scheduling," *Minnesota Cities*, Vol. 94, No. 3, March 2009, by the League of Minnesota Cities, St. Paul. Reprinted with permission of the publisher.

it's easier and more convenient for them to do business at city hall."

The St. Francis, Albertville, and Bayport administrators all report a positive response from citizens about the schedule change. The key to this, says Hylen, was communication. The city gave plenty of notice to residents about the new hours — posting it on the web site, the school district newsletter, and the front door of city hall. There were also newspaper articles about it.

The Employee Benefit

For employees, the longer days can be a difficult adjustment at first but, once they got used to it, most enjoyed the new schedule. Many reported that they felt more productive. "One positive thing I've noticed is that I see the piles of paper diminishing. Working the longer days gives you time to catch up on things because you have more time without distractions," says Hylen.

Bayport is offering even more flexibility for employees. They can choose to work 4/10s, or they can work 4/9s — a 36-hour workweek, with a proportionate 10 percent reduction in their gross pay.

In most situations, only the city hall office staff members are on the four-day work schedule. Public works is still covered five days a week and, of course, full police coverage is still provided in cities that have their own police departments.

Cost Savings

All three administrators say their city will save energy by closing city hall one extra day each week. It's hard to quantify right now, but some said they would track their energy costs and compare them to previous costs to try to calculate savings. They don't expect huge savings because they don't have large buildings, but every little bit helps. McGuire says he expects to save about $1,000 on the city's annual heating and cooling costs.

There will also be a small environmental impact as their employees reduce their commutes by 20 percent. "I look at the big picture," says McGuire. "If more businesses and other did the same, this could have a big impact on the environment and on the price of gas."

While Minnesota cities are just starting to experiment with a four-day workweek, some cities in other states have been doing it long enough to gather some solid data. One such city is Avondale, Ariz. (population 38,000). Avondale reports two specific cost savings: janitorial services and energy.

Reducing janitorial services from five days to four provides an annual savings of $9,444. In terms of energy, the city has seen a 13 percent reduction in electricity use, providing an annual savings of $13,624.

Hylen says he's had calls from several other cities that are also exploring the four-day workweek. These include Zimmerman (population 4,475), Rockford (population 3,903), Fridley (population 26,603), and Hanover (population 2,421). In fact, *Sun Newspapers* reported in February that Hanover has begun a trial four-day week for administrative staff and voted to continue it until May, when they will evaluate how it's going and decide whether to continue the new schedule.

Telecommuting

Another way some cities are considering offering more flexibility to employees is to allow them to work from home, at least on a part-time basis. Some cities have expressed an interest in this idea, but it seems that few Minnesota cities are actively pursuing this option yet.

The City of St. Paul has a telecommuting policy, which it created in 1998, but few employees currently work from home on a regular basis, says LeeAnn Turchin, St. Paul human resources manager. If they telecommute, they are generally working at a client site rather than at home.

The city has a virtual private network (VPN), which allows employees to access the city's network remotely, says Turchin. That makes telecommuting even easier. "If people are mostly doing office work, that situation lends itself well to working off-site. It doesn't matter whether the work is done at home or in the office."

According to the St. Paul policy, "the city considers telecommuting to be a viable work option that can be implemented at the discretion of the department or office management. Telecommuting, when appropriately applied, may benefit both the city and the employee. To telecommute, a city employee and supervisor shall enter a written telecommuting agreement."

Real-Life Example

Some cities may be able to learn from the example of their local government counterparts on the county level. For example, about 150 of Olmstead County's 1,100 employees telecommute three to four days a week, says Associate County Administrator Mary Callier.

"We started telecommuting in 1996 because we wanted to reduce our need for space and to be more flexible in meeting the needs of clients and staff," Callier explains. "We read about how telecommuting increases productivity and reduces turnover, and that's what really convinced us to try it."

The option is available to all country employees, but the employee's supervisor has to approve the arrangement. Some employees don't have a personality or work style that is compatible with telecommuting, Callier says. "I know I wouldn't be as productive working at home because I would be distracted by things at home."

So, employees have to take a compatibility survey before they can telecommute. The survey gives an indication of whether it would work well for that particular employee. The employee also has to meet with his or her supervisor and, as with St. Paul's policy, the supervisor and employee must sign a telecommuting agreement.

Advantages of Telecommuting

Callier says after having a telecommuting program for more than 12 years, the county has definitely seen some measurable benefits, including increased productivity and reduced turnover. In the county's Family Support and Assistance Unit, for example, telecommuters are taking on case loads that are 15 percent to 63 percent larger than those working in the office full-time.

The Community Services Department, which has the county's largest number of telecommuters, has seen turnover drop from 14.5 percent to 6 percent. "I can't say that's completely because of telecommuting, but I think it's partly because of that," Callier says.

Some of the other benefits are lower transportation costs for employees, reduced carbon emissions, and reduced space needs. And Callier says she doesn't see any reason why city governments can't also take advantage of the telecommuting option. If you want to try it, she recommends starting small with a department you think is a good fit with such an arrangement. "Look at metrics like turnover rates and figure out how you can measure and show success," Callier says.

Flexibility Is the Key

Turchin says telecommuting can be valuable in the right situation, but "the most important thing is just to allow flexibility — and that takes many forms, including part-time schedules, flexible hours, etc. Telecommuting is just one form."

For example, she says, she works four 10-hour days a week, and she has a part-time employee who works two 10-hour days. Some of her employees prefer working earlier hours — such as 6:30 A.M. to 3 P.M. — while some would rather work the more traditional 8:30 A.M. to 5 P.M. schedule and others like working 10 A.M. to 6:30 P.M.

"Whether you have baby boomers who are contemplating retirement or the new generation of workers, they all want flexibility," Turchin says. "People like to have control over their work and their schedules. When they have that, they're happier and less stressed."

CHAPTER 39

San Diego Uses Management and Labor to Solve Budget Problems

Jay M. Goldstone

The Great Recession has created a unique set of issues for each of our communities, but we've all had to balance the negative impact this has had on our budgets with our ability to meet community expectations. The depth of this recession has been unprecedented in recent history, with revenues declining and benefit-related costs escalating so dramatically at the same time. And while we may be seeing a little light at the end of the recession tunnel, no one is predicting the kind of rapid turnaround we have seen during previous economic cycles. If this is the new reality for the foreseeable future, the question we are all asking ourselves is how do we balance our budgets and still meet our core missions? One way is by turning to the jurisdiction's workforce for concessions.

Background: San Diego

The economic struggles this recession brought to San Diego, California, were nothing new to the city, which was already living beyond its means. Like many public agencies, in the late 1990s and early 2000s, San Diego was increasing wages and pension benefits as it attempted to compete with the private sector for talented employees. But unlike most other public agencies, San Diego's approach was to significantly underfund its pension system so it could provide services and programs the city couldn't afford without asking the community to pay more taxes. A number of articles have been written about how this combination of delivering services without having a means to pay for them finally caught up with the city.

Beginning with the fiscal 2007 budget, San Diego began a long process to "right-size" its budget. Over the next few years, the city made its pension payments in full and rebuilt its reserve balances, and most of the organization went through business process reengineering to determine more cost-efficient ways of delivering services. San Diego reexamined its core versus non-core services, eliminated several programs, reduced others, asked employees to take on more responsibilities with fewer resources, and raised selective fees. By fiscal 2010, the city was a trimmer organization, with approximately 875 fewer positions — nearly 8 percent of the total workforce; 12.5 percent, if you look at just the general fund workforce. The city also stopped increasing salaries, eliminated certain benefits for employees hired after July 1, 2005, and established a second tier pension plan for most employees hired after July 1, 2009. Fortunately for San Diego, much of this was done

Originally published as "Labor and Management: Teaming Up to Solve Budget Problems," *Government Finance Review*, Vol. 26, No. 6, December 2010, by the Government Finance Officers Association, Chicago, IL. Reprinted with permission of the publisher.

while the local economy was still strong. City officials explored every option for controlling costs while preserving critical services.

As a result, when the recession did hit, San Diego was probably better positioned than most other large cities, but it also had fewer easy options left to close the looming new deficit. After years of cuts, cost controls, and reorganizations, there were few places to turn without affecting services.

In October 2009, the city released its fiscal 2011–2015 five-year financial outlook. The picture was dire. The city projected a general fund budget deficit of about 16 percent in fiscal 2011—$179 million. This was in spite of having cut more than $150 million over the previous three fiscal years. Since total decimation of city services was not an option and raising revenues would have required voter approval, San Diego took a multifaceted approach to its budget problem, employing a combination of one-time solutions and permanent fixes and asking its employees to be a key part of the solution.

Like most public agencies, a significant portion of San Diego's budget is driven by salary and wages — as much as 70 percent to 80 percent for most departments. Given the severity of the projected deficits, the city turned to its workforce for concessions. Instead of offering no wage or benefit increases, this time, the city asked labor to give back a portion of the compensation it had previously negotiated. In anticipation of tough economic times, the city had negotiated its labor contracts to all expire at the same time, so every labor group would be at the negotiation table concurrently.

Often, both labor and management want multiyear labor contracts. This typically creates more certainty for both sides and allows for future salary and benefit adjustments to be structured to meet the particular economic conditions at the time. Having multiyear agreements also helps minimize the workload associated with negotiating the contracts, especially when a jurisdiction has multiple labor organizations. But there are times when the need for greater flexibility far outweighs the extra time and costs associated with negotiating four, five, or even ten separate labor agreements. As the City of Vallejo, California, has demonstrated, trying to unwind multiyear agreements can be extremely expensive and time consuming.

San Diego took a cautious approach. As we started to see the city's revenues decline and the stock mark plummet, we anticipated that the economic cycle was going to be unlike any we had experienced in the past. Therefore, we took the position that one-year labor agreements were in the city's best interest. This gave both sides more flexibility to maneuver through the economic storm. Since the duration and severity of the recession on city revenues and expenses was unknown, San Diego's approach allowed it to better control its costs, change course as necessary, and improve its financial planning. It probably also made it easier for the labor leaders to convince their members to accept labor contracts that did not include salary or benefit increases, since they knew these were only one-year agreements. In the end, the strategy of negotiating one-year agreements proved very beneficial to the city.

Balancing the Budget

As previously mentioned, San Diego took a multifaceted approach to developing a balanced budget. First, the city adopted its fiscal 2011 budget in December of 2009 and implemented most of the reductions by February 2010. The approximately $24.5 million the city saved in fiscal 2010 by implementing the reductions early was set aside in a separate account so it would be available to offset the fiscal 2011 deficit. The city also turned to a number of one-time solutions that preserved positions and services, accounting for nearly $72 million in additional savings. Approximately $32.5 million dollars came from actual service reductions, including substantial cuts to both the police and fire department budgets. For the first time in recent memory, the city not only reduced park and recreation programs, library hours, and numerous administrative positions, but it actually cut sworn police and fire positions from the budget. In the end, the city had cut another 539 positions, bringing the total number of positions eliminated from the budget to 1,414 since fiscal year 2007. The remaining $50 million in savings came from reducing every employee's compensation.

Labor Concessions

So how was the city able to obtain critical concessions from its labor organizations? The short answer is "It wasn't easy," but it was done in a mostly cooperative environment.

When management sat down at the negotiating table, all of the city's cards were laid out in plain view. The city presented its five-year financial outlook and discussed the details behind the numbers. Of course, the press was reporting about every other city, large or small, going through the same budget crisis, which made it slightly easier for San Diego to convey its message to the unions. Headlines throughout the state and across the country were all the same, and no one thought the recovery from this recession was going to be quick or easy.

Beyond the numbers, we talked to labor about the balanced approach the city was willing to take to close its budget gap. It was not all about layoffs. Since service levels had to be cut and some employees were going to lose their jobs, management felt strongly that labor had to be key part of the solution. Our primary goals were to minimize possible service reductions as much as possible, minimize layoffs in such a tough economy, and, unlike in previous years, spread out any service costs throughout the organization, including police and fire.

Through this process, dollar targets were established regarding how much the city needed from each budget-balancing alternative. In the end, it was determined that a 6 percent concession from every employee was required. San Diego's labor negotiators then sat down individually with each group to lay out the city's strategy. Needless to say, this was not initially well received, but again, there was at least a recognition that the city was facing a $179 million general fund deficit. One of the additional challenges the city faced was convincing labor that every employee must participate with the concessions, even if their position was funded with enterprise funds or some other non-general fund source.

Once the discussion moved past the 6 percent target, the city decided to offer a menu of options in order to achieve the target. This menu varied from bargaining group to bargaining group, depending on the particular needs of each group. In addition, the city ultimately allowed some flexibility on an individual employee basis within the group. While most groups had to pick up a large portion of their retirement costs, the balance of the 6 percent could come from other benefit reductions or salary reductions.

Not Without Its Challenges

Of course, trying to apply something of this magnitude to every employee is never easy, especially when you are negotiating with five labor groups at once, each with unique needs. Reaching full agreement was no different in this case. In the end, the city did reach an agreement with three of its five labor groups and had to declare impasse with the other two. The next challenge for management was getting a majority of the city council to accept the mayor's last, best, and final offer and to impose the last, best, and final offer on those two remaining groups. What worked in San Diego's favor was the fact that management's objectives were ultimately aligned with the objectives of the three groups that had already reached an agreement with the city. These groups were not willing to make the necessary concessions unless they applied to everyone. As such, clauses were built into the agreements of the three groups that would allow them out of the agreement if the city council did not impose at least the same terms on the two remaining groups.

To convince all the groups that it was in everyone's best interest to reach an agreement with the city, San Diego's last, best, and final offer to the two remaining groups included reductions or concessions that were more severe and less flexible than those agreed to by the other three groups. Even with that, these two groups felt that they had enough influence with the city council to avoid the concessions and get a better offer. In the end, these two groups underestimated the resolve of the city, especially in light of the "most favored nation" clauses that were put into the three initial agreements and the impact that failing to reach an agreement with the final two groups would have had — the city would have been forced to further cut critical services.

At the end of a very long day, the city council came out of closed session and voted on each agreement, one at a time. They first approved the three agreements with the groups that had settled with the city. Then, one at a time, they agreed to impose the mayor's last, best, and final offer on the remaining two groups. The room got deafeningly silent.

Conclusions

In the end, these agreements saved the city's general fund approximately $50 million a year. Even with this savings, police and fire services were reduced, along with library hours and recreation programs. It is hard to imagine what the city's service levels would have looked like with $50 million in additional cuts. Fortunately, we did not need to find out.

CHAPTER 40

San Jose Solicits Feedback on Services from Employees

Brooke A. Myhre

How do you get from "Let's not try to fix what ain't broke" to "My job is to maintain a park that I'd want to bring my own family to"? Both quotes are from employees participating in implementation of a performance measurement system in San Jose, California. They represent the challenge and the benefit of the journey toward a customer-focused and results-driven organization. Public employees, and their acceptance of such a significant culture change, are critical to achieving — and even to initiating — a better government organization through performance measurement and public involvement.

Five lessons were learned about preparing employees, as well as other partners, to build a successful performance measurement system that integrates meaningful and useful public participation and promotes understanding among decision makers, service providers, and the range of "customers" for local government services.

Deal with the Fear Factor

Performance measurement and increasing public involvement are often proposed as means to hold governments accountable, make them

more efficient, or even make them behave "more like a business." From the management level to the front line, however, many employees view performance measures and public involvement as threats, despite the best intentions of those who proposed these measures. The implication is that public employees are untrustworthy, professionally or technologically challenged, unmotivated, overstaffed and overpaid, or noncompetitive compared to the private sector. Obviously, no government employee wants to hear these things stated or implied about his or her performance. When proposed as an across-the-board initiative, it is like hearing that the entire organization has been placed on the auditor's next work plan.

Fear and uncertainty may affect other major "stakeholder" groups as well. Unions, employee associations, executives and senior staff, and even elected representatives may take a position on the effort. Outside stakeholders such as neighborhood associations, advocacy groups, or private development customers may see both positive and negative impacts from changes to increase "public" input and communication and introduce performance data into decision-making criteria.

Individual employees assess this potential change and its impact on their job, or the role

Originally published as "Public Employees as Partners in Performance: Lessons from the Field," *National Civic Review*, Vol. 97, No. 1, Spring 2008, pp. 29–34, by the National Civic League, Denver, CO. Reprinted with permission of the publisher. www.wileyonlinelibrary.com/journal.ncr.

they play in the organization. From their assessments, employees will decide whether to fight change, ignore it until it goes away, accept it as something they must do, or actively advance the concepts in performance of their job and role. Typical questions are, "Who owns the initiative? Who is for or against it? Is there strong leadership, as well as broad-based and top-to-bottom employee support (or at least acceptance) of the effort? Will it affect me? What's in it for me?" If not acknowledged and dealt with early on, employee and stakeholder questions and concerns can at a minimum create more mistrust of the effort, necessitate more watchdog processes, create demands for representation in or review of any decisions, and ultimately stop the effort before it gets going.

Outside of hearing complaints, public employees may have had little involvement with customers that generates feedback on how, or how well, they do their job. Most are unprepared to use, or lack access to, communication systems that enable outreach to and input from customers. Furthermore, involvement efforts are received with cynicism if they do not facilitate meaningful communication and useful input from all parties.

Every jurisdiction has its own set of circumstances generating the call for the proposed performance measurement initiative and its own cast of players and spectators. Although each jurisdiction is unique, two common elements of successful implementation are to ensure that (1) all key participants are clear on the why and the what and (2) good-faith efforts are made to involve all parties meaningfully. In short, employees and others need to jointly discover what is and ain't broken and then make informed decisions about what to fix and how to fix it.

Here are two suggestions from the San Jose experience to manage the fear factor and prepare employees to participate effectively as partners in the effort.

First, it is essential to prepare the organization and the employees to understand the *why* and *what*— the rationale, goals, scope, priority, and amount of time and resources needed for the performance measurement and public involvement effort. Plan an inclusive employee rollout event or process to announce the effort, with real opportunities to ask questions and comment freely on the purpose and process ahead. This should include leadership, with participation by employees from all levels of the organization as well as representatives of key stakeholder groups such as unions. Deliver a united leadership message on the purpose, priority, and goals of the effort, but make it clear that everyone's input is a valued part of the process. Prove this by acknowledging all suggestions and responding as to why suggestions are incorporated or not. Employees and others will judge by this response whether their input really matters.

Second, schedule a series of meetings with employees at each major step in the implementation process to ensure consistent communication and allow free discussion of issues. In San Jose, these meetings were conducted by members of a central implementation team alongside representatives of employee bargaining groups. No supervisors or managers were present. Issues and concerns were freely voiced. Misunderstandings and factual errors were addressed immediately. Suggestions and unresolved concerns were communicated anonymously to management and leadership for an appropriate response. Plan to offer additional meetings as often as necessary. A major communication challenge to those responsible for leading the effort is to compete favorably with the amazingly efficient rumor mill.

Understand What Governments Really Do and for Whom (or, It's About Service Delivery...)

Another way to help employees engage effectively is to build the conversation about government performance around service delivery, rather than policies, procedures, or people. Focus on which services are delivered, and the results experienced by customers. This not only reinforces the relationship of the public to the employees and their work but helps depoliticize and depersonalize the atmosphere and promote the kind of frank, factual discussion needed to allow all parties to learn how they are doing now and how they might be able to address any performance issues creatively and positively.

For a performance measurement effort to be meaningful, employees as well as customers, managers, and policymakers must share a clear understanding of why the government exists, where it is going, and the services it delivers. It is fundamental to review an organization's mission, vision, and goals, but remember that what local governments really do is deliver services. To keep the focus of the performance measurement effort on service delivery rather than the organization, San Jose created a "service delivery framework" to be used to inventory services and evaluate the alignment of the service being delivered with accomplishment of the city's mission, vision, and goals. The basic question is, "Are we doing the right things?"

An important role for employees in this evaluation is to help develop the inventory of services. Once given the knowledge and tools to inventory and describe services, employees are potentially the best source of information on what services are actually being delivered.

In San Jose, hundreds of employees from all levels of the organization were invited to participate in this effort on the basis of their knowledge of or direct responsibility for key functions or services. Training and facilitation were conducted to guide employees through these steps:

1. *Inventory and define services delivered.* Employees learned to focus on groups of activities that result in a distinct deliverable to customers, one that can be measured. The inventory included the internally delivered services of the administrative departments in the organization.

2. *Refine and check alignment of services.* Employees checked for duplication and opportunities for consolidation or elimination, and they confirmed that each service aligned with and contributed to accomplishment of the mission, vision, and goals of the organization.

3. *Identify who your customers are.* For many government services, this is not a simple question. The analysis should identify all types of customers. For example, who receives (directly or indirectly), pays for, or cares about the service you deliver?

4. *Validate using customer input.* Employees gathered input from identified customers in focus groups to clarify service descriptions, or restructure the service inventory to ensure they were meaningful from the customers' perspective.

After these steps, the city council — in a public setting — considered and approved service inventory and service descriptions.

When Determining Performance Measures and Targets, Put Learning Before Scorekeeping

Employees should participate in creating what is measured as well as in establishing baseline performance levels and future targets. To ensure constructive participation, ascertain whether the measurement and evaluation scheme is perceived as valid, fair, and forgiving when necessary. Employees must agree that the measures fairly represent the results of their work in order for them to take ownership. If the performance measurement effort stresses performance against targets too soon, employees may challenge the data or how the targets were set, or worse they may engage in game-playing to set targets that will always be met.

The key and continuing question here is, "Are we measuring the right things correctly?" A primary goal of a performance measurement system should be to improve service delivery, not just meet targets. Performance data should not be reported just for accountability purposes but must be used to better understand why results occurred and to evaluate actions taken to address performance issues.

In the San Jose model, a balanced set of performance measures including quality, cost, cycle time (if applicable), and customer satisfaction were developed for each service. Measuring each service on multiple dimensions is intended to generate data on internal aspects (how well, how much, how fast) as well as external customer perception of the overall success in meeting customer needs.

Communication among employees, customers, and stakeholders is also critical at this stage to validate existing perceptions of satisfaction with service delivery results and determine desired levels of performance and satisfaction. Every participant can benefit from others' perspectives. Two factors to consider are, first, how well services are being provided now. Customers are often unaware of the overall performance of a service because they have experienced a horror story, some incident that may occur only rarely. Though both are important, input from a customer satisfaction survey gives a much different perspective from a review of complaint data.

Second, what do customers want from our services? What they really want, need, or value may be very different from what employees currently believe. Through closer interaction, employees can learn that customers may value quick acknowledgment that their request is being worked on and can feel satisfied with a longer response time so long as it is reasonable and they know what to expect.

Just Try It—The Actual Experience May Not Be So Bad

Once the performance measurement and public involvement systems are established, what can employees expect? In place for more than five years, San Jose's system can offer examples.

A citywide resident survey is conducted every other fiscal year, asking respondents about issues the city should address and their satisfaction with city services, both overall and with individual services. Between the baseline year 2000 survey and the 2005 survey, San Jose's economy experienced the dot com crash and city revenues declined, creating the need for operating budget reductions, including hiring freezes, position cuts, and service-level reductions every year. Surprisingly, the 2005 survey showed residents' satisfaction with overall city service remained steady, and satisfaction with several individual services actually increased from 2000. A prime example was library services, reflecting the results of a bond-funded capital program to rebuild neighborhood branches, as well as implementation of new operating

practices within the branches designed to meet changing customer needs.

Overall maintenance of resident satisfaction, despite significant reductions in staffing and funding, may well be the result of employees being more productive as well as understanding which services are most important to residents.

A service delivery analysis of the city's vehicle abatement service was performed, using performance data and customer surveys to establish baseline performance and evaluate a six-month pilot program to restructure the service. San Jose's vehicle abatement policy is to cite and, if necessary, remove abandoned vehicles parked for more than seventy-two hours on city streets. To respond to a very high volume of service requests and numerous complaints of long resolution time, the service was reassigned to a new department on a pilot basis. New procedures were developed to improve initial response (warning citations) and reduce the time taken to remove abandoned vehicles. Performance measures were set up for initial response and case resolution with time frames that were reasonable to customers.

After the six-month pilot, the percentage of response time targets met increased significantly. In addition, a follow-up customer satisfaction survey of those requesting service showed a ten-percentage-point increase in satisfaction at every step of the process from initial complaint to resolution. When the results were shared with a city council committee in a recommendation to approve continuation of the new procedures, one council member asked several members of the public in attendance if the service had improved under the pilot. Despite the group's earlier presentation of a six-foot banner of photos of abandoned cars, they confirmed that things had definitely improved under the pilot program.

At the operational level, developing a better understanding between employees delivering service and their customers can produce unexpected benefits. A park maintenance worker shared a story about a customer he had thought of as a "nosy neighbor" who would regularly confront him on his rounds to clean up at a park playground. After initially finding this to be irritating, the worker realized that the customer was a good source of "field" intelligence, pointing out that teenagers would regularly have parties in the park on a particular night and the park would remain dirty for days until the next scheduled cleanup. On the basis of this information, the park worker could revise the maintenance route schedule to take care of the cleanup on the day immediately following.

The Three C's: Commitment, Capacity, Communication

Commitment

To ensure employees' continued constructive participation, leadership must display an initial and sustained commitment to the performance measurement effort and its public involvement elements. Introduction of any new effort will compete with many other priorities and demands on employees, but given the long list of organizational development initiatives introduced over the last ten to fifteen years, efforts such as these must also pass the "flavor of the month" test. Employees constantly evaluate not only statements from leadership but their actions as well, to judge the relative priority of the effort amid competing demands.

In local governments, public involvement and performance measurement efforts are often viewed as important though not urgent, and when competing needs arise, leadership's immediate priorities may change. However, it is particularly important for leaders to maintain a long-term commitment because once employees do choose to buy in to the effort, they will be increasingly sensitive to whether leaders are "walking the talk." If leaders' good faith is questionable, employees will quickly bail out, and it will be difficult if not impossible to regain their constructive participation.

To mitigate this potential, one suggestion is to develop an enduring statement of values to serve as a reminder of what remains important to the organization, through good budget times and bad; the statement may help to sustain public involvement and performance measurement efforts over time.

Capacity

Along with leadership commitment, these efforts require significant new resources or redirection of existing ones for a lengthy period of time to accomplish something that is worthwhile:

- Designated staff and funding to establish and sustain the performance measurement and public involvement systems at an effective level
- A sustained central training and coaching program to introduce new employees to the systems and update skills of existing employees
- Membership and participation in professional associations and peer or benchmarking groups to stay current with developments in the field as well as to share data and techniques
- Valid and consistent survey development methodology, templates, software, and other tools that give employees the knowledge and capacity to receive customer feedback on individual services
- Expertise and assistance in outreach to customers of specific services to communicate successes and receive input through more face-to-face methods such as presentations and focus groups

Communication

As mentioned previously, communication with employees during implementation of performance measurement and public involvement efforts is critical to allay fears, stop rumors, and obtain employees' participation as a major partner in the efforts. Once the system is established, open and timely communication about how the system is being used is critical in maintaining their constructive participation. Employees as well as their collective bargaining representatives need to be kept in the communication loop when performance is reported and when public input is given.

Final Thoughts

To be sustainable, performance measurement and public involvement cannot be seen as something extra. These efforts must become an integral part of the employees' job and expected as the way business is done. If not seen as an integral part of service delivery, these efforts may be an easy target for cuts when budget times are bad.

Sometimes government is seemingly inefficient for good reason. Although customers focus mainly on results, all parties must recognize that when it comes to government services, due process requirements and limits of legal authority cannot be ignored. Requirements such as public input or appeal processes, local policies and ordinances, and state and federal laws are significant factors in evaluating performance of government — especially when comparisons are made to the private sector. Employees must work to innovate and improve services within these requirements unless legislators, leadership, policymakers, and customers take action to change these requirements.

Resources affect the limits of what can be delivered, despite customer desires, and relative priorities and optimum service levels need to be decided on at every level, from the front line to elected representatives. Realistically, not every performance target can or should be set at 100 percent of what is ultimately desired for that service. Preparing employees to make these judgments on the basis of awareness of various customers' needs is vital.

Events and changing priorities affect the best planned service levels; permission to revise those plans and targets has to be an element of the system. Employees' exercise of good judgment and innovation should be encouraged and rewarded, as well as whether all performance targets are met.

Finally, expect to continuously check what is working and what needs improvement. Remember, failure is how we learn.

CHAPTER 41

Sandy Springs and Other Cities Contract for Public Works Services

Robert Barkin

With the clock ticking last fall, Centennial, Colo., officials had a tough decision to make. For the first time since it incorporated in 2001, the Denver-area city soon would be responsible for its own public works services, which previously were provided by Arapahoe County. City leaders had to make a choice: go it alone or hire out the operation to a contractor.

So, Public Works Director Dave Zelenok opened his spreadsheet and calculated the options. He could either build his department from scratch, buy all the equipment and hire a staff, or he could outsource the whole operation to a third-party provider. After running the numbers, he and other city leaders decided to outsource. "I was pleasantly surprised," he says. "The outsource option was competitive against the public sector model in a large city."

On July 1, 2008, Englewood, Colo.–based CH2M HILL OMI began conducting all public works functions for the city of 110,000 residents, from water and wastewater system optimization and operation to community development and public works administration. "This is a turning point," Zelenok says. "Outsourcing has now moved into a major city of over 100,000 people. There's never been a conversion of this size."

Centennial is just the latest city to contract with a private firm to take on traditionally public responsibilities. While Centennial is contracting with a single provider, others have chosen to use a variety of vendors. But in all the cases, cities are motivated to consider the move in an effort to improve service and control costs through competition and reduced overhead. Whether more cities will outsource may depend on economics, community acceptance and potential political opposition.

Picking and Choosing Services

The trend toward outsourcing entire public works departments is more of a trickle than a gusher at this point. While acknowledging that there have been cities that have moved to the private sector model, Dennis Houlihan, a labor economist for the Washington-based American Federation of State, City and Municipal Employees, says that the number has been "tiny" and mostly among smaller communities. Public works remains primarily a municipal department, Houlihan says, because of conflicts between the goals of the private and public organizations and lack of control of the public works function.

However, Richard Norment, executive director of the National Council for Public-

Originally published as "Public Works, Private Works," *American City & County*, Vol. 123, No. 8, August 2008, by Penton Media, Inc., Overland Park, KS. Reprinted with permission of the publisher.

Private Partnerships (NCPPP), says the concept of privately run public works departments is attracting increasing interest, nationally and internationally. "This started out popping up here and there," he says, "but now this is a serious emerging trend."

The model for outsourcing public works operations has been around for decades in the Los Angeles area. Lakewood, Calif., has relied on public works services supplied by outsiders for more than 50 years, ever since it incorporated in the early 1950s. Rather than allowing themselves to be annexed by Long Beach, homeowners in the development chose self-government. But that meant the new city could no longer rely on Los Angeles County to supply its services.

Initially, in 1954, the city contracted with the county for all of its services, including law enforcement, fire and public works. By 1957, the city had moved to a "hybrid" arrangement that meshed services from the county and private vendors, says Don Waldie, Lakewood's assistant to the city manager. "We learned early to mix services," he says. "We pick and choose which route is the most efficient and lowest cost. It depends on the character of the work."

The city of 83,000 residents has only 170 employees and a budget of $60 million. Rather than a large work force, the city has 20 people who manage vendor contracts. Waldie says that 25 percent of California cities now are organized following Lakewood's hybrid model. "I can't say whether this is a better way of performing these services or not," he says. "We have always done it this way. It would be impossible to change. We would be another kind of city."

Pleasant Ridge, Mich., a community of about 2,500 residents near Detroit, decided one year ago to end its 10-year public works contract with a single private company to move to a hybrid model that now depends on five different companies and services from neighboring municipalities. The city contracts with nearby Royal Oak for water and sewer services and with Oak Park for its curbside leaf pick-up. For landscaping and tree maintenance, it contracts with a local company. "After working entirely with one company, we realized there are strong areas and weak areas, as any other department under city auspices," says City Manager Sherry Ball. "This way, we have each provider's strong suit. We can capitalize on the best of the best."

Pleasant Ridge has no public works employees or legal costs, no overhead, no equipment or maintenance building; it just has to manage the contracts. The city is discussing with other communities the possibility of regionalizing public works services. "There's no reason not to form more of an alliance and share services," Ball says.

Going Solo

Given the same choice, though, Sandy Springs, Ga., leaders decided to hire a single provider when their city of 90,000 residents incorporated in 2005. Residents had been receiving services as an incorporated area of Fulton County, which includes Atlanta, but decided they could do better on their own.

The city hired one private firm for all city services — everything except police and fire, which the city provides. Since then, other nearby cities, including Johns Creek and Milton, also have adopted the sole-source model. Sandy Springs Mayor Eva Galambos says the ability to work with a single vendor has given the community "more flexibility than working through a civil service system."

One improvement has consolidated all city information on a single database that allows residents to expedite their permits. An application for a home-owner to build a new deck can take 10 to 15 minutes, instead of the previous three weeks, and business permits are approved much faster. "We're sticking with this model," Galambos says. "It's definitely more efficient."

According to Norment, the Sandy Springs decision to use outsourcing for the whole city was a breakthrough for the model of providing public works services. Previously, he says, cities contracted just for pieces of their operation, like water systems. But difficult times are making cities rethink how they deliver services, he says, noting that renewal rates on contracts for private sector services are more than 95 percent.

In theory, nothing is preventing a much larger city from outsourcing its public works functions, Norment says. "The only impediment is developing the public consensus," he says.

NCPPP has developed keys for successful private-public partnerships, and the list includes establishing the laws to allow such an operation, developing a receptive political environment and strong political leadership. "Cities are in a declining revenue stream," because of falling tax revenues, he says. "This allows them to maximize their revenue and maintain control."

Comparing Apples

Maximizing revenue and maintaining control were among the key objectives of Centennial, Colo., leaders as they debated whether to build their own public works department or hire an outside company to perform and manage the city's daily operations. Zelenok, the city's public works director and the key staffer behind the ultimate decision, came to the position from a unique perspective. Previously, as public works director for Colorado Springs, a city with about 375,000 residents, he had managed a department that performed everything from paving streets to operating a local toll road.

When Zelenok joined the city staff, Centennial had about eight months to figure out how to deliver public works services to the community. "I compared a fully burdened insource model with an outsource model," he says, "and outsource won, but not by a huge amount." In comparing the two formats, Zelenok considered costs such as training, retirement plans and insurance. "Apples to apples," he says.

In the end, other considerations entered into the decision to use the private sector alternative. Zelenok points out that there is now a call center that will respond to residents' questions around the clock, seven days a week.

The final five-year contract, which includes a number of built-in penalties and performance incentives, is worth about $4 million for the second half of 2008 and about $8.6 million in 2009. The city will review the contract annually.

Most importantly, the outsourcing model gives the city more control, Zelenok says. "I don't have to worry about the budget for the next five years," he says.

For Zelenok, the outsource model allows him to spend less time on personnel issues, like hiring and firing, and more time crafting a strategic vision for the city. "It's what I really want to do," he says, "charting a way ahead for the community."

CHAPTER 42

Savannah Uses a Budgeting for Results Process

Eva Elmer *and* Christopher Morrill

The art of leadership in today's world involves orchestrating the inevitable conflict, chaos, and confusion of change so that the disturbance is productive rather than destructive.[1]

At the end of 2008, city leadership determined that the City of Savannah, Georgia, needed a long-term structural approach to lowering expenditures, and they decided to make the transition to budgeting for outcomes (BFO) in 2009. The changeover was challenging, not only because of the intensity of the learning and implementation process for all involved, but also because the city was under great financial pressure in the midst of a steep economic downturn. However, the priority-driven BFO process helped focus available revenue while supporting the city's most important goals.

The city realized many benefits from this process, but the top four are:

- **Financial Resiliency**. Meeting budget reduction targets without increasing taxes or resorting to balancing gimmicks that would simply increase financial problems in later years.
- **Clarity of Outcomes**. Opening up the budget process and financial information to the entire organization in order to focus all employees on assisting with the financial challenges.

- **Internal Engagement**. Training hundreds of employees to identify outcomes, develop performance measures, and prioritize services.
- **Cross-Departmental Cooperation**. Changing the organizational culture to one of service collaboration in order to meet community priorities.

Why Budgeting for Outcomes

The city's financial team had first been introduced to budgeting for outcomes at a Government Finance Officers Association (GFOA) conference in June 2008. The immediate reaction was that this was a great approach to budgeting but extremely time-consuming and a major challenge to the status quo. If things ever got bad enough, maybe Savannah would try it. Then, in the fall of 2008, things did get bad enough; the economic crisis became global and hit Savannah's major industries hard.

The City of Savannah, like local governments around the country, was faced with the greatest financial challenge in decades. While

Originally published as "Budgeting for Outcomes in Savannah," *Government Finance Review*, Vol. 26, No. 2, April 2010, by the Government Finance Officers Association, Chicago, IL. Reprinted with permission of the publisher.

Savannah's diverse economy spared the city from the beginning stages of the recession, the downturn hit city revenues beginning in the fall of 2008. Since that time, sales tax revenue and property tax revenue declined substantially, and other elastic sources of revenue such as hotel/motel taxes and rental vehicle taxes declined by more than 10 percent. Additionally, the state of Georgia prohibited property reassessments until 2012. The cumulative impact of these challenges compelled the city to reduce the 2010 general fund budget by more than $10 million. Fortunately, when times were good and revenues were increasing, Savannah had done the right things. The city had reduced general fund debt by more than 40 percent in the previous eight years, increased the capital maintenance program, increased reserves — including establishing a special sales tax stabilization fund to smooth out the volatility of elastic revenue sources — and invested in projects that reduced ongoing costs (e.g., energy retrofits).

The financial challenges were clearly structural and not short term. Therefore, city officials decided to avoid short-term fixes; they would not make across-the-board-cuts, draw down reserves, delay maintenance, take a pension holiday, or undertake other cost-reduction methods that would not lead to long-term budget reductions. Instead, Savannah's financial leaders chose to realistically determine the amount of funds available and then direct them to services and programs that best met the city's priorities — in other words, budgeting for outcomes.

Assessing the City's Capabilities

The first step in the BFO process was to find out if the city had the talent, technical capabilities, and will to adapt to this challenging new process. The core financial team, which consisted of representatives from the finance, research and development, human resources, and auditing departments, was brought together to study the issue. Team members had mixed reactions to BFO, but generally the concern was about change. Of the major issues that came out of these meetings, the first was that the change would be too labor-intensive for staff to deal with, especially when there was so much to cope with as a result of the financial crisis. There were also concerns about whether city staff actually had the skills necessary to carry out the change. And finally, the research and development department staff was worried that it would be difficult to adapt BFO to the city's existing financial software system. A new system would have to be created to accommodate and adapt BFO and then translate it back to the legacy financial system.

In the end, the city determined that it had the talent, will, and sufficient technology to adopt the new system. Implementing BFO would force the city to take a more strategic, thoughtful, collaborative, and innovative approach to closing the projected budget gap in 2010 and beyond. Furthermore, the new system would have the added benefit of involving more people in the budget process, tapping into more talent, and creating an environment that promoted teamwork. The most controversial aspect of BFO is that it puts a great deal of trust in thoughtful non-experts to make good decisions and to encourage or force experts to start thinking outside the box. If this basic premise is not accepted, BFO will not generate the preferred results.

Introducing BFO to the Organization

In February 2009, the city manager and assistant city manager gathered key financial staff, bureau chiefs, and department heads for a two-day meeting to introduce BFO. They knew they had to make a strong case to staff to help employees understand that the city could not continue with business as usual. External consultants presented an overview of BFO and case studies from other cities to help illustrate the process and its desired outcomes. They were also on hand to help newly minted teams and team leaders understand their roles and get organized.

The initial introduction of BFO overwhelmed the majority of staff and created a lot of confusion. There were a handful of employees, however, who left the meeting feeling like they had a fairly clear understanding of what BFO was. Many of these employees had come into public service from the private sector and the BFO system was much more in line with what they had been accustomed to as private-sector workers. They were happy with the change because, it emphasized efficiency and strategic thinking. The conversion was less traumatic for them than it seemed to be for their colleagues who were career public administrators. The city leadership team has determined that it would be worth the effort to tap into the experience and insight of these employees as Savannah continues working through the process.

Developing the Priorities

The executive staff put together a list of priorities based primarily on the Savannah City Council's vision statement and existing goals. However, existing council goals focused on where to direct new resources, and they did not include all community values. For example, the city council did not have goals for culture and recreation or financial management, although these were clearly community values. The priorities were expanded to be more inclusive through feedback from citizen survey data, ongoing interaction with neighborhoods, and staff input. Each priority was given a priority statement. Each statement was written from the citizen's point of view:

- **Economic Growth**. "I want to live in a community that has appropriate economic growth that creates jobs, expands city revenue, and improves neighborhoods and commercial corridors."
- **Poverty Reduction**. "I want to live in a community that reduces poverty by empowering motivated people to become economically self-sufficient."
- **Neighborhood Vitality**. "I want to live in a city of strong and vibrant neighborhoods that are clean, safe, and encourage a sense of community."
- **Public Safety**. "I want to be safe and feel safe from crime, fire, and other hazards anywhere in the community."

- **Culture and Recreational Opportunities**. "I want to live in a community that provides a recreational and cultural opportunity that will keep my mind and body active and that recognizes the needs of all citizens."
- **Health and Environment**. "I want to live in a community that promotes health through good infrastructure while preserving the environment for future generations."
- **High-Performing Government**. "I want a fiscally responsible, accessible, and responsive government that maximizes use of public resources for services I need."

Sellers and Offers

BFO is based on the premise that instead of being organized through individual departments, budgeting should be based on services one department or several departments (as well as outside agencies) provide to the city. One or more departments or authorized outside agencies offer services to "sell" to the city at a certain price. The city "buys" the service based on how closely it aligns with the indicators, factors, and strategies detailed in the "request for results" (RFR) associated with each priority. An offer includes a description of the service, its justification, and an explanation of how the service addresses a priority. It details any collaboration efforts with outside agencies and departments, performance measurements (output, quality, and outcomes), and a summary of total expenditures.

Department heads and outside agencies were given a training session on writing offers, and the research and development department provided a guidebook with step-by-step instructions for filling out the online Excel forms and calculating expenditures. Although information and support were provided, there was still a great deal of confusion, and research and development spent a lot of time cleaning up expenditure calculations. More targeted training for different types of departments would have been helpful. Authorized outside agencies were especially vulnerable in the new system and felt that they were at a disadvantage in competing with city departments when submitting offers.

Some of the issues that came up during this part of the process had to do with ensuring that sellers were accounting for all expenditures in their offers and that they had effective performance measurements. An important part of the BFO system is making staff see and understand the total cost involved in providing a program or a service. This involved accounting for all overhead costs, monies that departments would not normally include in traditional budgeting (e.g., gas costs for vehicles, risk management allocations, pensions, and longevity bonuses for personnel). Performance measurements are also an essential component of the BFO model. Many sellers struggled to put together quality performance measurements, and consequently, the priorities team will focus on this issue for the 2011 budget cycle.

Teams: Key to Success

The city's financial team developed the teams that would help lead the city through the BFO process. The BFO framework suggests having a priorities team to provide overall leadership; a process team to monitor progress, set deadlines, and help clarify procedural and process issues; and a results team for each priority. The results teams put together the indicators (specific measures of success), craft the strategy maps (visual representations of a cause-effect pathway to a desired outcome), develop the RFR from which the offers are written, and then rank the offers.

In the Savannah model, the city eliminated the process team, adding those responsibilities to the priorities team, and expanded the budgeting team structure. A values team and efficiency task forces were also added. The values team was made up exclusively of bureau chiefs (the seven individuals who answer directly to the city manager). The hope was that bureau chiefs would be in the best position to identify channels leading toward inter-bureau cooperation and reveal efficiencies that could be implemented throughout the city. Each efficiency task force was a temporary cross-bureau group focusing on identifying cost savings in one operational area. For example, task forces looked at the city fleet, office space, mowing — all areas where there were possibilities for reducing costs through shared use and collaboration. The theory was that these task forces, through reporting to the values team, would make recommendations that departments could use to reduce the costs of their offers.

Results Teams. The city was interested in choosing people for the results teams who could think beyond the limits of their own departments, who could be critical thinkers and put themselves in the role of an average citizen or non-expert when reviewing offers and linking them to desired outcomes. Furthermore, and perhaps most importantly, team members needed to not only deal with change in a positive way, but also to embrace the experience and inspire others to do the same. In the end, results teams took ownership of the process and became committed to its success. Out of this process, new leaders emerged who otherwise might never have been identified.

The target for completing the 2010 budget was October 2009. Results team meetings began in February 2009 with the teams' first task: Identify three to five indicators that would serve as broad measurements of success for each priority. After the indicators were in place, teams started working on strategy maps, which provide a succinct look at what matters most. The maps consist of identifying three to five primary factors that contribute to achieving the priority, and then identifying three to five secondary factors that directly contribute to the primary factors. The teams researched and found evidence that these factors demonstrated a direct causal relationship to the priority, even if it seemed counterintuitive. For example, "well-maintained streets" is a secondary factor that contributes to a primary factor "prevention of risk" under the public safety priority.

After developing the strategy maps, each results team developed RFR documents. Each RFR included a description of the desired outcome, the factors that contribute to the outcome, the strategies that will influence each outcome, and the indicators that will serve as a gauge in determining if the results have been achieved. RFRs were submitted at the beginning of May 2009.

City-wide Priorities Team. The priorities team's responsibilities included overseeing the process, establishing a timeline, making procedural decisions, allocating funds for each priority, handling communication with teams and executive staff, and training or offering guidance to results team leaders. As results teams were working on indicators, strategy maps, and RFRs, the priorities team spent a great deal of time discussing the details of each step. Issues that came up and the subsequent decision made about them include:

- How do capital improvement projects fit in with BFO? (Capital improvement projects were not included in the process for this year but will probably be included in subsequent years.)
- How are overhead departments handled? (All overhead departments were included in the "high-performing government" priority.)
- Will team members submitting offers be allowed to vote on their own offers? (Yes.)
- Will team members assigned as recorders and facilitators be allowed to vote on offers? (Yes.)
- What will the criteria be for ranking offers? (There will be forced ranking with a third ranked "excellent," a third ranked "very good," and a third ranked "good." Team members give offers 3 points for excellent, 2 points for very good, and 1 point for good. All offers should be scored individually first and then by the team, and finally ranked after discussion and debate.)
- How are outside social service agencies effectively incorporated in BFO? (A presentation was given to all outside organization, and a separate results team was set up to review and rank offers from outside agencies.)

The priorities team set up regular meetings with results team leaders and facilitators, allowing them to vent, voice concerns, exchange ideas, ask questions, and learn successive steps in the process. These meetings proved vital in keeping the teams working within the same framework of rules and in ensuring the integrity of the system. Feedback from results team and priority team members underscored how critical they were to the success of the process.

Challenges Ranking Offers

When offers were submitted, the results teams began working on the first-round ranking. Each offer was ranked without regard to cost and only on the merits of how well it met key results. Feedback from team members revealed certain challenges in the ranking process:

- **Bias.** Results teams took the issue of bias in ranking very seriously. Some teams went to great lengths to minimize any appearance of bias throughout the process. In the end, each team relied on a team member's good judgment and objectivity. Final decisions were based on team consensus, and most felt satisfied with their final rankings. Many team members commented that the biggest challenge they had was taking themselves out of their own departments and acting in the best interests of the city.
- **Team Makeup.** The most important issue about the makeup of the results teams had to do with the balance between subject area experts and non-experts. Some sellers believed their offers ranked low because they didn't have enough subject experts on a team, while others saw the involvement of non-experts as essential to moderating issues of bias and supporting the goal of staff looking at programs from the point of view of the city and its citizens.
- **Offer Size.** There was concern that opportunities to find efficiencies were missed because of the sheer size of an offer. Small offers tended to have a higher casualty rate than large ones because the small offers were more easily handled and researched and thus easier to cut.
- **General Fund vs. Enterprise Fund.** All offers, regardless of funding sources, were ranked together. This did cause some confusion for team members, and many supported the notion of either disclosing all

funding sources during the second round of ranking or ranking offers funded from the general fund and enterprise or other funds separately.

After the priorities team established funding levels for each priority, second-round ranking began. Offers were re-ranked with funding taken into account. During the second-round ranking and post-ranking period, results teams analyzed offers and worked with sellers to reduce cost, create efficiencies, and identify avenues for collaboration and consolidation of services. Savings found with offers that were above the funding line helped fund programs and services that had fallen below the line. It was a challenging process, but in the end, the City of Savannah had relatively few programs that went unfunded.

Collaboration and Innovation

The race to save programs at the end of the BFO process served as an effective way of wringing out the efficiencies and cost-saving measures that were critical to balancing the budget. In traditional budgeting, there is an understanding that department heads and bureau chiefs will hang on to a "cushion" as a buffer against budget cuts they know will come. In the end, there were relatively few services that had to be cut because bureau chiefs were forced to look closely at all their programs to cut the fat from their budgets and find new ways to collaborate with other departments in order to reduce costs. Although somewhat slow to embrace this major change in budget preparation, the majority of bureau chiefs played important and critical roles to bring in a balanced budget.

As difficult, time consuming, and frustrating as many found the process to be, there was a lot of positive feedback on how much the exercise of creating indicators, strategy maps, and RFRs changed the way team members thought about the role of city government. Setting priorities and creating a visual roadmap to achieving those priorities had a powerful impact on the organization. Instead of status quo, city staff had to seriously examine what was impor-

tant, visualizing where the city was going and how it was going to get there.

Conclusions

The City of Savannah had to cut nearly $10 million from the 2010 budget because of the financial crisis, and BFO was an important tool — it helped the city identify its most important priorities and provided guidance on how to approach cost cutting strategically. Expenditures had to be reduced, which would have been the case regardless of the budgeting system in place. However, BFO made the painful budgeting process more constructive and purposeful.

The first year of BFO came with a great deal of anxiety and disorganization because of the newness of the system. Among other things, working on the BFO infrastructure in the same year as implementing the system (many experts recommend a two-year implementation) caused the budgeting cycle to become much longer. The entire process, from when BFO was introduced to staff to when the City Council adopted it, took 11 months, as opposed to the usual six-month cycle.

BFO introduced a process that energized staff and created an environment that rewarded innovation and collaboration across departmental lines. The city's mayor had established a paradigm for change at the beginning of his tenure in office, calling for the creation of "a distinctive environment in which employees feel an alignment with and a deep commitment to the ideals and mission of the organization." The mayor saw BFO as a continuation of that paradigm and indicated that he was proud of staff for committing themselves to setting aside the interests of their own bureaus or departments, taking ownership of the process, looking objectively at the city's most important priorities, and working toward achieving those goals. One of the best aspects of BFO, he noted, is that it involved so many people throughout the organization who were all focused on the same vision and set of priorities. BFO involved a greater number of staff members across all bureaus than traditional budgeting does, opening countless informal lines of communication and facilitating current and future avenues for co-operation. Staff interviewed during the assessment of the process consistently supported the premise of BFO because it took a more strategic approach to cost reductions and created a budget that focused on achieving the city's most important priorities.

Important Considerations in Developing a BFO System

1. **Make Culture Change Central to the BFO Process and Continuously Challenge the Status Quo.** Managing change requires dedicated, committed leadership in the face of resistance and a complex environment.

2. **Get Buy-In from the Governing Board Early On.** BFO represents a major change, so it is important to proceed with the approval of the governing board.

3. **Put the "Best and Brightest" on Your Teams.** Do not choose by title.

4. **Clearly Define an Organization-wide and Ongoing Communication Strategy.** Having an effective and ongoing communication strategy cannot be over-emphasized. Change is difficult in any organization, and it is even more difficult when the central leadership loses control of the message to the rumor mill. BFO training for all levels of the organization should be a key component of this strategy.

5. **Determine the Level of Outside Help You Need.** Be realistic about how much help your organization will need and bring in outside consultants to help with the whole transition, or with parts of it. The length of time you choose for implementing BFO — 12 or 24 months — will influence this decision.

6. **Define All BFO Staff Roles.** Without clear roles, the BFO process will not function effectively. Functions and responsibilities of BFO staff need to be defined, and these roles within the process need to be recognized and empowered by strong central leadership.

7. **The Chief Executive Should Take a Strong Role as BFO Leader.** Change that is not supported at the highest level is not likely to succeed.

8. **Establish a System Dedicated to Idea Generation, Selection, and Dissemination.** Create a database of ideas for innovation, cost savings, and cross-collaboration. Employ an evaluation process for idea selection and publish the best ideas — share them at team meetings or through targeted e-mails. Implement a system for keeping a record of ideas so knowledge is not lost.

9. **BFO Is Not a Process You Can Do Halfway.** The system must be fully implemented to produce results.

Questions to Ask: Is Your Organization Ready for BFO?

• Do you have the time?
• Do you have the talent?
• Are your elected officials on board?
• Do you have support from top management?
• Do you have the technology?
• Can your organization deal with change?
• Do you have a communication strategy?
• Can your organization deal with the fact that BFO is an art, not a science?

Unexpected Benefits

While the original goal of BFO was to produce a sustainable balanced budget, the city experienced some unanticipated but positive consequences:

• New leaders emerged.
• The level of discussion and debate in the organization was elevated.
• Performance measurements were finally linked directly to results.
• Tremendous capacity was built throughout the organization.
• Elected officials felt more involved in the process.

NOTE

1. Ronald Heifetz, Alexander Grashow, and Marty Linky, "Leadership in a (Permanent) Crisis," *Harvard Business Review*, July-August 2009.

Editor's note: The official team structure approved by Savannah's mayor and alderman for their Budgeting for Outcomes (BFO) process had the City-Wide Priorities Team and City-Wide Value Team reporting directly to their city manager, who reported directly to the elected officials.

CHAPTER 43

Seattle and Other Cities Implement Joint Purchasing Programs

Connie Kuranko

Increasing numbers of environmentally friendly products are available — from office supplies to furniture, and technology products to lab supplies — and government purchasing professionals are looking at new contracts with a green lens. As local government leaders institute environmentally preferable policies and programs, purchasing professionals are boning up on their product knowledge and trying new purchasing methods to meet environmental goals while staying within their budgets.

Following the Money

Having increased by more than 400 percent in the last three years, green building programs are on the rise among the top 200 most populated counties in the country, according to a recent report from the National Association of Counties (NACo) and the American Institute of Architects, both based in Washington. The growth in greener building is attributed to local leadership and the sharing of ordinances and resolutions among counties and cities.

But, green buildings can do only so much to help reduce energy use and waste. They have to be augmented with renewable energy credits, hybrid fleet vehicles, biofuels, reduced garbage collection coupled with increased recycling,

water use management, energy efficiency evaluations and more eco-friendly products and services.

The demand for greener products and services has prompted some cities and counties to hire sustainability directors and recycling experts, and has, in many cases, changed the government purchasing professional's role. Public purchasers are seeing a greater need for integration among departments and are looking for ways to work with other local and state agencies. They also have had to become versed in eco-labeling language to ensure the products they select have specific certifications and are not making false or misleading claims.

Buying in the Emerald City

Some cities and counties are taking the lead on sustainable purchasing and are becoming examples for others to follow. Seattle leaders, for example, have been "buying green" for years. "A series of local ordinances date back to the 1970s and provide the legal and policy framework to make green purchasing a priority and a mandate," says Nancy Locke, the city's purchasing manager. "Mayor Nickels and the city council have continued to renew and update the ordinances to stay up to date with the

Originally published as "Purchasing: The Green Standard," *American City & County*, Vol. 123, No. 9, September 2008, by Penton Media, Inc., Overland Park, KS. Reprinted with permission of the publisher.

most current knowledge and best practices. Having such clear ordinance authority, established early on, gives us our strongest tool to ensure all departments pursue a green purchasing standard."

Seattle's Green Purchasing Program aims to promote goods, materials, services and capital improvements that help reduce greenhouse gas emissions. In addition, purchasing contracts include several mandates, such as using 100-percent recycled paper for city work, duplex document production, toxin-free chemicals in pesticide and facility management contracts and reduced Persistent Bioaccumulative Toxic chemicals (PBTs) in products the city buys.

In selecting from the top-rated bids or proposals, the city requires bidders to identify any PBTs in their products and may require them to describe environmental benefits of their products or services. The city also has used environmental scoring as a substantial part of the selection criteria for computer hardware, cleaning chemicals, paint, copier equipment and paper products.

The Seattle Purchasing Department taps into green experts who work with the city to help prepare strategies and bids. "Sometimes these are champions that work for different organizations or companies, but their personal knowledge or commitment makes them extremely valuable to our base of expertise. These experts encourage us and are often the ones who point out opportunities and help prepare strategies and specifications for the city's bids," Locke says.

In the last five years, Seattle officials have made more specific efforts to use cooperative purchasing as a tool to accomplish their environmental purchasing objectives. It joined the Walnut Creek, Calif.–based U.S. Communities Green Purchasing Program to gain access to a broad line of environmentally certified products and services. The program identifies items in its contracts that meet third-party environmental certification standards, including EcoLogo, Green Seal and Energy Star, and public agencies can search the group's Web site to find products' environmental information. "Cooperative purchasing allows us easier access to environmentally preferable product lines. Some-

times the products are emerging technologies that don't yet lend themselves to an independent city bid; sometimes it allows us easy access to a wider share of green products," Locke says. "Our mayor has committed to serving as a model for our residents, companies and public agencies in our use of green products. Cooperative purchasing allows us to assist agencies with easy-access to our own green contract bid results."

No Rules, Just Right

Hennepin County, Minn., instituted its Environmentally Preferable Purchasing and Green Building Program in 1997 and changed the name in April 2001 to the Environmentally Preferable Purchasing and Waste Reduction Resolution after county officials studied waste growth projections and disposal trends. The resolution is not guided by a specific ordinance, but is purposefully unspecific in nature. "We feel it gives our program more flexibility in a time of changing technologies, products, priorities, certifications, etc.," says Nathan Reinbold, environmentally preferable purchasing/recycling specialist. "Our resolution is written in general language to allow us to accomplish the most without being restricted. Hennepin didn't want certain certifications or a detailed resolution/policy to hamper what we set out to do in the first place: buy green and be green, while saving green."

Without a specific ordinance, Hennepin County can choose the most appropriate products for its needs, rather than follow specific standards that can be restrictive. However, Reinbold says the county is moving to become more standardized to close loopholes that defeat the purpose of the green purchasing program.

Hennepin County purchasers look for environmentally preferable certifications, such as EcoLogo and Green Seal, when making purchasing decisions, and they consider the amount of waste that will be generated by the products they buy to help minimize the amount of toxic materials that are brought in and have to be disposed. They also aim to reduce the amount of packaging needed for products and often buy in bulk to limit packaging waste.

Hennepin County's Green Purchasing Program works with county departments to help purchase environmentally preferable products, create resolutions, lead workshops and report on green purchasing progress. "Being the largest county in Minnesota, we feel we have the role, responsibility and resources to pilot and implement green products and practices to show to the rest of the state that it can be done," Reinbold says. "Most importantly, purchasing can be done in a way that minimizes costs while still protecting the environment."

In 2005, the county established a Lead by Example Incentive Fund for county departments attempting to reduce waste or purchase green products. The fund offers $100,000 annually to be used on innovative waste reduction, recycling and environmentally preferable purchasing projects. The awards typically are between $5,000 and $25,000, and have helped with bulk computer purchases, using compost on roadway slopes to prevent erosion, and buying bulk dispensing supplies and chemicals to facilitate a switch to green cleaners.

To measure progress on green purchases, Reinbold receives reports from vendors detailing the lower toxicity rates of and recycled content in products. Hennepin County also measures its success by the number of buildings that are being cleaned in a "green" way.

Since the county instituted its environmentally preferable purchasing program, demand for guidance in sustainable purchasing has increased, creating an opportunity for the county to explore cooperative purchasing. "Being a part of a cooperative purchasing program like U.S. Communities, we realize substantial cost savings when we pool our purchasing powers," Reinbold says. "It is good business practice and common sense in the world of crunched budgets and trying to do more with less."

For local government purchasers in the early stages of instituting sustainable purchasing programs, Reinbold says, "Pick low-lying fruit first. Don't try to take on the world all at once. Going green is a never-ending, fluid process. You are always trying to do better over time with the resources you have to work with. When you understand this, environmentally preferable purchasing becomes a lot easier."

As Locke and Reinbold have found, creating partnerships and sharing information is key to the success of sustainable purchasing programs. Adapting to green purchasing policies and building a sustainable purchasing portfolio is not a task that can be done all at once, but is an exercise made easier and more effective when it is done cooperatively.

CHAPTER 44

Springfield and Other Cities Reduce Their Energy Costs

John W. DeWitt

America's local and state governments annually spend more than $10 billion on energy, and much of it is wasted. Driven to reduce energy consumption and its environmental effects, many are moving aggressively to "power down."

"The idea that sustainability is important is permeating the nation," says John Soladay, director of environmental health for Albuquerque, N.M. "There are 850-something cities that have committed to reducing greenhouse gases. We're all scrambling, but at least we're moving."

The recessionary economy has added another reason to become energy efficient, says Alan Shark, executive director of the Washington-based Public Technology Institute. "Everyone is in this hunker-down mentality, and governments don't want to ask residents for more money when they are already strapped," Shark says. "People want to do the right thing and save the planet, but when economic reality faces people, they become more pragmatic."

So, local governments of all sizes are retrofitting air conditioning and lighting systems in buildings, replacing streetlights with light-emitting diodes (LEDs) and buying alternative fuel vehicles. Albuquerque; Springfield, Mass.; and Palm Desert, Calif., are three communities that already have taken innovative energy-saving steps to build more efficient futures.

Sustainable Strategies

Albuquerque has been busy in the five years since three-term Mayor Martin Chávez signed onto the bipartisan Mayors' Statement on Global Warming, an early version of the Washington-based U.S. Conference of Mayors climate protection agreement. To start, the mayor assembled an executive-level "green team" of department directors and others to build a plan toward sustainability — reducing greenhouse gas reduction, the amount of natural resources burned and dependence on foreign oil, Soladay says. Nine months later, a sustainable development strategy with eight core components emerged. "This plan in itself is a huge step for most cities, but it establishes a base framework for moving ahead," Soladay says.

Though environmental sustainability has been a main focus for the mayor, Albuquerque has benefited from a succession of energy conservation initiatives dating back to the late 1980s, when the city began converting part of its fleet to compressed natural gas (CNG). "By the early '90s, we recognized the importance of doing things like changing out light fixtures and ballasts, so we funded a line item to do that," Soladay says. "By the late '90s, for bigger and more innovative projects, we adopted a program

Originally published as "Energy: Cutting Kilowatts," *American City & County*, Vol. 124, No. 1, January 2009, by Penton Media, Inc., Overland Park, KS. Reprinted with permission of the publisher.

setting aside 1 percent of total capital improvement funding to target energy conservation."

In 2007, the mayor and city council increased the set-aside to 3 percent, directing $4.6 million toward infrastructure energy improvements. "Albuquerque is the only city I've found that actually funds their improvements that way," Soladay says.

The city also tracks its transportation-related energy use and greenhouse gas emissions and has reduced them. Today, more than half the city's fleet operates on alternative power sources — E85 (85 percent ethanol/15 percent gasoline), B20 diesel, CNG and hybrid engines. "We developed internal purchasing policies that mandate not only alternative fuels, but the most efficient vehicle for the application," Soladay says. "There's a strict review process attached to the mandate, and we put our green report card on our city's Web site to show that the numbers are verified, can be duplicated and measurements are believable."

Other savings come from energy-efficient traffic signals and lighting on streets and parking lots. "The payback is very short on LED traffic light conversions," Soladay says, especially now that costs have been reduced from $150 to below $50 per 12-inch light fixture. Conventional bulbs are still cheaper at $15 each, but they have to be changed every 18 months, versus every 10 years for an LED.

Facilities First

Going green also is the new wave for the old New England industrial center of Springfield, Mass. Spurred by the 2006 election of a new mayor, Domenic Sarno, the city has moved aggressively over the past two years to reduce energy consumption in its fleet and in its aging infrastructure, where the average building age is 54 years and the oldest school dates back to 1896.

As a key component of its energy-saving efforts, Springfield hired Buffalo Grove, Ill.-based Siemens Building Technologies to replace the ancient oil-fired boilers in more than two dozen city buildings, and install automatic light sensors and energy misers on computers and vending machines. The heating system upgrades, financed through city bonds, will pay for themselves in 12 years, and electricity consumption has been cut by 2.5 million kilowatt hours.

Springfield is taking other steps toward the city's sustainable future, Sarno says, including piloting a single-stream recycling program, hosting an annual green forum, and hiring an executive to coordinate green initiatives, such as green design, sustainable development and attracting green business to the city. The city also has announced a pilot plan to purchase four hybrid Ford Escapes for the parks division. Solar energy — even in the northern, snow-belt city — also is playing a role. The city has installed solar-powered trash compactors from Needham, Mass.–based BigBelly Solar and soon will request bids for photovoltaic panels on school buildings.

Private Participation

Even the small city of Palm Desert, Calif., has made itself a force for energy conservation — in a desert locale where the demand for summertime air conditioning consumes 150 percent more power than other areas of southern California, according to Patrick Conlon, director of the city's office of energy management. With a self-imposed deadline of December 30, 2011, the city has committed to reducing energy consumption by 30 percent — and that includes homes and businesses.

Palm Desert's government already has made significant progress toward its goal. Harnessing 350 days a year of sunshine, about half of government's electricity comes from photovoltaic arrays. Additionally, all new government buildings must attain at least a silver rating by the Washington-based U.S. Green Building Council's Leadership in Energy and Environmental Design (LEED) Green Building Rating System.

Palm Desert also is challenging the private sector to cut energy use by 30 percent at the end of 2011, and it is offering to fund private-sector energy conservation through unlimited government-backed loans to businesses and homeowners. "Time and again people say, 'I know I have a 25-year-old air conditioner that needs to be replaced, and I know my energy bills are $800 a month, but it's not a good time to get a home equity loan to put in a new $10,000 air conditioner,'" Conlon says.

City officials worked with local state assembly representative Lloyd Levine to create the Energy Independence Act that passed in July to allow private-sector energy conservation loans. Now, cities and counties can set up special energy districts, where business and residential property owners can borrow from the government and pay back the loans through their property taxes. Furthermore, local governments in California now can sell bonds to fund their private-sector loan programs.

To jump-start the loan program seeded by grant funding from the California Public Utilities Commission, the city council appropriated $2.5 million from its general fund in late August. "We have already spent $1.6 million, and people are standing in line for the loans," Conlon says. "The bad news is I have to ask the city council for more money. Bond packages take about 90 days to put together, and I don't want to interrupt this program."

Palm Desert offers 20-year loans for improvements at a 7 percent interest rate, with a $5,000 minimum and no maximum. Authorized improvements include solar panels, natural gas fuel cells, white roofs and EnergyStar refrigerators. "It's not a personal loan, so we don't have to concern ourselves with credit history, loan-to-value ratios, and so on," Conlon says. "It's just an assessment on the property, just like a curb or gutter or sewer assessment, and it stays with the property."

Leadership Lessons

Governments that reduce energy consumption and improve sustainability do more than plan and implement good programs; they dedicate leaders to the task and ensure accountability. "Where you find successes, you find not just leadership, but what I call championship—an energized cheerleader with substance who is out there keeping the energy issue alive in a meaningful way," Shark says.

In Springfield, Mayor Sarno's leadership approach has combined energy conservation, environmentalism, urban redevelopment, and an emphasis on the arts as integrated quality-of-life issues that will attract green-oriented businesses and residents downtown. Sarno's long-term vision is closely tied to saving money and reducing pollution from energy consumption.

Palm Desert officials quickly recognized that meeting their goal required support beyond their capabilities. Residents and businesses have taken action, southern California utilities funded grants, and the state assembly and governor approved the bill allowing local governments to float bonds to loan money to the private sector for energy conservation. Next, seeking even lower interest rates on energy conservation loans, Palm Desert leaders and their U.S. congressional representative, Mary Bono Mack, have set their sights on the IRS tax code. "Cities historically have sold tax-free municipal bonds to fund public works, but the IRS has ruled that because our loan program involves improvements to private property, they have to be taxable municipal bonds," Conlon says. "The market for them is very small, whereas there's a big market for tax-free municipal bonds, which are 2 to 3 percent cheaper."

If Palm Desert's latest push is successful, "It would help cities throughout America, and also would help the loan applicants, because cities could pass on the savings to them," Conlon says.

And, in Albuquerque, the mayor's task force is plotting a comprehensive climate action plan. "When we're done, we will have established clear reduction targets and a plan for us to achieve those targets," Soladay explains, emphasizing that continued support from top leadership "is the driving force that makes things happen."

CHAPTER 45

Walnut Creek and Other Cities Implement New Budget Processes

Shayne Kavanagh, Jon Johnson *and* Chris Fabian

The traditional incremental approach to budgeting is not up to the financial challenges posed by the Great Recession. An incremental approach is workable (but not optimal) in periods of revenue growth because the new revenue increments can be distributed among departments and programs with relatively little controversy. There is much more potential for acrimony, though, when allocating revenue decrements during times of revenue decline. Hence, the popularity of across-the-board cuts — they are perceived as equitable and thus attenuate conflict. But by definition, across-the-board cuts are not strategic. They do not shape and size government to create value for the public.

Priority-driven budgeting (PDB) is a natural alternative to incremental budgeting. Using PDB, the government identifies its most important strategic priorities. Services are then ranked according to how well they align with the priorities, and resources are allocated in accordance with the ranking.[1]

This article identifies the essential steps in a PDB process and the major levers that can be pushed and pulled to customize PDB to local conditions. The following organizations contributed to the Government Finance Officers Association's research on PBD: the City of Savannah, Georgia; Mesa County, Colorado; Polk County, Florida; Snohomish County, Wash-ington; City of Walnut Creek, California; City of San Jose, California; and City of Lakeland, Florida.

Making the Process Your Own

Designing a process that is fair, accessible, transparent, and adaptable is a challenge. However, it is also an opportunity to customize a PDB process that fits your organization best. The GFOA's research has identified five key customization questions that need to be answered as you design a PDB process:

- What is the scope? What funds and revenues are included? What is the desired role of non-profit and private-sector organizations in providing public services?
- What is the role of PDB in the final budget decision? Is it one perspective that will be considered among many, or is it the primary influence? By what method will resources be allocated to services?
- What is the organizational subunit that will be evaluated for alignment with the organization's strategic priorities? Departments, divisions, programs? Something else?
- How will subunits be scored, and who will score them? The scoring mechanism is central to PDB.

Originally published as "Anatomy of a Priority-Based Budget Process," *Government Finance Review*, Vol. 26, No. 2, April 2010, by the Government Finance Officers Association, Chicago, IL. Reprinted with permission of the publisher.

- How and where will elected officials, the public, and staff be engaged in the process? Engagement is essential for democratic legitimacy.

Jurisdictions can tailor the process to their needs so long as they stay true to the philosophy of PBD, which is about how a government should invest resources to meet its stated objectives. Prioritizing helps a jurisdiction better articulate why its programs exist, what value they offer citizens, how they benefit the community, what price we pay for them, and what objectives and citizen demands they are achieving. PDB is about directing resources to those programs that create the greatest value for the public.

Steps in Priority-Driven Budgeting

A PDB process can be broken down into a few major steps. In addressing each step, there are several options for answering the five key customization questions.

1. **Identify Available Resources.** The organization needs to fundamentally shift its approach to budgeting before embarking on priority-driven resource allocation. An organization should begin by clearly identifying the amount of resources available to fund operations, one-time initiatives, and capital expenditures, instead of starting out by identifying the amount of resources the organization needs for the next fiscal year.

Many jurisdictions start developing their budgets by analyzing estimated expenditures to identify how much money the organizational units will need to spend for operations and capital in the upcoming fiscal year. Once those needs are determined, then the organization looks to the finance department or budget office to figure out how they will be funded. When adopting a PDB approach, the first step is to gain a clear understanding of the factors that drive revenues. Jurisdictions perform the requisite analysis to develop accurate and reliable revenue forecasts of how much money will be available for the upcoming year.

Once the amount of available resources is identified, the forecasts should be used to educate and inform all stakeholders about what is truly available to spend for the next fiscal year. As the organization begins developing its budget, everyone must understand and believe that this is all there is — that there is no padding beyond what is forecast. Sharing the assumptions behind the revenue projections creates a level of transparency that dispels the belief that there are always "secret funds" to fix the problem. This transparency establishes the level of trust necessary for PDB to be successful.

In the first year of implementing PDB, an organization might chose to focus attention on only those funds that appear to be out of alignment on an ongoing basis. This will usually involve the general fund, but the organization might decide to include other funds in the PCB process. Polk County, Florida, for instance, limits the scope to the general fund.

Intended Result: A common understanding throughout the organization about the amount of resources available, which limits how much can be budgeted for the upcoming fiscal year.

2. **Identify Your Priorities.** PDB is built around a set of organizational strategic priorities. These priorities are similar to well-designed mission statements in that they capture the fundamental purposes behind the organization — why it exists — and are broad enough to have staying power from year to year. The priorities are very different from a mission statement, however, in one respect: They should be expressed in terms of the results or outcomes that are of value to the public. These results should be specific enough to be meaningful and measurable, but not so specific that they outline how the result or outcome will be achieved, or that they will become outmoded after a short time. Mesa Country, California, has six priority results, which are expressed as citizen statements:

- Economic Vitality. "I want Mesa County to have a variety of industries that will promote a healthy and sustainable economy."
- Well-Planned and Developed Communities. "I want plans and infrastructure that maintain quality of life."

- Self-Sufficient Individuals and Families. "I want a community where citizens have opportunities to be self-sufficient."
- Public Safety. "I want to feel safe anytime, anywhere in Mesa County."
- Public Health. "I want a healthy Mesa County."
- Public Resources. "I want Mesa County to have well-managed resources."

A strategic plan, vision, or mission statement can be the starting point for identifying the priority results. Grounding the priority results in these previous efforts can be helpful, as it respects the investment stakeholders might have in them and gives the priorities greater legitimacy.

Developing the priorities is a critical point of citizen involvement. The governing board must also be closely involved. Familiar tools such as citizen surveys, focus groups, and one-on-one interviews work well, too.

Intended Result: A set of priorities that are expressed in terms of measurable results, are of value to citizens; and are widely agreed to be legitimate.

3. **Define Your Priority Results More Precisely**. The foundation of any prioritization effort is the results that define why an organization exists. Organizations must ask what makes them relevant to their citizens. Achieving relevance — providing the programs that achieve relevant results — is the most profound outcome of a prioritization process.

The challenge is that results can be broad, and what they mean for your community can be unclear. Take, for instance, a result such as "providing a safe community," which is shared by most local governments. Organizations talk about public safety, or the provision of a safe community, as if it were an obvious and specific concept. But is it?

In the City of Walnut Creek, California, citizens, together with city leadership, commonly identified issues of building safety specific to surviving earthquakes as an important influence on the safety of their community. In the City of Lakeland, Florida, however, not a single citizen or public official discussed earthquakes in their work to help define the very

same result. Hence, the uniqueness and relevance we seek is established through the specific definitions of the community's results. The process of defining results reveals the community's identity and the objective meaning of what is relevant.

Strategy mapping is a powerful method for defining results.[2] It is a simple way to take a complex and potentially ambiguous objective — such as achieving a safe community — and create a picture of how that objective can be achieved. Sometimes referred to as cause-and-effect diagrams, or result maps, strategy maps can help an organization achieve clarity about what it aims to accomplish with its results.

The result map from the City of San Jose, California, showed the desired result in the Center (i.e., a Green Sustainable City) and the various concepts shown around the result contained the definitions (i.e., related to resource conservation, minimal environmental impact, the promotion of new technology, and innovative business solutions). This map with its goals and definitions, clearly helped San Jose's public officials clearly articulate, "When the City of San Jose — (fill in the blank with any of the result definitions that were shown), then we achieve a green, sustainable city."

The City of Walnut Creek approached the process of defining results knowing that citizens and community stakeholders needed to be involved. Its rationale was that its prioritization efforts would be valid only if the community members were responsible for establishing the results and their definitions. The city was successful in reaching out to the community (via radio, newspaper, city newsletters, and the city's Web site) to invite any citizen who was interested in participating to attend one of several town hall meetings. After an orientation, citizens were invited to participate in a facilitated session where they submitted as many answers as they could to fill in the blank in the following question: "When the City of Walnut Creek _____, then they achieve (the result the citizen was focused on)." The response from citizens was tremendous and generated a host of answers to the questions posed by the city. Members of the city government, who participated in the meetings, were then responsible for summarizing the citizens' responses by developing result maps.

When defining the results that establish relevance in your community, consider if some results might be more important than other results. This could have an impact on how programs are valued and prioritized. Elected officials, staff, and citizens have participated in voting exercises where they receive a set number of "votes" (or dollars, or dots, etc.) that they can use to indicate the value of one result versus another. This process should not be perceived as a budget allocation exercise (whereby the budget of a certain result is determined by the votes attributed to it). Instead, participants are communicating and expressing that certain results (and therefore the programs that eventually influence these results) might have greater relevance than others.

Intended Result: Revealing the identity of your community and the objective meaning of what is relevant to it through the process of defining results.

What about Capital Projects? A priority-driven budgeting process can be used to evaluate capital projects or one-time initiatives in the same way it is used to evaluate programs and services. For instance, the capital improvement plan can be ranked against the priority results.

4. **Prepare Decision Units for Evaluation.** Evaluating the services against the government's priority results is at the crux of PDB. First, the decision unit to be evaluated must be defined. A decision unit is the organizational subunit around which budgeting decisions will be made. For PDB, the decision unit must be broad enough to capture the tasks that go into producing a valued result for citizens, but not so large as to encompass too much or be too vague. If the decision unit is too small, it might capture only certain tasks in the chain that lead to a result, rather than the overall result, and might overwhelm the process with too many decision units and details. Traditional departments and divisions are not appropriate decisions units for PDB because they are typically organized around functions rather than results. Hence, research subjects took one of two approaches to this issue: offers and programs.

Offers. Offers are customized service packages designed by departments (or cross-functional teams, or sometimes private firms or non-profits) to achieve one or more priority results. Offers are submitted to evaluation teams for consideration against the organization's priority results.

Offers are intended to be different from existing organizational subunits for several reasons: to make a direct connection between the subunits being evaluated and the priority results; to encourage innovative thinking about what goes into an offer; and to make it easier for outside organizations to participate in the PDB process. For example, multiple departments can cooperate to propose a new and inventive offer to achieve a result instead of relying on past ways of doing things. A private firm could submit an offer to compete with an offer made by government staff.

How many offers are there? Research participants that used the offer approach averaged one offer for every $1.5 million in revenue that was available in the priority-driven budgeting process.

The drawback of offers is that they constitute a radical departure from past practice and might be too great a conceptual leap for some. This could increase the risk to the process, but if the leadership's vision is for a big break from past practice, then the risk could be worth it. For example, Mesa County's board is interested in having private and non-profit organizations fully participate in its budget process at some point in the future, so the offer approach makes sense for that jurisdiction.

Programs. A program is a set of related activities intended to produce a desired result. Organizations that use the program method inventory the programs they offer and then compare those to the priority results. Programs are an established part of the public budgeting lexicon, and some governments already use programs in their financial management, so thinking in terms of programs is not much of conceptual leap. This means less work and process risk. However familiar the concept, though, the programs need to be sufficiently detailed to allow for meaningful decision making. Generally speaking, if a program makes up more than

10 percent of total expenditures for the fund in which it is accounted for, then the program should probably be broken down into smaller pieces. If a program makes up 1 percent or less of total expenditures, or less than $100,000, it is probably too small and should be combined with others.

Also, the program approach might provide less opportunity for outside organizations to participate in the budgeting process. That's because the starting point is, by definition, the existing portfolio of services. For that same reason, radical innovation in service design or delivery method is less likely.

Intended Result: Preparing discrete decision-units that produce a clear result for evaluation. Think about evaluating these decision-units against each other and not necessarily about evaluating departments against each other.

5. **Score Offers/Programs against Results.** Once the organization has identified its priority results and more precisely defined what those results mean in terms of meeting the unique expectations of the community, it must develop a process to objectively evaluate how the offers/programs achieve or influence the priority results. Scoring can be approached in several ways, but the system must ensure that scores are based on the demonstrated and measurable influence the offers/programs have on the results. In many organizations, such as the cities of Lakeland, Walnut Creek, and San Jose, programs were scored against all the organization's priority results. The idea was that a program that influenced multiple results must be a higher priority — programs that achieved multiple results made the best use of taxpayer money. Alternately, organizations such as Mesa County, City of Savannah, Polk County, and Snohomish County matched each offer with only one of the priority results and evaluated it based on its degree of influence on that result. Using this scenario, a jurisdiction should establish guidelines to help it determine how to assign an offer/program to a priority area and how to provide some accommodation for those offers/programs that demonstrate critical impacts across priority result areas. Both of these approaches have been used successfully in PDB.

There are two basic approaches to scoring offers/programs against the priority results. One approach is to have those who are putting forth the offers/programs assign scores based on a self-assessment. This approach engages the owners in the process and taps into their unique understanding of how the offers/programs influence the priority result. When taking this approach, it is critical to incorporate a peer review or other quality control process that allows review by peers in the organization and external stakeholders (citizens, elected officials, labor unions, business leaders, etc.). During the peer review, the owner of the offer/program would need to provide evidence to support the scores assigned.

A second approach to scoring establishes evaluation committees that are responsible for scoring the offers/programs against their ability to influence the priority result. Owners of offers/programs submit them for review by the committee, which in turn scores the programs against the result. The PDB process becomes more like a formal purchasing process based on the assumption that those doing the evaluations might be more neutral than those proposing the offers/programs. Committees could be made up entirely of staff, including people who have specific expertise related to the result being evaluated and others who are outside of that particular discipline. An alternate committee composition would include both staff and citizens to gain the unique perspectives of both external and internal stakeholders.

Regardless of who is evaluating the offers/programs and assigning the scores, there are two key points. To maintain the objectivity and transparency of the PDB process, offers/programs must be evaluated against the priority results as commonly defined (see step 3). Also, the results of the scoring process must be offered only as recommendations to the elected officials who have the final authority to make resource allocation decisions.

Organizations should establish the elected governing board's role at the outset. In some jurisdictions, the board is heavily integrated into the PDB process, participating in the scoring and evaluation step. They can question the assigned scores, ask for the evidence that supports a score, and ultimately request that a score be changed based on the evidence presented and their belief in the relative influence that an offer/program has on the priority result it has been evaluated against. In other organizations such as Snohomish County, Washington, the PDB process is implemented as a staff-only tool that is used to develop a recommendation to the governing body.

Intended Result: Scoring each unit of prioritization in a way that indicates its relevance to the stated priorities.

6. **Compare Scores Between Offers/Programs.** A real moment of truth comes when scoring is completed and the information is first compiled, revealing the top-to-bottom comparison of prioritized offers/programs. Knowing this, an organization must be sure that it has done everything possible prior to this moment to ensure that there are no surprises, that the results are as expected, and that the final comparison of offers/programs in priority order is logical and intuitive.

In the City of San Jose's peer review process, the scores departments gave their programs were evaluated, discussed, questioned, and sometimes recommended for change. The city established a review team specific to each of the city's results. The review teams first went over the result map to ensure that each member of the team was grounded in the city's specific definition of the result. Next, the review teams were given a report detailing every program that gave itself a score for the particular result under review. The teams met to discuss: whether they understood the programs they were reviewing; whether they agreed with the scores; whether they required further testimony or evidence to help them better understand the score given; and whether the score should stand, or if the team should recommend increasing or decreasing it. All programs were evaluated in this manner until a final recommendation was made regarding the final program scores.

What made San Jose's approach noteworthy is that in addition to including peers within the organization to review the scores, the city also invited the local business community, citizens representing their local neighborhood commissions, and labor leaders. According to San Jose's City Manager's Office, "The partic-

ipants found the effort informative as to what the city does; they found it engaging with respect to hearing staff in the organization discuss how their programs influence the city's results; and, most interesting, they found it fun."

Lastly, it is important to recognize that community stakeholders could be apprehensive about engaging in an evaluation that could result in losing support for their program. Even though program directors, or citizens who benefit from a particular program, might understand why their programs weren't ranked highly, they still won't be pleased with that outcome. Organizations must ask if the end result of their efforts in prioritizing programs is simply that finish line when it is clear what programs should be cut. Organizations such as the City of Lakeland have used prioritization not only to balance their budgets in a meaningful way, but also to understand how programs that might appear less relevant to the city as a whole might in fact be very relevant to other community stakeholders. These stakeholders might actually take responsibility for supporting or preserving a program. There are often opportunities to establish partnerships with other community institutions such as businesses, schools, churches, and non-profits.

Intended Result: A logical and well-understood product of a transparent process — no surprises.

7. **Allocate Resources.** Once the scoring is in place, resources can be allocated to the offers/programs. There are a number of methods for allocating resources. One method is to order the offers/programs according to their prioritization within a given priority result area and draw a line where the cost of the offers/programs is equal to the amount of revenue available. Revenues can be allocated to each result area based on historical patterns or by using the priority's relative weights, if weights were assigned. Those offers/programs that are above the line are funded, and those that are below the line are not. Discussion will ensue about the offers/programs on either side of the line and about moving them up or down, reorganizing them to move them above the line (e.g., lowering service levels), or even shifting resources among priority results.

An alternate method, used by the City of Lakeland, is to organize the offers/programs into tiers of priority (i.e., quartiles) and then allocate reductions by tier. For example, programs in the first tier might not be reduced, while programs in the lowest tier would receive the largest reductions. The programs could be forced to make the reductions assigned, or the reductions could be aggregated as a total reduction amount for each department, based on the programs within its purview (with the implication being that the department would weight its reductions toward the lower-priority programs, but this would provide more flexibility in deciding the precise reduction approach). Of course, under any PDB process, the prioritization is always just a recommendation to the governing board, and there is give and take to negotiate a final budget.

PDB can be used effectively for evaluating priorities in all funds, not just the general fund. One option is to handle special purpose funds (where there are restrictions placed on how monies can be used) separately. For example, perhaps enterprise funds or court funds would be evaluated on a different track or budgeted in a different way altogether. Another option is to rank offers/programs without respect to funding source, but then allocate resources with respect to funding source. Knowing the relative priority of all the offers/programs could generate some valuable discussion, even if there is no immediate impact on funding. For example, if a low-ranking offer/program is grant funded, is it still worth providing, especially if that grant might expire in the foreseeable future?

Intended Result: Aligning resource allocation with results of priority-driven scoring.

Creating Accountability

There can be a potential moral hazard in PDB; the owners of the offers/programs that are being evaluated might over-promise or over-represent what they can do to accomplish the priority result. Create methods for making sure that offers/programs deliver the results that their positive evaluations were based on. Many of the GFOA's research participants are striving toward performance measures for this purpose. For example, an offer/program might have to propose a standard of evidence or a metric against which it can be evaluated to see if the desired result is being provided.

Polk County has a conceptual approach to connecting priority result areas to key indicators. However, none of the research participants have worked this situation out entirely to their satisfaction. For those just starting out, the lesson is to be cognizant of the place for evidence in your process design, but also to be patient about when this part of the process will be fully realized.

Intended Result: Making sure that those who received allocations are held accountable for producing the results that were promised.

Conclusions

Priority-driven budgeting is a big change from traditional budgeting. You should have strong support for the PDB philosophy before proceeding, especially from the chief executive officer (who proposes the budget) and, ideally, from the governing board (who adopts the budget). If you move forward, study PDB carefully so you can design a process that works for your organization. Keep in mind the major levers and decision points mentioned in this article and use them to create a process that fits your organization.

NOTES

1. Priority-driven budgeting is also known as budgeting for results, and the best-known method of implementing PDB is budgeting for outcomes (see "The City of Savannah Uses Budgeting for Outcomes to Address Its Long-Term Challenges" in this issue of *Government Finance Review* for more information about BFO). BFO was the subject of *The Price of Government: Getting the Results We Need in an Age of Permanent Fiscal Crisis* by David Osborne and Peter Hutchinson (New York: Basic Books) 2006.

2. Robert S. Kaplan and David P. Norton, *Strategy Maps: Converting Intangible Assets into Tangible Outcomes* (Boston, MA: Harvard Business Press) 2004.

Editor's note: The following information regarding the funding priority placed on "support services" was also contained in GFOA's research results.

Are Support Services a Priority?

The jurisdictions that participated in the GFOA's research offered two alternatives for funding support services. Some suggested creating a "good governance" priority that addresses high-quality support services. This gives support services a clear place in PDB and allows them to evaluate program relevance against the strategic results they are asking to achieve. Here is how the City of Walnut Creek, California, defined its governance goals.

• Enhance and facilitate accountability and innovation in all city business.

• Provide superior customer service that is responsive and demystifies city processes.

• Provide analysis and long-range thinking that supports responsible decision making.

• Proactively protect and maintain city resources.

• Ensure regulatory and police compliance.

Other participants envisioned moving to a system that would fully distribute the cost of support services to operating programs. Thus, the impact of any changes in the funding of these services would be tied to the prioritization of the operating services they support.

CHAPTER 46

Waukesha and Other Cities Reduce Health Costs for Their Aging Employees

Robert Barkin

Like a huge cloud appearing on the horizon, the aging of the baby boom generation is moving closer to shore, carrying with it a storm of financial consequences. Employee benefit plan managers are bracing themselves and their employees for the effects of the aging of the largest demographic group in the nation's history. "We have been planning for this population increase," says Scott Streator, director of health care for the Ohio Public Employee Retirement System (OPERS). "We're the largest plan in Ohio. If anyone will feel it, we will."

Plan administrators are aligning their benefits programs to better meet the expected demands of older employees as they reach what will be a decades-long retirement. The changes are designed to help early retirees manage their expenses until Medicare is available at age 65 and to curb the rising costs of employers' health care obligations.

Many programs are focusing on encouraging employees to save for post-retirement medical expenses, trying to control costs through wellness programs for older employees and disease management programs that help them receive the right treatment for their illnesses. Some employers also are focusing on the generation following the baby boomers, whose saving and health habits have assumed different patterns from their older cohorts. "We need to

try new approaches and show that they work," says Dan Stewart, assistant vice chancellor for employee benefits and services at the University of Texas in Austin and a past president of the Richmond, Ky.–based State and Local Government Benefits Association. "These are taxpayer dollars [going to employee benefits]," he says. "We can't make a mistake. We have to be accountable."

Living Longer but Not Healthier

Although the 80 million baby boomers are expected to live longer than their parents, they are not as healthy as the smiling retirees bicycling in fast-paced television ads would suggest. In fact, studies indicate that baby boomers are not even as healthy as their parents.

According to the federally funded University of Michigan Health and Retirement Study, the nation's leading resource for data on the health and economic circumstances of aging Americans, there are some early warning signs about baby boomers' health. The 14-year study tracks 22,000 U.S. adults over age 50 every two years as they move toward retirement.

As reported in the Washington Post, when researchers examined the first wave of boomers

Originally published as "Employee Benefits: Fighting the Fight," *American City & County*, Vol. 122, No. 6, June 2007, by Penton Media, Inc., Overland, KS. Reprinted with permission of the publisher.

to enter the study — 5,030 adults born between 1948 and 1953 — they found that the group reported poorer health than groups born between 1936 and 1941 and between 1942 and 1947.

According to the study, baby boomers were much less likely than their predecessors to describe their health as "excellent" or "very good" and were more likely to report having difficulty with routine activities, such as walking several blocks or lifting 10 pounds. They also were more likely to report pain, drinking and psychiatric problems, and chronic problems, such as high blood pressure, high cholesterol and diabetes. "We're seeing some very powerful evidence point to these findings," says Mark Hayward, a professor of sociology at the University of Texas in Austin. "The trend seems to be that people are not as healthy as they approach retirement as they were in older generations. It's very disturbing."

Although the Health and Retirement study is based on self-reports, researchers indicate that it often reflects actual trends in the general population. While many consider the findings very reliable, others have raised questions about their accuracy, suspecting baby boomers have higher expectations for their health or may be more health conscious than their parents. But, if that were the case, the findings would lead to earlier diagnosis of problems that may actually reduce health issues later in life. The actual trends will not be known for years, but other surveys by British researchers and the National Center for Health Statistics' National Health Interview Survey have indicated results similar to the Health and Retirement Study.

Creative Cost Cutting

Whether baby boomers are actually less healthy than their parents may be debatable, but indisputably they are getting older and edging toward retirement. Stewart notes that the group of baby boomers that are now 50 to 65 years old is the most expensive for employee benefit programs to maintain because they have more health issues and are not yet eligible for Medicare.

OPERS leaders began developing a comprehensive health care preservation plan in 2003 to control costs without affecting quality, according to Streator. "We wanted to eliminate unnecessary costs without putting the burden on the back of our members," he says.

The Ohio health plan, now totaling almost $13 billion in assets, pays for health care services for its 200,000 retirees as part of its defined benefit pension plan. The preservation plan, which went into effect in January, is designed to make employees share responsibility for the program and maintain its long-term solvency. As one step, OPERS changed one brand name drug on its medications list to a generic and expects to save an estimated $13 million. "We can't just write checks and watch the draining of our plan," he says. "We need to be in partnership with our members."

OPERS also has established Retiree Medical Accounts (RMA) that share savings with members, says Doug Foust, assistant director. Under the new health care program, eligible members receive a monthly allowance to apply toward the monthly premium for their medical/pharmacy coverage. If the member chooses options that exceed the monthly allowance, the difference between the allowance and the cost is deducted from his or her monthly benefit check.

As an incentive to take a cheaper option, though, if the monthly allowance exceeds the cost of the coverage options selected, the allowance excess is deposited into an RMA, which can be used to offset deductibles and other uncovered health care costs. "This allows them to put money aside, so they can take care of themselves," Streator says. A winter 2006 survey of the International City/County Management Association (ICMA) membership by Philadelphia-based CIGNA HealthCare found that 30 percent of the respondents are likely to consider similar arrangements in the next five years.

In Waukesha County, Wis., the emphasis in benefits coverage for baby boomers has turned to planning initiatives and wellness programs, says Peter Hans, employee benefits administrator. County retirees have access to the employee health plan, but the county does not pay their premiums. "People find it financially hard to retire before 65 [when Medicare becomes effective]," he says.

To help, the county contributes to a medical care account for its 1,400 employees that can be used to offset health-related expenses after the employees retire. Because the program does not promise a benefit, it is not affected by the new accounting rules that are forcing many public employers for the first time to set aside in their annual operating budgets the costs of their retirement medical care benefits. "We think these accounts help them hurdle the obstacle to retirement," he says. "It's a mechanism to help the transition in the high pre-Medicare years."

The county also is emphasizing wellness and fitness programs that can cut costs by preventing illness, Hans says. "We are focusing on lifestyle-related health costs," he says. "We want people to know how to make the right lifestyle choices so they don't have problems down the road."

In addition, the county has adopted a patient advocate program to help participants manage their health care better. In particular, the county is concentrating on employees with asthma and diabetes, which often lead to even more serious problems if left untreated.

Preparing for Gen X

Harris County, Texas, benefits administrators are focusing not only on the issues with the aging of its large baby boom workforce, but also the very different needs of the employees that are following just behind. The Generation X group is less concerned about retirement and needs to be taught the value of retirement saving. "There is an opportunity to save, but generations differ in values," says David Kester, director of human resources and risk management

for the 14,000-employee workforce. "The next generation seems to spend more than they save today. So we are trying to help them understand that need."

For baby boomers, the county has increased its categories of disease management from six to 26, which provides more services to help people receive the right treatment from the health care system. The county also has recognized that older employees often are caring for their children and for their elderly parents at the same time. That has led to increased services through the Employee Assistance Program, which guides employees to counseling to help them through stressful interactions and social services to assist in caretaking.

Harris County also has expanded assistance for financial planning, giving pre-retirees the tools and information they need to plan for retirement and ensure that they have sufficient resources. "People are going to live longer," Kester says. "There is a need for extended resources."

And, with people living longer, there is a greater likelihood that long-term care may be involved, with its considerable cost implications. As a result, long-term care insurance has drawn some interest from county leaders, Kester says, but there has been very little experience in the public sector with how it works and who will benefit from the coverage. Employers, like OPERS, may provide access to a long-term care insurance plan in the future, but in general there have been few takers.

Without taking steps to control costs, public employee benefit plans will find themselves in increasingly difficult situations, Stewart says. "We have to educate people about health care in general," he says. "It's a difficult issue to manage."

CHAPTER 47

West Palm Beach Provides Successful Social Service Programs

Alan Brown

Public sector policymakers, including elected officials and local government managers, often make decisions about which public sector social service programs — for example, crime, substance abuse, violence prevention, education interventions — should be funded, at which levels, and for how long. Usually, however, these policymakers have little or no impartial evidence on which to base their investment decisions. Consequently, billions of dollars are being wasted on programs that aren't improving the well-being of communities.

In light of the limited availability of rigorous evidence about program effectiveness, how can policymakers and administrators determine whether their funded programs actually produce the desired results? What can managers do to assure that resources are invested in programs that work? What can managers do to help policymakers establish funding priorities? What must managers understand about the change process in order to effectively promote a new culture of evidence-based programs among policymakers, citizens, and staff?

This article highlights the development of what is called the accountability system. The system is a resource and performance management program that provides the needed infrastructure to determine which intervention programs are working best, identify the cost and benefit of each program, and reveal what's not working. This article also briefly touches on return on investment (ROI), which will help introduce a new way of identifying effective programs.

Underlying the accountability system is a portfolio of evidence-based programs — that is, programs that have been carefully researched and meet these five criteria:

1. Show strong effect.
2. Are built on research designs.
3. Are sustainable.
4. Are replicable.
5. Are cost beneficial.

The overriding goal of the accountability system is to enable the most effective use of public resources to prevent substance abuse, crime, and violence; to intervene when necessary; and to treat the effects of these problems. This is done in a manner that supports community-based efforts to assist children, families, and communities to remain healthy and free of substance abuse and violence.

Why Is Evidence-Based Programming Important?

Although human services funders finance successful programs and providers deliver many

Originally published as "Investing in Effective Social Service Programs," *Public Management*, Vol. 93, No. 2, March 2011, by the International City/County Management Association, Washington, D.C. Reprinted with permission of the publisher.

effective services, we also know that funders overfund programs with little evidence of effectiveness, underfund effective programs, and fund programs that continue fragmentation of services.

The reality is that there has been little success — or evidence of success — to date, despite a multitude of programs and billions of dollars. A program may appear on the surface to work and logically should work, but when evaluated formally it may show no results or may in fact be harmful to the population it serves. In fact, some of the most widely used crime, substance abuse, and education interventions have been shown to be ineffective or harmful, according to Jon Baron in a personal communication written on April 4, 2008.

These points are quoted from Baron's presentation to the Children's Services Council in Palm Beach County, Florida:

• Widely used crime prevention programs such as boot camps have been found ineffective, and Scared Straight programs have been determined to be harmful to participants.

• The United States has made no significant progress in preventing drug or alcohol abuse since 1990, and commonly used programs in schools, such as Drug Abuse Resistance Education (DARE) and Project Alert, have been found to be ineffective in preventing substance use.

• The United States has made almost no progress in raising K-12 educational achievement during the past 30 years, according to the respected National Assessment of Educational Progress, despite a 90 percent increase in public spending per student. Many programs aimed at increasing student performance (for example, select 21st Century Community Learning Centers for students in elementary school) have demonstrated no positive effect and have shown adverse effects on student behavior.

This is a problem not only for social services. Many fields have implemented programs and practices that, when rigorously studied, also have shown ineffective or harmful effects. Here are just three examples from the extensive list provided by Baron:

• Hormone replacement therapy for post-menopausal women: one trial found that it increased risk of stroke and heart disease for many women.

• Stents to open clogged arteries: a rigorous trial has shown the procedure is no better than drugs for most heart patients.

• Beta-carotene and vitamin E supplements (antioxidants) to prevent cancer: trials have shown them to be ineffective and harmful in some cases.

Because so many programs are being implemented without sound research showing effectiveness, and because much of the conventional wisdom about "what works" is probably wrong, it's imperative that practitioners and funders turn to evidence-based programming.

If prevention programming does not begin to move in this direction, vast sums of money will be wasted and, more important, the very people programs are meant to help may actually be harmed. According to Dee Elliott, a University of Colorado faculty member and director, Center for the Study and Prevention of Violence, in his personal communication of January 11, 2007, the benefits of using evidence-based programs are simple and can be described in these four ways:

• Harmful effects can be avoided by being ethical.

• Stronger and more consistent positive outcomes are possible.

• The well-being of our children can be improved.

• Cost savings can be provided to taxpayers.

Key Elements of an Accountability System

Here are the benefits of an accountability system:

• Promotes the use of resources to invest in and implement the most effective programs available.

• Assists communities to build the capacity to select and deliver the best programs.

• Targets resources to those areas of highest need.

- Assists policymakers to establish funding priorities.
- Promotes a culture of evidence, allowing science to inform and serve public policy.

Your leadership can guide the creation and implementation of these five important benefits.

Develop a Strategic Policy Agenda to Arrive at Priorities. To provide policymakers with unimpeachable data for making important decisions, it's important to understand key strategies of accountability:

1. Know that underlying the development of the accountability system is a policy agenda. Essential ingredients of a policy agenda include:

- Priorities — a short list — that matter more than other things.
- Deliberate connections among programs that affect children and families, rather than isolated projects.
- A budgetary dimension that answers the question, What does policy mean to the budget?
- Specific articulation of the intended results.

2. Start with a strategic plan and vision that focus on priorities and the future.

3. Determine the scale and scope of prevention, as well as the scale of intervention and treatment.

Develop and Implement a System of Measurement. What program metrics need to be built into your portfolio of evidence-based prevention programs so that you know the programs are making a difference? Community indicators must be selected and measured periodically to see whether changes occur.

The data from a metric system will inform elected officials about statewide trends regarding, for example, pressing needs, current resources, the ability of community-based service providers to deliver services effectively, and the ability to monitor the impact of state-funded efforts.

Likewise, this data system will reduce duplication of effort by state agencies, align resource delivery with community needs, support the development of a centralized community capacity-building training system, identify and promote evidence-based programming, and measure the impact of state agency programming for children and families.

For community-based service providers, this data system will help in the development of strong proposals that are based on data-driven needs assessments. It will also help local communities track local progress on targeted issues, reduce fragmentation, increase local collaboration, and measure impact for children and families.

Establish Reporting Programs. Here are items you should take into consideration when developing a reporting system:

- *Focus community strategies for action.* Monitoring such indicators as infant mortality, school dropouts, and adolescent suicide can help you develop and monitor your community strategy and determine where to focus your efforts.
- *Track the impact of new policies and programs.* When programs and policies are associated with favorable changes in indictors, community groups may be able to build or strengthen local support for these activities. When programs and policies are associated with unfavorable changes, they need to be cut back.
- *Address community perceptions.* Indicator monitoring can change the way communities perceive such problems as addiction and also how they take action.
- *Provide a common information base.* Although there will always be different interpretations of what the data show, indicators will provide a common starting point for collaboration and action planning.
- *Compare the level of local problems with other programs in similar communities.* This comparison can help detect relationships between substance use and other community characteristics or policies.

Return on Investment

The final section of this article touches on ROI in the public sector. In Joshua D. Bigham and Thomas R. Goudreau's 2004 master's thesis, "Return on Investment in the Public Sector" (Storming Media Publishing, www.storming-media.us/69/6969/A696924.html), the authors indicate that in an environment of scarce resources and rising federal deficits, people not only expect but also demand greater accountability for the spending of public funds. This demand has created a trend in the public sector — in the United States and worldwide — toward the importation of private sector business practices to improve accountability-oriented analysis.

One example is increased emphasis on ROI analysis in public sector organizations. Development and application of ROI analysis is challenging in the public sector since most government organizations do not generate profit necessary for calculation of ROI as is done in the private sector. Properly designed ROI analysis reveals how, and for what goods and services, money is spent; it provides a means for comparing the value derived from investment and work performed.

Government organizations, unlike the private sector, often do not have a choice in whether to initiate a project. Government agencies cannot assess their portfolios and promote or kill projects simply on the ROI or the value to the organization. Most public sector projects are prescribed either by law (e.g., legislature, Congress, or other law-making body) or by political influences.

The use of ROI as a tool to measure the success of programs, processes, and initiatives in federal, state, and local government agencies is growing. Dispelling the myths of ROI is the first step toward improving the evaluation processes within your organization.

Government organizations may not be able to assess ROI to the same degree as the private sector. But they are responsible for justifying their projects — if not to internal customers, then to constituents. Public servants must be able to defend their decisions. The decision to proceed with a project, while subjective, must be justified — if not with a percentage or objective measurement, at least with subjective measurements.

Closing Message

The current policy environment — that is, fundamental fiscal scarcity at all levels of government, partisan deadlocks in state and local political settings, and public skepticism about government — often leads to the expression of negative attitudes toward government. In such a climate, leadership is necessary in at least three realms:

- Leadership is needed to seek and accept accountability for better results from government.
- Leadership is needed to frame and make decisions about scarce resources available to state and local governments.
- Leadership is needed to take the risks to make the hard choices that now face local and state governments.

As a manager of your local government, your role in establishing the community's portfolio of social service programs entails:

- Promoting the use of resources to invest in and implement the most effective programs available.
- Assisting communities to build the capacity to select and deliver the best programs.
- Targeting resources to those areas of highest need.
- Assisting policymakers as they establish funding priorities.
- Promoting a culture of evidence, allowing science to inform and serve public policy.

In this manner, we can together make an impact in the seemingly intractable problems confronting our communities.

CHAPTER 48

Westminster Uses Performance
Results to Improve Services

Brent McFall

Over the last several years, performance measurement has become an important tool in the manager's toolbox in the city of Westminster, Colorado. Whether it is in strategic planning, budgeting, or core services analysis/prioritization, performance measurement has brought important data to the table that has been extremely useful in the decision-making process.

In one example, the city used performance measurement to allocate resources for park maintenance. Developed park acres maintained per FTE has increased slowly over the past five years, with a sharp increase at the end of 2010 based on staff eliminations resulting from core service reductions. Concern over the potential negative impacts of this increase and city staff's ability to continue to maintain parks standards that support the strategic plan goals and objectives necessitated a paradigm shift in the city's park maintenance practices.

To accommodate the recent economy-driven changes in staffing and operations budgets, staff implemented a Tier Maintenance Program. Under this program, four different service levels, or tiers, based on visitation, reservation availability, Recreation Services Division programming, and park classification were developed. Parks with greater use and visibility receive more maintenance and a larger percent-age of the irrigation budget over parks and greenways with lesser use and priority. The city will use performance measures to track, maintain, and improve efficiencies, as well as gauge citizen satisfaction with park maintenance and appearance.

The city continues to strengthen the linkages between performance measurement and the city's strategic plan goals and objectives. The strategic plan frames the internal goals of departments and then departments develop associated performance measures that help determine progress toward achieving these goals. All of the city's performance measures are tied back to a specific city council strategic plan goal or objective through an internal department goal. Through departments' annual "Performance Measurement Report to the City Manager," specific performance measurement outcomes are discussed in the context of how they relate to progress toward achievement of the city's strategic plan goals and objectives.

After gauging overall effectiveness and assessment of key outcomes in relation to the city's strategic plan, working towards maintaining and improving efficiencies is the second most important aspect of the city of Westminster's performance measurement program. Over the last several years, the city has realized cost savings and improvements in overall operational

Originally published as "Performance Measurement Program Report for 2010," *Annual Report to the Mayor and City Council*, March 2011, by the Performance Measurement Team, City of Westminster, CO.

efficiencies thanks to having performance measurement as a management tool.

The city's street division is another example, which works to maximize limited funds available for pavement preservation, rehabilitation, and reconstruction by focusing on preservation and rehabilitation. This results in extending the useful life of roadways, thus avoiding most costly reconstruction. When comparing rehabilitation efforts versus reconstruction efforts, the price rises dramatically from $11.30 per square yard for arterial preservation to $57.65 per square yard for arterial reconstruction. On the residential side, the price per yard for preservation if $3.19, whereas the price per square yard for residential construcion is $11.13, a 350 percent increase. These figures show that it is much more cost effective for the city to invest in preserving a roadway as long and as well as possible. Based on the 2010 National Citizen Survey™, 49 percent of residents reported street repairs in the city as "very good" or "good" (29 percent reported "neither good nor bad"). While at first glance this might seem low, this rating is significantly above the national average.

The use of performance measurement has shifted the dialogue with local citizens from anecdotes and impressions to data and empirical evidence. The city of Westminster has shared data and evidence with citizens for many years and the city's performance measurement program strengthens its ability to share pertinent quantitative and qualitative data on a variety of citizen concerns and issues. Whether it is concerning citizen complaints, citizen budget requests or citizen questions, city staff is able to bring important information to the discussion table and put issues into a better context with the help of performance measurement data.

Editor's note: The City of Westminster, Colorado, is a participant in the International City/County Management Association's (ICMA's) Center for Performance Measurement (CPM). ICMA has been sponsoring this program for the past 17 years. For more information about this program, the reader is directed to the ICMA web site, which is listed in the *National Resource Directory.*

The City of Westminster is recognized as a leader in performance measurement efforts by professional organizations and the local government community. In 2010, the City of Westminster received ICMA's "Certificate of Excellence" Award for exceptional accomplishments in performance measurement. This is the second year that Westminster has received this level of award. This award category is the highest recognition provided by ICMA regarding performance measurement. Westminster was one of only 21 cities across ICMA's worldwide membership to receive this honor.

CHAPTER 49

Worcester Uses an Independent Source to Measure Service Performance

Roberta R. Schaefer

For more than a century, local government in the United States has tried, among other things, to become more businesslike in its operations (as exemplified by the movement to appoint professional city managers) and to encourage greater citizen participation (typified by legal requirements for citizen-run boards for planning, zoning, and education). Research bureaus were also the product of the "good government" movement at the turn of the twentieth century, created to clean up political party corruption by making government more businesslike and creating independent watchdog agencies to keep a check on corruption. Citizen-based performance measurement and reporting can bring together these three developments of the Progressive Era to improve government performance.

Over the past few decades, governments have tried to adopt the business practice of developing strategic plans for setting goals and tracking accomplishments. In 1993, Worcester's city manager decided to involve the city's residents in developing Worcester's first strategic plan. He appointed a Strategic Planning Committee composed of twenty-four members from around the city, representing diverse interests and backgrounds. The committee held five public hearings across the city and then met

with a facilitator to sift the findings of those hearings into the five broad goals of a seven-year strategic plan:

1. Improve the academic achievement of students in the Worcester Public Schools
2. Increase economic development
3. Improve public safety
4. Improve municipal and neighborhood services
5. Improve youth services

Over the next several years, the city council and public were kept informed of the resources being devoted to these goals; however, no one was tracking outcomes such as decreases in the crime rate or improvements in student test scores. The Worcester Regional Research Bureau, which had served on the 1993 committee that established the plan and goals, decided to take on the task of measuring government performance.

The bureau was founded in 1985 by Worcester businesspeople who felt the need for an organization to conduct independent, nonpartisan research on public policy; assist Worcester's city manager with recommendations for more effective and efficient municipal government; and monitor charter changes on public policies and electoral politics. They were con-

Originally published as "Starting Performance Measurement from Outside Government in Worcester," *National Civic Review*, Vol. 97, No. 1, Spring 2008, pp. 41–45, by the National Civic League, Denver, CO. Reprinted with permission of the publisher. www.wileyonlinelibrary/journal/ncr.

cerned about the city's capacity to sustain services and quality of life during its transformation from an older industrial economy into one with growing strength in health care, related industries, and higher education. The bureau's mission is to serve the public interest of the Greater Worcester region by conducting independent, nonpartisan research and analysis of public policy issues to promote informed public debate and decision making. For the first fifteen years of the bureau's existence, both municipal government and citizens saw it as a watch-dog agency. Government officials viewed our studies as factual and objective, but they could ignore the recommendations unless a crisis compelled them to do otherwise. Businesses were pleased that someone was looking critically at how tax dollars were being spent, while residents thought that because we were supported by businesses the research bureau was largely concerned about the welfare of the business community.

In 1999, the bureau began working with groups of citizens (many of whom had been involved in developing the original strategic plan) representing a broad cross-section of the population to develop and refine measures that would benchmark Worcester's progress toward achieving the five goals of the strategic plan. As a result of multiple sessions with each group, who were selected by business associations, neighborhood associations, government agencies, and nonprofit organizations, we developed a consensus around five or six measures for each goal that would offer a fairly good indication of whether we were making progress toward achieving them. In 2000, the bureau received a planning grant from the Alfred P. Sloan Foundation to develop a three-year project to institute citizen-based government performance measurement in Worcester. While researching similar projects, we learned about a program designed by the Fund for the City of New York's Center on Government Performance called ComNET (Computerized Neighborhood Environment Tracking), which can be used to measure delivery of neighborhood services and document changes in neighborhood conditions.

ComNET involves local residents in the process of first identifying street-level conditions of concern to them and then using handheld computers to collect data on the exact location of those community problems and assets. The multiple aims of ComNET are for citizens to collect accurate data, systematically review them, learn what is and is not government's responsibility, and decide which issues they want to refer to government. The precise location and description of their findings must be verifiable so that their reports to government will be factual and trustworthy. Digital cameras document some of the conditions found, to furnish additional evidence when necessary. In the course of starting a ComNET project, residents learn the nomenclature of government so that they can communicate successfully with one another.

The bureau adapted ComNET to fit Worcester's specific character, circumstances, and challenges. Because this one measure has had considerable impact on service delivery such as streamlining the process for removing abandoned vehicles, and on relations among the bureau, government, and citizens, we focus our attention on it here.

Worcester's version of ComNET is a system of biennial, technologically assisted surveys of the physical conditions of Worcester's most socioeconomically challenged neighborhoods, in which almost one-third, or fifty-five thousand, of the city's residents live. Although the physical problems plaguing the neighborhoods are not news to their residents or municipal officials, before implementation of ComNET there was no centralized means of collecting and reporting these problems to the appropriate municipal agency or of tracking their resolution. ComNET surveys enable residents and officials to identify and document more than 275 specific problems affecting residents' quality of life — such as potholes, faded crosswalks, abandoned vehicles, illegal dumping, and overgrown vegetation. Once neighborhoods possess this inventory, they have not only a "punch list" of problems but also a baseline for gauging whether their fortunes are rising or declining.

Before employing the ComNET system and technology, the research bureau had to complete some important preparatory work. Our first step was to engage in extended discussion with neighborhood associations on how to define neighborhood boundaries as well as the problems to be recorded. The second step was to create detailed maps for each neighborhood that was to be surveyed, along with the routes to be followed, and then to program the handheld computers with those streets and the physical features and conditions to be recorded. This work benefited from the active assistance of staff at the Fund for the City of New York. They helped the research bureau start the project, providing guidance and examples of route maps, training presentations and materials, a list of commonly identified street features and problems, and field assistance on the first surveys.

The actual process falls into three parts: recording, analyzing, and distribution. Traveling in teams of three or four (typically a scout to keep the team on its prescribed route, the "mobile computer" user to input findings, and one or two others to point out trouble spots), participants record the deficiencies they observe on drop-down menus (for example, "lines fading" or "roof/chimney broken") falling under three dozen broad categories of physical features (for example, "crosswalks" and "building-residential"). Once the data are uploaded, via the Internet to *ComNET Connection*, the research bureau is able to generate a variety of spreadsheets depending on the desired analysis or action. After analyzing the data, bureau staff share the results with neighborhood associations, giving them a clearer picture of specific areas of need to be addressed and helping them set priorities.

Enlisting the city's cooperation to respond to the problems recorded is, of course, critical to the success of ComNET. This cooperation was the result of the city manager's leadership in letting his subordinates know that he considered this project a priority. But second, there was recognition that cooperation was inescapable since we were measuring progress toward achieving the goals of the strategic plan developed by the city manager and adopted by the city council. Thus, when each municipal department receives a detailed electronic listing of the location and type of problems for which it is responsible, and if these problems are not

already known to it, they are added to its workload. City departments and neighborhoods are then better able to identify problems, determine responsibility, plan actions, and record progress.

Four neighborhoods in Worcester piloted the program in 2001, and four more were added in each of the next two years. Two have been added more recently. The fifty-four surveys completed during the past five years have led to documentation of more than 516 assets (potential partners in addressing problems, such as schools, churches, and community centers) and more than twelve thousand problems — for example, litter in more than seventeen hundred locations, more than fourteen hundred sidewalk trip hazards, and thirteen hundred instances of overgrown vegetation.

ComNET has led to a long list of quantitative and qualitative improvements in Worcester.

- Although residents had long complained of a perceived increase in abandoned vehicles, ComNET surveys made it possible to document the extent of the problem by pinpointing the exact location of every one. Since Worcester's Department of Public Works and Parks (DPWP) assumed control of the abandoned vehicle removal program in 2003, more than seven thousand vehicles have been removed from the streets. The program, which was aided by the DPWP's abandoned vehicle hotline, now pays for itself through collection of fines and storage fees.

- Instead of having residents wait to resurvey their neighborhood to know whether a problem had been resolved, the DPWP established a customer service center with a single phone number to afford residents direct access to municipal government for registering complaints and making requests and inquiries. The center responded to more than 115,000 calls, 1,100 walk-ins, and 800 e-mails in fiscal year 2006. About one-quarter resulted in work orders logged and tracked electronically by call takers, who collect all necessary information before transmitting requests to the responsible municipal agency. The work order is tracked, allowing a resident to call the customer service center for updates, and closed when the issue is resolved.

- The customer service center has cut response time and saved $275,000 per year because fewer people are needed to answer phones. (Prior to this, there were fifteen service numbers for the DPWP.) It has recently incorporated handheld computers in the field to expedite further problem resolution, and a Web-based component to allow citizens to submit requests online is in development.
- The kind of quantitative evidence that ComNET is able to produce has swayed political priorities and funding. Even though Worcester residents and the DPWP have long been aware of the poor condition of the streets and sidewalks, it was ComNET's ability to generate numbers and locations that led to increased funding and a plan for remediation. The fiscal year 2007 budget included $2 million from tax levy funds for street and sidewalk repair, plus $6.9 million in capital funding. The city manager proposed a five-year funding plan of $44.5 million.
- ComNET has also improved how city residents understand the work of the municipal government. ComNET data, for example, have dispelled the perception that some neighborhoods get favored treatment from municipal government, because there have been similar resolution rates for problems across neighborhoods. About two-thirds of all the problems recorded have been resolved since the program began six years ago.
- It has also led the residents to take on more responsibility for physical deficiencies in their neighborhood. For example, according to the commissioner of public works and parks, whose department has responsibility for the largest proportion (57 percent) of the identified problems, because of the process of documenting deficiencies residents now understand the issue of demand versus resources and that the city does not have the budget to address every issue at the same time. This same process

of documentation has led to a more complete understanding of who exactly is responsible for remedying which kind of deficiency. ComNET's spreadsheets not only list deficiencies but also clearly designate the agency responsible for remedying each; in about 25 percent of the cases, responsibility lies with the community itself. Community responsibilities include overgrown shrubs and broken fences on private property.

- With the ComNET survey findings in hand, neighborhood residents have shown admirable willingness to step in and deal with these deficiencies themselves. If there is debris accumulating in someone's driveway or yard, for example, neighborhood activists learn how to approach the homeowner and discuss the issue non-confrontationally, pointing out the importance of neighborhood appearance for quality of life and maintaining property values. In the case of residents who might not have the physical or financial wherewithal to repair or clean up their property, community members have frequently chipped in to get the work done.
- Finally, the ComNET program is helping break down some of the traditional town-and-gown barriers between Worcester and its institutions of higher education. The bureau has teamed up with Holy Cross College to incorporate ComNET into the service-learning component of its curriculum. As part of two courses in urban policy and politics, Holy Cross students join up with the neighborhood teams in conducting the surveys. To accommodate the academic calendar, four surveys are conducted in the fall and four in the spring. As a result of this partnership, the neighborhoods gain volunteers and get to know students as more than intruders in their neighborhoods, and the students become more integrated in the city and gain practical knowledge of the challenges facing urban areas.

Clearly, the same sort of problems that plague Worcester affect most urban areas in

Massachusetts and across the nation. However, ComNET is not merely a technology; it depends on the right institutional configuration and community commitment. One key factor in Worcester has been that a credible, independent third party, such as the bureau, has taken responsibility for the project. Although the bureau did not have a long history of working with neighborhood associations, as mentioned earlier it built credibility as an independent, nonpartisan agency over the previous fifteen years before undertaking this project. Neighborhood groups in Worcester tended to be skeptical about municipal government because of a history of unkept promises. Knowing that the bureau was not an arm of municipal government gave these neighborhood groups the comfort level they needed. After working with the first set of four neighborhoods in conducting the surveys, sharing the results, and transmitting them to appropriate municipal agencies, many other neighborhoods applied to participate in the project. Residents continue to participate because they have been able to document improved conditions during resurveys of their neighborhood.

ComNET, and our performance measurement project as a whole, have transformed relations between municipal government and the Worcester Regional Research Bureau as well. As a result of our systematic collection and analysis of data for such an array of measures municipal government uses regularly, we now get steady requests from government agencies (as well as from the private and nonprofit sectors) to conduct additional research and data collection and analysis. This would seem to indicate a greater level of trust between municipal government and the bureau.

As the program has matured, it and the role of the bureau have changed. In what we see as a mark of the program's success, a couple of neighborhoods have withdrawn from the program for the time being because their residents are now confident they can get results dealing directly with the customer service center. In general, as the neighborhoods gain experience with the surveys they are taking on more responsibility. The bureau expects to play a large role again only when a particular neighborhood wishes to undertake a more comprehensive survey or when we are opening up a new territory, as we expect to do in the spring of 2008 in conducting the first survey of Worcester's downtown neighborhood.

As the results of ComNET clearly indicate, citizen-based performance measurement and reporting have led to more effective and efficient delivery of municipal services and a more involved, satisfied, and better-informed citizenry.

PART III. THE FUTURE

CHAPTER 50

City Revenues, Budgets and the Future

Christopher W. Hoene

While the nation's economy may be approaching the late stages of the worst economic downturn since the Great Depression, local government budget tightening and spending cuts over the next several years could well impose a significant drag on the nation's economic recovery. Cities face layoffs, canceled contracts with small businesses and vendors, reduced services and sizable budget shortfalls for 2009 that are expected to grow much more severe and widespread from 2010 to 2012.[1] With the pace of recovery still sluggish, the consequences of the recession will be playing out in America's cities and towns, on Main Street and in the lives of families for years to come.[2]

This chapter provides projections about municipal budget shortfalls over the next three years and reviews city leaders' responses to those conditions. Among the findings:

- The municipal sector will likely face a fiscal shortfall of between $56 billion and $83 billion from 2010–2012, driven by declining tax revenues, ongoing service demands and cuts in state revenues;
- The low point for city fiscal conditions typically follows the low point of an economic downturn by at least two years, indicating that the low point for cities will come sometime in 2011; and

- City leaders are responding with layoffs, furloughs and payroll reductions; delaying and canceling capital infrastructure projects; and cutting city services.

The Municipal Sector Shortfall

The municipal sector — as if all city budgets were totaled together — likely faces a combined, estimated shortfall of anywhere from $56 billion to $83 billion from 2010–2012. The range of the projected shortfall is wide because of the number of factors that can potentially affect municipal bottom lines. Chief among these is the impact of the economic recession on municipal revenue collections. In 2009, city finance officers surveyed by NLC reported that sales tax and income tax collections were declining, but property tax collections were relatively flat.[3]

Nationwide, housing values are down 9.5 percent since 2007, which eventually will translate into residential property tax revenue declines for cities — the brunt of which will hit in 2010, 2011 and 2012. More recently, the commercial property market also has been affected by economic conditions, which will result in declines in commercial property tax collections. At the same time, ongoing and increased de-

Originally published as "City Budget Shortfalls and Responses: Projections for 2010–2012," *Research Brief*, December 2009, by the National League of Cities, Washington, D.C. Reprinted with permission of the publisher.

mands from residents for municipal services and increasing municipal costs will make it difficult for city leaders to offset revenue shortfalls through spending cuts alone.

Revenue declines and spending pressures will conspire to produce municipal budget shortfalls that will have to be filled through increases in fees for services, laying off workers or cutting back their hours, delaying and canceling capital infrastructure projects and drawing down municipal reserves.

For 2009, based on NLC's survey of city finance officers, cities faced an estimated budget shortfall of nearly 3 percent of total general fund budgets. Applying a similar shortfall estimate to each year of the next three years results in a combined, projected shortfall of $35 billion for 2010–2012. However, based on previous recessions, it is highly likely that cities will face larger shortfalls in 2010, 2011 and 2012 than they experienced in 2009. A 4 percent shortfall over the 2010–2012 period would total $46 billion, while a 5 percent shortfall over the period would total $53 billion.

Cuts in State Aid and Transfers

The other major factor that will influence municipal sector shortfalls from 2010–2012 will be actions state governments take in response to their own budget shortfalls. The Center on Budget and Policy Priorities estimates state budget gaps of $190 billion for 2010, $180 billion for 2011 and $118 billion for 2012.[4] The 2010 gap, alone, comprises 28 percent of state budgets for that year. As a means of covering these gaps, many state governments will make cuts in transfers to local governments. Similar actions were taken in response to the 2001 recession, coming mainly in 2003 and 2004. Over that two-year period states reduced total transfers to cities by 9 percent.[5]

In comparison, the current recession is by nearly all measures more severe than the 2001 recession, suggesting that state cuts in transfers to cities will, if anything, be more severe as well. Using a conservative estimate of reductions in state transfers to cities of 10 percent per year from 2010–2012 adds $21 billion to the shortfall in the municipal sector. If state governments were to make cuts in transfers to cities that more closely approximate their own budget shortfalls, those cuts might come more in the range of 15 percent, adding $30 billion to the shortfall in the municipal sector.

Using conservative projections of the municipal budget shortfall and state cuts for 2010–2012, the total range is between $56 billion (a 3 percent municipal budget shortfall and 10 percent reduction in state transfers) and $83 billion (a 5 percent municipal budget shortfall and 15 percent reduction in state transfers).

City Spending Cuts and Responses to Shortfalls

In response to declining economic conditions and the prospect of budget shortfalls, NLC's annual survey of city finance officers revealed that nine in 10 (91 percent) cities reported making spending cuts in 2009, and 82 percent expect to make further cuts in 2010. When asked about the most common responses to prospective shortfalls in 2009, by a wide margin the most common responses were workforce reductions, such as laying off staff, furloughs, and hiring freezes (67 percent), and delaying or canceling capital infrastructure projects (62 percent)— the types of projects that also result in investment in small businesses and other private sector vendors, as well as generating jobs beyond city government. One in seven cities (14 percent) has already made cuts to public safety services — police, fire, and emergency — a number that will inevitably rise as the municipal budget shortfalls increase.

The Need for Federal Intervention

City governments are important components of the U.S. economy. The local and state sector comprises about one-eighth of GDP and cities make up a significant portion of that sector. Consequently, the fiscal actions taken by cities affect the health of the local and regional economies that drive national economic performance. In the absence of additional federal intervention, a deepening local fiscal crisis could hobble the nation's incipient recovery with more layoffs, furloughs, cancelled infrastructure projects, and reduced services.

Estimates from Goldman-Sachs for 2010 and the Center and Budget and Policy Priorities for 2011 suggest that cuts in the state and local sector could reduce U.S. Gross Domestic Product (GDP) by 0.6 percent to 0.7 percent for 2010 and 0.9 percent for 2011. The President's Council of Economic Advisors estimates that each percentage point of GDP translates into approximately one million jobs, meaning that state and local sector cuts could cost the economy 600,000–700,000 jobs in 2010 and 900,000 jobs in 2011.[6]

In short, federal investment in a jobs package that helps stabilize city budgets will help cities save and create jobs locally, both city government jobs and private jobs via small businesses and other enterprises that are dependent on public sector investment.

At an event sponsored by NLC and the Brookings Institution Metropolitan Policy Program in November 2009, Philadelphia Mayor Michael Nutter said "Cities are too important to fail." Federal investment in local jobs and fiscal stabilization will help ensure that actions by cities are helping national economic recovery.

City Fiscal Conditions Typically Lag Economic Conditions

City fiscal conditions typically lag economic conditions, in much the same way that state fiscal conditions lag economic conditions and the unemployment rate lags overall economic recovery. For city budgets, this lag is typically two years, depending on the factors driving the changes in the economy and the depth of those changes. Current economic indicators suggest that the U.S. economy has recently passed the low point of the current recession, which means that the low point for city fiscal conditions will likely be experienced sometime in 2011.

This lag is a function of tax collection and administration issues in cities, particularly for the property tax, which is the most common form of city taxation. Property tax bills represent the value of the property in some previous year, when the last assessment of the value of the property was conducted. A downturn in real estate prices may not be registered for one to several years after the downturn began because property tax assessment cycles vary across jurisdictions: some reassess property annually, while others reassess every few years, and many jurisdictions only reassess a portion of all property in any given year.

Consequently, property tax collections, as reflected in property tax assessments, lag economic changes (both positive and negative) by varying periods of time, depending on the jurisdiction. Sales and income tax collections also exhibit lags due to collection and administration issues, although the lags are typically shorter.

Notes on Methodology

Projections for the budget shortfall in the municipal sector and cuts in state transfers from 2010–2012 were tabulated using U.S. Census of Governments data for municipal general revenues for fiscal year 2006, projected to 2009 using the U.S. Bureau of Economic Analysis (BEA) National Income and Product Accounts (NIPA) estimates for inflation in the state and local government sector, and estimated for 2010–2012 based on conservative projections that were informed by NLC's annual survey of *City Fiscal Conditions* and other NLC research.

Some of the data and findings reported here are drawn from NLC's *City Fiscal Conditions* Survey, a national mail survey of finance officers in U.S. cities. Surveys were mailed to a sample of 1,055 cities, including all cities with populations greater than 50,000 and, using established sampling techniques, to a randomly generated sample of cities with populations between 10,000 and 50,000. The survey was conducted from April to June 2009. The 2009 survey data are drawn from 379 responding cities, for a response rate of 36.0 percent.

NOTES

1. All references to specific years are for fiscal years as defined by the individual cities.

2. The use of "municipal," "municipalities," "cities" or "city" in this report refers to municipal corporations.

3. Christopher W. Hoene and Michael A. Pagano, *City Fiscal Conditions in 2009*, National League of Cities, September 2009, http://www.nlc.org/ASSETS/29BFCBD454 A442E9BF89645017277767/CityFiscalConditions_09.pdf.

4. Iris J. Lav, Nicholas Johnson, and Elizabeth McNichol, "Additional Federal Fiscal Relief Needed to Help States Address Recession's Impact," Center on Budget and Policy Priorities, November 19, 2009, http://www.cbpp.org/cms/index.cfm?fa=view&id=2988.

5. Christopher W. Hoene and Michael A. Pagano, "Fend-For-Yourself Federalism: The Effect of Federal and State Deficits on America's Cities," *Government Finance Review*, October 2003.

6. Goldman-Sachs U.S. Economic Analyst, "The State and Local Sector: What a (Fiscal) Drag," July 10, 2009 and Iris J. Lav, Nicholas Johnson, and Elizabeth McNichol, "Additional Federal Fiscal Relief Needed to Help States Address Recession's Impact," Center on Budget and Policy Priorities, November 19, 2009.

Editor's note: This research report also revealed several examples of fiscal distress in cities, and the operational impact of these anticipated revenue reductions. These examples primarily include the impact of budget reductions brought about by a decrease in selected revenue sources. The operational impact of these financial reductions included employee layoffs, employee work furloughs, early retirement programs, a reduction in scheduled street repairs, and other departmental public service reductions (e.g., police, fire, library, public works, and senior services), as well as a deferral of needed capital improvement projects to future fiscal year.

For a complete copy of the research brief, and related municipal research briefs, the reader is referred to the website for the National League of Cities, which is included in the *National Resource Directory*.

CHAPTER 51

Financial Constraints and New Service Opportunities
William Barnes

Michael Pagano says that we are in a "unique time in the history of public finance," a time when leaders and citizens can and should broach fundamental issues.

Pagano knows a thing or two about finance — the "lifeblood of municipalities." He speaks from more than a quarter century of widely respected scholarly and practical work in this field and from amidst his own budgetary turmoil as a dean at the University of Illinois at Chicago.

In recent presentations to an NLC Staff Seminar and to workshops at the NLC Congress of Cities in Denver, Pagano said that the recession and financial fiasco and the political responses to them have combined with, exacerbated, and highlighted long-term trends in the basic "architecture of public finance." The result is a combustible and excruciating situation that will linger for at least several more years.

He predicts that, to cope responsibly, communities will have to negotiate "new social compacts" upon which city finances can be reconstructed.

This will not be easy, especially in the current, nasty environment. Responding to the horrible shootings in Tucson, NLC President James E. Mitchell Jr., councilmember, Charlotte, N.C., said that "we cannot let fear limit the openness of public discourse" because "the open exchange of ideas in public settings ... is, in fact, at the heart of our democratic system."

A New Play Book

Similarly, Ronald O. Loveridge, mayor of Riverside, Calif., and now immediate past president of NLC, told delegates at the NLC conference that this is "not the time to hunker down or to withdraw within our city limits." He called instead for "a new play book" for municipal strategies.

He also cited author Richard Florida's claim, in "The Great Reset," that we are in midst of one of the nation's "broad and fundamental transformations of the economic and social order." City governments will need to understand what that means for them — what their new normal can be and will be — and then adapt and lead accordingly.

Elsewhere, URBACT, a consortium of cities and researchers in the European Union, observes that, because EU member states are financially debilitated, "The downturn has empowered local communities." Moreover, the situation "pushes on habits and overcomes taboos"; it "is raising questions that, by habit, we have not asked in a long time."

Originally published as "A Unique Time in Public Finance: Not for Hunkering Down," *Research Brief*, June 2011, by the National League of Cities, Washington, D.C. Reprinted with permission of the publisher.

Fundamental dollars and cents challenges lead directly to fundamental governance challenges, including questions that may not be part of the normal budgetary discussions. However diverse the focus in the variety of localities, the underlying commonality is that these are wicked policy/political matters, not easily subject to technical/administrative standards.

Questions

What kinds of questions are at issue here?

By way of example, Pagano mentioned the fairness of revenue systems; the pro-cyclical nature of local budget practice; accumulated long-term liabilities (pensions and infrastructure); definition of "core services" pricing infrastructure and services; and partnerships in service delivery.

That's a daunting list and thoughtful officials will formulate more items. What, indeed, are "core municipal functions?" If "public safety" and "economic development" and "strengthening families" are among them, what do we really mean by those concepts?

Loveridge suggested that the 21st century will be "the century of regions." Are there steps cities can take that are useful in the budget crisis and that also build a capacity for inter-local collaboration and shared services?

President Obama has called for fundamental federal tax reform (not just tax cuts.) Is it also time for fundamental municipal and state tax reform (not just tax cuts)?

Are tax exemptions for non-profits, especially the big institutional ones, appropriate? Some cities are already grappling with this.

Are we yet past the "do more with less" mantra? What will it mean to do less with less or to do differently with different?

And what about the even deeper issues, questions of purpose and values? What will be the mix in city budgets of investment versus current consumption? Who will pay and who will benefit? Will budgets facilitate economic growth? Stable neighborhoods?

Whether or not these and other questions are posed publicly and explicitly, the process will willy-nilly result in answers. And the effects will re-shape the future.

Public Deliberation

So, leaders may as well frame and pose such questions and try to debate the answers thoughtfully and in public. Does the government have a relationship with the residents and stakeholders of the community that will allow for and support such discussions? Do all the potential participants have the skills to take part effectively?

The view that government is per se bad is "not a useful place to start," such public discussions, says Pete Peterson, Director of the Davenport Institute at Pepperdine University.

It's important for officials to accept that "everything we're doing now is the right thing" is also not a useful place to start.

"The key question facing city leaders," observes Christopher Hoene, who analyzes public finance conditions as NLC's director of research and innovation, "is when do they move from managing cutbacks to rethinking the work of cities?"

The answers that evolve to such underlying questions will constitute a new normal or a new social compact. More prosaically, they will be new rules of the game about how the community is going to solve its problems and seize its opportunities.

CHAPTER 52

Redefining the Quality of Life in Your Community

Thomas L. Miller *and* Shannon E. Hayden

If you enjoyed the last week of 2010, you probably were in Papua New Guinea, where you had only a spotty Web connection and cannibals to contend with. Those local government managers who stayed at home to enjoy the plenty of 2010 ushered in 2011 with headlines like these:

"Bill Would Allow Indiana Cities to Declare Bankruptcy"[1]
"Cuomo's Consolidation Plan a Work in Progress"[2]
"[El Paso, Texas] City Manager Denies Huge Police Shortage"[3]
"Winnebago County [Illinois] May Trim Funding for 10 Service Programs"[4]
"Defaults by Cities Looming as U.S. Mayors Say Deficits Hinder Debt Payment"[5]

Word on the street is that this country's future holidays will be brighter than the last couple, now that the tax compromise has become law, consumer spending is noticeably improved, and the stock market is returning household wealth that investors saw spin down the rabbit hole in late 2008. But if you don't yet see the turnaround, don't blame yourself: most pundits argue that government will remain sickly for months after the private sector has revitalized. What could be worse than the economic tornado that swept away street

sweeping, along with public safety personnel, library hours, the foliage in our street medians, and the lights on our streets? What could do more damage to the reputation of our hard work and the goodwill of our residents than to either deny services long expected or charge more for even less service than before?

This could be worse: your fine community could ruin your winning track record by slashing service ratings. Wouldn't attitudes of residents denied snow removal, code inspection, road repair, jobs, and economic development be as depressed as the housing and consumer markets that first impelled the service cuts? It is expected that with the country's fall off the economic cliff, those who received local government services fueled by revenue back when times were good will now record their dissatisfaction with lower service delivery ratings.

Background and Methodology

National Research Center, Inc. (NRC) has been leading innovation in citizen survey methods and reporting since 1990, and we have conducted more than 1,000 surveys to gather residents' perspectives since 1995. In 2001 NRC partnered with ICMA to offer The National

Originally published as "The Hurt Dividend: Residents' Appreciation for Local Government Services in Tough Times," *The Municipal Yearbook 2011*, by the International City/County Management Association, Washington, D.C. Reprinted with permission of the publisher.

Citizen Survey™ (The NCS™) to local governments. After nine years of responses to core questions asked of a representative sample of residents in hundreds of locales from Honolulu, Hawaii, to Montpelier, Vermont, we have grown a hardy repository of opinions of over 180,000 residents, a database that we tend meticulously. Over time, we have tested different wording and methods. From the thousands of responses we have received regarding scores of local government services and many characteristics of community quality, we (and others) have been able to reflect on current trends in resident opinions.

Sometimes we have found ourselves with an opportunity to analyze the impacts of phenomena of historic proportions. (Did residents' perspectives in surveys received just before September 11, 2001, differ from those in surveys received just after it? No. Does a once-in-100-year snowstorm shake residents' confidence in their local government's snow removal service? Yes. Can residents return to feeling safe even after a sniper terrorizes their city? Yes.)

So the fall 2008 financial meltdown and subsequent world economic crisis offered NRC the opportunity for another experiment. NRC researchers examined how residents reacted to the steep economic decline and, after comparing results across several years of data, found — as expected — that downbeat opinions reflected the bad times. It should be noted that the set of jurisdictions surveyed each year is not identical (some jurisdictions respond to the survey every year and most respond every other year) and does not represent a random subset of all U.S. cities and counties. Nevertheless, the volume of data gathered each year (from a couple thousand respondents in the first year to over 15,000 in each subsequent year) and the nature of broadly similar experiences among communities across the country during this time make these findings compelling.

The data for these analyses come from The NCS™, administered in a methodologically rigorous and transparent way in each community. The standard survey protocol involves a mailed survey with multiple contacts to a scientifically selected random sample of households. Surveys for participating jurisdictions

are conducted year-round, and unless the questions are inapplicable to specific communities (e.g., questions pertaining to snow removal where snow removal is not an issue), the same questions are asked of all communities.

Findings

When residents were asked to speculate about the likely impact of the economy on their own household's financial well-being in the upcoming months, we found a slow but steady leading indicator of worsening worry that started in 2006, with 32 percent of respondents anticipating a negative impact, and spiked in 2009, the year following the worst quarter of stock market losses in generations. By August of 2010, when the data for this report were analyzed, pessimism was abating, down from 37 percent to 33 percent, but economic doubts about the future remained about as strong as they had been in the time leading up to the start of the recession.

Another expected finding relates to residents' sentiments about population growth. Although for many years the word *growth* had virtually been an expletive that majorities in communities wanted deleted from the lexicon, as the economy worsened in 2008 (but even beginning in 2006), residents became less worried about their communities growing too fast — no doubt because migration had slowed as jobs, the engine of population growth, had slowed. After peaking in 2005, worry about speedy population growth started to decline just as pessimism about personal economic futures began to grow.

Two years later, the ever-present worry about two few jobs rose steeply. Over the decade, the fraction of respondents assessing job growth as being too slow rose by over 25 percent.

Considering the noticeable and predictable disquiet of residents during this period, NRC researchers and our clients wondered if personal concerns about the economy might have spread to an overall negative view of community and service. This point of view might be considered the "Pervasive Pain" suspicion. It assumes that the economic cloud that shadows our own homes and jobs pervades the entire landscape of local government services, darkening residents' sentiments about service quality and their communities as well. If that is what occurred, one might also expect to see a decline in community ratings (e.g., for quality of life, the city as a place to live or retire or raise children) and service ratings (e.g., for police, fire, trash haul) over this period if the need to trim or eviscerate budgets impaired the quality of community and service delivery. If opinions get worse because services are cut, we might call this the "Poverty Penalty," a cut assessed to quality ratings concomitant with services that are not delivered at formerly high levels because of revenue shortfalls.

As it happened, all this common sense speculation about service ratings going down when cupboards go bare turned out to be wrong. Across the thousands of residents and hundreds of jurisdictions in our database, we found that dismal personal economic forecasts over these troubled times have not been predictive of feelings about the community. Nor have residents reported dissatisfaction with service delivery from their local government — at least not yet. While portents of a difficult personal economic future have not fully abated and worries about flagging job growth deepen, residents currently are either holding steady in their opinions of community life and service delivery or giving them even higher ratings than they did in better times past.

One dividend of the economic downturn has been a greater availability of affordable quality housing. While the spate of foreclosures that has accompanied the economic crisis has created a severe hardship for many who have lost their homes, the steep drop in housing prices across the country has meant, for others, homes that are more affordable. From 2007 to 2010, respondents' awareness of the opportunity presented in lower-cost housing rose by more than 10 percentage points. Although the greater availability of affordable quality housing is a sad benefit of a market collapse, the drop in home prices, like respondents' growing pessimism about their personal economic futures or worries about job growth, still represents a direct measure of resident sentiment about the economy.

What about general ratings of community quality or service delivery that are not proxies for economic conditions? Here is where the surprise comes in. Ratings of the overall quality of life have held relatively steady since 2004, with close to two-thirds of respondents giving positive ratings; moreover, partial results from 2010 show a possible uptick. The same trend appears in answers to questions about the neighborhood or city as a place to live or retire. Despite the economic storm, residents still feel positively about where they live. Could these be signs of gratitude for the stability that community offers in tough times?

But even if we see stability or improvement in community ratings, what about ratings of local government services? Here, too, we find an unexpected dividend of the bad economy — something we call the "Hurt Dividend," indicative of an appreciation for local government services in distressed times. For example, since 2006, satisfaction with police services has been climbing steadily, reaching an all-time high of nearly 70 percent in 2010.

Opinions about fire and emergency medical services have shown the same trend, as have opinions about street repair. In fact, virtually all examined services — trash haul, code enforcement, parks and recreation, library, and services overall — at least held steady in resident opinion over the two years following the economic crisis. Hypotheses to explain the unanticipated buoyancy of resident opinion abound but none with compelling proof.

- Are residents acknowledging that their local government despite praise when it tries harder despite the turn of the screws? (The Hurt Dividend)
- Have local governments tried harder to provide top-quality services when the going got tough — and did they succeed? (Call it the "Too Good to Fail" theory)
- Has the press painted such a gloomy picture that residents expected worse than they actually experienced? Have the real problems in places depicted in the news made people in communities with less economic hardship more appreciative of the services they are receiving? Have cuts been more strate-

gic — excising much more fat than muscle — than what the press has led residents to believe was required? (Name it "Oversold Gloom")
- Will the real impact of service cuts only begin to be felt in 2011 and beyond? (The "Hang onto Your Hat" hypothesis)

Conclusion

As the puzzle presented by our findings is contemplated, it is important to remember that these responses have been culled from the broadest cross-section of residents represented in well-conducted citizen surveys. And these residents do not sound like disgruntled citizens who come to public meetings every Tuesday night to gripe about how their local government is letting them down. Most residents in most communities across America are pleased with where they live and with the services their local government provides. That this sentiment of general approval has been (at least so far) sustained through this deep recession may say as much about real service delivery as it does about expectations and community engagement.

Local government managers should read several opportunities into these findings:

- If the Hurt Dividend keeps resident opinion strong about community and local government services because residents are especially grateful for the extraordinary effort when things get tough, managers could seek to harness that community goodwill by offering more opportunities for residents to participate in local governance and community service.
- If residents are pleased that good work continues through cutbacks caused by lean times because services are ramped up to overdrive, managers could continue to show that they are too good to fail by running lean and letting residents know how much has been and can be accomplished economically, even when the economy rebounds.

- If the media have oversold the gloominess of the downturn, managers could see how the local press can help them harness the goodwill that such pot-stirring creates.
- If the downturn's real impact on service delivery is just around the corner, managers could alert residents about the sacrifices to come and engage them in replacing some services with community labor and sweat.

Whatever the reasons for residents' sustained support of local government services, the prospect for the future in any one town, city, or county depends on unique local conditions — for example, a strong economic development plan, new programs to purchase green spaces, better recycling, improved transportation connections. Managers must keep the relatively small investment in their trend line solid so that whatever happens in local government service delivery can be read in the spikes and turns of resident perspective.

NRC researchers will continue to cultivate the growing database of citizen survey opinions to find answers as they become apparent. In the meantime, managers should cash in on that Hurt Dividend.

NOTES

1. Associated Press, "Bill Would Allow Indiana Cities to Declare Bankruptcy," (Fort Wayne) *Journal Gazette*, December 27, 2010, journalgazette.net/article/20101227/NEWS07/101229608 (accessed February 18, 2011).

2. Joseph Spector, "Cuomo's Consolidation Plan a Work in Progress," (Binghamton) *Pressconnects.com*, October 25, 2010, pressconnects.com/article/20101025/NEWS01/10250329/Cuomo-s-consolidation-plan-a-work-in-progress (accessed January 20, 2011).

3. Monica Balderrama, "City Manager Denies Huge Police Shortage," *KFOXTV.com*, December 21, 2010, kfoxtv.com/news/26211469/detail.html (accessed January 20, 2011).

4. Mike Wiser, "Winnebago County May Trim Funding for 10 Service Programs," *RRSTAR.COM*, November 22, 2010, rrstar.com/carousel/x1892562439/Winnebago-County-may-trim-funding-for-crime-fighting-programs?photo=0 (accessed January 20, 2011).

5. William Selway, "Defaults by Cities Looming as U.S. Mayors Say Deficits Hinder Debt Payment," *Bloomberg*, January 19, 2011, bloomberg.com/news/2011-01-19/cities-may-default-on-borrowings-amid-financial-strains-u-s-mayors-say.html (accessed January 20, 2011).

CHAPTER 53

The Condition of America's Infrastructure
Roger L. Kemp

Introduction

The term "infrastructure" refers to the basic facilities and installations necessary for the citizens in a society to operate, as well as to carry on the activities of their daily lives. These include transportation and communication systems (e.g., highways, airports, bridges, telephone lines, cellular telephone towers, post offices, etc.); educational and health facilities; water, gas, and electrical systems (e.g., dams, power-lines, power plants, aqueducts, etc.); and miscellaneous facilities such as prisons, asylums, national park structures, and other improvements to real property owned by government.

In the United States, the infrastructure components are divided into the private and public sectors. Public facilities are owned by the municipal, county, state, and/or federal governments. There are also many special district authorities, such as the Port Authority of New York and the Los Angeles Department of Water and Power, as well.

The American Society of Civil Engineers (ASCE) — the only professional membership organization in the United States that has graded our nation's public infrastructure — recognizes 15 major categories of the government infrastructure. These infrastructure categories include:

- Aviation,
- Bridges,
- Dams,
- Drinking Water,
- Energy,
- Hazardous Waste,
- Inland Waterways,
- Levees,
- Public Parks and Recreation,
- Rail,
- Roads,
- Schools,
- Security,
- Solid Waste,
- Transit, and
- Wastewater.

Managing America's Infrastructure and Fiscal Crises

All levels of government are facing a new era of capital financing and infrastructure management. Revenues that once were available for capital construction, restoration, and maintenance, have either diminished or evaporated entirely in recent years. Portions of the public infrastructure that were once adequate are now experiencing signs of distress, even decay, with no end in sight to the ongoing deterioration of our nation's infrastructure.

Local and state, as well as the federal, government are subject to unprecedented fiscal demands for public services in an environment of limited taxation and dwindling financial resources. State government deficits are increasing. At the same time, the federal deficit is at an all-time high — exacerbated by the fact that our nation is concurrently financing an undeclared war in the Middle East and suffering from a weakened economy. These negative fiscal circumstances, experts believe, are likely to continue for many years to come.

Congested highways, overflowing sewers, and corroding bridges, are constant reminders of the looming crisis that jeopardizes our nation's prosperity and the quality of life for our citizens. With new grades published in 2009, the condition of our nation's infrastructure has shown little to no improvement since receiving a collective grade of C- in 1988 — and with some areas sliding toward failing grades.

The American Society of Civil Engineers' *2009 Report Card for America's Infrastructure* assesses the same categories as it did in the previous survey. The grade comparisons of America's infrastructure between the ASCE's original survey in 1988 and its most recent survey in 2009 are highlighted below.

- **Aviation**— Received a grade of B- in 1988, and a grade of D in 2009.
- **Bridges**— Received a grade of C+ in 1988, and a grade of C in 2009.
- **Dams** —While not graded in 1988, they received a grade of D in 2009.
- **Drinking Water**— Received a grade of B- in 1988, and a grade of D- in 2009.
- **Energy**— While not graded in 1988, this category received a grade of D+ in 2009.
- **Hazardous Waste**— This category receive a grade of D in 1988 and again in 2009.
- **Inland Waterways**— While not graded in 1988, they received a grade of D- in 2009.
- **Levees** —While not graded in 1988, they received a grade of D- in 2009.
- **Public Parks & Recreation**— While not graded in 1988, they received a grade of C- in 2009.
- **Rail**— While not graded in 1988, this category received a grade of C- in 2009.
- **Roads** —Received a grade of C+ in 1988, and a grade of D- in 2009.
- **Schools**— While not graded in 1988, this category received a grade of D in 2009.
- **Solid Waste**— Received a grade of C- in 1988, and a grade of C+ in 2009. This is the only infrastructure category to increase during its grade since the original "graded" evaluation some 21 years ago.
- **Transit**— Received a grade of C- in 1988 and a grade of D in 2009.
- **Wastewater** —Received a grade of C in 1988, and a grade of D- in 2009.

In short, U.S. roads, bridges, sewers, and dams are crumbling and need a $2.2 trillion overhaul, but prospects for improvement are grim. This is the amount of money necessary over the next five years to restore and rebuild major components of our nation's public infrastructure. The nation's drinking water system alone needs a public investment of $11 billion annually to replace facilities and to comply with regulations to meet our future drinking water needs. Federal grant funding in 2005 was only 10 percent of this amount. As a result, aging wastewater systems are discharging billions of gallons of untreated sewage into surface waters each year, according to the ASCE's report.

And the signs of our deteriorating infrastructure go on! Poor roads cost motorists $54 billion a year in repairs and operating costs, while American's spent 3.5 billion hours a year stuck in traffic jams. The country's power transmission system also needs to be modernized, the report said. While demand continues to rise, transmission capacity failed to keep pace and actually fell by 2 percent in 2001. As of 2003, 27 percent of the nation's bridges were structurally deficient or obsolete, a slight improvement from the 28.5 percent in 2000. It is alarming to note, but since 1998 the number of unsafe dams in the country rose by 33 percent to more than 3,500.

A dozen national professional associations have officially endorsed the ASCE's *Report Cards for America's Infrastructure* over the years. Some of these organizations include:

- the American Public Works Association (APWA),
- the National Stone, Sand and Gravel Association (NSSGA),
- the U. S. Conference of Mayors (USCM),
- the National Heavy and Highway Alliance (NHHA),
- the American Road and Transportation Builders Association (ARTBA),

- the Association of State Dam Safety Officials (ASDSO),
- the National Association of Clean Water Agencies (NACWA), and
- the American Shore and Beach Preservation Association (ASBPA).

For a complete listing of these endorsing organizations please refer to ASCE's website <www.asce.org>.

National Leadership Is Needed

The views expressed by many experts who research and write on infrastructure issues point to a general agreement on the magnitude and complexity of this problem. However, little agreement exists on a consensus on how to achieve a comprehensive nationwide solution to restoring and maintaining America's public infrastructure. One point, though, seems obviously clear: *The necessary leadership and policy direction required to properly address this national issue must come from the highest level of government.* It is only within a national policy framework that states, counties, and cities can work together to improve the current condition of our public works facilities. Local and state governments alone, because of their many diverse policies, multiple budget demands, and varied fiscal constraints, cannot be relied upon to achieve the comprehensive solution required to solve this national problem.

The prevailing philosophy of our national government has been to let the lower levels of government (states, counties, and cities) solve their own problems, regardless of the nature of their complexity or the magnitude of funds needed. If a solution is to be forthcoming, the political posture of our national government needs to become more positive and proactive. Assertive leadership from the federal government must make the difficult policy decisions, as well as approve the funding required, to solve our country's infrastructure problem. Fundamental changes are needed to redirect national priorities about how public capital investments are made. Officials at all levels of government must recognize that they can no longer build public facilities without adequately maintaining them in future years.

The Future

As the severity of this issue escalates and citizens become more aware of the increased costs of postponing a decision on public infrastructure, taxpayers may become more politically involved in solving this issue in the future. Local taxpayers cannot be expected, however, to foot the entire bill for a solution, since the majority of our country's capital assets have been constructed over the past several decades — some over a century ago — and frequently with the assistance of grant funds from our federal government. Cities, counties, and states have relative degrees of wealth based on their taxing capacity, bonding levels and ratings, and budgetary reserves. Because of this, many lower levels of government do not have the financial capability, even with increased taxation, to adequately address those issues related to restoring and maintaining America's infrastructure.

This bullet is "too big to bite" by lower levels of government alone.

It is safe to say that most citizens throughout the country already feel overtaxed by all levels of government. Even though citizens may be willing to assist financially, a major redirection of federal government funds will be required for a truly comprehensive and coordinated nationwide response to our country's outstanding infrastructure problems and issues.

Even with some additional taxes and user fees, funding will be limited from the lower levels of government. For this reason, argue those who deal with infrastructure issues, national priorities must be established for the replacement and restoration of capital facilities for all levels of government, starting with those projects that are necessary to ensure the public's security, health, and safety. Funds from existing federal grant programs must be targeted for infrastructure projects nationwide — such as from less-important operational programs with limited or only special interest constituencies.

To the President: Our nation is not "on

the road to ruin," as some experts explain, but merely going through the transition period required to properly sort-out and arrive at a politically acceptable long-term solution to this critical and complex policy issue that plagues all levels of government — federal, state, county, and city alike.

If our country's infrastructure is allowed to deteriorate even further in the future, possibly to the point of decay, the cost of resolving this issue will escalate significantly in future years for all taxpayers. If this happens, economic development programs will also continue to suffer, and the revenues they could generate will not be available to assist in restoring our public infrastructure. For these reasons, I strongly urge President Obama to make the restoration of America's public infrastructure a national funding priority.

The New Administration, headed by President Obama, with the assistance of Congress, recently passed the American Recovery and Reinvestment Act of 2009. This legislation, for the first time in a number of years, includes substantial funding (upwards of $150 billion) for public investment in new infrastructure projects, as well as the restoration of our nation's existing infrastructure network. This new *federal stimulus package* is certainly a step in the right direction! The amount of funds allocated by our national government for the restoration of America's public infrastructure, however, is only a portion of what is actually needed to restore and maintain our nation's various public works components.

It is now up to the public officials in our states, and their cities, to invest wisely in those public works projects most important to the citizens that they serve. Now that this issue has been acknowledged as a national priority, hopefully additional funding will continue for this essential purpose in future years. This legislation and funding, and hopefully future actions of this type, prove that America is "not on the road to ruin" but rather "on the road to recovery." Only time will tell if our nation, characterized by the very historical essence of democracy and capitalism, can sustain its critical position at the forefront of advanced nations throughout the world during the coming century!

Note: To develop the *2009 Report Card for America's Infrastructure*, ASCE assembled a panel of 24 of the nation's leading civil engineers, who analyzed hundreds of studies, reports, and other sources, and surveyed more than 2,000 engineers throughout the nation to determine the condition of America's infrastructure. Base grades were then reviewed by ASCE's Advisory Council. For more details about this process, refer to ASCE's website <www.asce.org>.

CHAPTER 54

Cities, New Technologies and Public Services

Marcel Bullinga

In the future, new technologies will give us much better control of the world around us. We'll surround ourselves with self-service dashboards and carry a multipurpose self-service card and a self-service mobile phone. This techno-control will allow us to perform continuous checks on everything (and everyone) in our environment: Is the air polluted? Is the taxi driver cheating me? Is this doctor licensed? We also will be able to control any use of our own personal data and to prevent misuse. This will greatly enhance our privacy.

At the same time, government will gain power as well. In the years ahead, technology will provide government and society at large with tools for a safer world and for automatic law enforcement. Permits and licenses will be embedded in smart cars, trains, buildings, doors, and devices. Laws will automatically download and distribute themselves into objects in our physical environment, and everything will regularly be updated, just as software is now automatically updated in your desktop computer.

Innovations in government will enable us to have a safer environment for law-abiding citizens because built-in intelligence in our environment will minimize fraud, global crime, pandemic diseases, accidents, and disasters.

Law-abiding citizens will *gain* privacy, while criminals will lose it.

Innovations in ambient intelligence — rooms full of networked smart devices that adapt to our needs and respond to our whims — are accelerating and offer the promise of automatic control over our world. Right now, innovation in government worldwide is about creating parts of this infrastructure, with the goal of a paperless world with fewer mistakes, fewer flaws, and real-time ID checks.

Only a combination of smart control and smart technology will solve major current problems. I stress the phrase *smart technology* since a lot of today's technologies are simply too dumb. They are not compatible, exchangeable, or reusable.

Successful governance of these technologies requires that they meet human needs by providing safety, shelter, communication, health, happiness, better care, less waiting, better rules, better public services, more-efficient mobility, less criminality.

So how do we achieve this ideal through automatic governance, using smart knowledge and citizen control? What consequences will we face when our world turns intelligent and transparent in the next 10 years? And what should we do to make it happen?

Originally published as "Intelligent Government: Invisible, Automatic, and Everywhere," *The Futurist*, Vol. 38, No. 4, July-August 2004, by the World Future Society, Bethesda, MD. Reprinted with permission of the publisher.

Government in Control: Automatic Law Enforcement

Making rules and enforcing them are important government tasks. Right now, laws are written down on paper and enforced by individuals. In the future, all rules and laws will be incorporated into expert systems and chips embedded in cars, appliances, doors, and buildings — that is, our physical environment. No longer will police officers and other government personnel be the only law enforcement. Our physical environment will enforce the law as well. I call this trend automatic law enforcement.

A cigarette machine, for example, would only allow you to purchase cigarettes if you were of legal age, a fact that is stored on a smart card and can be verified. You would put the smart card in the machine or wave at it, and once your information is verified the cigarettes would be dispensed. The smart card is the key to obtaining legal services or products (in this case, cigarettes). If you are not of legal age, you cannot obtain the restricted product or service.

In the same way, an elevator would stop accepting passengers if the government license that is embedded in it has expired. If it has not expired and if the elevator still meets all government demands, then it would just keep working.

Automatic law enforcement or governance will find its most useful application in the intelligent car. Toyota exhibited a concept car in early 2004 that would recognize a change in speed limit as the car moves onto a new road, then tell the driver when he or she is exceeding that limit. It would not be smart or powerful enough to disable the car if the driver is disobedient, but that ability is feasible.

Starting this future intelligent car would be like launching a spaceship: The system would perform a lot of network checks before it actually started. Are the safety belts on? If not, then the car doesn't start. Are you the rightful owner? If not, then the car doesn't start. Is there a police warrant for your arrest? If yes, then the car won't budge. Only when the car and driver have satisfied all the network checks — which will require just milliseconds to complete — will the car start. Once it does, the smart car will do most of the work of driving. It will be self-steering, for instance. While driving, you will pay road taxes by the mile, and you won't be allowed to drive into a noise-restricted zone or exceed the speed limit. This kind of real-time government control has been tested already in satellite-steered cars. The motor continuously checks if it meets the environmental laws. If it fails, it does not work. And finally, driver identification and authentication systems will make attempts to steal the vehicle futile. The car simply will not work for a thief.

The intelligent car is an environment filled with invisible, networked information systems. All kinds of databases about the car and its owner are linked with government databases that together manage the vehicle to protect the owner's safety, prevent theft, improve traffic flow and public safety, and safeguard the environment both inside and outside the car.

Updateable Laws, Updateable Machines

Future governments will no longer supply paper laws but will instead supply open-standards software with the appropriate regulatory information and protocols to all citizens' intelligent cars, appliances, buildings, and machines. Intelligent devices will become self-aware to the extent that they will "know" what laws or regulations apply and how to act upon them. They will make decisions and self-enforce them. Automatic law enforcement will be used for environmental regulations, traffic and safety laws, bookkeeping rules, and all social-security issues involving proof of identity. In the future, when asking for reports and statistics, government will use a company's own software to extract and upload the reports automatically; by the same method, the government authority could download a license in real time. The machines and buildings would continuously update themselves with new rules.

If the value of the digits stored on a smart card is guaranteed, if the context and the ownership of the digits is guaranteed and packaged in the same data, then we could get something like an intelligent beer tap that links the dispenser to the cashier's register for automatic billing. And bartenders could keep track of who has had too much to drink.

If we can make a connection between the beer tap and the cashier, we can also make a link to government tax-collection agencies, enabling them to collect sales taxes in real time. We are already using our mobile phones for many more purposes than just calling people. We now pay bills, parking tickets, and train fares by phone, setting the stage for the development of "intelligent money": The European Central Bank is already planning to put a chip in paper money to guarantee authenticity, so it shouldn't be long before we get rid of the paper and keep the chip.

In medieval city-fortresses, there were huge walls and gates where everyone was checked thoroughly before being admitted. If you could not contribute to the city, or if you were a criminal, then you were not allowed inside.

Today, cities lack walls and gates, but illegal or harmful immigration and the spread of diseases such as SARS and mad cow disease may lead to a countertrend toward more-limited access and the old defense mechanisms of medieval cities. Old national borders will be replaced by new physical city borders and by virtual administrative borders. For instance, Rome has a video tracking system installed to help reduce traffic congestion. All over the world, police forces argue that we should use such systems not only for tracking cars but also for tracking people, checking on who wants to get into a city, and preventing them from doing so if they are illegal immigrants or criminals. Networked smart environments, continuously updated by governments, will thus help the fight against terrorism while respecting and promoting a decent civil society.

Citizen in Control: Self-Service and Self-Control Dashboards

Imagine the potential of having multiple self-service dashboards in your car, office, or home. This would evolve from the current concept of an organizer or mobile phone, which, if properly equipped with validated, real-time knowledge, can be a command and control center for any profession and for any moment of the day.

An intelligent sports machine equipped with your personal sports dashboard could maintain your sports records. It would track what you did last time and what you do now, and encourage you to do it better than yesterday. You might get real-time information on whether you sweat enough, helping you to stay trim.

In the future, you may wear computerized eyeglasses specific to your profession. Outfitted with monitors, the glasses would be like a dashboard for your professional work, containing all the information needed for doing a job properly. You would not only see the physical machinery you are working with, but you would also see the virtual content surrounding that machine. The computer glasses could thus tell you how to repair it and with what kind of equipment.

We as citizens, customers, employees, and civil servants will each possess many transactional dashboards, by which we will conduct all our business virtually with companies and government authorities, bypassing intermediary clerks and other workers. This trend of humans being replaced by technology is old, but it is now accelerating. We no longer need the aid of a staff of workers for many kinds of routine services.

We are heading for *smart knowledge*— that is, knowledge that knows its owner and its owner's wishes, so that we will become the real center of the knowledge environment. We will be able to maintain our profile in all business and government databases and trace the use of our data anywhere in the world. Whether in the physical environment or in a virtual environment, we can control how and when our data is used, according to the rules of our Personal Terms of Use embedded in every device, building, or environment under our control.

For that to work, we also need a validated identity to attach to all of these self-service dashboards: a self-service card.

Self-Service Cards

It's incredible how many IDs, membership cards, and passes people typically possess: Besides a driver's license, you may have a shopper's club card, a housing pass, a bicycle pass, a disco pass, and, in some countries, even an addict pass, which controls the distribution of drugs. In 2005, Malaysia will have a smart card citizen ID; in 2006, the Dutch will have a public-transport pass.

These smart cards are mostly local and single-function, covering only a tiny segment of daily life. Now is the time to reflect on whether these countless cards — essentially information-management and access-control devices — are actually meeting our needs. In the future, these various smart cards and passes will likely merge into one multifunctional, all-purpose pass, because having dozens of passes is simply not manageable for the individual. We will thus see a trend toward reduction of all these different passes over the next 10 or 20 years.

Security of these multifunctional identification and access cards will be a big issue, and all future passes will need multiple, redundant biometric security systems to ensure safe and valid transactions. The automaker Renault advertises a new vehicle that people can unlock and start without a key. The car identifies them by their hands and smart cards.

Self-Service Mobile Phones

Smart cards will likely be inserted into our mobile phones, which will gain more and more new functions, becoming personal communication control centers. The smart phone will prove your identity, pay your bills, collect your bonus points, and render services based on where you are (if you're waiting at a bus stop, for example, it will tell you when the next bus will arrive).

More crucially, though, the smart mobile device will be a lie detector, allowing you to perform everyday checks in real time, such as whether the driver of a taxi cab has a valid government license, whether the driver has tampered with the meter, and whether he is taking the shortest route as determined by your smart mobile's real-time GPS check.

Other things you'll be able to check include whether the city air is polluted or not, whether a pub has passed its fire-safety inspection, or whether a new doctor really earned all the diplomas hanging on her wall. This type of transparent information means we'll be able to check anything we need to — and make new choices as a result.

Self-Service Privacy

The ability to bind all of our activities and tap into transparent information will help strengthen our control as citizens.

Self-service smart dashboards will enable self-service privacy. That is, you will decide which databases you want information about you to be in and under what conditions others may use the data you voluntarily give to a company or government agency. (Some government relationships obviously are not voluntary. If you are a criminal, for instance, you won't be able to delete yourself from the police records.)

In a world of ambient intelligence, your privacy will be much more closely guarded and protected than ever before, so long as you stick to the rules. But if you commit criminal acts, you lose your privacy immediately.

Digital technology makes it relatively easy to make personal information anonymous so that it can only be used in aggregated statistical information. While driving an intelligent car, you will be monitored, but your privacy will not be lost. No one knows it's you who is driving there or why, unless you choose to reveal your status to people you trust. A traveling salesman, for instance, might want his employer and his clients to be able to track him down.

But when something bad happens, like an accident, this self-service privacy will be superseded by the smart environment of the car: no more hit-and-run accidents, thanks to intelligent automatic governance. If you hit someone and try to drive on without taking care of the victim, the car itself will reveal your identity to another car, a passenger, or a nearby police officer.

Similarly, in a virtual transaction such as voting or using electronic payments, your legitimate transaction would be anonymous and private, but if you try to fraudulently vote or spend your money twice, the system would reveal your identity and location, then cancel the transaction or deny entrance.

Automatic governance made possible by the smart knowledge environment will not be about "Big Brother." Rather, it will be about giving citizens more information about, access to, and control over both the knowledge environment and the physical one.

Choosing the Future for Intelligent Governance

Automatic, intelligent governance will require a new sense of citizenship that stresses the duties and responsibilities of citizens and not just individual rights. For instance, societies and their leaders will need to decide whether they want criminals to have the same privacy rights as law-abiding citizens. Will we help criminals or punish them? Criminal law at present is about punishing people *after* the crime.

A combination of better civil law and new technologies to enforce it will make it possible to *prevent* crimes from happening.

Government agencies can take the first step toward creating a smart knowledge infrastructure by reducing all government passes into one self-service card. Authorities could also build networked knowledge systems and interactive Web services instead of static, information-only Web sites. And they could create and use only open standards for data and open source for software.

I believe that the future "automatic government," though it may have the grim potential of authoritarian abuse, will have more than just a human face. The humans who will use these technologies will be living their lives without really noticing them. No technology will be visible. The intelligent environment is about living and being comfortable and having a nice time and relaxing and resting. The technology is embedded.

It has been said that the best government is that which governs least. Invisible technology and smart knowledge may help us attain that ideal.

CHAPTER 55

City Government Options for Public Service Innovations

Christopher Hire

Where is Starbucks without Seattle; Coca-Cola without Atlanta; or HP, Apple, and Xerox without the broader Bay area?

None of the modern behemoth enterprises and engines of economics could survive without succouring at the breast of their city. For no matter how global business becomes, each business calls a city home. There are no multinationals. There are merely businesses writ large and gone global. But, all business anchors in a city.

Cities are where we live, work, meet our significant others, give birth to children, raise families, enjoy arts and culture, learn new ideas, remember forgotten ideas, and most of all, where we spend our time. When we plan cities, we forget these passionate connections between ourselves and our cities.

In reality, cities are not one person's vision. The best cities are layers — layers of dreams, hopes, fights, and internecine rivalries; of passions; of tears, hopes and dashed dreams — all forged in a crucible of steel, iron, green trees, lattes, and irony.

There is no "right way" to build the "right city." So much of what is written about cities, in business and economics, is formulaic. Much of "city thinking" assumes that what works in one city works in another.

And, when things fail, these failures are scrutinized and criticized harshly by cities and their media. But, for a great city, it is more useful to study *success* than study failure. Sometimes, it is the tepid initiative that wins the battle of ideas — but does not necessarily succeed.

Once again, there is no "right" success. The London Eye works, as does the Eiffel Tower (originally temporary); so do the "Gherkin," Sydney Opera House, Statue of Liberty, Chrysler Building, and Seattle's Space Needle. These are big engineering projects that became big branding icons.

But the small works too: the I Heart New York logo; Berlin's Green Man; Melbourne's Laneways and street art; Cheeseheads and Green Bay USA — in a town that thrives on its football team. Sometimes, the small matters *more* to a city, and to the citizens who love it.

No Single Right Answer

It is not enough to say that innovation in cities is merely a phenomenon of big massive budget projects, nor incubators, nor industry roundtables, nor property development, nor direct foreign investment. Nor is it enough to say that attracting "creative people" alone is sufficient direction to build a great city.

All these things may assist, and be a cata-

Originally published as "Innovative Cities: How Cities Can Change the World," *Municipal World*, Vol. 119, No. 9, September 2009, by Municipal World Inc., St. Thomas, Ontario, Canada. Reprinted with permission of the publisher.

lyst for the forging of innovation. But, there is no "single right answer, right for all times and places." Any model needs to recognize cultural differences, and be flexible enough to integrate them.

The 2009 Innovation Cities Program is unique as the first flexible model of comparative city performance on 162 innovation indicators. Innovation Cities models optimal social and economic performance of a city looking forward and can identify unique opportunities.

Since 2007, the Innovation Cities model has produced a growing index ranking all major cities social and economic performance, based on current trends.

Rather than a concept, the key to Innovation Cities model is the flexibility to make changes year-on-year, as old city issues are solved and new issues arise. Cities or urban researchers may also consult with us to add or remove data points easily on a city, national, regional, or global basis, and may suggest future data points.

Informative City Concepts

When speaking of rankings, the two most quoted existing rankings of cities are livable cities (Mercer and Economist) with a lifestyle focus; and sustainable (various) cities (or Eco-Cities[1]) with a green focus. MasterCard puts out some excellent City Commerce rankings, which we reference.

In terms of concepts, leading academic thinkers like Landry and Carrillo have focused on the Creative City[2] for generating ideas, the Knowledge Cities[3] for making knowledge work. These leading theories inform the Inspiration and Implementation segments of the Innovation Cities model.

Finally, there is the remarkable Richard Florida,[4] the public face of the cities field for the past decade. Florida's chief achievement has been popularizing culture and digital thinking as a key part of city planning — a critical counter-reaction to urban renewal and infrastructure only approaches of prior decades. Richard Florida's models measure "tolerance," with a resultant focus on "hip and cool."

As practical advice, though, not all cities should have an instant make-over into LA or SoHo on a global scale, with 24-hour bars and dark spaces full of cool and hip. Local food, energy, and manufacturing matter increasingly.

Rather than asking "how to attract the creative class," we should ask how cities "grow a creative class, out of a larger economic pie." Economist Hernando De Soto[5] answers this question in part.

Before the Florida concept, in a historical context, Joel Kotkin[6] in his sweeping concise work informed our thinking, as cosmopolitanism; evolving from within economics and trade. Kotkin relies on views of commerce, security, and power as important to cities future performance. Jared Diamond,[7] in some contrast, also influenced often-overlooked concepts of city prosperity.

Along with economics, this is integral and unique as third "markets" element, factoring in critical trade, economic, and geo-political consideration. Trade, commodities, foreign direct investment, ability to enforce terms, currencies — within emerging or behavioral economics — are all mid-term, more critical than "cool" in serious modeling of cities. After all, individual "unquestionable" urban theories of the 1970s are gone today.

Innovation Cities draws together these dominant paradigms of cities thought — *markets* (economic, political, commercial, health, geo-political, military, and economic factors), along side *inspiration* (largely cultural), and *implementation* (business, infrastructure, urban) with flexibility for change.

Beyond One Size Fits All

Our goal with Innovation Cities is a 2.0 adaptive model that people can change and rebuild within a structure that makes sense. Ultimately, a working model must be flexible and comparative, and admit the need to adapt to different current theories — a model beyond any single current world view, that can adapt and grow as trends and city issues change.

At the base of the framework is a concept of innovation. "Innovation is a broad congregation" is the 2thinknow view. A Socratic dialogue on innovation could turn up many views.[8] Beyond purely digital approaches to innovation often assumed, we include in a cities context agricultural, manufacturing, viticulture, sports, technology usage, science, business models, and network innovations.

For Innovation Cities, innovation is "improved economic and social performance in cities mainly over a mid-term of up to 15 years." In short, measuring what winners do, and then creating winners. One example of the direct relevancy of this concept in 2009 is, as the OECD recently expressed,[9] that Finland and Korea used innovation to improve their economic recovery out of the last recession.

However, innovations follow a relatively known time frame of two to 15 years before they deliver economic returns. Since 2006, we've expressed that productivity and innovation, not asset bubbles, are the two key mid- to long-term drivers of economic growth. Most economists agree — at least, at home in the dark. Why, then, is it so hard to breach the walls of these silos and create a coherent measure for cities?

A Model for Now-Forward

If one was to make a list of all the things in a city that matter, all the performance indicators, it would need to be a big list. The Innovation Cities Index has 162 data points. Ideally, with that many data points, no city scores well on every area; but, no city scores badly on all areas.

The Innovation Cities Program and Index models and captures comparative data across this wide range of innovation indicators in 31 streams, within the three segments of *inspiration*, *implementation*, and *markets*. All 162 innovation indicators are then weighted based on current trends.

So, what should a city do to face the three city challenges of economics, environment, and equity? In 2009, in the 2ThinkNow view, equity is a sleeper issue in many "real world" cities. The least optimal outcome is an underclass serving a "fought-over" creative class.

Florida led the way for measuring culture — although tolerance is the outcome, rather than the precedent — in a critical counter-reaction to a focus on urban renewal and infrastructure only.

Inspiration: Measuring Culture Matters

Culture matters. Arts and culture, sports, tourism: these contribute massive amounts of money to the economy. So, why do some cities get them so right, and other cities get them so wrong? Measuring what matters is different to measuring what's easy. Measuring GDP per capita is easy; culture is harder to measure.

Measuring the subjective — art galleries, museums, sports — is not an academic issues, however. Economically, socially, and locally, these things matter. Do you count the paintings, admission days, square meters, or the bolts? Should we use "hard" as an excuse to not measure? Those are dilemmas that a few scientists and academics ponder, seeing a need for an overtly quantitative approach.

How then do we account for an exhibition such as the Sistine Chapel? Visitor numbers? What about a beautiful art gallery in a country at war, or closed because of a pandemic? These may seem obtuse questions; but, if we assume uncertainty or non-linearity as the norm, then we may ask these questions with a straight face.

2.0 MEANS MARKETS MEASURE

The reality is the market and the people: the crowd decides. The Sistine Chapel, Michelangelo's master work, as well as the galleries of the Louvre are two of the world's best art exhibitions — and, every year, tourists vote with their feet. In much the same way, great newspapers have loyal readers, even in downturns.

The market, the citizens, the crowd — over the mid-term, they often reflect a value — not captured by academics. In Innovation Cities, we band them. Cities like Paris and Vienna are a perfect five for public art galleries, and few could argue. For scope, diversity, types of art galleries, these cities stand out.

Public library collections are another area,

as are business school rankings. These areas are hard to measure without markets — but too valuable not to measure. Meals. Theatre. Music. Restaurants. All these things are discussed anecdotally, and opined online and in print by thought-leaders, venerable food critics, and bloggers alike. And yet, surprisingly, a Socratic dialogue and truth again emerge, as we find the words to encapsulate what is a perfect representation; but, it is never so perfect as to be a perfect description.

For every arts and culture city, or sports city, in the 2010 world-view, there needs to be a manufacturing or business city; and vice versa. The 2thinknow City of Excellence, from the Innovation Cities model, recognizes that each city has different innate strengths over a long period of time. For example, in 2009, Barcelona was awarded a 2thinknow City of Excellence for Architecture.

Implementation and Markets: Measure What Matters

In the Innovation Cities Analysis (ICA) Report 2009[10] (accompanying Innovation Cities), 2thinknow explains all the innovation indicators for cities — including implementation and market indicators, as well as all rankings.

Implementation indicators include infrastructure with sustainable elements — especially public transport, rail, green buildings, ports — but also traditional roads (shorter journey times), universities, business, finance, and a range of critical factors in cities' success. Often overlooking, energy is a critical element of city innovation — especially in a digital economy.

In a broader sense, Professor Snow Barlow spoke of "food, water, energy" as the most serious challenge of our time.[11] Innovation Cities is the only model or ranking to capture strategic pre-conditions of city performance. As a way of focusing the mind, it is worth noting that any city where you have to import all food and energy, and build your own road or railway to do something is probably not a lasting centre of innovation. Hip or cool bars at 2 A.M. matter far less than these factors.

DYNAMIC IDEA EXCHANGE

But, what about engineers and scientists? It is the presence of engineering marvels like bridges and airports, or retail stores with every type of electro-mechanical gadget that inspires these people. For musicians, it may be musical venues across multiple genres. For farmers, agricultural industries. And then there's cross-pollination, as multiple clusters exists in and around cities like Melbourne or San Francisco.

In markets, the often-termed concept of "clusters" inspires the creativity of each profession. And, it is that creativity that the European Year of Creativity and Innovation 2009 <http://create2009.europa.eu> — recognized — a program of which the Innovation Cities Index is part. Clustering builds creative inspiration, and goes some way towards providing the implementation structures and markets for the outputs of creativity. All this is explained in detail in the ICA Report published by 2thinknow.

In some periods, some specific clusters become critical. Arts and culture often are the force that inspires designers, and designers are increasingly the forces within the 21st century city that engineers were to the 19th and 20th centuries. The city presence of design and media clusters matters now.

Trends: Measuring When It Matters

Cities take time to change. And, in given periods of history, certain cities prosper more than others. Consider the rivers of gold of 19th century Gold Rush Melbourne. Pre-Bazalgette London was a centre of the financial world, yet sewers and other infrastructure birthed new London. Buenos Aires was, and is, a wonderful city; yet Argentina has declined from economic parity with Australia a century ago.

At the 2008 Metropolis congress in Sydney, a participating planning department chose to focus on financial services and the service economy. The papers were distributed before the September 2008 global financial crisis events, and were invariably out-of-date before distribution. In 2004, the papers would have seemed contemporary. The service economy has suffered post-crisis, as has the retail economy.

Sports and sports business, however, are booming — as they did in the 1930s Depression. In Australia, cafes have been growing in popularity, while high-end restaurants are forced to create lunch specials and see reduced wine spending. As the global director of a consulting firm once sneered at me in 2007, there are, indeed, "just winners and losers." But, how do we predict future winners? R&D alone is a very narrow measure. It misses more than it captures — yet, this is the basis of much self-serving slipshod analysis.

A simple example of this is the importance of the sports industry in recessions. Another is the increased reliance on public institutions such as libraries and art galleries during an economic downturn. These public cultural spaces pour the creative fuel that fires the mental furnaces of designers and other creatives — leading to billions in sold products. This is the "inspiration" in Innovation Cities.

Many cities do contribute immeasurable economic and social value to their citizens. How much depends in large part on the current paradigm, and the mid-term future of a city. The world we *feel* about in 2009 is different from the world we felt about in 2007. And, that feeling, the sense of change, predated the hard data. Half of negative growth is always a posthumous pronouncement of recession; we *feel* it first. GDP per capita and infant mortality rates are important trailing indictors of past success and past investment.

PREDICTIVE ANALYSIS

As a nation, in May 2009, France was the healthiest in Europe — according to John Mickelthwait of *The Economist* magazine. Few foresaw that in 2007, calling France the "sick man of Europe." In 2007, though, Paris and Vienna were found to be ranked #2 and #1 respectively as Innovation Cities in Europe — and these are cities now less affected by the global financial crisis.

France has been the world's largest beneficiary of USD $234 billion in relocating corporations, at the cost of USA, UK, Canada, and

others according to *Harvard Business Review*, June 2009.

In October 2007,[12] 2thinknow foresaw the global financial crisis as a "September 2008 ... shock turmoil event" using nascent trend analysis — a new analysis framework for balancing lead trend indicators. Tools like change maps and change waves are related ways 2thinknow maps trends as they impact lives. These tools, once again, are too long and involved to cover here; each is an article of its own.

What the Innovation Cities Index (the ranking part of the cities model) does is rank and analyze cities based on weighted change trends. The index is re-weighted for trends — for example, "Is sport more important economically and socially than art, in the mid-term? Local manufacturing or imports?"

In reality, by measuring the hard-to-measure, we can measure the paradigm-shift before it occurs (before what Gladwell calls the "tipping point"). Other times, we can see the points in the change cycle to apply various forms of assistance and stimulus; or change strategy for specific cities.

CURRENT TREND INSIGHTS

Inevitably re-localizing and greener manufacturing are trends of the next 25 years. Local manufacturing may rise in value in lockstep (after a lag period) with protectionism, a prominent trend.

Fast rail is of increasing importance to cities — something 2thinknow predicted clearly as "ready to start" in 2007, around the time of Warren Buffett's purchase of railway stocks.

Irrespective of your position on carbon-drive climate change, economic investment in clean and green tech is a *fait accompli* — few can argue that genuinely cleaner air and water will not improve quality of life.

It is necessary to take a position as to what trends will impact the world, so as to understand our cities.

Right Now

In 2009, Innovation Cities indicators and change trend analysis are leading-edge; but, they are also open to further refinement. The Innovation Cities Model gives cities perspective over short-, mid-, and long-term time frames. And, by consulting with cities, we change the data to model targeted local scenarios.

According to the change trend analysis for the next few years, the current trends for cities are not the manias and fads of terrorism, but rather the three city challenges we define: economics, equity, and environment.

Economics is most obviously manifested in forced-house sales, quantitative easing, jobs figures, deflation, stagflation, or inflation — depending on where you live.

The environment is manifested in the twin challenges of climate change and the economic opportunity of green tech and clean tech.[13] There are undoubtedly rivers of green gold in the greening of the world, and some companies will profit from deploying that innovation (assuming they use the right models).

Finally, equity is the sleeper issue, constantly there. As Azar Gat argued,[14] it impacts the potential for war, drives terrorism, may impact the economic viability of gangs in urban spaces, and thus reaches the livability of cities and their survivability.

Every city conference in 2003 was decrying terrorism as the challenge of the 21st century. Security is important, but economic opportunity (i.e., jobs) is the key determinant of security. The driver, in many respects, is equity of opportunity.

Putting It Together

The Innovation Cities model is a framework for measuring innovation. This model generates both big number scores on cities' innovation potential — as any ranking index does. But then, it takes it further. In a given year, it weights those scores, to reflect current trends for the mid-term. And, it provides the data to analyze potential opportunities to improve performance.

These are all ideas. The strength of the In-novation Cities lies in not judging which of these ideas is right for all time, but rather scoring all data points, and then weighting them to reflect the current time. And the priorities of a city in a given year.

Now is a time for us to challenge the assumptions we make about cities, and to carefully model which criteria matter more to the future economic and social performance of our communities.

Cities are a dream in a time, and we should dream them as the best dream for each of their marvelous citizens. Right now, there is no better time. Innovation starts now.

NOTES

1. Richard Register, *EcoCities: Rebuilding Cities in Balance with Nature,* revised ed. (Gabriola, BC: New Society, 2006).

2. Charles Landry, *The Creative City* (London: Earthscan, 2006).

3. Francisco Javier Carrillo, *Knowledge Cities: Approaches, Experiences, and Perspectives* (New York: Elsevier Butterworth Heinemann, 2005).

4. Richard Florida, *The Flight of the Creative Class: The New Global Competition for Talent* (New York: HarperBusiness, 2005).

5. Hernando De Soto, *The Mystery of Capital: Why Capitalism Triumphs in the West and Fails Everywhere Else* (New York: Bantam, 2000).

6. Joel Kotkin, *The City: A Global History* (New York: Modern Library, 2006).

7. Jared Diamond, *Collapse: How Societies Choose to Fail or Succeed* (New York: Penguin, 2005).

8. Christopher Hire, *Global Innovation Review 2007 Annual: The World's Top Innovation Cities and Global Innovation Rankings* (2thinknow, 2007; available in reprint from 2thinknow directly).

9. Kenneth Davidson, "Not Debt Size, but How It's Used, Is Crucial," *The Age,* June 15, 2009, http://business.theage.com.au/business/not-debt-size-but-how-its-used-is-crucial-20090614-c7dr.html.

10. Innovation Cities Analysis Report 2009, 2think now www.2thinknow.com.

11. Professor Snow Barlow, associate dean, University of Melbourne, Festival of Ideas, June 16, 2009.

12. "3 Predictions for Life in Australia in 2008," INNOVATION Journal [Global Innovation Conversation], October 2, 2007, www.2thinknow.com/innovation/2007/3-predictions-for-life-in-australia-in-2008/121 (part of a series of predictions until April 2008).

13. "Where Smart Money Is Going in Cleantech," *Der Spiegel,* June 18, 2009, www.spiegel.de/international/business/0,1518,631123,00.html.

14. Azar Gat, *War in Human Civilization* (New York: Oxford University Press, 2006).

CHAPTER 56

The Financial Future of America's Cities
Roger L. Kemp

The various case studies presented in this volume focused on the budgetary and the financial options used to balance public budgets, primarily during these difficult economic times. No doubt, when the pressure is on local public officials, they will come up with various creative ideas to balance their respective public budgets — from a budget reduction as well as revenue enhancement standpoint, or an appropriate balance between these two political options.

A budget is based on providing an acceptable level of public services and financing them with anticipated available public revenues during the coming fiscal year. There are, however, other cost-saving and revenue-generating measures to consider during normal budget years. From a budgetary and financial management perspective, certain basic common best practices make sense regardless of the condition of the local, state, or national economy.

To assist public officials, and citizens, with options to balance their respective public budgets, which involves generating sufficient revenues to cover expenses, the following budgetary, financial, and operational options are set forth to accomplish this goal. While many of these best practices were obtained from the case studies presented in this volume, other best practices, primarily for normal and future budget years, were added to give public officials and

citizens additional budgetary and financial options to lessen the impact of these difficult economic times.

If public officials and citizens properly plan for their financial future, it should make dealing with economic hard times much easier in the coming fiscal years. Primarily because they should have already taken measures to reduce costs and increase revenues based on generally accepted, and increasingly common, municipal budgetary and financial practices.

Best Practices

In summary, taking the best practices from the numerous case studies presented in this volume, the various budgetary, financial, and process options evolving in this dynamic field are highlighted below, and explained in greater detail in the in the next section of this chapter. The common terms used during normal budget years, bad budget years, and future budget years, are summarized and described below.

NORMAL BUDGET YEAR PRACTICES

Appropriate Charges
Budget Guidelines
Contracting for Public Services

Employee Hiring Practices
Energy Audits
Enterprise Funds
Grants Availability
Joint Purchasing Programs
One-Time Revenues
Overtime Expenses
Printing Expenses
Public Services
Revenue/Expenditure Projections
Surplus Properties
User Fees and Charges
Vehicle Purchases

BAD BUDGET YEAR PRACTICES

Bond Indebtedness
Budget Information
Budget Reductions
Budget Reduction Statements
Budget Reviews
Capital Projects
Contractors and Vendors
Employee Expenses
Employee Hiring Practices
Employee Layoffs
Employee Unions
Public Information
Public Services
Ranking Public Services
Tax Collection Rates
User Fees and Charges
Volunteer Services

FUTURE BUDGET YEAR PRACTICES

Budget Surpluses
Capital Improvement Programs
Citizen Input Practices
Consolidation of Public Services
Economic Development Incentives
Enterprise Funds
Financial Policies
Public Funds and Balances

These best practice terms are explained in greater detail below. When citizens and public officials review the case studies presented in this study, and find examples that might be applicable to their respective communities, they can directly contact a public official at the city they desire by checking out the city's website in the

Regional Resource Directory, which is located in the appendix section at the end of this volume. A greater level of detail regarding these best practices is provided in the following paragraphs.

Normal Budget Year Practices

Appropriate Charges. Review, and make sure that, selected user fees and charges are appropriate for those public services that are used by non-profit organizations, and other public agencies, that utilize your city's municipal services.

Budget Guidelines. Develop appropriate budget preparation guidelines based on professionally-developed revenue and expenditure projections. These projections form the basis of the financial resources available to fund the approved level of public services during the coming fiscal years.

Contracting for Public Services. Public officials owe it to their taxpayers to periodically go through the contracting for services, or bidding, process to compare private sector costs of providing a public service against the in-house governmental cost. It makes sense to contract out selected public services if the quality is the same and the cost is less. State and local laws and labor agreements must be checked before undertaking such a bidding process.

Employee Hiring Practices. Hire all new employees at the entry level of the salary ranges for their respective positions. Do not hire "experienced" employees at higher than entry level salary steps when filling vacant positions. This practice should be common during difficult economic times.

Energy Audits. Have energy audits conducted for all major public buildings. These audits, frequently performed free of charge by utility companies, may lead to the use of low energy illumination, automated on/off switches, heating/air conditioning controls, and the installation of double-pane windows to reduce daily energy expenses.

Enterprise Funds. Check the financial structure of all existing Enterprise Funds to make sure that their user fees/charges cover all expenses for the services that they provide. User fees and charges should be adjusted to ensure that the revenues generated from each fund totally finances the services that it provides.

Grants Availability. Always seek available public operational and infrastructure grants from higher levels of government. The availability of federal and state grant programs is always changing, especially when a new administration assumes office after an election takes place.

Joint Purchasing Programs. It is common for cities to work together to undertake the joint purchasing of larger items. Counties, councils of governments, and states are also providing joint purchasing services to their communities. The larger the quantity of something purchased, the lower the unit cost. Joint purchasing programs are increasing at all levels of government in all regions of the nation.

One-Time Revenues. Always use one-time revenues wisely since they will not be available in future fiscal years. Ideally, one-time revenues should be used to finance one-time budget expenses. This action will reduce the financial magnitude of any future budget deficits.

Overtime Expenses. Try to keep overtime expenses for all employees to a minimum. Police and fire employees are sometimes exceptions to this fiscal savings goal, since constant staffing levels may be required for the services that they provide. Existing labor agreements may also impact overtime expenses.

Printing Expenses. As many public documents as possible should be scanned and placed online on the organization's website. This action reduces unnecessary printing and publishing costs associated with duplicating various official publications, legal notices, and other public documents.

Public Services. Avoid laying off municipal employees to maintain existing approved public service levels. The goal of the professional staff should be to maintain the levels of public services during the fiscal year that were previously approved by their elected officials.

Revenue/Expenditure Projections. Always have the administration, typically through the professional finance staff, prepare a mini-mum of 3 to 5 year revenue and expenditure projections. Longer projections may be desirable, depending upon the nature of your community's financial resources.

Surplus Properties. Inventory all unused municipally-owned real properties. Then determine which ones will not be needed in the future for any public purpose. Sell surplus municipal properties to the highest bidder using the public bidding process.

User Fees and Charges. Update your city's existing user fees and charges, taking appropriate measures to accommodate the truly needy. The use of selected reduced fee rates, and/or free use periods during low-activity times, may be appropriate for qualifying "needy" citizens.

Vehicle Purchases. Purchase four-cylinder replacement vehicles for the workforce. This reduces ongoing gasoline consumption and maintenance expenses. Selected public safety vehicles may be excluded from this vehicle replacement process.

Bad Budget Year Practices

Bond Indebtedness. The management staff should check with their city's financial advisor/bond counsel to determine if the refinancing of outstanding bond indebtedness would save the city money. Proceed according to their recommendations with regard to refinancing existing outstanding bond indebtedness.

Budget Information. Provide timely budgetary information to everyone. This information should be provided to elected officials, the management staff, the employee unions, the public, as well as the local news media. Financial and budgetary information should be disseminated to everyone as soon as it is available.

Budget Reductions. Evaluate the impact of all budget reductions relative to the existing service levels. Four stages of service reductions can be used for this purpose. They include the following:

Stage 1: Maximum Service Impact— Those budget reductions that would substantially reduce or eliminate an entire program or service.

Stage 2: Medium Service Impact— Those budget reductions that may reduce a sizeable portion of a service or program, but do not affect the basic, or essential, service or program levels.

Stage 3: Small Service Impact— Those budget reductions that only reduce a small portion of a program or service, but not impact essential or critical public services or programs.

Stage 4: No Service Impact— Those budget reductions that would have little or no impact on the prevailing levels of public services or programs.

Role of Elected Officials— The criteria used to rank budget reductions should be recommended by the management staff, but should be reviewed and approved by elected officials as they consider the impact of their possible budget reductions on existing program and service levels.

Budget Reduction Statements. Always prepare a Public Service Impact Statement (PSIS) for each proposed budget reduction to properly inform elected officials and citizens of the anticipated operational impact of all budgetary decisions. These statements should be prepared jointly by the city administrator and the department manager for each department's budget reductions.

Budget Reviews. Direct all department managers to review their respective departmental budgets to look for possible accrued/potential savings in their operating budgets for the remainder of the current fiscal year. Such budgetary savings will help reduce the magnitude of the projected budget deficit for the coming fiscal year, and help to avoid service reductions and employee layoffs.

Capital Projects. The management staff should review all important capital projects with elected officials to defer the less important ones to future fiscal years. The available limited funds should be used to focus on maintaining adequate levels of existing public services, and the approval of only critical and important capital projects.

Contractors and Vendors. Ask contractors and vendors to hold their costs down, or to keep them constant, for the coming fiscal year, or you may have to go to bid, or drop their service entirely. Many contractors and vendors will work with local government public officials to help them hold down their expenses during difficult financial times.

Employee Expenses. Every effort should be made to reduce discretionary travel and professional development expenses, such as training and conferences. Telecommunications technology should be used, such as teleconferencing, to help reduce these expenses. Certain mandated and contractually obligated professional development and travel expenses may be required.

Employee Hiring Practices. Implement an organization-wide hiring freeze. The city council may wish to adopt a resolution to make this an officially approved public policy. It is better not to fill vacant positions, then to fill them and have to lay-off employees during the following fiscal year.

Employee Layoffs. Keep in mind that employee layoffs are always a last resort when balancing a public budget. This goal should be embraced by both management and the employee unions, as well as the city's elected officials. This mindset helps facilitate joint negotiations to achieve this mutually advantageous goal.

Employee Unions. Form a union-management cost-savings working committee. The city council may wish to adopt a resolution to make this an officially approved public policy. The chief executive officer and finance director should meet with the presidents of all of the employee unions to look for avenues of cost-savings. These may include:

Salary Increase Deferral— Many, if not all, city employees may already be entitled to an annual salary increase based upon previously approved labor agreements. Due to these difficult economic times, consideration may be given to rescinding or deferring this salary adjustment to avoid employee layoffs. A revised labor agreement would require the approval of both the unions involved as well as the elected officials.

Early Retirements— Consider early retirements for their employees by offering incentives to facilitate the retirement of senior employees. These positions can be left vacant for the duration of the fiscal year. Even if some of them are filled, savings results from lower salary and fringe benefit costs.

Fringe Benefits— Consider a reduction in their employees' vacation and sick leave benefits. Such changes can focus on senior employees, newly hired employees, or both groups of employees. Each bargaining unit must approve these agreements too.

Healthcare Expenses— Consider a reduction in healthcare benefit costs. Options to reduce these costs include increased co-pays, partial payment of benefit costs, a reduction of existing coverage levels, employee wellness programs, and possible cost limitations. Each bargaining unit must also approve these cost reductions.

Work Furloughs— Consider work furloughs, the duration of which would be based on the magnitude of the projected budget deficit for the coming fiscal year. Overtime costs may increase with some bargaining units, such as the police and fire unions, where constant staffing may be required.

Working Hours— Consider a reduction in working hours, and a corresponding percentage decrease in existing salary levels for those employees that will be working fewer hours. Each bargaining unit must approve such agreements.

Public Information. The Public Service Impact Statements (PSIS) should also be distributed to the management staff, the employee unions, and made available to the news media, citizens, and other interested parties that have requested copies of these statements. Public information, when it becomes available, should be provided to everyone as soon as possible.

Public Services. Do not provide any new public services. The city council may wish to adopt a resolution to make this an officially approved public policy. Such a policy makes it easier to deal with special interest groups seeking special public services from their elected officials.

Ranking Public Services. Rank the importance of all public service that are provided to your citizens. Four service levels may be used for this purpose. They include:

Level 1: Essential Services— You may not want to reduce these services or programs under any circumstances. They would include minimal levels of police, fire, health, and public works services.

Level 2: Desirable Services— This category includes programs and services that are highly desirable, but not absolutely essential or critical, or required by law.

Level 3: Nice-but-Not-Necessary Services— Comprises those public services and programs that have significant value, but do not provide essential, critical, or necessary services to the public.

Level 4: First-to-Go Services— These services and programs include those that are not essential or critical, and not required by law, and only serve a small portion of the community.

Role of Elected Officials— The criteria used to rank public services should be recommended by the management staff, but should be accepted and approved by elected officials as they consider budget reduction options to balance their operating budget.

Tax Collection Rates. Take appropriate measures to increase all existing tax collection rates. Taxpayers should be informed that if all taxes due are paid in a timely manner that this will decrease the need to increases their taxes in the future.

User Fees and Charges. Review all existing programs for the possible application of appropriate user fees and charges. Since salaries and fringe benefits tend to increase over time, user fees and charges should be adjusted periodically as costs increase, such as every other fiscal year, or so.

Volunteer Services. Public officials may wish to consider using citizens to provide volunteer services, consistent with any restrictions that may exist in local labor agreements and applicable state laws. Local policies and state laws frequently set forth restrictions or limitations on the use of citizen volunteers to provide selected public services. Citizens can be used, however, to provide public services within any established limitations and restrictions that may exist.

Future Budget Year Practices

Budget Surpluses. The balances of any funds no longer needed, or that have surpluses in excess of what is reasonable, can be transferred to the un-appropriated General Fund balance. This is usually done by the adoption of a resolution by the elected officials at a public meeting.

Capital Improvement Programs. The management staff, annually, should prepare a five-year Capital Improvement Program (CIP). After the preparation of the CIP, its processing and review, it should be presented to the elected officials for their consideration. The major steps in the CIP development process are highlighted below.

Role of the City Administrator—The City Administrator should form a CIP Committee. The usual members of such a committee typically include the Planning Director, Public Works Director, Finance Director, and other appropriate department managers with planned major capital projects.

Department Head Involvement—The CIP Committee should solicit qualifying capital projects from all department managers for the next five-years. These projects should then be reviewed, prioritized, with appropriate funding sources noted. Typical funding sources may include operating funds, General Obligation Bonds, Revenue Bonds, and other appropriate approved funding sources.

Role of the Planning Commission—Once this five-year plan has been reviewed with the City Administrator, and he/she approves of it, it should be forwarded on to the City's Planning Commission for their review and approval. The CIP approved by the Planning Commission should then be forwarded on to the city's elected officials for their consideration.

Role of Elected Officials—The elected officials typically hold public study sessions on this plan, with the City Administrator and respective department managers in attendance to explain this plan, and the various capital projects

contained in it, to the public. Ultimately, the CIP should be approved by the elected officials. Typically, the capital projects contained in the first year of the plan are recommended and approved for funding, and concept approval is granted for the rest of the capital projects in the remaining years of the plan.

Citizen Input Practices. It is quite common to seek comments and opinions from citizens on a city's budget and financial practices, especially proposed ones. Various techniques and processes can be used to achieve this goal, including the use of city-wide meetings, neighborhood meetings, focus groups, questionnaires, the use of online resources, such as websites, and related information sources.

Consolidation of Public Services. Public officials should always consider available alternatives to jointly provide public services, at a reduced cost, using other service provision options. These would include joining with other public agencies to provide the service, or working jointly with other public agencies to prepare a request for proposal to solicit services from a private-sector provider. Any consolidation of public services must be approved by elected officials at a public meeting.

Economic Development Incentives. Public officials may wish to consider new economic development incentives, or modify existing ones, to help attract private-sector investment to their community. Such incentives typically include low-interest loans, financing off-site improvements, providing employee job training, approving tax abatements, and other desired incentives that may be approved by local public officials.

Enterprise Funds. Review existing public services with the goal of creating possible additional Enterprise Funds where the user fees/charges make the services cost covering. The creation of such funds is appropriate when only the users benefit from a public service.

Financial Policies. Implement prudent financial policies to ensure the future integrity of your budgetary and financial practices and operations. Financial policies should focus on:

Bonding—Set criteria for the minimum capital project value/cost to qualify for bonding, plus the types of bonds that can be used for different capital projects. Such a policy should also include an assessment of the fiscal impact that each capital project has on the organization's operating budget. When such capital projects are completed, departmental operating budgets must be adjusted accordingly.

Budget Reserves— This policy should set forth the desired size of the annual budget/financial reserve. The size of a budget reserve is usually determined as a percent of the overall operating budget (e.g., 5 percent, 8 percent, 10 percent, etc.), depending upon the size of the operating budget, and how much was spent during the previous fiscal years.

User Fees and Charges— This policy should include the desired periodic updates to review and update the city's departmental user fees and charges. Updating user fees and charges every other fiscal year would be an appropriate cycle for most communities.

Role of Elected Officials— Financial policies approved by elected officials at public meetings remain in place until they are officially changed by them at a future public meeting, while administrative policies come and go with the administrators that issued them.

Other Financial Policies— Every effort should be made for elected officials to officially adopt financial policies proactively so budgetary and financial problems that happened in the past do not take place again. If such policies are adopted by elected officials, they stay in place until they are officially changed again in the future by majority vote of the elected officials at a public meeting.

Public Funds and Balances. Thoroughly review all existing public funds, and their respective balances, for their appropriateness. Assess the desire to continue them as they were originally designed and approved. Also, assess the adequacy of their respective fund balances. Any unnecessary funds, and their balances, including fund balances that may be larger than required, may be transferred to the city's General Fund. This is done by the approval of a resolution at a public meeting.

The Future

There is no doubt that these are difficult financial times for local public officials who represent the citizens they serve, and who approve funding for their respective governmental organizations. All of these budgetary, financial, and operational options and choices are difficult to make, but are a sign of the times due to the pressures brought about by negative external economic conditions. The sorting and prioritizing of public programs and services, and the rational reduction of government spending, include some of the most challenging issues and problems facing public officials today.

It is a good practice to analyze the political and administrative choices and options approved and implemented by other public officials in similar local governments in recent years. This should facilitate the use of orderly and proven budgetary and financial options selected by public officials as they strive to balance their respective budgets to properly serve the public, their constituents. Learning what works from other public officials in comparable communities will facilitate this process.

These suggested guidelines and options are provided with the intention of lending insight and clarity into this difficult political process. Budget reduction and revenue enhancement strategies that reflect responsibility, not only to the beneficiaries of public services, but also to those citizens who must foot-the-bill, the taxpayers, must ultimately prevail.

Welcome to the difficult world of sorting out the relative value of public services and programs, and making sound financial and budgetary decisions so that public budgets are balanced in the most rational and equitable way possible to meet available revenues! The above budgetary and financial planning options may represent the best available practices for both citizens and public officials at the present time.

No doubt, however, that other appropriate and suitable alternatives will emerge in future years as public officials in cities throughout the nation continue to cope with the ongoing economic challenges that they face. By balancing their respective budgets, both operating and capital, and by maintaining an acceptable level of tax revenue from their constituents, this difficult process can become somewhat routinized. The need will exist to update these budgetary and financial alternatives within the next few years to continue to provide the most up-do-date alternatives to our citizens, as well as their elected and appointed public officials, as they successfully cope with future budget cycles in their respective communities.

Appendices

A. *Local Government Financial Terms*

It is helpful to have a list of common terms used to describe local government financial processes, fund accounts, and budgets. This glossary should make it easier for citizens to understand and monitor local public finances. This listing was prepared by the Local Government Center, University of Wisconsin, which is listed in the *National Resource Directory* section of this appendix.

Account A classification established for the purpose of recording revenues and expenditures. (The various classifications used are likely to be drawn from a "chart of accounts" developed or adopted by the unit of government.)

Account Basis The method adopted for treating revenues and expenditures. The methods most likely to be found in use among small and medium-size units of government include:

1. The **Accrual Basis** of accounting under which revenues are recorded when earned (whether or not actual payment is received at that time) and expenditures are recorded when goods and services are received (whether or not payment is made at that time).
2. The **Cash Basis** of accounting under which revenues are recorded when received in cash and expenditures are recorded when payment is made in cash.
3. The **Modified Accrual Basis** under which (most kinds of) revenues are recorded when received in cash, but (most kinds of) expenditures are recorded when goods and services are received.

Activity A specific, identifiable unit of work or service performed.

Adopted Budget Every governing body must adopt by a majority vote a financial plan for the ensuing fiscal year. It must contain a general summary, detailed estimates of all anticipated revenues, all planned expenditures, and a compensation schedule.

Amended Budget Legal alternations to the Adopted Budget as provided by Wisconsin Statutes that require a two-thirds vote of the governing body.

Appropriation A legal authority granted by the governing body which permits public officials to incur obligations and make expenditures up to the amount of money allocated and within time limits set by the governing body. Does not mean it will be fully expended.

Assessed Valuation A dollar value placed upon real estate for personal property by the local assessor, to be used as a basis for levying property taxes.

Audit A careful examination, using generally accepted accounting principles and practices, giving the independent auditor's opinion whether or not revenues are fairly reported and whether expenditures are fairly reported. Audits are reported with an "opinion."

1. An "**Unqualified**" audit opinion suggests that the audited government has satisfactorily met all audit requirements, is in general compliance with GAAP, and there are no significant deficiencies in how funds are being managed. It is essentially a "clean bill of health."
2. A "**Qualified**" audit opinion suggests there is some deviation from Generally Accepted Accounting Procedures (GAAP). An auditor presenting a "qualified" audit will often use the term "except for." In most cases, a qualified audit means there is some policy or pro-

cedure that needs to be changed, updated or corrected but it is not so critical as to place the organization in financial jeopardy.

3. An "**Adverse**" opinion is offered when the auditor concludes the financial statements are so misstated or misleading that they do not fairly present the income, financial position or cash flows of the organization. Adverse audits are relatively rare but, when expressed, indicate severe problems with how the organization is accounting for its finances.

Balance Sheet A statement which discloses the financial condition of an entity by assets, liabilities, reserves, and equities of a fund or account group at a specific date to exhibit financial position.

Bond A bond is a debt security, in which the authorized issues owes the holders a debt and, depending on the terms of the bond, is obliged to pay interest (the coupon) and/or to repay the principal at a later date, termed maturity. A bond is a formal contract to repay borrowed money with interest at fixed intervals. Thus a bond is like a loan: the *issuer* is the borrower (debtor), the *holder* is the lender (creditor), and the *coupon* is the interest. Bonds provide the borrower with external funds to finance long-term investments, or, in the case of some government bonds, to finance current expenditures. Certificates of deposit (CDs) or commercial paper are considered to be money market instruments and not bonds. Bonds must be repaid at fixed intervals over a period of time.

A municipal bond is a bond issued by a city or other local government, including schools, special purpose districts, airports and seaports to secure funding for major projects. Municipal bonds may be general obligation bonds repaid by general funds or special revenue bonds secured by specified revenues and may be tax exempt, depending upon the circumstances and type of bond.

Budget The managerial and political document in which the costs associated with various activities are estimated, anticipated revenues projected and decisions made which result in appropriations, tax levies and borrowing authority.

Also a plan forecasting the amounts of money to be expended, revenues and their sources. Two kinds of budgets are commonly used:

The **Operating Budget** is the plan for current or annual expenditures and the proposed means of financing them.

The **Capital Budget** is the financial plan that details expenditures for (many kinds of) equipment, repair projects, the purchase or construction of buildings and facilities, and the means of financing each over longer periods of time.

(Also see "Performance budget," "Program budget" and "Zero based budget.")

Budget Calendar The schedule of events that need to occur and the date or period of time for each to occur in the preparation, review and adoption of a budget.

Capital Assets Buildings, machinery, equipment or other items having a useful life of several years and/or costing a significant amount of money to acquire. (Also called fixed assets. Local policy determines the criteria for treating proposed budget items as capital assets.)

Capital A plan listing priorities for major capital improvement.

1. **Improvement Plan** projects anticipated over a fixed number of years, their costs, and methods of financing the expenditures. (Among small to medium size units of government, a capital improvement program will typically span three to seven years.)

2. **Capital Outlay** Expenditures for the acquisition of new or replacement of current capital assets.

Cash Flow Plan A projection of the cash receipts and disbursements anticipated during each week or month of the fiscal year. Usually requiring a cooperative effort by the clerk and treasurer, the plan helps determine the most opportune time to expend funds, helps avoid unnecessary short term borrowing, and earns the highest return on idle funds.

Contingency Funds Assets or other resources set aside to provide for unforeseen expenditures or for anticipated expenditures of uncertain amounts.

Coupon A bond's **coupon** is the annual interest rate paid on the issuer's borrowed money, generally paid out semi-annually on individual bonds. The coupon is always tied to a bond's face or **par value** and is quoted as a percentage of par.

For example, you invest $5,000 in a six-year bond paying a coupon rate of five percent per year, semi-annually. Assuming you hold the bond to maturity, you will receive 12 coupon payments of $125 each, or a total of $1,500.

Debt An obligation resulting from the borrowing of money or purchase of goods and services. Government debt includes bonds, time warrants and notes.

Debt Limit The maximum amount of debt legally permitted. In Wisconsin, General Obligation debt is limited to 5 percent of the jurisdiction's equalized value.

Debt Service The amount of money a unit of government must spend to repay in full and on schedule the principal and the interest owed on what it borrows from outside lenders.

Deficit An excess of expenditures/uses over and above revenues/resources.

Depreciation That portion of the total expended to acquire a capital asset charged as an expense during a particular period of time. Depreciation usually estimated in a straight line calculation in which the original value is decreased each year as a percentage of full value over the expected life of the asset.

Eminent Domain The power of a government to acquire private property for public purposes. It is used frequently to obtain real property that cannot be purchased from owners in a voluntary transaction. When the power of eminent domain is exercised, owners normally are compensated by the government in an amount determined by an independent appraisal of the property.

Encumbrance Commitments to pay for equipment, goods or services without payment actually being made. Purchase orders and contracts are typical ways in which government agencies encumber funds charged against an appropriation for contracts yet to be performed.

Endowment Funds or properties that are donated with either a temporary or permanent restriction as to the use of the principal and/or interest. Such funds are "restricted" and their balances cannot be used to offset deficits in General Funds.

Enterprise Fund An accounting method for revenues and expenditures of an activity that is treated much like a business enterprise because it is expected to be self supporting, with little or no subsidy provided from general funds, and with an ongoing independent revenue source.

Equalized Valuation The statutory full market value of all real property within each jurisdiction (except agricultural land which is valued based on production/earning potential). The State Department of Revenue analyzes market sales statewide to estimate the full market (or equalized) value for each jurisdiction. Equalized values provide a means of comparing different jurisdictions, even if they are assessed at different percentages of market value. Equalized values are used to apportion the levies of overlying districts (for example, schools and counties) to the municipalities within them. The state values are needed because municipalities assess property at varying percentages of the market value.

Expenditures Expenditures include current operating expenses which require the current or future use of net current assets, service and capital outlays.

Fixed Assets See "Capital assets."

Fiscal Year A twelve-month period of time used for budgeting, accounting and tax collection purposes which may differ from a calendar year. Wisconsin municipal entities operate on a calendar basis from January 1 to December 31 while the State operates on a July 1 to June 30 basis.

Forecasting A forecast of the expected financial position and the results of operations and cash flows based on expected conditions. In local government, this generally means anticipating what revenues are anticipated from property taxes, state shared revenues and fees for services and comparing those "forecasted" revenues with expected obligations and expenditures.

FTE (Full Time Equivalent) A term used to compare the hours budgeted for regular full-time and regular part-time, temporary part-time and overtime based on 2,080 hours annually of a full time position.

Fund An independent accounting entity with its own set of accounts to record revenues and expenditures, obligations and reserves. (Most local units of government establish a general fund along with several special revenue funds and, if appropriate, enterprise funds.)

GASB The mission of the independent, not-for-profit, nongovernmental **Governmental Accounting Standards Board** is to establish and improve standards of state and local governmental accounting and financial reporting that will result in useful information for users of financial reports and guide and educate the public, including issuers, auditors, and users of those financial reports. Most local governments adhere to GASB standards.

General Reserves Revenues received but not needed until a future date in order to meet obligations; these revenues can be invested in a variety of authorized ways to generate additional income. (The investment of idle funds requires coordination between cash flow planning and budget planning.)

GFOA (Government Finance Officers Association) The professional organization for government finance officers that provides training and a venue for discussion of issues related to government finance.

ICMA The **International City/County Managers Association** is the professional organization for City Managers and County Administrator and provides professional training, information sharing, and guidance on local government issues.

Impact Fees Fees charged to developers to cover,

in whole or in part, the anticipated cost of improvements (e.g., parks, sidewalks, etc.) that will be necessary as a result of the development.

In-Lieu of Tax Payment made in place of a tax or taxes. Payments can be negotiated with nontaxable property owners who will make a payment on property not subject to property tax.

Levy To impose taxes, special assessments or service charges for the support of government activities and services.

Liquidity The ability to convert an investment (of idle funds) quickly in order to meet obligations with minimum loss of earning power.

Line-Item/Object The classification of expenditures on the basis of categories call

1. **-of- expenditure** objects-of-expenditure (personal services, contractual services,
2. **budget** capital outlay, etc.) and within each category more detailed line-items (salaries, travel, telephone expense, etc.). (This type of budget, traditionally used among local units of government, focuses attention on how much money is spent and for what purpose rather than the activity affected or its outcomes.)

Management Letter A letter from the independent auditors that is usually a series of findings or recommendations on ways the financial management policies and practices may be improved.

Mil Rate The amount of taxes levied for each $1,000 (mil) of assessed property valuation. For example, a tax levy budget of $2.5 million (total property tax assessment) with a property tax base of $1 billion (value of all taxable property) would generate a levy rate of $2.50 per $1,000 of assessed value. On a house value of $100,000, the property tax would equal $250 (100X $2.50).

Municipal Any county, city, village, town, technical college district, special purpose district or board or commission and any public or quasi-public corporation or board or commission created pursuant to statue, ordinance, or resolution, but does not include the state, a state agency, or corporation chartered by the state or a school district.

Municipal Bond A municipal bond is a bond issued by a city or other local government. Municipal bonds may be general obligations of the issuer or secured by specified revenues. Interest income received by holders may be tax exempt.

Obligations Amounts a government may be required legally to meet out of its resources.

Operating Budget A financial, programmatic, and organizational plan for furthering the goals of the governing body for the current year.

Par Value The stated value of a security as it appears on its certificate. A bond's par value is the dollar amount on which interest is calculated and the amount paid to holders at maturity. Par value of preferred stock is used in a similar way in calculating the annual dividend.

Performance The classification of expenditures on the basis of specific activities.

Budget (resurfacing streets, investigating traffic accidents, etc), the number of units performed and their costs. (This type of budget focuses attention on what a work unit does, how frequently it does it, and at what cost rather than a detailed, line-item accounting of expenditures.)

Per Capita Income Total income divided by the population.

Personnel Costs Budget category used to denote salaries and wages as well as all associated benefits such as employer paid pension costs; social security; health, life, dental, and disability insurance; vacation; holidays; and sick leave.

Principal In the context of bonds, the face value or par value of a bond or issue of bonds payable on stated dates of maturity.

Program Group of activities, operations, or organizational units directed to attaining specific purposes or results. (A group of activities related to crime prevention can be made part of the same program even though the activities involve separate work units within the same program under the same governing body. The same may be true of activities related to fire prevention, health care centers, road maintenance, etc.)

Program Budget The classification of expenditures on the basis of programs, significant problems or policy issues each attempts to deal with, and alternatives for dealing with them. (This type of budget focuses attention on the kinds of problems and policy issues chief executives and governing bodies are expected to resolve and, in a summary fashion, the resources needed to resolve them.)

Property Tax Taxes levied and revenue received based on both real and personal property assessed valuation and the tax rate.

Reimbursements Payments remitted on behalf of another party, department, or fund. Recorded as expenditures, or expenses, in the reimbursing fund, and as reductions of the expenditure, or expense, in the fund that is reimbursed.

Restricted Assets An account set up to control

monies or other resources, the use of which is restricted by legal or contractual requirements.

Reserve For An account, included as part of most budgets, set aside for **Contingencies** emergencies or other unanticipated needs not otherwise included as part of a budget. (Since a contingency fund is usually included in the adopted budget, it takes a simple majority of the governing body to approve spending from it.)

Special Assessment A compulsory levy made against certain properties to defray all or part of the cost of a specific capital improvement or service deemed to benefit primarily those properties.

TIF Tax Increment Financing is a tool to use future gains in taxes to finance current improvements (which theoretically will create the conditions for those future gains). When a public project such as a road, school, or hazardous waste cleanup is carried out, there is often an increase in the value of surrounding real estate, and perhaps new investment (new or rehabilitated buildings, for example). This increased site value and investment sometimes generates increased tax revenues. The increased tax revenues are the "tax increment." Tax Increment Financing dedicates tax increments within a certain defined district to finance debt issued to pay for the original improvement project. TIF is designed to channel funding toward improvements in distressed or underdeveloped areas where development might not otherwise occur. TIF creates funding for "public" projects that may otherwise by unaffordable to localities, by borrowing against future property tax revenues.

Transfer of Funds An approved movement of monies from one separate fund to another fund. Other budgets call for Transfers In to the General Fund to pay for centralized expenditures such as utilities, insurance, or fringe benefits. Transfers Out from the General Fund may be required to subsidize new special activity funds or those with insufficient or unreliable revenue source.

Unreserved Available funds from prior year budgets that the local fund balance auditors have determined are not pledged for any purpose that may be used as a guarantee for the credit of the government's long term bonds, or for any legal general purpose. (Unreserved funds are considered outside the normal operating budget unless applied as "Funds Forwarded" to reduce the tax levy. Expenditure of these funds requires a 2/3 vote.)

Zero-Base Budget A budget approach whereby the expenditure amount for each line item is examined in its entirety each year, regardless of prior funding. Those items that cannot be justified are subject to elimination. In most cases, Zero-Base Budgeting (ZBB) organizes information into decision packages, i.e., incremental spending levels that reflect varying levels of effort and costs. In theory, each department prepares at least three (3) packages: a base-level, meeting the program's minimum requirements; current-level funding; enhanced package — to address unmet needs. Packages from all departments are then ranked according to perceived need for the package. The packages are then ranked and either selected for adoption or rejected.

B. Regional Resource Directory

The municipal governments included in the best practices section are listed below alphabetically by their name. Additional information, including personal contacts, may be obtained from their respective organizational websites.

Ann Arbor: (http://www.ci.ann-arbor.mi.us/)
Arlington: (http://www.arlington.gov/)
Auburn: (http://www.auburnmaine.org/)
Boca Raton: (http://www.ci.boca-raton.fl.us/)
Chandler: (http://www.chandleraz.gov/)
Charlotte: (http://charmeck.org/)
Chicago: (http://www.cityofchicago.org/)
Cincinnati: (http://www.cincinnati-oh.gov/)
Colorado Springs: (http://www.springsgov.com/)
Coral Springs: (http://www.coralsprings.org/)
Denver: (http://www.denvergov.org/)
Des Moines: (http://www.dmgov.org/)
Elgin: (http://www.cityofelgin.org/)
Eugene: (http://www.eugene-or.gov/)
Gardena: (http://www.ci.gardena.ca.us/)
Hanover: (http://www.co.hanover.va.us/)
Harrisburg: (http://www.harrisburgpa.gov/)
Las Vegas: (http://www.lasvegasnevada.gov/)
Lewiston: (http://www.ci.lewiston.me.us/)
New York: (http://www.nyc.gov/)
Peoria: (http://www.peoriaaz.gov/)
Philadelphia: (http://www.phila.gov/)
Portland: (http://www.portlandonline.com/)
Provo: (http://www.provo.org/)
Redlands: (http://www.ci.redlands.ca.us/)
Roanoke: (http://www.roanokeva.gov/)
Rochester: (http://www.ci.rochester.mi.us/)
Rockland: (http://www.ci.rockland.me.us/)
St. Paul: (http://www.stpaul.gov/)
San Diego: (http://www.sandiego.gov/)
San Jose: (http://www.sanjoseca.gov/)
Sandy Springs: (http://www.sandyspringsga.gov/)
Savannah: (http://www.savannahga.gov/)

Seattle: (http://www.seattle.gov/)
Springfield: (http://www.springfield-ma.gov/)
Walnut Creek: (http://www.walnut-creek.org/)
Waukesha: (http://www.ci.waukesha.wi.us/)
West Palm Beach: (http://www.cityofwpb.com/)
Westminster: (http://www.ci.westminster.co.us/)
Worcester: (http://www.worcesterma.gov/)

C. National Resource Directory

The following list represents major national professional associations, foundations, research organizations, and citizen associations, focusing on issues and problems relating to local governments, including their financial issues and problems.

Academy for State and Local Government: (http://www.usa.gov/)

American Accounting Association: (http://co borgs.isu.edu/aaagnp/)

American Association for Budget and Program Analysis: (http://www.aabpa.org/)

American Economic Development Council: (http://www.aedc.org/)

American Finance Association: (http://www.afaj of.org/)

American Financial Services Association: (http://www.americanfinsvcs.org/)

American Real Estate and Urban Economics Association: (http://www.areuea.org/)

American Society for Public Administration: (http://www.aspanet.org/)

Association for Budgeting and Financial Management: (http://www.abfm.org/)

Association for Enterprise Opportunity: (http://www.microenterpriseworks.org/)

Association of Government Accountants: (http://www.agacgfm.org/)

Association of Local Government Auditors: (http://www.governmentauditors.org/)

Association of Public Treasurers: (http://www.aptusc.org/)

Community Associations Institute: (http://www.caionline.org/)

Community Development Society International: (http://comm-dev.org/)

Congress for New Urbanism: (http://www.cnu.org/)

Corporation for Enterprise Development: (http://www.cfed.org/)

Council for Urban Economic Development: (http://www.cued.org/)

Government Accounting Standards Board: (http://www.gasb.org/)

Government Finance Officers Association: (http://www.gfoa.org/)

Government Research Association, Stamford University: (http://www.graonline.org/)

Institute of Internal Auditors: (http://www.the iia.org/)

Institute of Public Administration, University of Delaware: (http://www.ipa.udel.edu/)

International Association of Assessing Officers: (http://www.iaao.org/)

International City/County Management Association: (http://www.icma.org/)

International Institute of Public Finance: (http://www.iipf.org/)

International Municipal Lawyers Association: (http://www.imla.org/)

Local Government Center, University of Wisconsin: (http://lgc.uwex.edu/)

Local Government Commission: (http://www.lgc.org/)

National Association of Counties: (http://www.naco.org/)

National Association of Development Organizations: (http://www.nado.org/)

National Association of Local Government Auditors: (http://www.nalga.org/)

National Association of Towns and Townships: (http://www.natat.org/)

National Civic League: (http://www.ncl.org/)

National Community Development Association: (http://www.ncdaonline.org/)

National Council for Urban Economic Development: (http://www.ncued.org/)

National Institute of Governmental Purchasing: (http://www.nigp.org/)

National League of Cities: (http://www.nlc.org/)

Partners for Livable Communities: (http://www.livable.com/)

Smart Growth America: (http://www.smart growthamerica.org/)

Urban Affairs Association, University of Delaware: (http://www.udel.edu/uaa/)

The Urban Institute: (http://www.urban.org/)

U. S. Conference of Mayors: (http://www.usmay ors.org/)

The U.S. Governmental Accountability Office: (http://www.gao.gov/)

World Future Society: (http://www.wfs.org/)

D. City Management Officials State Chapter Directory

Many states have state-wide chapters of the national professional association for local government managers, called the International City/County Management Association (ICMA), which is listed in the *National Resource Directory* section of this appendix. Those states with ICMA chapters, or closely related organizations, are shown below (in alphabetical order by state name; not all organization names start with the state name).

Alabama City/County Management Association: (http://www.accma-online.org/)

Alaska Municipal Management Association: (http://www.alaskamanagers.org/)

Arizona City/County Management Association: (http://www.azmanagement.org/)

Arkansas City Management Association: (http://www.arml.org/)

California City Management Association: (http://icma.org/ca/-icma/)

Colorado City/County Management Association: (http://www.coloradoccma.org/)

Connecticut Town and City Management Association: (http://www.cttcma.govoffice3.com/)

City Management Association of Delaware: (http://www.allg.org/)

Florida City and County Management Association: (http://www.fccma.org/)

Georgia City/County Management Association: (http://www.gccma.com/)

Idaho City/County Management Association: (http://www.idahocities.org/)

Illinois City/County Management Association: (http://ilcma.org/)

Indiana Municipal Management Association: (http://www.citiesandtowns.org/)

Iowa City/County Management Association: (http://www.iaccmanagement.govoffice2.com/)

Kansas Association of City/County Management: (http://www.kacm.us/)

Kentucky City/County Management Association: (http://www.kccma.org/)

Louisiana City Management Association: (http://www.lma.org/)

Maine Town and City Management Association: (http://www.mtcma.org/)

Maryland City/County Management Association: (http://www.icma.org/mccma/)

Massachusetts Municipal Management Association: (http://www.massmanagers.org/)

Michigan Local Government Management Association: (http://www.mlgma.org/)

Minnesota City/County Management Association: (http://www.mncma.org/)

Mississippi City and County Management Association: (http://www.mmlonline.com/)

Missouri City Management Association: (http://www.momanagers.org/)

Nebraska City/County Management Association: (http://www.nebraskacma.org/)

Local Government Managers Association of Nevada: (http://icma.org/logman/)

New Hampshire Municipal Management Association: (http://www.nhmanagers.org/)

New Jersey Municipal Management Association: (http://www.njmma.org/)

New Mexico City Management Association: (http://www.nmml.org/subsection-city-managers/)

New York State City/County Management Association: (http://www.nyscma.govoffice.com/)

North Carolina City and County Management Association: (http://www.ncmanagers.org/)

Ohio City/County Management Association: (http://www.ocmaohio.org/)

City Management Association of Oklahoma: (http://www.cmao-ok.org/)

Oregon City/County Management Association: (http://www.occma.org/)

Association for Pennsylvania Municipal Management: (http://www.apmm.net/)

Rhode Island City and Town Management Association: (http://www.rileague.org/)

South Carolina City and County Management Association: (http://icma.org/scccma/)

South Dakota City Management Association: (http://www.sdmunicipalleague.org/)

Tennessee City Management Association: (http://www.tncma.org/)

Texas City Management Association: (http://www.tcma.org/)

Utah City Management Association: (http://www.ucma-utah.org/)

Vermont Town and City Management Association: (http://www.vlct.org/)

Virginia Local Government Management Association: (http://www.vlgma.org/)

Washington City/County Management Association: (http://www.wccma.org/)

West Virginia City Management Association: (http://wvmanagers.org/)

Wisconsin City/County Management Association: (http://www.wcma-wi.org/)

E. Finance Officials State Chapter Directory

Many states have state-wide chapters of the national professional association for finance directors, called the Government Finance Officers Association (GFOA), which is listed in the *National Resource Directory* section of this appendix. Those states with GFOA chapters, or closely related organizations, are shown below.

Alabama GFOA: (http://www.gfoaa.org/)
Alaska GFOA: (http://www.agfoa.com/)
Arizona GFOA: (http://www.gfoaz.org/)
Arkansas GFOA: (http://www.agfoa.org/)
California Society of Municipal Finance Officers (CSMFO): (http://www.csmfo.org/)
Colorado GFOA: (http://www.cgfoa.org/)
Connecticut GFOA: (http://www.gfoact.org/)
District of Columbia Metro Area GFOA: (http://gfoa-wma.org/)
Florida GFOA: (http://www.fgfoa.org/)
Georgia GFOA: (http://www.ggfoa.org/)
Idaho City Clerks, Treasurers & Finance Directors Association (ICCTFOA): (http://www.idahocities.org/)
Illinois GFOA: (http://www.igfoa.org/)
Iowa Municipal Finance Officers Association (IMFOA): (http://www.imfoa.org/)
Kansas GFOA: (http://www.ksgfoa.com/)
Kentucky GFOA: (http://www.kgfoa.org/)
Louisiana GFOA: (http://www.lagfoa.org/)
Maine GFOA: (http://www.nesgfoa.org/)
Maryland GFOA: (http://www.mdgfoa.org/)
Massachusetts GFOA: (http://www.mgfoa.org/)
Michigan GFOA: (http://www.migfoa.org/)
Minnesota GFOA: (http://www.mngfoa.org/)
Missouri GFOA: (http://www.gfoa-mo.org/)
Montana Municipal Clerks, Treasurers, & Finance Officers Association (MMCTFOA): (http://www.mlct.org/)
Nebraska Municipal Accounting & Finance Committee (NMAFC): (http://www.lonm.org/)
Nevada GFOA: (http://www.ngfoa.org/)
New England States GFOA (NESGFOA): (http://www.nesgfoa.org/)
New Hampshire GFOA: (http://www.nhgfoa.org/)
New Jersey GFOA: (http://www.gfoanj.org/)
New Mexico Municipal Clerks and Finance Officers Association (NMMCFOA): (http://www.nmml.org/)
New York State GFOA: (http://www.nysgfoa.org/)
North Carolina GFOA: (http://www.sog.unc.edu/node/108/)
North Dakota Finance Directors (NDFD): (The GFOA Directory referred inquiries to the North Dakota League of Cities website)

Ohio GFOA: (http://www.ohgfoa.com/)
Oklahoma Municipal Clerks, Treasurers, and Finance Officials Association (OMCTFOA): (http://www.omctfoa.com/)
Oregon Municipal Finance Officers Association (OMFOA): (http://www.omfoa.org/)
Pennsylvania GFOA: (http://www.gfoapa.org/)
Rhode Island GFOA: (http://www.rigfoa.org/)
South Carolina GFOA: (http://www.gfoasc.org/)
South Dakota GFOA: (http://www.sdmunicipalleague.org/)
Tennessee GFOA: (http://www.tngfoa.org/)
Texas GFOA: (http://www.gfoat.org/)
Utah GFOA: (http://www.ugfoa.com/)
Vermont GFOA: (http://www.nesgfoa.org/)
Virginia GFOA: (http://www.vgfoa.org/)
Washington Finance Officers Association (WFOA): (http://www.wfoa/)
West Virginia GFOA: (http://www.wvml.org/)
Wisconsin GFOA: (http://www.wgfoa.org/)
Wyoming Association of Municipal Clerks and Treasurers (WAMCT): (http://www.wamcat.org/)

F. State Municipal League Directory

Most states have a municipal league, which serves as a valuable source of information about city government budgets and taxes. Additional information on budgets and taxes is available from the various state municipal league websites, which are shown below (in alphabetical order by state name; not all organization names start with the state name).

Alabama League of Municipalities: (http://www.alalm.org/)
Alaska Municipal League: (http://www.akml.org/)
League of Arizona Cities and Towns: (http://www.azleague.org/)
Arkansas Municipal League: (http://www.arml.org/)
League of California Cities: (http://www.cacities.org/)
Colorado Municipal League: (http://www.cml.org/)
Connecticut Conference of Municipalities: (http://www.ccm-ct.org/)
Delaware League of Local Governments: (http://www.ipa.udel.edu/localgovt/dllg/)
Florida League of Cities: (http://www.flcities.com/)

Georgia Municipal Association: (http://www.gmanet.com/)

Association of Idaho Cities: (http://www.idahocities.org/)

Illinois Municipal League: (http://www.iml.org/)

Indiana Association of Cities and Towns: (http://www.citiesandtowns.org/)

Iowa League of Cities: (http://www.iowaleague.org/)

League of Kansas Municipalities: (http://www.lkm.org/)

Kentucky League of Cities: (http://www.klc.org/)

Louisiana Municipal Association: (http://www.lamunis.org/)

Maine Municipal Association: (http://www.memum.org/)

Maryland Municipal League: (http://www.mdmunicipal.org/)

Massachusetts Municipal Association: (http://www.mma.org/)

Michigan Municipal League: (http://www.mml.org/)

League of Minnesota Cities: (http://www.lmnc.org/)

Mississippi Municipal League: (http://www.mmlonline.com/)

Missouri Municipal League: (http://www.mocities.com/)

Montana League of Cities: (http://www.mlct.org/)

League of Nebraska Municipalities: (http://www.lonm.org/)

Nevada League of Cities and Municipalities: (http://www.nvleague.org/)

New Hampshire Local Government Center: (http://www.nhmunicipal.org/)

New Jersey State League of Municipalities: (http://www.njslom.com/)

New Mexico Municipal League: (http://www.nmml.org/)

New York Conference of Mayors and Municipal Officials: (http://www.nycom.org/)

North Carolina League of Municipalities: (http://www.nclm.org/)

North Dakota League of Cities: (http://www.ndlc.org/)

Ohio Municipal League: (http://www.omunileague.org/)

Oklahoma Municipal League: (http://www.oml.org/)

League of Oregon Cities: (http://www.orcities.org/)

Pennsylvania League of Cities and Municipalities: (http://www.plcm.org/)

Rhode Island League of Cities and Towns: (http://www.rileague.org/)

Municipal Association of South Carolina: (http://www.masc.sc/)

South Dakota Municipal League: (http://www.sdmunicipalleague.org/)

Tennessee Municipal League: (http://www.tml1.org/)

Texas Municipal League: (http://www.tml.org/)

Utah League of Cities and Towns: (http://www.ulct.org/)

Vermont League of Cities and Towns: (http://www.vlct.org/)

Virginia Municipal League: (http://www.vml.org/)

Association of Washington Cities: (http://www.awcnet.org/)

West Virginia Municipal League: (http://www.wvml.org/)

League of Wisconsin Municipalities: (http://www.lwm-info.org/)

Wyoming Association of Municipalities: (http://www.wyomuni.org/)

G. State Library Directory

Most state libraries have copies of state laws relating to the various tax and revenue options available to the local governments within their jurisdiction. The amount of state funds allocated to cities is also available. The contact information for the various state libraries is shown below.

Alabama: (http://www.apls.state.la.us/)
Alaska: (http://www.www.library.state.ak.us/)
Arizona: (http://www.www.lib.az.us/)
Arkansas: (http://www.www.asl.lib.ar.us/)
California: (http://www.www.library.ca.gov/)
Colorado: (http://www.cde.state.co.us/)
Connecticut: (http://www.cslib.org/)
Delaware: (http://www.state.lib.de.us/)
District of Columbia: (http://dclibrary.org/)
Florida: (http://dlis.dos.state.fl.us/)
Georgia: (http://www.georgialibraries.org/)
Hawaii: (http://www.librarieshawaii.org/)
Idaho: (http://www.lili.org/)
Illinois: (http://www.cyberdriveillinois.com/departments/library/)
Indiana: (http://www.statelib.lib.in.us/)
Iowa: (http://www.silo.lib.ia.us/)
Kansas: (http://www.skyways.org/KSL/)
Kentucky: (http://www.kdla.ky.gov/)
Louisiana: (http://www.state.lib.la.us/)
Maine: (http://www.state.me.us/msl/)
Maryland: (http://www.sailor.lib.md.us/)

Massachusetts: (http://www.mass.gov/mblc/)
Michigan: (http://www.michigan.gov/hal/)
Minnesota: (http://www.state.mn.us/libraries/)
Mississippi: (http://www.mlc.lib.ms.us/)
Missouri: (http://www.sos.mo.gov/library/)
Montana: (http://msl.state.mt.us/)
Nebraska: (http://www.nlc.state.ne.us/)
Nevada: (http://dmla.clan.lib.nv.us/)
New Hampshire: (http://www.state.nh.us/nhls/)
New Jersey: (http://www.njstatelib.org/)
New Mexico: (http://www.stlib.state.mn.us/)
New York: (http://www.nysl.nysed.gov/)
North Carolina: (http://statelibrary.dcr.state.nc.us/)
North Dakota: (http://ndsl.lib.state.nd.us/)
Ohio: (http://winslo.state.oh.us/)
Oklahoma: (http://www.odl.state.ok.us/)

Oregon: (http://oregon.gov/OSL/)
Pennsylvania: (http://www.statelibrary.state.pa.us/libraries/)
Rhode Island: (http://www.olis.ri.gov/)
South Carolina: (http://www.statelibrary.sc.gov/)
South Dakota: (http://www.sdstatelibrary.com/)
Tennessee: (http://www.tennessee.gov/tsla/)
Texas: (http://www.tsl.state.tx.us/)
Utah: (http://library.ut.gov/index.html/)
Vermont: (http://dol.state.vt.us/)
Virginia: (http://www.lva.lib.va.us/)
Washington: (http://www.secstate.was.gov/library/)
West Virginia: (http://librarycommission/lib.wv.us/)
Wisconsin: (http://www.dpi.state.wi.us/dltcl/pld/)
Wyoming: (http://www-wsl.state.wy.us/)

About the Editor and Contributors

The affiliations of the contributors are as of the time the articles were written.

Michael Bailey, director, Finance Department, City of Redmond, Washington.

Robert Barkin, free-lance writer, Bethesda, Maryland.

William Barnes, director, Center for Municipal Programs and Resources, National League of Cities, Washington, D.C.

Gordon Berlin, president, MDRC, New York, New York, and Oakland, California.

Barbara J. Cohn Berman, vice president, Fund for the City of New York, and its sister organization, the National Center for Civic Innovation, New York, New York.

David Bigos, mayor and council assistant, City of Chandler, Arizona.

John Borget, director, Administrative Services Department, City of Provo, Utah.

Donald J. Borut, executive director, National League of Cities, Washington, D.C.

Alan Brown, president, Prevention Matters, LLC, Scottsdale, Arizona.

Marcel Bullinga, futurist, keynote speaker, and government adviser on Internet trends, Amsterdam, Netherlands.

John Buntin, staff writer, *Governing Magazine*, eRepublic Inc., Washington, D.C.

Jacqueline J. Byers, director, research and outreach, National Association of Counties, Washington, DC.

Joe Casey, deputy county administrator, Hanover County, Hanover, Virginia.

Craig Chavez, management intern, ICMA Knowledge Center, Fullerton, California.

Peter Christensen, senior budget analyst, Management and Budget Department, City of Peoria, Arizona.

Jeff Clark, free-lance writer, Bath, Maine.

Linda C. Davidson, director, Financial Services Department, City of Boca Raton, Florida, and member, Executive Board, Government Finance Officers Association, Chicago, Illinois.

John W. DeWitt, Marketing Consultant and Business Writer, New Salem, Massachusetts.

Eva Elmer, graduate intern, Office of the City Manager, City of Savannah, Georgia.

Chris Fabian, senior manager, Research and Advisory Services, Center for Priority Based Budgeting, Denver, Colorado.

Karen Feher, coordinator, Capitol Budget Program, Metro Regional Government, Portland, Oregon.

Melissa Germanese, manager, Program Development and CityFutures Program, National League of Cities, Washington, D.C.

Amanda M. Girth, instructor, School of Public Affairs, American University, Washington, D.C.

Jay M. Goldstone, chief operating officer, City of San Diego, California.

Kathleen Gray, staff writer, *Detroit Free Press*, Detroit, Michigan.

Katie Gregory, budget coordinator, Management and Budget Department, City of Peoria, Arizona.

Shannon E. Hayden, senior research associate, National Research Center, Inc., Boulder, Colorado.

Christopher Hire, executive director, 2thinknow and Innovation Cities Program, Melbourne, Victoria, Australia.

Christopher W. Hoene, director, Center for Research and Innovation, National League of Cities, Washington, D.C.

Claudia Hoffacker, publications manager, League of Minnesota Cities, St. Paul.

259

Nancy Mann Jackson, free-lance writer, Florence, Alabama.

Jon Johnson, senior manager, Research and Advisory Services, Center for Priority Based Budgeting, Denver, Colorado.

Jocelyn M. Johnston, director and associate professor, MPA Program, School of Public Affairs, American University, Washington, D.C.

Shane Kavanagh, senior manager, Research and Consulting Center, Government Finance Officers Association, Chicago, Illinois.

Elizabeth Kellar, president and chief executive officer, Center for State and Local Government Excellence, Washington, D.C.

Alan Kemp, executive director, Iowa League of Cities, Des Moines.

Roger L. Kemp is a practitioner in residence, Department of Public Management, College of Business, University of New Haven and has been a city manager of cities on the West and East Coasts of the United States for more than 25 years.

Connie Kuranko, director, U.S. Communities Going Green Program, Walnut Creek, California.

Laura Kushner, director, Human Resources Department, League of Minnesota Cities, St. Paul.

Josh Lerner, codirector, Participatory Budgeting Project, Brooklyn College, Brooklyn, New York.

Brent McFall, city manager, City of Westminster, Colorado.

Melanie McKinney-Gonzales, graduate student, Department of Political Science, University of Colorado, Denver, and intern, Town of Bayfield, Colorado.

Monte Mercer, deputy executive director, North Central Texas Council of Governments, Arlington.

Thomas L. Miller, founder and president, National Research Center, Inc., Boulder, Colorado.

Liz Chapman Mockler, free-lance writer and editor, Augusta, Maine.

Christopher Morrill, city manager, City of Roanoke, Virginia, and former assistant city manager, Office of the City Manager, City of Savannah, Georgia.

Brooke A. Myhre, principal, Brook Myhre Consulting, San Jose, California.

Russell Nichols, staff writer, *Governing Magazine*, eRepublic Inc., Washington, D.C.

Derek Okubo, senior vice president, National Civic League, Denver, Colorado.

Zach Patton, staff writer, *Governing Magazine*, eRepublic Inc., Washington, D.C.

Lynn Peisner, free-lance writer, Atlanta, Georgia.

James Ricco, director, Low-Wage Workers and Communities Policy Area, and research director, Opportunity NYC–Family Rewards, MDRC, New York, New York, and Oakland, California.

Douglas Rooks, free-lance writer and regular contributor, West Gardiner, Maine.

Lisa Rund, manager, Human Resources Department, League of Minnesota Cities, St. Paul.

Walter Rybeck, director, Center for Public Dialogue, Silver Spring, Maryland.

Roberta R. Schaefer, founding executive director, Worcester Regional Research Bureau, Worcester, Massachusetts.

Jeff Schott, program director, Institute of Public Affairs, University of Iowa, Iowa City.

Sheryl Sculley, city manager, City of San Antonio, Texas.

Ann H. Shawver, director, Finance Department, City of Roanoke, Virginia.

James H. Svara, professor, School of Public Affairs, and director, Center for Urban Innovation, Arizona State University, Phoenix.

Karen Thoreson, president and chief operations officer, Alliance for Innovation, Phoenix, Arizona.

Index